This Era of
Black Activism

This Era of
Black Activism

Edited by
Mary Marcel and Edith Joachimpillai

LEXINGTON BOOKS
Lanham • Boulder • New York • London

Chapter One was published in Sociological Forum, Vol. 34, No. S1, December 2019. Permission to reprint from John Wiley and Sons.

Published by Lexington Books
An imprint of The Rowman & Littlefield Publishing Group, Inc.
4501 Forbes Boulevard, Suite 200, Lanham, Maryland 20706
www.rowman.com

86-90 Paul Street, London EC2A 4NE

British Library Cataloguing in Publication Information Available

Library of Congress Cataloging-in-Publication Data

Names: Marcel, Mary, editor. | Joachimpillai, Edith, editor.
Title: This era of Black activism / edited by Mary Marcel and Edith Joachimpillai.
Description: Lanham : Lexington Books, [2023] | Collection of essays by Jozie Nummi and 14 others. | Includes bibliographical references and index. | Summary: "While much focus has been placed on Black Lives Matter activism in response to police and civilian murders of Black people, authors argue that Black activism in this era addresses a broad range of issues both on the street and inside institutions and communities"— Provided by publisher.
Identifiers: LCCN 2023030395 (print) | LCCN 2023030396 (ebook) | ISBN 9781666940640 (cloth ; alk. paper) | ISBN 9781666940657 (ebook)
Subjects: LCSH: African Americans—Politics and government—21st century. | Black lives matter movement. | African Americans—Violence against. | African Americans and mass media. | Mass media and race relations—United States. | Citizen journalism—United States. | Police brutality—United States. | Racial profiling in law enforcement—United States. | Organizational change—United States. | African Americans—Civil rights.
Classification: LCC E185.615 .T493 2023 (print) | LCC E185.615 (ebook) | DDC 323.1196/073—dc23/eng/20230725
LC record available at https://lccn.loc.gov/2023030395
LC ebook record available at https://lccn.loc.gov/2023030396

♾️™ The paper used in this publication meets the minimum requirements of American National Standard for Information Sciences—Permanence of Paper for Printed Library Materials, ANSI/NISO Z39.48-1992.

For Eval Silvera
Keep bending the arc
and
For Roderick Silvera
Rest in Power

Amuthu Pulavar, Amma, and Edward
I inherit my activism from you
My communities, near and far
You support and inspire me

Contents

Acknowledgments

We would both like to thank Kiana Pierre-Louis, JD of Northeastern University School of Law, who along with Mary Marcel facilitated the NEH-funded seminar "From Scapegoats to Citizens: This Era of Black Activism" at Bentley University during 2021–2022. Her commitment to racial and social justice for all people and her passion in action throughout and beyond this seminar continue to humble us. Hans Eijmberts generously supported the seminar through the Valente Center for the Arts and Sciences at Bentley. Neelangi Gunasekera provided our meetings with all we needed, but most of all with her joy. The Bentley Faculty Affairs Committee provided timely and generous funding for permissions and indexing. Liz DePhillipis and Joey Huang volunteered a summer of research time at the height of Covid, and their work informs this and future research projects on Stand Your Ground cases. Rohan Rao cheerfully provided excellent research assistance.

Mary would like to thank Jette Hawley, John Sims, Lorraine Perez, Earl Avery, Claudette Blot, Sharon Seivert and Peri Onipede for their companionship, critical conversations and unwavering support over the two years this book has been taking shape. My family of choice, Allison, Craig, Harper, Foster and Wyatt, reminded me to enjoy the holidays. Most of all, my beautiful and funny husband Thomas Williams made sure the waters stayed calm so that I could get my part of this book safely into harbor. Sine qua non.

Edith would like to relay her gratitude to the individuals and institutions who have helped shape her insights on both this era and Black activism. Kemal Dervis, Karim Foda and the Brookings Institution and Scott Sumner, David Gulley, Aaron Jackson, Michael Quinn, Kristen Sorensen and Charlie

Hadlock from Bentley University provided the early tools necessary to examine *du jour* issues. My dear friends, most especially Kirsten Dean and Derek Hess, provided tremendous personal support before, throughout, and beyond this process. Last, but not least, Mom, Dad, Cynthi, Tony, Lola, Coco, and (hopefully a future activist) Theo—I love you "past the end of the universe." You challenge me, inspire me, and love me. Thank you.

Introduction

This Era of Black Activism

Edith Joachimpillai and Mary Marcel

There has never been a day in US history when our nation fully lived up to the promises of our Declaration of Independence and our democracy for Black people. As Ashley Hall wrote in 2020, "American civic identity and citizenship are founded on and confirmed through the active denial of Black humanity" (125). Likewise, there has hardly been a day when Black people somewhere somehow haven't decided to change that reality. Those determined steps—ideas, actions, plans and manifestations—have taken many forms in our nation's history. Progressive social and political activism by ordinary Black people may not ever have single-handedly changed our nation; we are a complex society and there are few mechanisms we can imagine which could achieve progressive change in a single stroke. But activism by Black people before and after the slavery era has gotten questions asked and cases litigated. It has set the stage for laws to be passed and the constitution changed. It has gotten the attention of companies and their stockholders. It has brought to light the truths and lived realities of people who were and are often expected to sacrifice their lives and well-being "for the greater good," in which white society presumes they have no part. And it has demanded to have the full voices of Black people heard and heeded (Campney 2019; Collier-Thomas and Franklin 2001; Davis 2022; Farmer 2017; Finley et al. 2015; Ford 2022; Hahn 2003; Hedin 2015; Hill 2017; Hinton 2021; Holsaert et al. 2010; House 1988; McGuire 2010; Olson 2001; Ransby 2003). Protests are, as Daniel Gillion (2020) recently noted, a vital and influential part of our electoral system. Black activists have been the bringers of our more perfect union. And as the last ten years have witnessed, they have ushered in a new era of attention and action on a whole range of issues in response to these definitely not post-racial times. So how did we get here?

1

In the introduction to Michelle Alexander's 2010 book *The New Jim Crow: Mass Incarceration in the Age of Colorblindness*, she writes of her growing awareness that, despite the gains made by the Civil Rights movement of the 1950s–1970s to legally overturn many of the racist and discriminatory policies that had plagued and proscribed the lives of African Americans, a thicket of new laws had sprung up in the intervening years which had nullified many of those gains. The stigmas formerly attached to legal definitions of race were migrated onto those with records of arrest and incarceration. The political right wing had found new ways to use legal processes to circumvent equal justice. Likewise, starting in 2005, Florida and then dozens of other states passed so-called "Stand Your Ground" laws, which set the stage for white civilians to kill people of color with no or diminished legal consequences (Ackerman et al. 2015; Sweeney 2015). Then in 2012, Trayvon Martin was shot dead by George Zimmerman in Florida. The Stand Your Ground defense loomed in the background as Zimmerman won acquittal on the murder charge. In the summer of 2014, it was the unprovoked murders by police of Eric Garner in New York and Michael Brown in Missouri that widened the floodgates of public protest (Bunn et al. 2021; Cobbina 2019; Hillstrom 2018; Jacobs, Thompson Taiwo and August 2021; Lowery 2016; Ransby 2018). The Movement for Black Lives would also encompass the murders of Black women by police, including Shantel Davis in 2012 in New York and Breonna Taylor in 2020 in Kentucky (Jones 2021). The resulting protests and ongoing activism against both civilian and police murders of Black people constitute the Black Lives Matter movement.

In 2006 Tarana Burke, trained to be an activist for Black issues starting in high school (Burke 2021), founded the online #MeToo movement. A survivor of sexual abuse herself, she wanted to enable Black women and girls to come forward and talk about their experiences of sexual harassment, sexual assault and rape within the Black community. She was shocked as her movement went viral in 2017, when her hashtag was used by Alyssa Milano to call forward any woman who had been sexually harassed or assaulted. Milano's spark were the allegations surfacing against megaproducer Harvey Weinstein, and the #MeToo movements that broke forth from that moment continue to progress. But Tarana Burke's focus on the experiences and needs of Black women and girls has been pushed into the background. Scholars writing about #MeToo rarely even acknowledge her contribution to creating this movement (Cossman 2021; Phipps 2020).

Benjamin Chavis, Jr. initiated the movement against environmental racism in 1982 (Bullard 1993). The water crisis in Flint, Michigan starting in 2014 devastated a largely Black city (Pauli 2019). As a result, greater awareness of the avoidable and yet profoundly damaging health and economic consequences of pollution concentrated in poor and often predominantly Black communities gained some traction. This kind of "slow death" is generally a lower priority for journalists because it tends to be less sensational than the catastrophe created by government officials in Flint. Yet local activists continue to wage campaigns against both governments and companies to stop such pollution in their communities, address the resulting health effects, and mitigate the environmental damage, which invariably also has negative economic impacts on Black households.

As long as there have been movies and television, Black Americans have actively sought to appear on screen, tell their own stories and shape the society's ideas about Black people (Bodroghkozy 2012; Erigha 2019). But after snubs in what should have been a winning year for Black movie artists, in 2015 April Reign took on the industry with the #OscarsSoWhite campaign. This social media phenomenon drew the support of many Hollywood actors and directors and forced the Academy of Motion Picture Arts and Sciences to respond. Without a dedicated on-the-ground organization, #OscarsSoWhite was a movement of a moment; it made visible the failure of Hollywood, despite generations of work by those in the entertainment industry as well as by external critics and even politicians to make the entertainment landscape in the United States fully representative of the stories and talents of its Black citizens. By the same token, Black social media users jumped on the possibilities of social media. Using video and digital photos as well as texts, they began to create spaces online to correct the narratives of news and commentary, build community, and offer each other real-time support and safety (Bailey 2021; De Kosnik and Feldman 2019; Jackson, Bailey and Foucault-Welles 2020; Jones 2019; Richardson 2020).

And then, in the winter and spring of 2020, the coronavirus pandemic hit. At a time when the public had heightened awareness of racial disparities in so many spaces of American life, the profoundly different rates of illness and death from the virus for Black and white Americans served as proof that healthcare was still as racialized as ever (Gonsalves and Kapczynski 2020). And yet arguably because of Black Lives Matter activism, awareness of these disparities made the center stage of public attention, to call for access to medical care, vaccinations, and preventative public health interventions.

All these movements and more were created by Black Americans. Along with Native Americans, they are the US constituency, across their multiple identities and subject positions, most likely to be subjected to violence and legal discrimination, incarceration, exaggerated levels of policing both during school years and after, barriers to upward economic mobility, and to everyday incidents of racist micro- and macroaggressions as they live their lives (Alvarez, Liang, and Neville 2016; Ansell 2017; Carroll 1998; Currie

2020; Gonsalves and Kapczynski 2020; Harris 2020; Hill 2016; Hoberman 2012; Kendall 2020; Living Cities and Pilgrim 2022; Washington 2006). In a system built upon the protection of privileges for some and the denial of basic rights for others, African Americans for centuries have been defined and treated as scapegoats for violence Whites might otherwise direct against each other. The movements which this current era builds upon have always worked to contest this status and sue for inclusion under the umbrella of full citizenship and social and economic rights.

While rooted in the experiences of Black, Indigenous and People of Color (BIPOC), these movements have developed widespread impacts, as well as broad and diverse support. They continue to reveal both active and passive complicity with racist and misogynist agendas in politics, policing, environmental protection, education and business. And they have held up a mirror to the Black community to address the sexual abuse and rape of Black girls and women by Black men. We believe this is a moment when scholars would do well to focus on how these Black-led movements, building upon but also building beyond the Civil Rights Movement of the 1960s, are working to transform the lives of Blacks in America as well as US society as a whole. It is a moment to reflect upon and engage in research on the goals, the means, the leaders, the supporters, and the outcomes so far during this period of activism.

This era of black activism has taken many forms: protests, online spaces, changes to law and public policy, and corporate responses. This volume seeks to bring together research and reflections on many of them, to show the reach of racism across social, political, economic, public and personal spaces, so that readers may begin to appreciate that Black activism, especially in this era, is never about only one issue or one strategy. We believe it has been the sustained, creative and adaptive work of activists who have continually found ways to bring forth a more perfect democracy, and a more beloved community.

To contend with the vast set of challenges that this era of black activism highlights, the activist community that has stepped forward is extremely diverse. It is multigenerational, ranging from veterans of the Civil Rights Era to generations of young leaders who came of age in a world with greater intersectionality. It has been led by Black women and included the issues of the LGBTQ community. And it has utilized the most contemporary media technologies to build support and mobilize the public. We reprint here an article by Jozie Nummi, Carly Jennings and Joe Feagin which explores these dynamics and sets a context for the Movement for Black Lives.

Two deaths that ushered in this era of black activism were the murders of Trayvon Martin and Michael Brown. Protest-based activism after these two murders shed light on two major structural issues: Stand Your Ground Laws and racist policing. Mary Marcel's chapter discusses Dream Defenders, a group that formed to protest the murder of Trayvon Martin by George Zimmerman. Their work, which began in 2012, has consistently focused on repealing Stand Your Ground laws in Florida, where Trayvon was killed, but has also expanded to a wider range of issues affecting Black and Brown Floridians. Jozie Nummi and Ammorette T. Young focus on the massive protests which took place in Ferguson, Missouri in August 2014 over the police shooting of Michael Brown. They examine official, media and citizen accounts of the disproportionate use of force and police interference with reporting. They establish the omissions in government reports, biased framing in news media accounts, and the volume of citizen reports on social media which paint a clear and disturbing picture of policing which targeted protesters but left their community and residential spaces unprotected.

To sustain this activism, Black individuals and communities have formed intentional spaces to correct the dominant narrative of White supremacy about Black lives and serve as a sanctuary for their community. Digital tools in the modern era have enabled citizens to capture video of racist murders by both police and citizens (Richardson 2020). This evidence has served to mobilize protests and substantiate judicial claims about police and civilians engaging in unlawful brutality against Black citizens. Joyce Hope Scott explores the history and meaning of Black Americans' use of cameras, photographs and film and the active resistance it has enabled. On both sides of the Atlantic, the camera as an agent of witnessing has empowered activists demanding justice and the rebuilding of cultures devastated by racism.

The impact of trauma from both experiencing and witnessing racialized violence in countless forms has been a newly framed issue in the twenty-first century (Buhuro 2019; Hinderliter and Peraza 2022). Social media has also been used to propagate claims and ideas which are not factual and intended to damage Black people and push back their social, political, and economic gains. David Stamps explores online Black digital spaces which create sanctuary across many dimensions and reflect the collective nature of Black community. He explores Black influencers who daily correct racist political and news narratives and create safe spaces to find collective healing from trauma and build community.

Unlike previous eras of Black activism, BIPOC women and queer individuals have been leading in this era without relying on the validation of Black male leaders, including church leaders, or White leaders. Activists like Alicia Garza, Patrisse Khan-Cullors and Opal Tometi have put the era of respectability politics behind us (Carruthers 2018; Cooper 2017; Garza 2020; Greenlee, Alabi, and Zinzi 2021; Khan-Cullors and Bandele 2017; Knight

Steele 2021). Their vision says you do not have to be middle-class or heteronormative to affirm the value of your life. Moussa Hassoun picks up the thread of this vision through the activist work of Black New York queers like Marsha P. Johnson, who led the Stonewall Uprising in 1969. Their demands for protection from police brutality inside and outside of the prison system, and for housing and safety for Black and minority queer people, were largely sidelined by White activists seeking to gain acceptance through assimilation to white middle-class norms (Hanhardt 2013; Rimmerman 2014; Schneider 2019). Queer activists in the Movement for Black Lives have challenged the corporatization of Pride marches and, since 2020 especially, have created Queer Black Power marches centering Black queer lives still threatened by violence, homelessness and marginalization.

This era of Black activism also emphasizes the importance of facing structural racism. The Civil Rights Era set the groundwork for changing the structure of knowledge to include Black narratives by Black scholars. The inception of African American studies was a result of the Civil Rights-era contestations of White higher education and structures of knowledge (Rojas 2010; Rooks 2007). This era is building on the work of the Civil Rights era, trying to center Black research and narratives in academic, public, and private institutions. In academic settings we include two chapters which discuss this work. Anne Rawls focuses on the work of White sociologists who sought to build on W. E. B. Du Bois's foundational contributions to the role of race in that field and challenge White-centric theories about society and social relationships within it. Utz McKnight and Greg Austin explore perspectives of Black scholars on defining their work not from behind the veil in relation to a White-created system and structure of knowledge, but as core and foundational to all human knowledge, without inflection or diminution.

By 2020, after years of murders of Black women and men by both citizens and police, the death of George Floyd brought a sea change in public awareness of the Movement for Black Lives. Its strength and power were manifested in large scale protests, but also new calls to defund the police and fundamentally redefine what justice means for Black and White America. It was not only activists but the public itself who now expected corporations and businesses to respond to this grievous injustice. Ziyuan Zhou analyzes the responses of Fortune 100 companies in their corporate social advocacy by examining public statements made on their company websites. He expands the analysis of public relations responses by utilizing both Corporate Social Activism theory, and Corporate Responsibility to Race theory. These represent major advances in public relations thinking developed and refined in response to current Black activism.

At the same time, there has been a somewhat greater acknowledgement of complex challenges *within* the Black community, like cultural betrayal and sexual abuse. Tarana Burke's #MeToo movement, which she created in 2006, was the spark that set off a worldwide movement in 2017 (Burke 2021). But as the movement in the US widened and was taken over largely by White women, as it moved forward, few White women reached back to support the work of Tarana Burke for Black women and girls who have experienced sexual assault and abuse by Black men (Cossman, 2020; Phipps, 2019). Standing in solidarity with Black women and girls who face these grievous challenges, our book contains a chapter by Jennifer Gómez that directly defines the experiences of sexual violence and trauma from within the community and develops pathways and hope for healing in both clinical and non-clinical settings.

In the midst of this decade of intensified Black activism, COVID-19 brought the world to a standstill. Melissa Hector's chapter addresses the disproportionate morbidity and mortality of Black individuals throughout the pandemic, and the work of activists in public health and medical care to address and reduce these disparities. She demonstrates another pathway by which activism can take place, namely through governmental organizations and agencies. We can pose the question of whether these disparities in rates of COVID-19 deaths and lack of access to treatment would have achieved the visibility that they did without the heightened urgency about saving and protecting Black lives brought about by the thousands of protests which preceded the onset of the pandemic.

Moving beyond private institutions, individual outcomes, and public health, it is clear that extensive long term structural policy changes must be made to fully realize the demands and vision of Black humanity (Livingstone Smith 2020; Winship et al. 2021). Through a discussion about the past and present, Edith Joachimpillai shares how unmet basic needs have led to poorer life and income outcomes for Black people. She then details how a new social contract can produce a set of race-conscious policy measures across social welfare programs. This is necessary to overcome the life outcome gaps that Black Americans face as compared to their peers of other races.

Finally, we wanted to include a bibliography of materials from 2000–2023 which address three other important areas of Black Activism. We collected books, chapters, and journal articles which address *activism around environmental racism* from throughout the United States. These efforts tend to be localized and therefore do not generate widespread journalistic attention, with the exception of Flint. But many other sites of community organizing and activism have taken place since 2000, and we include here the scholarship which has been produced about them. A second very notable area is *activism by Black athletes*, starting with Colin Kaepernick. There has been a great deal of scholarly attention to the many instances of such protests and their relationship to fan attitudes as well as corporate and league responses. We include those materials here. Third, we include materials discussing *activism by the Black church*. Black churches were situated at the center of much of the activism of the 1950s–1970s. We wanted to include materials which discuss trends and developments in Black church-related activism and the ways it connects to broader, non-church-based activism in this era.

This Era of Black Activism is multidimensional, intersectional, and interdisciplinary. In the 1960s, the movements for Black liberation, women's liberation, and gay liberation were distinctive and often separate efforts. Black Studies as an academic discipline emerged out of Black Liberation. Corporations have become more accountable to public demands, and issues of sexual assault and abuse are no longer in the shadows, thanks to generations of activists. We wanted to resist the tendency to narrowly focus on one area of activism to the neglect of others. Our hope is that an exploration of these many aspects of this era of Black activism showcases how they are interconnected, continuously developing, and additive in their impact.

REFERENCES

Ackermann, Nicole, Melody Goodman, Keon Gilbert, Cassandra Arroyo-Johnson, and Marcello Pagano. 2015. "Race, Law, and Health: Examination of 'Stand Your Ground' and Defendant Convictions in Florida." *Social Science & Medicine* 142 (15): 194–201. http://dx.doi.org/10.1016/j.socscimed.2015.08.012.

Alexander, Michelle. 2010. *The New Jim Crow: Mass Incarceration in the Age of Colorblindness*. New York: The New Press.

Alvarez, Alvin, Christopher Liang, and Helen Neville. 2016. *The Cost of Racism for People of Color: Contextualizing Experiences of Discrimination*. Washington, D.C.: American Psychological Association.

Ansell, David. 2017. *The Death Gap: How Inequality Kills*. Chicago: University of Chicago Press.

Bailey, Moya. 2021. *Misogynoir Transformed: Black Women's Digital Resistance*. New York: NYU Press.

Bodroghkozy, Aniko. 2012. *Equal Time: Television and the Civil Rights Movement*. Urbana: University of Illinois Press.

Buhuro, Danielle, ed. 2019. *Spiritual Care in an Age of #BlackLives Matter*. Eugene: Wipf and Stock Publishers.

Bullard, Robert. 1993. *Confronting Environmental Racism: Voices From the Grass Roots*. Boston: South End Press.

Bunn, Curtis, Michael Cottman, Patrice Gaines, Nick Charles, and Keith Harriston. 2021. *Say Their Names: How Black Lives Came to Matter in America.* New York: Grand Central Publishing.

Burke, Tarana. 2021. *Unbound: My Story of Liberation and the Birth of the Me Too Movement.* New York: Flatiron Books.

Campney, Brent. 2019. *Hostile Heartland: Racism, Repression, and Resistance in the Midwest.* Urbana: University of Illinois Press.

Carroll, Grace. 1998. *Environmental Stress and African Americans: The Other Side of the Moon.* Westport, CT: Praeger.

Carruthers, Charlene. 2018. *Unapologetic: A Black, Queer, and Feminist Mandate for Radical Movements.* Boston: Beacon Press.

Cobbina, Jennifer. 2019. *Hands Up Don't Shoot: Why the Protests in Ferguson and Baltimore Matter, and How They Changed America.* New York: NYU Press.

Collier-Thomas, Bettye and V. P. Franklin, eds. 2001. *Sisters in the Struggle: African American Women in the Civil Rights-Black Power Movement.* New York: NYU Press.

Cooper, Brittney. 2017. *Beyond Respectability: The Intellectual Thought of Race Women.* Urbana: University of Illinois Press.

Cossman, Brenda. 2021. *The New Sex Wars: Sexual Harm in the #MeToo Era.* New York: NYU Press.

Currie, Elliott. 2020. *A Peculiar Indifference: The Neglected Toll of Violence on Black America.* New York: Metropolitan Books.

Davis, Thulani. 2022. *The Emancipation Circuit: Black Activism Forging a Culture of Freedom.* Durham: Duke University Press.

De Kosnik, Abigail and Keith Feldman, eds. 2019. *#Identity: Hashtagging Race, Gender, Sexuality and Nation.* Ann Arbor: University of Michigan Press.

Erigha, Maryann. 2019. *The Hollywood Jim Crow: The Racial Politics of the Movie Industry.* New York: NYU Press.

Farmer, Ashley. 2017. *Remaking Black Power: How Black Women Transformed an Era.* Chapel Hill: University of North Carolina Press.

Finley, Mary Lou, Bernard Lafayette, Jr., James Ralph Jr., and Pam Smith, eds. 2015. *The Chicago Freedom Movement: Martin Luther King Jr. and Civil Rights Activism in the North.* Lexington: University of Kentucky Press.

Ford, Melissa. 2022. *A Brick and a Bible: Black Women's Radical Activism in the Midwest During the Great Depression.* Carbondale: Southern Illinois University Press.

Garza, Alicia. 2020. *The Purpose of Power: How We Come Together When We Fall Apart.* New York: One World/Random House.

Gillion, Daniel. 2020. *The Loud Minority: Why Protests Matter in American Democracy.* Princeton: Princeton University Press.

Gonsalves, Gregg and Amy Kapczynski. 2020. *The New Politics of Care: From COVID-19 to Black Lives Matter.* Cambridge, MA: Boston Review.

Greenlee, Cynthia, Kemi Alabi, and Janna Zinzi, eds. 2021. *The Echoing Ida Collection.* New York: The Feminist Press.

Hahn, Steven. 2003. *A Nation Under Our Feet: Black Political Struggles in the Rural South from Slavery to the Great Migration.* Cambridge, MA: Belknap Press.

Hall, Ashley R. 2020. "Slippin' In and Out of Frame: An Afrafuturist Feminist Orientation to Black Women and American Citizenship." *Quarterly Journal of Speech,* 106 (3): 341–51. doi:10.1080/00335630.2020.1785630.

Hanhardt, Christina. 2013. *Safe Space: Gay Neighborhood History and the Politics of Violence.* Durham: Duke University Press.

Harris, James. 2020. *Black Suffering: Silent Pain, Hidden Hope.* Minneapolis: Fortress Press.

Hedin, Benjamin. 2015. *In Search of the Movement: The Struggle for Civil Rights Then and Now.* San Francisco: City Lights Books.

Hill, Marc. 2016. *Nobody: Casualties of America's War on the Vulnerable, from Ferguson to Flint and Beyond.* New York: Atria/Simon & Schuster.

Hillstrom, Laurie. 2018. *Black Lives Matter: From a Moment to a Movement.* Santa Barbara: ABC-CLIO.

Hinderliter, Beth and Steve Peraza, eds. 2022. *More Than Our Pain: Affect and Emotion in the Era of Black Lives Matter.* Albany: State University of New York Press.

Hinton, Elizabeth. 2021. *America on Fire: The Untold Story of Police Violence and Black Rebellion Since the 1960s.* London: W. W. Norton.

Hoberman, John. 2012. *Black and Blue: The Origins and Consequences of Medical Racism.* Berkeley: University of California Press.

Holsaert, Faith, Martha Noonan, Judy Richardson, Betty Garman Robinson, Jean Smith Young, and Dorothy Zellner, eds. 2010. *Hands on the Freedom Plow: Personal Accounts by Women in SNCC.* Urbana: University of Illinois Press.

House, Ernest. 1988. *Jesse Jackson and the Politics of Charisma: The Rise and Fall of the PUSH/Excel Program.* Boulder: Westview Press.

Jackson, Sarah, Moya Bailey and Brooke Foucault-Welles. 2020. *Hashtag Activism: Networks of Race and Gender Justice.* Cambridge, MA: MIT Press.

Jacobs, Walter, Wendy Thompson Taiwo, and Amy August, eds. 2021. *Sparked: George Floyd, Racism and the Progressive Illusion.* St. Paul: Minnesota Historical Society.

Jones, Feminista. 2019. *Reclaiming Our Space: How Black Feminists Are Changing the World from the Tweets to the Streets.* Boston: Beacon Press.

Jones, Solomon. 2021. *Ten Lives, Ten Demands: Life-and-Death Stories, and a Black Activist's Blueprint for Racial Justice.* Boston: Beacon Press.

Kendall, Mikki. 2020. *Hood Feminism: Notes from the Women That a Movement Forgot.* New York: Viking.

Khan-Cullors, Patrisse and Asha Bandele. 2017. *When They Call You a Terrorist: A Black Lives Matter Memoir.* New York: St. Martin's Griffin.

Knight Steele, Catherine. 2021. *Digital Black Feminism.* New York: NYU Press.

Livingstone Smith, David. 2020. *On Inhumanity: Dehumanization and How to Resist It.* Oxford: Oxford University Press.

Lowery, Wesley. 2016. *They Can't Kill Us All: Ferguson, Baltimore, and a New Era in America's Racial Justice Movement.* Boston: Little, Brown & Co.

Living Cities and Amina Pilgrim. 2022. *Systemic Racism 101: A Visual History of the Impact of Racism in America*. New York: Adams Media.

McGuire, Danielle. 2010. *At the Dark End of the Street: Black Women, Rape, and Resistance—A New History of the Civil Rights Movement from Rosa Parks to the Rise of Black Power*. New York: Vintage Books.

Olson, Lynne. 2001. *Freedom's Daughters: The Unsung Heroines of the Civil Rights Movement from 1830 to 1970*. New York: Scribner.

Pauli, Benjamin. 2019. *Flint Fights Back: Environmental Justice and Democracy in the Flint Water Crisis*. Cambridge, MA: MIT Press.

Phipps, Alison. 2020. *Me, Not You: The Trouble with Mainstream Feminism*. Manchester, UK: Manchester University Press.

Ransby, Barbara. 2003. *Ella Baker and the Black Freedom Movement: A Radical Democratic Vision*. Chapel Hill: University of North Carolina Press.

———. 2018. *Making All Black Lives Matter: Reimagining Freedom in the 21st Century*. Oakland: University of California Press.

Richardson, Alissa. 2020. *Bearing Witness While Black: African Americans, Smartphones, and the New Protest #Journalism*. Oxford: Oxford University Press.

Rimmerman, Craig. 2014. *The Lesbian and Gay Movements: Assimilation or Liberation?* New York: Routledge.

Rojas, Fabio. 2010. *From Black Power to Black Studies: How a Radical Social Movement Became an Academic Discipline*. First edition. Baltimore: Johns Hopkins University Press.

Rooks, Noliwe. 2007. *White Money/Black Power: The Surprising History of African American Studies and the Crisis of Race in Higher Education*. Boston: Beacon Press.

Schneider, Jr., Richard. 2019. *In Search of Stonewall: The Riots at 50, the Gay & Lesbian Review at 25: Best Essays, 1994–2018*. Boston: G & LR Books.

Sweeney, Daniel. 2016. "Standing Up to 'Stand Your Ground' Laws: How the Modern NRA-Inspired Self-Defense Statutes Destroy the Principle of Necessity, Disrupt the Criminal Justice System, and Increase Overall Violence." *Cleveland State Law Review*, 64, 715–746. http://engagedscholarship.csuohio.edu/clevstlrev/vol64/iss3/10.

Washington, Harriet. 2006. *Medical Apartheid: The Dark History of Medical Experimentation on Black Americans from Colonial Times to the Present*. New York: Doubleday.

Winship, Scott, Christopher Pulliam, Ariel Shiro, Richard Reeves, and Santiago Deambrosi. 2021. *Long Shadows: The Black-White Gap in Multigenerational Poverty*. Washington, D.C.: The Brookings Institution. https://www.brookings.edu/wp-content/uploads/2021/06/Long-Shadows_Final.pdf.

Part 1

BLACK ACTIVISM

Chapter One

#BlackLivesMatter

*Innovative Black Resistance**

Jozie Nummi, Carly Jennings, and Joe Feagin

Since 2013, extrajudicial police killings of black people have captured the attention of United States and international media, substantially because of the work of leaders in the Black Lives Matter (#BLM) movement. #BLM is simultaneously a group of localized organizations and a broad online social movement. In this article, we examine the #BLM movement in detail, with particular emphasis on the following aspects of the movement: (1) its innovative organizational practices and social media use; (2) its accent on black perspectives (counterframing) of systemic racial oppression, heteronormativity, and capitalism; and (3) its broad emphasis on oppressed Americans, including black women and LGBTQ+ people. We also situate the #BLM movement within the surrounding system of racial oppression, including the historical role of racialized policing in maintaining social control of blacks. We detail the long tradition of black social movements, especially black feminist organizing, against systemic racial oppression. In doing so, we intend to contribute social movement theorizing that more fully considers powerful counterframed perspectives of black activists in US social movements. Although the #BLM movement reflects black feminism and past civil rights movement struggles, it is a uniquely twenty-first-century social movement that uses new technologies for innovative social protest.

INTRODUCTION

Historically, African Americans and other Americans of color have experienced extensive exploitation, violence, and other oppression at the hands of

---

Reprinted from Sociological Forum 2019.

various policing agents—white slave patrols, vigilantes, and law enforcement agents—ever since Europeans violently stole and colonized territory occupied by indigenous nations and forced work on that land by enslaved African Americans. Researchers have shown that one factor in the development of numerous US policing agencies has been an explicit goal of subordinating African Americans and other Americans of color. Some early policing agencies, such as early slave patrols, had this as a major responsibility (Feagin 2012; Hadden 2003; Roth and Kennedy 2012). Black social movements resisted these discriminatory and oppressive police agents, court systems, and prisons since the days of slavery (Dillon 1990; Morris 1984). To better understand what Black Lives Matter (#BLM) is, it is important to understand this context and background, including the persisting white-controlled use of police agencies and other parts of the US criminal justice system to target, criminalize, and subordinate black Americans and other people of color.

For centuries, black people have actively resisted this system of racial oppression, especially its racist policing and other control aspects, in their own counterframing and protest actions, although much of this historical background remains little known. #BLM is a continuation of past social movements but is innovative in its own right. In this article we provide an overview of #BLM, their goals and innovations, the online social movement and the counterframing of online users and organizations. First, we review the political and social conditions the #BLM movement emerged within and their claims for justice. Second, we examine their policy goals as part of the policy platform of the Movement for Black Lives (M4BL). Third, we review the use of social media to produce counterframes to the white racial frame. This article aims to highlight how #BLM is aiming to bring the United States closer to providing liberty and justice for all, especially black Americans.

THE DEEP HISTORICAL BACKGROUND

This historical resistance is necessary because in the US case, systemic racism is based on a broad white racial frame (worldview) that penetrates all social institutions, public consciousness, and political bodies. This white frame puts whites constantly at the top of the racial hierarchy, constructing them as good and virtuous, while constructing people of color as the "other" and negatively framed as unvirtuous. Feagin (2013) details how this white frame includes a beliefs aspect (racial stereotypes), integrating cognitive elements (racial narratives), visual elements (racialized images), racialized emotions, and an inclination to discriminate. It includes a very positive orientation toward whites as generally virtuous (a pro-white subframe) and a negative orientation to racial "others" as substantially unvirtuous (anti-other subframes). This white racial frame generates, legitimates, and reproduces the patterns of racial discrimination and racially stratified institutions in society, including its central policing and other criminal justice organizations. Police departments and the criminal justice system are the violent and militarized implementation of the white racial frame in the daily lives of black communities.

Much of the historical background of the resistance to systemic racial and gender oppression is not well known in mainstream white America. Over these centuries, black people have developed an assertive counterframing very critical of the dominant white-racist framing and its well-institutionalized discriminatory actions targeting them and others of color. The contemporary black counterframe includes a strong critique of white oppression, a vigorous countering of negative framing of African Americans, a positive assertion of the full humanity of African Americans, a clear assertion of the Americanness of African Americans, and a strong accent on liberty, justice, and equality for all. This counterframing also includes a recognition of the gendered racism black people face (Collins 2009 (2000); Combahee River Collective 2015 (1977); Crenshaw 1991; Feagin 2013).

For example, historian Herbert Aptheker (1943) documented 250 slave uprisings, along with many other rebellions by enslaved African Americans on both an individual and a group level. In the mid-eighteenth century, David Walker's (1829) *Appeal to the Coloured Citizens of the World* was one of first published African American statements to present an antioppression resistance framework, with many elements still being present today in the counterframing African Americans use to counter racial oppression. David Walker, Maria Stewart, and other black people worked courageously to address systemic racism and sexism in this black protest tradition. Stewart, like Walker, worked unapologetically for black liberation and advocated for black collective action. Unfettered by structural barriers to black intellectual development, she utilized her writing and public speaking talents to create change in systemic racism in nineteenth-century America (Stewart and Richardson 1987).

This fight for black liberation did not end with slavery, as white oppression evolved into new forms of social control—such as lynching-enforced Jim Crow segregation. In the late 1800s Ida B. Wells-Barnett, an African American journalist and anti-lynching activist, continued the African American tradition of speaking out and publishing sharp critiques of white racism and pressing for racial change, in this case against white vigilante violence to police and control black communities (Barnett 1993; Wells-Barnett 1991). Later on in the twentieth century, black women's leadership in the civil rights movement and in organizations such as the Student Nonviolent Coordinating Committee (SNCC), Third World Women's Alliance (TWWA), and Black

Panthers was substantially impactful on that critical movement, though often unrecognized (Poirot 2015). Black women such as Angela Davis, Ella Baker, Diane Nash, Fannie Lou Hamer, Prathia Hill, and Rosa Parks, among countless others, contributed greatly to shaping the civil rights movement's strategies and tactics and its active demonstrations against white racist institutions, including racialized policing institutions and their white violence against African Americans (Hogan 2007; Wells-Barnett 1991).

Although the civil rights movement produced legislative changes affecting housing and voting rights, the problem of police brutality persisted. On August 28, 1963, at the March on Washington, current US congressman John Lewis, who was then chair of the SNCC, emphasized the constant failure to protect black citizens from white police brutality in the Jim Crow era. Underscoring what would affect future protests, he said, "In good conscience, we cannot support wholeheartedly the administration's civil rights bill. There's not one thing in the bill that will protect our people from police brutality. This bill will not protect young children and old women from police dogs and fire hoses, for engaging in peaceful demonstrations" (Lewis 2015, 219). Lewis's criticism of what became the 1965 Civil Rights Act brings us to our discussion of extrajudicial police killings and other abuses of black Americans in the contemporary US criminal justice system.

Similar white policing practices contributed to the underlying conditions of black uprisings and revolts in racially marginalized communities in the 1960s and 1970s. Substantial data collected for the famous 1960s "ghetto riots" in US cities provide some context for and congruencies with the contemporary #BLM movement. A majority of the major black uprisings in the cities had a precipitating event that involved conflict between a white police officer and black person. Much research shows that the causes of the urban uprisings in the 1960s–1970s and the nonviolent civil rights movement included policing oppression and other economic, political, and social oppression of African Americans by whites (Feagin and Hahn 1973; Feagin and Sheatsley 1968; Hahn and Feagin 1970). Unsurprisingly, the 1960s protests are similar to contemporary #BLM protests in which black communities targeted by white-run police departments again protest these same discriminatory conditions that remain central to systemic racism.

THE BLACK LIVES MATTER MOVEMENT

The goals of the contemporary #BLM movement address this continued oppression of black Americans and other people of color in the US criminal justice system, schools, and other institutions. Alicia Garza, Patrisse Khan-

Cullors, and Opal Tometi founded #BLM after George Zimmerman's acquittal for this extralegal killing. Zimmerman shot Trayvon Martin, an unarmed young black man on February 26, 2012. Acting without legal authority as a self-appointed policing agent, Zimmerman pursued Martin, who was visiting his father in the subdivision, with a gun after he called 911 to report a "suspicious person" (Botelho and Yan 2013). After a struggle with Martin, who was unarmed, Zimmerman shot him. However, he was found not guilty on July 13, 2013. As with past black movements, Zimmerman's murder of Trayvon Martin initiated many new black protests across the country.

Garza, Khan-Cullors, and Tometi were longtime organizers when they reflected on Trayvon's murder by Zimmerman. They reflected on Garza's Facebook post expressing anger following the acquittal for murder and stating that "Black Lives Matter" (Craven 2015). After reading the post, Khan-Cullors started using the #BlackLivesMatter hashtag on Twitter. Subsequently, Kahn-Cullors, Tometi, and Garza discussed how this emerging black movement needed its own organizations and social platform. Their website states that their goal is to "(re)build the Black liberation movement" (Garza 2014). Yet again, this ongoing movement is influenced by the injustice of extralegal killings, connecting past and present white oppression and black resistance.

#BLACKLIVESMATTER STRUCTURE AND GOALS: MAJOR SOCIAL MOVEMENT INNOVATIONS

The #BLM movement has three important organizing aspects: (1) local chapter-based, member-led organizations, (2) a distinctive #BLM hashtag and impactful online social movement, and (3) a larger black movement with national organizing and training programs (Freelon, Mcilwain, and Clark 2016). It is supported by an online news network and by "Black Twitter," the black cultural phenomenon on Twitter (Brock 2012; Clark 2014; Florini 2014). #BLM has more than forty chapters around the United States and in Canada, as well as a few in Europe. Each is locally member-led while being supported by the national organization's organizing principles and important training programs. The movement is innovative in at least two respects: (1) in their constant emphasis on supporting all black lives and (2) in amplifying their message through new social media networks and platforms.

#BlackLivesMatter's members often describe themselves as building an infrastructure—accenting the goal of building more black political-economic power across the country, and indeed abroad. Local chapters are working to address community needs and histories. These chapters and structure make the movement "leaderful," which is a strategic choice of #BLM founders.

These black activists are "adaptive and decentralized" to address local needs and time-sensitive events (Matthews and Noor 2017). This decentralized structure is a purposeful choice, and it reflects the collective nature of their organizing around the country as well as the unique needs and actions identified by chapters leaders. This network of organizations often links to past social networks that supported the 1960s civil rights movement, which consisted of SNCC, Southern Christian Leadership Conference, Congress on Racial Equality, National Association for the Advancement of Colored People, other civil rights organizations, and black churches. Despite this similarity in their structure, they are innovative in choosing to stay secular and in their use of social media platforms that allow members everywhere to support individual chapter efforts, such as local protests, through rapid responses.

While #BLM founders describe their organization as a continuation of past black rights movements, they strongly emphasize that they aim to avoid the "harmful practices that excluded so many in past movements for liberation" (Garza 2014). They assert that past liberation movements have too often centered on "black heterosexual, cisgender men" and thereby marginalized "women, queer and transgender people, and others" (Matthews and Noor 2017). Part of avoiding harmful practices involves accenting an important array of socially marginalized voices, including LGBTQ people and undocumented immigrants (Garza 2014). In contrast, the 1960s civil rights movement relied heavily on the African American church for much labor, organizational structure, and leaders, as well as for legitimacy and respectability (Morris 1984). Civil rights advocates such as Bayard Rustin and Barbara Jordan, among others, are often forgotten or downplayed in civil rights history because of the homophobic and transphobic thinking long prevalent within many black churches and communities at times, as well as in the larger white supremacist society (Garza 2017; Poirot 2015). The #BLM's localized and adaptive network of chapters provides significant space for the development of new African American leaders of diverse gender and class backgrounds, and for these leaders to determine the needs of their specific communities (Matthews and Noor 2017).

#BlackLivesMatter activists addressed larger US government foreign policy issues. This work is similar to activism by Frantz Fanon, Pauli Murray, and others. #BLM raised these issues to be a central concern of the national and international M4BL, which makes these issues more central to black activism than the past national civil rights movement platform. They emphasize that the US government not only colonized indigenous lands using genocidal tactics and established slavery in the United States but also later expanded US imperialism worldwide through recurring US military actions—the latter including intervention into other countries' political and economic systems.

This white imperialism is not limited to some distant past but has persisted in US corporations' exploitation of workers of color in the Global South (formerly the "third world"), usually with US government backing (Glenn 2015; Massey and Pren 2012; Paradies 2016). In foregrounding these ongoing structures of US colonialism and imperialism, #BLM activists and their organizations have established more space for solidarity and inclusion for many populations of color, including undocumented immigrants and indigenous populations in the United States and other countries (Garza 2014; Matthews and Noor 2017). These commitments and actions in solidarity with other groups reflect the #BLM goal of social justice for all lives of peoples of color, at home and abroad.

The #BLM movement is rare among contemporary anti-oppression movements in addressing what Feagin and Ducey (2017) term the US "triple helix of oppression" through their important guiding principles and consequent action. Drawing from intersectionality theorists such as Crenshaw and Collins, Feagin and Ducey define the triple helix of oppression as the interlocking systems of systemic racism, systemic sexism, and systemic classism. In this manner, they operate in the tradition of pioneering black women author-activists such as Zora Neale Hurston, Audre Lorde, and women in the group called the Combahee River Collective (Combahee River Collective 2015 (1977); Crenshaw 1991; Lorde 2007; Smith, Hull, and Scott 1982). The #BLM activists use their major social platform to deconstruct and critique the sexism that systemically oppresses black women, transgender people, and queer people, including within black patriarchal family structures. In addition, this black feminist perspective recognizes there are no single-issue struggles, for black women are always black, women, and workers simultaneously. From this critical perspective, #BLM founders recognize that the "personal is political" and seek to eliminate all systems of oppression targeting black communities, including systemic racism, sexism, and classism (capitalism). Their stated principles include a commitment to racial, gender, and class diversity—indeed, they are unapologetically black, queer, and transgender affirming—and to restorative justice and global resistance connections among peoples of color (Matthews and Noor 2017).

The distinctive approach of the #BLM chapter leaders and the M4BL to contemporary social organizing also incorporates concerns with community healing and social justice, with black feminism and intersectional social justice. This approach has a long tradition in black communities, albeit one mostly unrecognized in the social movement literature of the social sciences (Bracey 2016; Collins 2009 (2000); Smith 2017). These practices, for instance, are reflected in the contemporary #BLM Healing Justice Working Group, which aims to provide healing justice to black communities. This broad healing

Jozie Nummi, Carly Jennings, and Joe Feagin

practice orientation is innovative because it is elevated as a regular part of the broad counterframing of this major national black liberation movement, rather than being delegated to only black women participants and thus unrecognized as critical movement labor (as happened in some earlier civil rights movements). The pioneering #BLM founders Tometi, Khan-Cullors, and Garza follow a long line of black female activists who have addressed major intersectional types of racial, gender, and class oppression that black Americans (and other people of color) routinely and frequently experience (Garza 2017).

GOALS

As in the 1960s civil rights movement, protests by #BLM chapters have very specific community goals. They aim to affect local government actions to improve black freedom and living conditions in communities, including pointed messages to the mostly white officials that police malpractice will no longer be tolerated. Central to #BLM is the foundational claim that black perspectives matter. Their goals are proclaimed and developed through social media such as Twitter, even though they are often ignored by mainstream news media. For example, during the Ferguson protests, black users posted fliers from the protests. These protesters included Antonio French, a black local alderman; Wesley Lowery, a black Washington Post journalist; and Michael Skolnik, a Jewish American editor-in-chief of GlobalGrind. Antonio French sent out a flier on Twitter on August 11, 2014, at 10:26 a.m. (Central Standard Time). By the next day, at 7:47 p.m., it had been retweeted 1,567 times, signaling rapid and widespread dissemination. According to the flier, the demands of the black Ferguson protesters included that:

1. The officer involved in the shooting death of Michael Brown be immediately identified.
2. The same officer should be immediately fired and charged with murder.
3. The Ferguson Police Department "Protocol Handbook" be distributed throughout the Ferguson community.
4. The racial composition of the Ferguson Police Department should reflect the racial demographics of the community.

These specific community goals also exemplify the larger objective of #BLM to call for localized data and institutional changes, again often centered on changes in white-run policing and other aspects of the criminal justice system. Thus, the political purpose of the protesters was very clear within two days of the shooting, because of the speed of the use of social media.

While #BlackLivesMatter is now a well-known slogan, the group's specific public policy goals, such as these, are much less known. According to a Pew Research Center (2016) survey, only 12 percent of whites said they knew the goals of #BLM well. Comparatively, a third of blacks reported they knew the goals of #BLM well.

However, this lack of knowledge is not due to a #BLM failure to state clearly their goals but from a lack of mainstream media attention. Thus, in 2016 some #BLM leaders and other organizations outlined their broader public policy goals as part of the M4BL (Anonymous 2016), again accenting that black perspectives matter on specific criminal justice issues. Their broad platform targets the modern expression of white-on-black policing and subordination in a white-run government framework, education reform, healthcare reform, and other issues. Their goals have not been widely circulated by the white-run news media. Furthermore, the complexity and full recognition of effort of the more than fifty organizations is not publicized. #BLM's organization cosigned a policy agenda as part of the Movement for Black Lives Policy Table. The M4BL addresses violence against black communities in the United States and globally. To address the lack of attention to this movement, we briefly state some of the M4BL goals:

- Direct democratic community control of local, state, and federal law enforcement agencies, ensuring that communities most harmed by destructive policing have the power to hire and fire officers, determine disciplinary action, control budgets and policies, and subpoena relevant agency information.
- An end to money bail, mandatory fines, fees, court surcharges, and "defendant-funded" court proceedings.
- An end to the use of past criminal history to determine eligibility for housing, education, licenses, voting, loans, employment, and other services and needs.
- An end to the mass surveillance of black communities and the end to the use of technologies that criminalize and target our communities (including international mobile subscriber identity-catchers, drones, body cameras, and predictive policing software).
- The demilitarization of law enforcement, including law enforcement in schools and on college campuses.
- An immediate end to the privatization of police, prisons, jails, probation, parole, food, phone and all other criminal justice-related services.

Repeatedly, the goal statements of #BLM activists and the M4BL accent much more than a modestly reformed criminal justice system. Here, they are calling for major reforms in and/or substantial replacement of the current white-run criminal justice system and justice in education, health care, and politics for trans lives and larger LGBQ communities. These reforms address long-standing patterns of racial discrimination in the US criminal justice system, which often date back to the slavery and Jim Crow eras (Alexander 2012; Davis 2014; Henricks and Harvey 2017).

Indeed, in examining the #BLM local and national objectives, one quickly sees that systemic racism in policing and other aspects of the white-run criminal justice system are constant and central themes. Current policing institutions are the continued militarized and violent articulation of the white racial frame against populations of color. For example, although the mainstream media and police organizations usually frame police killings as individualized incidents of "bad apples" or single officers abusing their power, #BLM activists have regularly addressed systemic abuses of police power, such as the well-institutionalized pattern of discriminatory racial profiling. Furthermore, they have protested the discriminatory actions of white-run police unions and the use of military equipment by many police departments, which are often used to aggressively police communities of color (see Apuzzo 2014; King 2018). Numerous official reports and research studies have supported #BLM claims of substantial injustice in the criminal justice system.

Protests in Ferguson, Missouri, in August 2014 provide an example of the systemic racism and use of militarized equipment by police departments and criminal justice organizations. Specifically consider the findings from the US Department of Justice (DoJ) report on Ferguson, Missouri, where protests took place in which #BLM was involved (United States Department of Justice 2015). Despite African Americans constituting about 67 percent of the population in Ferguson, there were only four African American officers compared to 50 white officers. The DoJ found staggering amounts of racial profiling and excessive use of violence by local police. The investigation also found that "African Americans are more likely to be searched but less likely to have contraband found on them" (United States Department of Justice 2015, 71). An investigation of the Ferguson Police Department (FPD) by the DoJ found that explicit and implicit racism was pervasive in the FPD and associated court system. The discriminatory FPD actively supported itself with substantial revenue from citations, fines, and tickets issued to the city's mostly black residents. The report found that the FPD is running what is termed a debtor's prison, "the arrest and jailing of poor people for failure to pay legal debts they can never hope to afford, through criminal justice procedures that violate their most basic rights" (ACLU 2016). The investigation noted that the racist culture of the predominantly white FPD had resulted in excessive, often illegal, arrests and use of police force against ordinary residents. Unsurprisingly, the US Department of Justice (2016) sued the city of Ferguson, citing "a pattern or practice of law enforcement conduct that violates the First, Fourth and 14th Amendments of the Constitution and federal civil rights laws." Thus, #BLM criminal justice system concerns are not unwarranted, as many mainstream commentators insist, but are backed up by much social science and other research on racial profiling and other police malpractice (Davis 2002; Hirschfield 2015; Hyland, Langton, and Davis 2015; Russell 1988; Worden 1996).

WHITE FRAMING, BLACK COUNTERFRAMING: OLD AND NEW MEDIA

Social movement theorists in the social sciences have often suggested that movement protests may be less successful in effecting change without significant media attention (Gitlin 2003; Lipsky 1968; McAdam 1999; Tarrow 2011 (1994)). Today, when the white-run media attempt to delegitimize protests, the social media platforms add an important space for black social movements to critique mainstream white framing online. They are very important in giving marginalized communities of color a much stronger voice, in providing an innovative organizing mechanism, and in enabling better coverage of movements' offline antiracist protests. The counterframing taking place online analyzed within this article is produced by #BLM activists, member organizations of M4BL, and online users not directly involved with any organization per se. The use of the #BlackLivesMatter hashtag has become an important political choice for black activists and their opponents alike (Anderson et al. 2018). Even the 2016 US presidential debates included a mainstream media question on #BlackLivesMatter, which illustrated these contemporary activists' ability to significantly affect the national political agenda (Flores 2015).

MAINSTREAM NEWS MEDIA AND BLACK SOCIAL MOVEMENTS

Because of white framing in and control of the mainstream media, for more than a century black rights activists and groups have utilized an antiracist counterframe to press for racial justice, especially as presented in alternative black media (Feagin 2013; Morris 1984). African Americans have a long tradition of using alternative media to amplify their antiracist counterframe (Dillon 1990). To take another example, in May 1835 the American Anti-Slavery

Society—created by mostly white abolitionists but soon a major platform for the black leader Frederick Douglass and other black abolitionists—published antislavery pamphlets detailing the suffering of enslaved Americans. These abolitionists were able to "flood the nation" with publications distributed in the North and South (Dillon 1990, 178). This tradition carried into the twentieth century's civil rights movements. Ida B. Wells-Barnett, the previously mentioned African American woman activist, led the fight against lynching in that same period through her activism and journalism, including use of extensive use of her own printing press. Her columns on racism issues were printed and reprinted nationwide, once landing her the title of "Princess of the Press" (McMurry 1998, 102).

News of protests and editorial persuasion in alternative black newspapers were central in raising consciousness on, and organizing for, racial justice during the 1910s–1960s civil rights movements (McAdam 1999; Morgan 2010). These were necessary to counter white-racist images of black rights activists. Later on in the 1960s, white news organizations framed SNCC and other black activists negatively as "rebellious youth," "outside agitators," or "hyper-militants" (Morgan 2010, 76, 71, 77). Mainstream discourse delegitimized nonviolent protests and black "riots" (uprisings), ignoring the underlying policing and socioeconomic conditions generating black anger. Morgan (2010, 90) concluded that much white media coverage about the 1960s social movements "failed to take their grievances and arguments seriously," which marginalized the movements and cast them "outside the bounds of legitimate discourse," at least among whites. However, police brutality images in the same media following the black protest campaign in Birmingham "electrified" and energized the black audiences who saw them (Morgan 2010, 122). Graham and Smith (2016) also emphasize the use of television coverage of the civil rights movement to provide political pressure nationally and internationally. Thus, both alternative black news media and the protesters' images in black and mainstream media were crucial elements in spurring the 1960s civil rights movement (Graham and Smith 2016). Similar to that earlier civil rights movement, #BLM has sought out and used alternative black media space—for example, much of the black social media—to address the extrajudicial and other unjust killings of black people by white vigilantes and police officers (Gamson 1992; Johnston 2005).

NEW SOCIAL MEDIA AND BLACK ACTIVISM

Today, Twitter and other social media often function as alternative black media spaces and thereby lend themselves to facilitating successful civic participation (Conover et al. 2013; Gleason 2013; Halpern and Gibbs 2012; Murthy 2013; Theocharis et al. 2015; Varnali and Gorgulu 2015). When major social networking sites are used to gather information, there is frequently a positive impact on individuals' level of engagement in civic and political action, whatever their racial background (Gil de Zu'n~iga, Jung, and Valenzuela 2012). Although participation in a social movement in the past traditionally required a physical presence at an event or participation in a letter-writing campaign, now activism can be from users' cell phones, tablets, and laptops (Earl et al. 2015). This frequently results in "a more engaged, informed group of citizens" (Gleason 2013, 980; Murthy 2013). As we see it, rather than analyzing or considering social media posts as just individual matters, it is very important in many cases to analyze them as collective social phenomena, which can often create major political pressures that enable social movements to significantly affect the public policy agenda.

Discussions of racist issues and black political issues on Twitter are facilitated by Black Twitter. That is, news of important racist events go trending on Twitter because there is a very strong black network online, especially of black women activists (Freelon et al. 2016). There is a flourishing analytical discussion surrounding what is described as Black Twitter (Brock 2012; Clark 2014; Florini 2014; Graham and Smith 2016; Sharma 2013). Florini (2014, 225) describes the phenomenon of Black Twitter as "millions of black users on Twitter networking, connecting, and engaging with others who have similar concerns, experiences, tastes, and cultural practices." Black Americans have taken quickly to these new social media and are now disproportionately represented among social media users. Graham and Smith (2016) defined Black Twitter as a counterpublic, because it is a major place to provide information and news unavailable in the mainstream media. That is, this is a major space for black users to produce uniquely black views and discussions, like those discussed for decades in all-black spaces such as black barbershops and beauty salons (Graham and Smith 2016; Lei 2018). Clearly, these crucial black discussions of social justice matters are ordinarily not part of the mainstream media, which signals again the importance of these new social media to the #BLM campaigns for social justice. Black Twitter is yet another important form of alternative news media in the long tradition of African Americans using their own publishing media as platforms to change a racist US society.

Comprehensive studies of the hashtags #Ferguson and #BlackLivesMatter have been done by Freelon et al. (2016), and other studies have analyzed Ferguson Twitter data in some detail (Bonilla and Rosa 2015; Harris 2015; Jackson and Welles 2016). Bonilla and Rosa (2015) have assessed how this "hashtag activism" helps to foster political activism more broadly. Various studies on Twitter activity during Ferguson protests confirm hashtag activism took place and support Black Twitter as a counter public. Jackson and Welles (2016) analyzed specific Ferguson data on Twitter between August 9 and August 15, 2014, and found that both white elites and less powerful black Americans used many tweets to try to influence the national debate over Michael Brown's death. Some black users criticized the use of the word mob and suggested community as a better descriptor (Jackson and Welles 2016:407). In addition, Freelon et al. (2016) analyzed nine periods of Twitter data from June 1, 2014, to May 31, 2015, providing a comprehensive overview of the online social movement and #BLM organization. They found that the online social movement integrated alternative news networks to elevate issues important to the movement onto the national stage. Ray et al. (2017) concludes that the widespread use of the hashtag #Ferguson on Twitter has come to represent a collective racial identity, illustrating black solidarity in regard to the significance of racialized policing in the United States. Furthermore, black Ferguson hashtag users online were much more likely than others to find and retweet Twitter accounts that exemplified "marginalized public (framing) over mainstream framing" of these Ferguson events. In this way Twitter was a "tool for subverting traditional citizen—state power structures, enabling counterpublics to drive national conversations" (Jackson and Welles 2016:406, 413). Our findings detailed below reflect the use of Black Twitter as a counterpublic being integral to #BLM and anti-brutality protests.

Still, there are major critics of this type of movement participation. Although many people post on social media with the belief they are making a significant difference, some critics suggest that this is a rather low level of participation, one described by some as "slacktivism" (Cadei 2014; Murthy 2013). Slacktivism is a valid critique of the motivation and participation of some social media users, but criticism misses other examples where there are powerful impacts. For instance, important activist hashtags often reach major cable television news shows; they are commonly featured in the "trending" list for Twitter and on other social media sites. This requires a significant number of activists to be posting about the same topic using that hashtag. This strategy is helpful as activist-users on Twitter and other websites like Instagram can follow hashtags to gain significant information about ongoing protest topics and events. Murthy (2013, 99) argues that despite the low level of energy needed to post on social media, such "modes of communication have historically been integral to revolutions." Thus, we analyze hashtags and posts as applying political pressure, providing new information about protests, and defining social movement goals further.

The data we analyze here that we identify as counterframing is produced by #BLM organizations, organizations that are part of M4BL, and online users not involved in an organization. The authors analyzed #BLM social media guides, social media activity during Ferguson protests, online news articles about #BLM, and reviewed articles analyzing social media data to determine the opportunities provided by social media platforms, specifically Twitter. The Twitter data were obtained by purchasing publicly available randomly sampled tweets from Twitter. The data set included 176,000 public tweets between August 9 and August 31, 2014, about Ferguson protests, using specific filters. Four hundred fifty-five of the most retweeted tweets were coded. The authors determined from these data sets online users provided counterframing to mainstream news reporting on Ferguson protests following the shooting of Michael Brown by Officer Darren Wilson.

In this data set and analysis of #BLM reports, we confirmed prior findings that Twitter is utilized as a counterpublic because of Black Twitter and online user participation. We extend these findings to illustrate that counterframing was present in 443 of the 455 tweets analyzed. As a reminder, the contemporary black counter-frame includes a strong critique of white oppression, an aggressive countering of negative framing of African Americans, a positive assertion of the full humanity of African Americans, a clear assertion of the Americanness of African Americans, and a strong accent on liberty, justice, and equality for all. These counterframes were found in various forms on Twitter and emphasize a continuation of past struggles online.

Although the post-civil rights era is thought by many white analysts to be relatively free from significant racist framing in most white minds, black social media users have regularly provided a window into the lives of black Americans and other people of color that demonstrates that racial discrimination is still regularly experienced by them (Boyd 2013; Daniels 2013; Feagin 2014; Nakamura 2008). The use of Twitter by #BLM illustrates the significance of modes of communication, as many #BLM activists have used the platform to critique mainstream media framing of police brutality victims and of the often militarized police forces. The Black Twitter network and community, and the essential cultural critique they provide, have accelerated the development and circulation of black counterframing against white racism, the latter being central to the online efforts critical to the #BLM movement. Social media users who contribute to the #BLM organization and its related online activities delineate and regularly critique many explicit examples of current institutional racism, such as the negative coverage of those who are the actual black victims of recurring police brutality. For example, on Twitter the typical pro-white racist framing of white criminals in mainstream media has been compared to the often antiblack biased framing of Michael Brown and other men and women of color. The mainstream media framing of Michael Brown frequently used multiple racist stereotypes and images from old antiblack elements of the dominant white frame, in effect justifying his being shot by Officer Darren Wilson. This media framing portrayed the black teenager as criminal, delinquent, and dangerous, and with language such as "he was no angel" (Eligon 2014; Sullivan 2014). Countering this mainstream approach, the hashtag #iftheygunnedmedown was utilized by many as a discursive technique that highlighted the differences between the negative pictures of Brown in the mainstream media versus more positive school photographs these media utilized for white victims or white mass shooters. These social media users explicitly reframed the African American teenager as a contributing member of society and a college student. This strategy was emphasized through a #BLM report instructing users to share the following tweet: "Trayvon was a high school student, a son, and a Black child with his whole life ahead of him #RememberingTrayvon." This reflects the counterframe illustrating a positive assertion of the full humanity of African Americans. Again, social media use accents that African American perspectives matter and are too often missing in mainstream media.

Most users articulated the counterframing by stating that they were sharing an image that mainstream news networks did not show. They often counterframed the negative framing of black Americans by the mainstream media during #BLM protests. #Sonsandbrothers and #SOB (Save Our Brothers) was used in reference to police brutality victims in the data set. Thus, using such hashtags, one user shared the statistic that "every 28 hours a black male is killed in the United States by police or vigilantes. #Ferguson." They also provided insight into the socialization of black children titled "Survival Lessons for Black Youth" (Fig. 1). These tweets frequently link the racist past with the racist present and thus strongly suggest the fight for racial equality never ended. This these tweets counterframe the mainstream media's numerous negative images of African Americans, emphasizing their full humanity and a call for liberty and justice for all.

Black rights protesters are reframed by black social media users; the latter have provided more context or positive framing of protesters. In the #BLM online movement, a common action involved sharing street and other photos that black users felt would not be passed along by the mainstream media. These included pictures of peaceful protesters, of youthful black gang members protecting a store from being looted, and of young black men cleaning up Ferguson after the protests. The online #BLM movement and associated social media activities aggressively and regularly brought to light the struggles of being black in America, especially by using many striking images neglected in the mainstream media. This counterframing reflects an aggressive countering of negative framing of African Americans.

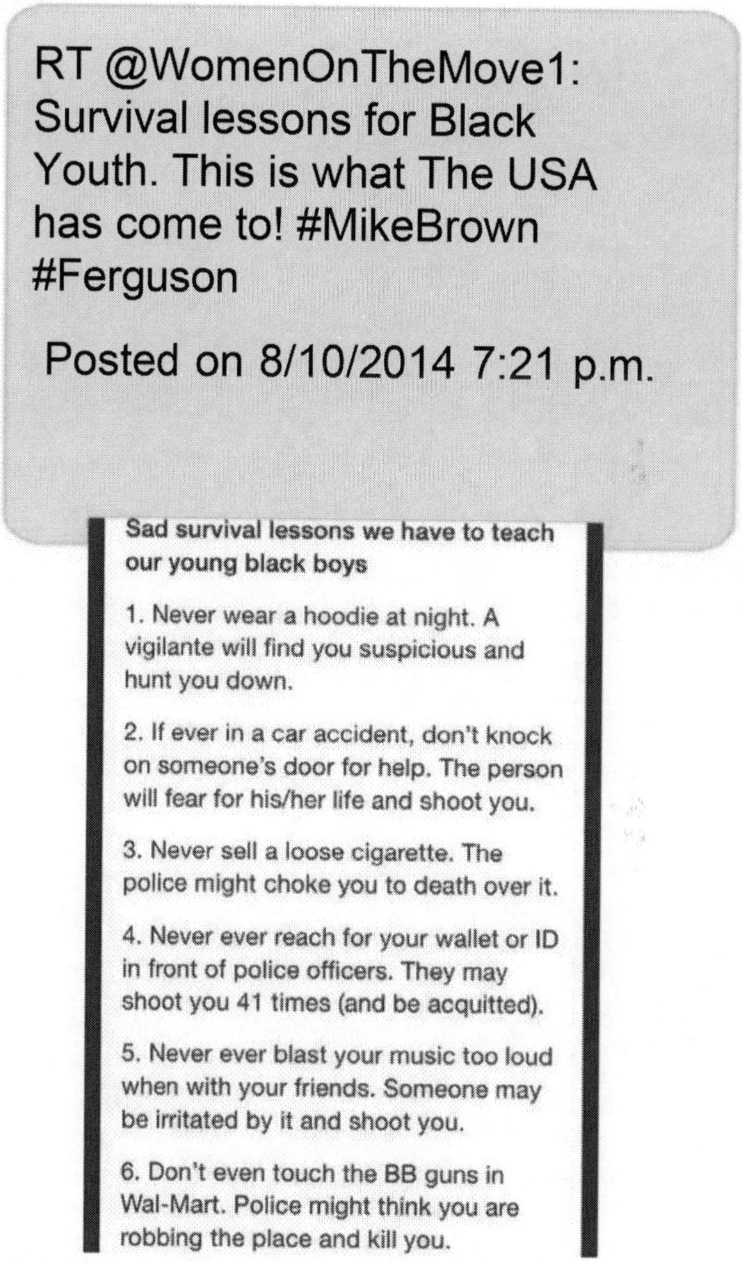

RT @WomenOnTheMove1:
Survival lessons for Black
Youth. This is what The USA
has come to! #MikeBrown
#Ferguson

Posted on 8/10/2014 7:21 p.m.

Sad survival lessons we have to teach
our young black boys

1. Never wear a hoodie at night. A
vigilante will find you suspicious and
hunt you down.

2. If ever in a car accident, don't knock
on someone's door for help. The person
will fear for his/her life and shoot you.

3. Never sell a loose cigarette. The
police might choke you to death over it.

4. Never ever reach for your wallet or ID
in front of police officers. They may
shoot you 41 times (and be acquitted).

5. Never ever blast your music too loud
when with your friends. Someone may
be irritated by it and shoot you.

6. Don't even touch the BB guns in
Wal-Mart. Police might think you are
robbing the place and kill you.

Figure 1.1.   Tweet About Survival Lessons for Black Youth
[Color figure can be viewed at wileyonlinelibrary.com]

Twitter has also been used creatively to share much practical information for black and other civil rights protesters targeting police malpractice. For example, on August 14, 2014, at 1:21:39 a.m., one Twitter user explicitly mentioned this in a tweet: "say what you will about social media, but I've learned more about #Ferguson through Twitter in 1 hour than from national news in 4 days." Black users shared images of peaceful protests and protesters to counterframe the protests and police violence shown on television and in other mainstream media. Black Twitter users have tweeted out hashtags like #medialiteracy and #mediablackout to criticize the mainstream media's (white) framing of blacks killed by police (such as Michael Brown) and of the black protesters. These social media users also asserted that the mainstream media's blackout included ignoring the substantial police brutality being directed at the disproportionately black protester. Such actions further highlight the effectiveness of these online social networks in providing information for anyone seeking to document the policing oppression.

Our analysis of the #BLM Twitter data supports Fleming and Morris's (2015, 115) argument that "blacks' political engagement on social media both extends and diverges from prior forms of mobilization." #BLM and other black use of the social media has created a major black counterpublic that continues today, one reflecting the long history of alternative news media as a form of African American resistance strategy. However, the earlier black communication media had many consumers but relatively few producers, whose pattern is significantly altered by the use of contemporary social media (Castells 2012; Fisher 1998; Tilly and Wood 2013; Wellman and Haythornthwaite 2008). As Ito (2008, 7) emphasizes, there are now "peer-to-peer" and "many-to-many" informational relationships between users across numerous social media platforms, and such relationships around the world, rather than just a top-down dissemination of information that emanated from mainstream print media previously. The current #BLM use of social media such as Twitter is innovative in part because it is decentralized and broadly available and in part because individual users can utilize cell phone photos, immediate personal experiences, and developing local events to effectively critique mainstream news media and police department actions in real time. The contemporary social media have resulted in new forms of media connecting and of mobilizing people from different cultures and communities, in a certain sense collapsing space and time (Ito 2008; Jenkins 2006). The #BLM online presence—including millions of social media tweets and other posts—has forced civil rights and other key social values from the edges of society into the white-controlled center, and thereby has resulted in new political pressures on that center's powerful white figures.

In the contemporary United States, as the #BLM material we examine here shows, the dissemination of critical information in social media has been central to antiracist activism and to pushing systemic racism issues back into the national conversation. General recognition and use of social media have increased. According to a Pew Research Center (2016) survey, roughly half of Americans in the past year have posted in various social media about political topics. Other surveys show that the importance of these media varies somewhat by racial group. Eight in ten black respondents stated that the social media "highlight important issues that may not get a lot of attention" (Anderson et al. 2018, 11). In contrast, 62 percent of whites and Hispanics agreed. Some 78 percent of blacks agreed that these social media enable underrepresented groups to have an important voice, in contrast to roughly 60 percent of white and Hispanic respondents. About 65 percent of blacks and 60 percent of Hispanics agreed that social media help to hold powerful people more responsible, as compared to 53 percent of whites (Anderson et al. 2018). Black Americans further assert that the new social media are essential for amplifying critical issues not discussed in mainstream media, such as police brutality, racism, and other injustices (Lei 2018). Unsurprisingly, in the #BLM organizational toolkit posted on their website, they strongly accent the importance of social media for social change.

As we see it, posting substantial and frequent movement tweets on Twitter or commentaries on other major social media like Facebook is today well within the realm of contemporary political activism, as these posts contribute to movement consciousness-raising activities and build political pressures to address issues such as racialized police malpractice. Indeed, in our data on the #BLM movement we find that the trending of #BLM issues on social media platforms such as Twitter was regularly associated with offline #BLM and related black protests. Clearly, Twitter and other social media platforms have become critical parts of the larger societal environment in which social movements now operate and thereby provide major spaces of resistance in building the black liberation movements.

The #BLM movement has stimulated and affected other civil rights movements. The #BLM founders translated their anger over unjust killings of black people into an innovative social movement, one whose goals eventually expanded to protest racial injustices experienced by all people of color. Thus, the successes of the #BLM movement—accompanied by the failure of mainstream media to recognize racialized policing also targets black women—helped to generate the important #SayHerName social media campaign and hashtag. That social media campaign has been led by Kimberlé Crenshaw, Andrea Ritchie, Rachel Anspach, and Rachel Gilmer (2015) as part of the

African American Policy forum. They have vigorously emphasized the reality
that black women, not just men, are major and recurring targets of police brutality and other antiblack violence at the hands of whites (Crenshaw 1991).

CONCLUSION: WHITE RESISTANCE
AND CONTINUING BLACK CHALLENGES

Today, there is continuing large-scale resistance by elite and ordinary
white Americans to contemporary black protest movements, just as there
was against the 1960s civil rights movement and, much earlier, against
the mid-1800s abolitionist movement (Feagin 2014; Morris 1984). Many
commentators in the white-controlled mainstream media and in the white
public have continued to delegitimize persisting #BLM protests and their
recurring calls for fairness, justice, and structural reforms in policing and
other aspects of the still racialized criminal justice system. In response to
#BLM, many whites have in response proclaimed on Twitter that stated
#Alllivesmatter, attempting to erase or marginalize essential societal discus-
sions of the systemic racism repeatedly demonstrated in the criminal justice
system and other major institutions (Feagin 2014). Other conservative media and political attacks have regularly targeted the #BLM movement. In
2016 a white-generated petition addressed to the White House even called
for #BLM to be labeled a "terrorist group" (Flores 2016). In the social
media, the aforementioned political #TCOT (Top Conservatives on Twitter) hashtag has been coupled with attacks on #BLM as "too radical" and
used to direct white racial stereotypes toward #BLM protesters (Ray et al.
2017) and hashtag-themed resistance using the tag #HandsUpDontShoot. A
white #Pantsupdontloot (a counter to #HandsUpDontShoot) campaign online raised several thousand dollars to try to buy a billboard to display that
aggressive hashtag (Anonymous 2014; Catalan 2014). The endorsement of
the conservative #Pantsupdontloot meme by mainstream journalists, and the
mainstream media's antiblack framing of police victims discussed earlier,
reflect a continuation with past white news media attempts to delegitimize
black civil rights movements against systemic racism (Eligon 2014; Sullivan
2014). Indeed, according to the Pew Research Center, a 2016 survey found
that only 14 percent of white respondents strongly supported the #BLM
movement, as compared with 41 percent of black respondents. In recent
years, there has been a significant increase in white nationalist and other
white hate groups in the United States, some of which have specifically
targeted #BLM organizations and associated black protesters (Potok 2016).
Black Americans, including #BLM activists, have suffered much white dis-

crimination, including increased, often violent, hate crimes and racialized police practices (Matthews and Cyril 2017; Potok 2016; Viets 2016).

Despite widespread #BLM and other similar black protests, substantive legislation has not been passed by state and federal legislatures that would implement serious consequences for extrajudicial police killings, for not reporting such police killings, or for not prosecuting police officers. Only rarely have legislatures acted to make major structural reforms in our still highly racialized criminal justice system. As noted previously, the DoJ has sued the Ferguson Police Department for violations of federal civil rights laws, but there is no result yet; and twenty legislative bills have been introduced in the Missouri legislature to address racial profiling and other injustice in the criminal justice system, but the only one that passed was a cap on traffic ticket revenues (Davey 2015). These political actions indicate some official shift in recognizing the malpractice of individual police officers and departments but do not address the deeper institutional racism that underpins a criminal justice system that continues to harass, imprison, and disenfranchise black people at very disproportionate rates.

Nonetheless, #BLM chapters continue active campaigns addressing local police accountability and discriminatory bail bonding, among other specific racial issues in the criminal justice system. #BLM activists also continue to work actively with other Americans of color to bring significant change, illustrating their commitment to such broader solidarity. For instance, in order to address environmental injustice, they stood in solidarity with the Standing Rock Native American protesters against the construction of the Dakota Access Pipeline (Matthews and Noor 2017).

The #BLM movement has also generated numerous global connections to people of color in other countries who are also struggling to end racialized police oppression and for other human rights. It has also helped to create more US links to major international officials and agencies seeking to expand the protection of human rights in all countries. Indeed, some black activists, including the parents of Michael Brown, have pressed for the intervention of international organizations in regard to US police killings of black Americans. In 2014, Brown's parents testified to the United Nations Committee Against Torture, asking that agency for "global intervention" in the United States to provide substantial redress for the injustice in their son's police killing (Kelly 2017). Additionally, in summer 2016, a United Nations Special Rapporteur and distinguished Kenyan lawyer, Maini Kiai, made an official visit to the United States and did a study of US conditions regarding the rights to freedom of peaceful assembly and of association. In his report, he found "justifiable and palpable anger in the black community" over discriminatory policing and other injustice and that it was "this context that gave birth to the non-violent Black Lives Matter protest movement." He interviewed #BLM activists and concluded that their movement was "a reaffirmation that black lives do in fact matter, in the face of a structure that systematically devalues and destroys them." He also found increased intimidation of #BLM and other black protesters by police agencies, including officers who went to #BLM activists' homes "to warn them off impending protests" and an undercover officer at a #BLM protest "marching with demonstrators and filming them." This international human rights lawyer concluded that African Americans "have good reason to be angry and frustrated at the moment. And it is at times like these when robust promotion of assembly and association rights are needed most" (Kiai 2016).

Our analysis of the #BLM movement reveals that its principal founders—Tometi, Khan-Cullors, and Garza—represent a long and distinguished tradition of African American feminists calling out, challenging, and protesting the elite-white-male dominance system, which has for centuries encompassed not only systemic racism but also systemic sexism and systemic classism (Feagin and Ducey 2017). These courageous #BLM chapter leaders, along with thousands of activist-protesters from diverse racial groups, continue to put their bodies on the line to confront and protest an array of human rights violations and injustices, most centrally in the U.S. criminal justice system. They are clearly seeking more than more one-way assimilation into a still largely white-dominated society; they seek great structural change. The #BLM movement has taught all Americans another visible lesson about what it takes in cognitive, emotional, and organizational labor to make "liberty and justice for all" real in this oppressive country. They have sought and continue to seek to transform U.S. society by ending all structures of racial, gender, and class oppression so as to finally provide black communities and other oppressed communities with full self-determination and the country with real "liberty and justice for all."

NOTE

1. These tweets were public as of June 26, 2015. These filters required the tweet to include a hashtag and include the words *Ferguson, Wilson, Brown,* or *Pantsupdontloot* and excluded the phrases *blacklivesmatter* and *handsupdontshoot*. The sample was further reduced to be under one million tweets by randomly sampling 5 percent of the data. These hashtags were excluded to initially theorize racism on Twitter. During this period, Freelon et al. (2016) found 581 tweets using #BlackLivesMatter out of the 12,589,097 tweets they analyzed, making the hashtag used in less than 1 percent of the tweets. Although this is a limitation of the data, #BLM founders give particular relevance to Ferguson protests, so we feel comfortable generalizing these data as affecting the discussion of #BLM and counterframing of police brutality cases.

REFERENCES

Alexander, Michelle. 2012. *The New Jim Crow: Mass Incarceration in the Age of Colorblindness*. New York: The New Press.

American Civil Liberties Union. 2016. "Ending Modern-Day Debtors' Prisons." ACLU. Accessed May 1, 2016. https://www.aclu.org/issues/smart-justice/sentenc ing-reform/ending-modern-day-debtors-prisons.

Anderson, Monica, Skye Toor, Lee Rainie, and Aaron Smith. 2018. "Activism in the Social Media Age." Pew Research Center. Accessed August 16, 2018. http://assets .pewresearch.org/wp-content/uploads/ sites/14/2018/07/11095520/PI_2018.07.11 _social-activism_FINAL.pdf.

Anonymous. 2014. "Closed." IndieGOGO. Accessed May 2, 2015. https://www.indie gogo.com/projects/closed–172.

Anonymous. 2016. "About Us." A Movement for Black Lives. Accessed January 13, 2019. https://policy. m4bl.org/about/.

Aptheker, Herbert. 1943. *American Negro Slave Revolts*. New York: Columbia University Press.

Apuzzo, Matt. 2014. "War Gear Flows to Police Departments." *New York Times*, June 8, 2014. https://www.nytimes.com/2014/06/09/us/war-gear-flows-to-police -departments.html?ref=us&_r=1;.

Barnett, Bernice. 1993. "Invisible Southern Black Women Leaders in the Civil Rights Movement: The Triple Constraints of Gender, Race, and Class." *Gender & Society* 7 (2): 162–182. https://doi.org/10. 1177/089124393007002002.

Bonilla, Yarimar and Jonathan Rosa. 2015. "#Ferguson: Digital Protest, Hashtag Ethnography, and the Racial Politics of Social Media in the United States." *American Ethnologist* 42 (1): 4–17. https://doi. org/10.1111/amet.12112.

Botelho, Greg and Holly Yan. 2013. "George Zimmerman Found Not Guilty of Murder in Trayvon Martin's Death." CNN, July 14, 2013. https://www.cnn .com/2013/07/13/justice/zim merman-trial/index.html.

Boyd, Danah. 2013. "White Flight in Networked Publics? How Race and Class Shaped American Teen Engagement With Myspace and Facebook." In *Race After the Internet*, edited by Lisa Nakamura and Peter Chow-White, 203–222. New York: Routledge.

Bracey, Glenn. 2016. "Black Movements Need Black Theorizing: Exposing Implicit Whiteness in Political Process Theory." *Sociological Focus* 49 (1): 11–27. https:// doi.org/10.1080/00380237.2015.1067569.

Brock, André. 2012. "From the Blackhand Side: Twitter as a Cultural Conversation." *Journal of Broadcasting & Electronic Media* 56 (4): 529–549. https://doi.org/10 .1080/08838151.2012.732147.

Cadei, Emily. 2014. "Hashtag Activism 2.0: Sites Aim to Turn Attention Into Change." NPR, November 8, 2014. https://www.npr.org/2014/11/08/362367236 /hashtag-activism-2-0-sites-aim-to-turn-attention-into-change.

Castells, Manuel. 2012. *Networks of Outrage and Hope: Social Movements in the Internet Age*. Cambridge, MA: Polity.

Catalan, Julissa. 2014. "#PantsUPDontLOOT." Diversity Inc. Accessed January 3, 2015 http://www.diversityinc.com/news/pantsupdontloot/.

Clark, Meredith. 2014. "To Tweet Our Own Cause: A Mixed-Methods Study of the Online Phenomenon 'Black Twitter.'" PhD diss., University of North Carolina at Chapel Hill.

Collins, Patricia H. 2009 (2000). *Black Feminist Thought: Knowledge, Consciousness, and the Politics of Empowerment*. New York: Routledge.

Combahee River Collective. 2015 (1977). "A Black Feminist Statement." In *This Bridge Called My Back: Writings by Radical Women of Color*, edited by Cherríe L. Moraga and Gloria E. Anzaldúa, 210–218. Albany: State University of New York Press.

Conover, Michael, Clayton Davis, Emilio Ferrara, Karissa McKelvey, Filippo Menczer, and Alessandro Flammini. 2013. "The Geospatial Characteristics of a Social Movement Communication Network." *PloS One* 8 (3): 1–8. https://doi .org/10.1371/journal.pone.0055957.

Craven, Julia. 2015. "Black Lives Matter Co-Founder Reflects on the Origins of the Movement." *Huff-Post Politics,* September 30, 2015. http://www.huffingtonpost .com/entry/black-lives-matter-opal-tometi_560c1c59e4b0768127003227.

Crenshaw, Kimberlé. 1991. "Mapping the Margins: Intersectionality, Identity Politics, and Violence Against Women of Color." *Stanford Law Review* 43 (6): 1241–1299. https://doi.org/10.2307/1229039.

Crenshaw, Kimberlé, Andrea Ritchie, Rachel Anspach, and Rachel Gilmer. 2015. "Say Her Name: Resisting Police Brutality Against Black Women." African American Policy Forum. Accessed May 2, 2016. http://www.aapf.org/sayhernamereport.

Daniels, Jessie. 2013. "Race and Racism in Internet Studies: A Review and Critique." *New Media & Society* 15 (5): 695–719. https://doi.org/10.1177/1461444812462849.

Davey, Monica. 2015. "A Year Later, Ferguson Sees Change, but Asks If It's Real." *New York Times*, August 5, 2015. http://www.nytimes.com/2015/08/06/us/in-year -since-searing-death-ferguson-sees-uneven-recovery.html?_r=0.

Davis, Angela Y. 2002. "Chapter 5: Masked Racism." *Race and Resistance: African Americans in the Twenty-First Century*, edited by Herbert Boyd, 53–59. Cambridge, MA: South End Press.

———.2014. "Deepening the Debate Over Mass Incarceration." *Socialism and Democracy* 28 (3): 15–23. https://doi.org/10.1080/08854300.2014.963945.

Dillon, Merton. 1990. *Slavery Attacked: Southern Slaves and their Allies, 1619–1865*. Baton Rouge: Louisiana State University Press.

Earl, Jennifer, Jayson Hunt, R. K. Garrett, and Aysenur Dal. 2015. "New Technologies and Social Movements." In *The Oxford Handbook of Social Movements*, edited by Donna Della Porta and Mario Diani, 355–366. Oxford: Oxford University Press.

Eligon, John. 2014. "Michael Brown Spent Last Weeks Grappling With Problems and Promise." *New York Times*, August 24, 2014. http://www.nytimes.com/2014/08/25 /us/michael-brown-spent-last-weeks-grappling-with-lifes-mysteries.html?_r=0.

Feagin, Joe. 2012. *White Party, White Government: Race, Class, and US Politics*. New York: Routledge.

———.2013. *The White Racial Frame: Centuries of Racial Framing and Counter-Framing*. New York: Routledge.

———.2014. *Racist America: Roots, Current Realities, and Future Reparations*. New York: Routledge.

Feagin, Joe and Kimberley Ducey. 2017. *Elite White Men Ruling: Who, What, When, Where, and How*. New York: Routledge.

Feagin, Joe and Harlan Hahn. 1973. *Ghetto Revolts: The Politics of Violence in American Cities*. New York: Macmillan.

Feagin, Joe and Paul Sheatsley. 1968. "Ghetto Resident Appraisals of a Riot." *Public Opinion Quarterly* 32 (3): 352–362. Accessed July 19, 2019. www.jstor.org /stable/2747641.

Fisher, Dana R. 1998. "Rumoring Theory and the Internet: A Framework for Analyzing the Grass Roots." *Social Science Computer Review* 16 (2): 158–168. https://doi .org/10.1177/089443939801600204.

Fleming, Crystal M. and Aldon Morris. 2015. "Theorizing Ethnic and Racial Movements in the Global Age: Lessons from the Civil Rights Movement." *Sociology of Race and Ethnicity* 1 (1): 105–126. https://doi.org/10.1177/2332649214562473.

Flores, Reena. 2015. "Democratic Debate: Do Black Lives Matter?" CBS News, October 13, 2015. https://www.cbsnews.com/news/democratic-debate-do-black -lives-matter/.

———.2016. "White House Responds to Petition to Label Black Lives Matter a 'Terror' Group." CBS News, July 16, 2016. https://www.cbsnews.com/news/white -house-responds-to-petition-to-label-black-lives-matter-a-terror-group/.

Florini, Sarah. 2014. "Tweets, Tweeps, and Signifyin': Communication and Cultural Performance on 'Black Twitter.'" *Television and New Media* 15: (3): 223–237. https://doi.org/10.1177/1527476413480247.

Freelon, Deen, Charlton Mcilwain, and Meredith Clark. 2016. "Beyond the Hashtags: #Ferguson, #Blacklivesmatter, and the Online Struggle for Offline Justice." Center for Media & Social Impact, February 29, 2016. www.cmsimpact.org/sites/default /files/beyond_the_hashtags_2016.pdf.

Gamson, William A. 1992. *Talking Politics*. Cambridge: Cambridge University Press.

Garza, Alicia. 2014. "A Herstory of the #BlackLivesMatter Movement by Alicia Garza." Feminist Wire, October 7, 2014. https://thefeministwire.com/2014/10 /blacklivesmatter-2/.

———.2017. "Alicia Garza." In *How We Get Free: Black Feminism and the Combahee River Collective*, edited by Keeanga-Yamahtta Taylor, 145–175. Chicago: Haymarket Books.

Gil de Zuñiga, Homero, Nakwon Jung, and Sebastian Valenzuela. 2012. "Social Media Use for News and Individuals' Social Capital, Civic Engagement and Political Participation." *Journal of Computer-Mediated Communication* 17 (3): 319–336. https://doi.org/10.1111/j.1083-6101.2012.01574.x.

Gitlin, Todd. 2003. *The Whole World Is Watching: Mass Media in the Making and Unmaking of the New Left.* Berkeley: University of California Press.

Gleason, Benjamin. 2013. "#Occupy Wall Street: Exploring Informal Learning About a Social Movement on Twitter." *American Behavioral Scientist* 57 (7): 966–982. https://doi.org/10.1177/ 0002764213479372.

Glenn, Evelyn N. 2015. "Settler Colonialism as Structure: A Framework for Comparative Studies of US Race and Gender Formation." *Sociology of Race and Ethnicity* 1 (1): 52–72. https://doi.org/10.1177/ 2332649214560440.

Graham, Roderick and Shawn Smith. 2016. "The Content of Our #Characters: Black Twitter as Counterpublic." *Sociology of Race and Ethnicity* 2 (4): 433–449. https:// doi.org/10.1177/2332649216639067.

Hadden, Sally. 2003. *Slave Patrols*. Boston: Harvard University Press.

Hahn, Harlan and Joe Feagin. 1970. "Rank-and-File Versus Congressional Perceptions of Ghetto Riots." *Social Science Quarterly* 41 (2): 361–373. www.jstor.org /stable/42858601.

Halpern, Daniel and Jennifer Gibbs. 2012. "Social Media as a Catalyst for Online Deliberation? Exploring the Affordances of Facebook and YouTube for Political Expression." *Computers in Human Behavior* 29 (3): 1159–1168. https://doi .org/10.1016/j.chb.2012.10.008.

Harris, Fredrick. 2015. "The Next Civil Rights Movement?" *Dissent* 62 (3): 34–40. https://doi.org/101353/dss.2015.0051.

Henricks, Kasey and Daina Cheyenne Harvey. 2017. "Not One but Many: Monetary Punishment and the Fergusons of America." *Sociological Forum* 32 (S1): 930–951. https://doi.org/10.1111/socf.12360.

Hirschfield, Paul. 2015. "Lethal Policing: Making Sense of American Exceptionalism." *Sociological Forum* 30 (4): 1109–1117. https://doi.org/10.1111/socf.12200.

Hogan, Wesley. 2007. *Many Minds, One Heart: SNCC's Dream for a New America*. Chapel Hill: University of North Carolina Press.

Hyland, Shelley, Lynn Langton, and Elizabeth Davis. 2015. "Police Use of Nonfatal Force, 2002–11." Bureau of Justice Statistics, November 2015. Accessed December 5, 2016. www.bjs.gov/content/pub/pdf/punf0211.pdf.

Ito, Mizuko. 2008. "Introduction." In *Networked Publics*, edited by Kazys Varnelis, 1–14. Cambridge, MA: MIT Press.

Jackson, Sarah and Brooke Welles. 2016. "#Ferguson Is Everywhere: Initiators in Emerging Counterpublic Networks." *Information, Communication and Society* 19 (3): 397–418. https://doi.org/10.1080/ 1369118X.2015.1106571.

Jenkins, Henry. 2006. *Convergence Culture: Where Old and New Media Collide*. New York: New York University Press.

Johnston, Hank. 2005. "Talking the Walk: Speech Acts and Resistance in Authoritarian Regimes." In *Repression and Mobilization*, edited by Christian Davenport, Hank Johnston, and Carol Mueller, 108–137. Minneapolis: University of Minnesota Press.

Kelly, Kate. 2017. "Extrajudicial Killings in the United States: The International Human Rights Perspective." Law Professor Blogs, December 10, 2017. Accessed September 3, 2018. http://lawprofessors.typepad.com/human_ rights/2017/12 /extrajudicial-killings-in-the-united-states-the-international-human-rights-perspec tive. html.

Kiai, Maini. 2016. "Statement by the United Nations Special Rapporteur on the Rights to Freedom of Peaceful Assembly and of Association at the Conclusion of His Visit to the United States of America." United Nations Office of the High Commissioner for Human Rights, July 27, 2016. https://www.ohchr.org/en/newsevents /pages/DisplayNews.aspx?NewsID=20317&LangID=E.

King, Shaun. 2018. "Law Enforcement Groups Gave $420,000 to DA Deciding Whether to Bring Charges Against Cops Who Killed Stephon Clark." *The Intercept*, April 25, 2018. . https://theintercept.com/2018/04/25/stephon-clark-police -shooting-district-attorney/.

Lei, Cecilia. 2018. "Majority of Black Americans Value Social Media for Amplifying Lesser-Known Issues." NPR, August 5, 2018. https://www.npr.org/2018/08/05 /635127389/majority-of-black-americans-value-social-media-for-amplifying -lesser-known-issue?utm_source=twitter.com&utm_medium=social&utm _campaign=npr&utm_term=nprnews&utm_content=20180805.

Lewis, John. 2015. *Walking With the Wind: A Memoir of the Movement*. New York: Simon & Schuster.

Lipsky, Michael. 1969. *Protest in City Politics: Rent Strikes, Housing, and the Power of the Poor.* Chicago: Rand McNally.

Lorde, Audre. 2007. *Sister Outsider: Essays and Speeches*. Berkeley, CA: Crossing Press.

Massey, Douglas, and Karen Pren. 2012. "Unintended Consequences of US Immigration Policy: Explaining the Post-1965 Surge From Latin America." *Population and Development Review* 38 (1): 1–29. https://doi.org/10.1111/j.1728 -4457.2012.00470.x.

Matthews, Shanelle, and Malkia Cyril. 2017. "We Say Black Lives Matter. The FBI Says That Makes Us a Security Threat." *Washington Post*, October 19, 2017. https://www.washingtonpost.com/news/posteverything/wp/2017/10/19/we-say -black-lives-matter-the-fbi-says-that-makes-us-a-security-threat/?utm_term =.c3472693528b.

Matthews, Shanelle, and Miski Noor. 2017. "Celebrating Four Years of Organizing to Protect Black Lives." Black Lives Matter. Accessed June 15, 2018 https://drive .google.com/open?xml:id= 0B0pJEXffvS0uOHdJREJnZ2JJYTA.

McAdam, Doug. 1996. "The Framing Function of Movement Tactics: Strategic Dramaturgy in the American Civil Rights Movement." In *Comparative Perspectives on Social Movements: Political Opportunities, Mobilizing Structures, and Cultural Framings*, edited by Doug McAdam, John McCarthy, and Mayer Zald, 339–355. Cambridge: Cambridge University Press.

McAdam, Doug. 1999. "Decline of the Civil Rights Movement." In *Waves of Protest: Social Movements Since the Sixties*, edited by Jo Freeman and Victoria Johnson, 325–348. Oxford: Rowman & Littlefield.

McMurry, Linda. 1998. *To Keep the Waters Troubled: The Life of Ida B. Wells*. New York: Oxford University Press.

Morgan, Edward P. 2010. *What Really Happened to the 1960s: How Mass Media Culture Failed American Democracy*. Lawrence: University Press of Kansas.

Morris, Aldon D. 1984. *The Origins of the Civil Rights Movement.* New York: Simon & Schuster.

Murthy, Dhiraj. 2013. *Twitter.* Cambridge, UK: Polity.

Nakamura, Lisa. 2008. *Digitizing Race: Visual Cultures of the Internet.* Minneapolis: University of Minnesota Press.

Paradies, Yin. 2016. "Colonisation, Racism and Indigenous Health." *Journal of Population Research* 33 (1): 83–96. https://doi.org/10.1007/s12546-016-9159-y.

Pew Research Center. 2016. "On Views of Race and Inequality, Blacks and Whites Are Worlds Apart." Pew Research Center, June 27, 2016. http://assets.pewresearch.org/wp-content/uploads/ sites/3/2016/06/ST_2016.06.27_Race-Inequality-Final.pdf.

Poirot, Kristan. 2015. "Gendered Geographies of Memory: Place, Violence, and Exigency at the Birmingham Civil Rights Institute." *Rhetoric & Public Affairs* 18 (4): 621–648. www.js tor.org/stable/10.14321/rhetpublaffa.18.4.0621.

Potok, Mark. 2016. "The Year in Hate and Extremism." Southern Poverty Law Center, February 17, 2016. https://www.splcenter.org/fighting-hate/intelligence-report/2016/year-hate-and-extremism.

Ray, Rashawn, Melissa Brown, Neil Fraistat, and Edward Summers. 2017. "Ferguson and the Death of Michael Brown on Twitter: #BlackLivesMatter, #TCOT, and the Evolution of Collective Identities." *Ethnic and Racial Studies* 40 (11): 1–17. https://doi.org/10.1080/01419870.2017.1335422.

Roth, Mitchel and Tom Kennedy. 2012. *Houston Blue: The Story of the Houston Police Department.* Denton: University of North Texas Press.

Russell, Kathryn. 1988. *The Color of Crime.* New York: New York University Press.

Sharma, Sanjay. 2013. "Black Twitter? Racial Hashtags, Networks and Contagion." *New Formations: A Journal of Culture/Theory/Politics* 78 (1): 46–64. https://doi.org/10.3898/NewF.78.02.2013.

Smith, Barbara. 2017. "Barbara Smith." In *How We Get Free: Black Feminism and the Combahee River Collective,* edited by Keeanga-Yamahtta Taylor, 29–69. Chicago: Haymarket Books.

Smith, Barbara, Gloria Hull, and Patricia Scott, eds. 1982. *All the Women Are White, All the Blacks Are Men, but Some of Us Are Brave: Black Women's Studies.* New York: Feminist Press.

Stewart, Maria and Marilyn Richardson. 1987. *Maria W. Stewart, America's First Black Woman Political Writer: Essays and Speeches.* Bloomington: Indiana University Press.

Sullivan, Margaret. 2014. "An Ill-Chosen Phrase, 'No Angel,' Brings a Storm of Protest." *New York Times,* August 25, 2014. Accessed August 15, 2018. https://publiceditor.blogs.nytimes.com/2014/08/25/an-ill-chosen-phrase-no-angel-brings-a-storm-of-protest/.

Tarrow, Sidney. 2011 (1994). *Power in Movement: Social Movements and Contentious Politics.* New York: Cambridge University Press.

Theocharis, Yannis, Will Lowe, Jan Van Deth, and Gema García-Albacete. 2015. "Using Twitter to Mobilize Protest Action: Online Mobilization Patterns and Action Repertoires in the Occupy Wall Street, Indignados, and Aganaktismenoi Movements." *Information, Communication and Society* 18 (2): 202–220. https://doi.org /10.1080/1369118X.2014.948035.

Tilly, Charles and Lesley Wood. 2013. *Social Movements 1768–2012*. Boulder, CO: Paradigm.

United States Department of Justice. 2015. "Investigation of the Ferguson Police Department." Civil Rights Division, March 4, 2015. Accessed May 2, 2016. https:// www.justice.gov/sites/default/files/opa/press-re leases/attachments/2015/03/04 /ferguson_police_department_report.pdf.

United States Department of Justice. 2016. "Justice Department Files Lawsuit to Bring Constitutional Policing to Ferguson, Missouri." U.S. Department of Justice, February 10, 2016. Accessed April 29, 2016. https://www. justice.gov/opa/pr/jus tice-department-files-lawsuit-bring-constitutional-policing-ferguson-missouri.

Varnali, Kaan and Vehbi Gorgulu. 2015. "A Social Influence Perspective on Expressive Political Participation in Twitter: The Case of #OccupyGezi." *Information, Communication and Society* 18 (1): 1–16. https://doi.org/10.1080/13691 18X.2014.923480.

Viets, Sarah. 2016. "Meet White Lives Matter: The Racist Response to the Black Lives Matter Movement." Southern Poverty Law Center, March 18, 2016. https://www.splcenter.org/hatewatch/ 2016/03/18/meet-white-lives-matter-racist -response-black-lives-matter-movement.

Wellman, Barry and Caroline Haythornthwaite. 2008. *The Internet in Everyday Life*. Malden, MA: Blackwell.

Wells-Barnett, Ida. 1991. *The Selected Works of Ida B. Wells-Barnett*. New York: Oxford University Press.

Worden, Robert. 1996. "The Causes of Police Brutality: Theory and Evidence on Police Use of Force." In *Police Violence: Understanding and Controlling Police Abuse of Force*, edited by William Geller and Hans Toch, 23–51. New Haven, CT: Yale University Press.

Chapter Two

Dream Defenders

The First Ten Years and the Transition to This Era of Black Activism

Mary Marcel

When #BlackLivesMatter broke on our national consciousness, for many people it felt like something entirely new. Many of us who had lived through the Civil Rights era, whether as children or adults, felt that while the struggles had continued, this new era of Black activism was taking shape differently than its predecessor. The existence of social media and a hash-tagged movement were part of that newness. No longer were activists constrained by broadcast news and newspaper editors who selected and framed what the public would see and hear about their goals and actions. Smart phones and social media meant that direct sharing of information but also photographs and videos was now possible, and that certainly changed the dynamics of what we knew and how we responded through activism. And then there were the three Black women who started the Movement for Black Lives: Alicia Garza, Patrisse Khan Cullors and Opal Tometi. They were young, confident, educated women who were immersed in the daily struggles facing Black communities, experiencing the effects of mass incarceration, underemployment, and lack of access to healthcare (Cullors and Bandele 2017). They were not pastors affiliated with any Christian denomination; they were not members of the NAACP; and in 2014 they would for the first time become household names. They weren't interested in the politics of respectability because they found it exclusionary and too deeply rooted in unjust systems they believed needed to be retired and replaced. They were queer and trans inclusive; women's issues and women's leadership were central to their platforms. They were the new faces of a new era of Black activism, in a nation that had just elected its first Black president. The struggles were not new, but the energy was.

Between the era of the Civil Rights movement of the 1950s–1970s and the 2010s, however, activism around racial justice had certainly continued. Dr. Robert Bullard started the movement for environmental justice and against environmental racism in the 1980s (Bullard 1993, 2000, 2005). Rev. Jesse Jackson, MLK's chosen successor and twelve years younger than his mentor, carried forward with Operation PUSH (Stanford 2002). The Rainbow Coalition, which he brought together in the 1980s, was an attempt at bringing together men and women of color fighting for racial justice, women of all races fighting for gender equity, lesbians and gays, union organizers and environmental activists under one tent. Likewise, Rev. Al Sharpton, thirteen years younger than Jackson, became a force for bringing attention and protests to cases of racial injustice, both as an organizer with his National Action Network and as a media presence and TV host (Johnson and Stanford 2002). In 1991, Anita Hill changed US history by finding the language to describe sexual harassment in the confirmation hearing for future Supreme Court Justice Clarence Thomas (Hill 2021). And of course, the NAACP continued in its efforts unabated (Smith 2002).

As Michelle Alexander pointed out in *The New Jim Crow* (2010), however, the gains of Civil Rights movement had now been undermined by a new and more insidious form of racism, which used incarceration and conviction as a proxy for race. By changing laws to make it easier to convict and incarcerate people for a variety of offenses, millions of men and increasingly women—disproportionately BIPOC and poor—were having their entire lives upended and their life chances permanently diminished because of what Alexander referred to as the new Jim Crow.

Another effort by conservatives to reinforce White supremacy centered on loosening controls on gun ownership and then on the use of guns for self-defense. In 2005, Florida became the first in a large group of states to pass legislation which has come to be known collectively as Stand Your Ground laws (Weaver 2008). These laws took various forms, but generally removed the legal requirement to retreat from a threatening situation when outside one's home. Despite being touted as protecting women, those suffering domestic violence, especially Black and trans women, have found little legal protection when attempting to invoke Stand Your Ground (Franks 2014; Ijoma 2018; Messerschmidt 2016). Stand Your Ground laws were criticized widely for contributing to a rise in homicides rather than lowering crime rates. More disturbingly, several reviews of SYG cases revealed that when a shooter was Black and the victim white, there was a significantly greater likelihood that a SYG claim would be *denied* than if the shooter was white and the victim Black (ABA 2015; Ackerman et al. 2015; Mack and Roberts-Lewis 2016; National Urban League 2013).

This takes us to the threshold of the murder of Trayvon Martin by George Zimmerman. In 2017 Patrisse Khan-Cullors, one of the founders of the Movement For Black Lives, wrote:

> At some point Al Sharpton hears about what happened to Trayvon and a huge rally is held in New York. An arrest is demanded. And at first it seems ignored. But the demand is elevated in Florida by a group of brilliant and brave young organizers, the Dream Defenders, led by (Phillip) Umi Agnew. They occupy the governor's office, bringing direct action back into the fore for our generation. They use social media to amplify their voices, and they inspire a nation of organizers, including me. . . . (167)

This chapter explores the protests, organizing and activism of a group which calls itself the Dream Defenders. It made the murder of Trayvon Martin a reckoning for white supremacy and Stand Your Ground laws. The Movement for Black Lives (M4BL) coalesced in 2013 after the not guilty verdict for George Zimmerman, the killer of Trayvon Martin, but arguably gained national and international scale after the murder by police of Michael Brown on August 9, 2014 in Ferguson, Missouri. While police killings of Black men, women and children have continued since Ferguson, opposition to Stand Your Ground (SYG) legislation in Florida was core to the work of a young Black man, Phillip Agnew and the Black and Brown activists known as Dream Defenders.

This group has been acknowledged as a predecessor to and partner of Black Lives Matter, but none of its leaders have written a book. Three books have dealt in small part with Dream Defenders, primarily in connection to Trayvon Martin: Barbara Ransby's *Making All Black Lives Matter* (2018); Wesley Hogan's *On the Freedom Side* (2019) and Charles Davis's *Rise Up!: Activism as Education* (2019). These three offer in-depth accounts of the group's 2013 sit-in at the Florida Governor's office as well as interviews and quotes from speeches not reported extensively in the press. My goal in this chapter is different. I want to explore the history of Dream Defenders over its first decade of existence, using Florida newspapers, including university papers, as primary sources of information. I begin with Phillip Agnew's previous activism, involving protests over the murder of Martin Lee Anderson while in detention at a juvenile detention camp in Panama City, Florida on January 6, 2006. I then discuss Agnew's formation of Dream Defenders and the broadening of its affiliations and actions. I examine three subsequent streams of activism in which Dream Defenders have taken part. I report on media frames used in Florida newspaper coverage of the group. I conclude with reflections on ways in which this coverage, which departs from an expected overall negative framing, nevertheless also mutes many of the group's own values and commitments.

I use two sources of information about Dream Defenders. The first is newspaper coverage. I have only used newspapers (including campus newspapers) from Florida to focus on how Dream Defenders were being perceived and presented in their home state. The Student Coalition for Justice, the group which preceded Dream Defenders in Tallahassee, organized in 2006 to protest the juvenile boot camp killing of Martin Lee Anderson, a 14-year-old Black boy whose killing was caught on security camera (Francois 2007). Facebook had only been created in 2005, with other social media platforms following. So in those early years, newspapers were still a core source of news. While social media and cell phones were certainly used to help organize actions, the major onset of digitized news and social media sharing was still in the offing. Using this medium, we will be able to assess how newspapers were framing Dream Defenders, starting with references to prior eras of activism and activists as it became a stable and recognized new activist organization in its own right.

The second source is the Dream Defenders' website and posts on Instagram, Twitter and Facebook. I am most concerned with the messages and programming Dream Defenders have put out to both define themselves and engage others in their organizing. On March 28, 2023 there is no online platform where DD have more than one hundred thousand followers. By contrast, Black Lives Matter on Twitter has over 1 million followers on that same day. For an organization of its age, this suggests to me that Dream Defenders remain a largely on the ground organization rather than a hashtagged or purely digital phenomenon.

PHILLIP AGNEW AND ORGANIZING PROTESTS OVER THE MURDER OF MARTIN LEE ANDERSON 2006–2007

In spring 2005, Phillip Agnew, a business major at Florida A&M (FAMU), an historically Black university in Tallahassee, was running for student government vice-president (Costly Campaigns 2005). He won the election (Hordge 2005). In January 2006, he was angered by the apparent murder of Martin Lee Anderson, age fourteen, a Black youth who died while in detention at a juvenile camp in Panama City, Florida (McGrory 2013). When no charges were brought against the staffers who had physically restrained and brutalized Anderson, in April 2006 Agnew and two friends organized a sit-in at Governor Jebb Bush's office in Tallahassee which lasted thirty-three hours (Pecquet 2006). After the sit-in, Agnew and other activists vowed to keep the case in the media spotlight, holding a press conference at the quarterly State Medical Examiners Commission meeting to question the initial autopsy findings. And they joined an NAACP-sponsored rally in Panama City on May 15. On May 31, Governor Bush signed a bill outlawing juvenile justice "boot camps," to be replaced by facilities that offered treatment (*Florida Today* 2007) but without providing for additional funding. Students rallied again in October when no charges had yet been brought (Price 2006). However, when camp staff members were subsequently tried, they were acquitted on all counts (Krause 2007). Agnew and hundreds of other FAMU, Tallahassee Community College and Florida State University students turned out for another protest on October 13, 2007, shortly after the acquittals were announced (Pecquet 2007). Agnew and twelve other Tallahassee activists subsequently travelled to Washington to join a rally of many thousands around the Justice Department (Kim 2007), to protest the death of Martin and other racist hate crimes that were not being adjudicated. That protest was organized by Reverend Al Sharpton.

After December 2007 (Mallard 2007), I was not able to find any references to Student Coalition for Justice, the group which Agnew had been a part and which had spearheaded protests surrounding the Martin Lee Anderson killing. As many college student groups do, this one may have continued to meet but engaged in work that did not receive press coverage.

At this juncture, I want to make a few observations on continuities and new developments in the organizing work of Phillip Agnew and his fellow activists. First, the NAACP, Reverend Al Sharpton and Reverend Jessie Jackson, all fixtures of twentieth-century activism, were present and engaged in the cause of Martin Lee Anderson (Kam 2006; Mallard 2007). Students turned out for protests organized by these leaders, both in Florida and in Washington, DC. Florida and national NAACP leaders issued statements and called for investigations and charges (for example Ensley 2007; Price 2008). In that sense, they used their now-institutionalized voices to deliver criticisms of both Bush administrations (US and Florida).

To illustrate this point, I searched the ProQuest US Newsstream database for newspaper stories mentioning Martin Lee Anderson and known activists and organizations between 2006 and 2008. I found 215 stories mentioning the NAACP and Martin Lee Anderson; 88.4 percent were Florida papers. In Florida papers from throughout the state there were 31 stories *with NAACP in the headline* between 2006 and 2008, out of 190 stories mentioning the organization. There were 103 stories mentioning Al Sharpton and Martin Lee Anderson; 62.1 percent were Florida papers. There were 112 stories mentioning Jesse Jackson and Anderson; similarly to Sharpton, 67 percent were in-state papers. There were only 44 stories mentioning Anderson and the Student Coalition for Justice, of which Phillip Agnew was a member. Of these, 77.3

percent were from the *Tallahassee Democrat*, and 100 percent were in-state. I found twenty stories mentioning Anderson and Phillip Agnew. Of these, 65 percent were from the *Tallahassee Democrat* and 100 percent were in-state newspapers. In contrast, there were 1,620 stories in the same period which mentioned Martin Lee Anderson *but not* the NAACP, Jesse Jackson or Al Sharpton. Of these, 81.2 percent were Florida newspapers. This suggests that while activists and organizations were being mentioned in news stories, they constituted a relatively small proportion of overall US news coverage. Martin Lee Anderson's case remained most intensively covered within Florida, with those newspapers constituting 81.2 percent of newspaper coverage. The out-of-state newspapers with the heaviest coverage were the *Houston Chronicle*, the *New York Times*, the *St. Louis Dispatch*, the *Chicago Tribune*, and the Memphis *Commercial Appeal*, all running between twelve and nineteen stories in that period.

Clearly decades of activism and media presence would ensure Sharpton and Jackson a place in the public eye. Patterns of coverage suggest that they were more likely to get out-of-state attention than the NAACP. By the same token, coverage of Anderson's death which mentioned these activists and organizations tended to be localized to Florida, and even more so to Tallahassee where student activists were involved.

Sharpton, who describes himself as the generation between MLK and the "hip hop" generation of activists (TV Worth Watching 2008), clearly connected with Anderson's killing. But for college students and other young Black people like Agnew, Anderson was the age of their little brothers. There was a visceral connection that was different from Sharpton's voice as a Black "spokesman" or that of the NAACP or Reverend Jackson. Without discounting the commitment of longstanding organizations like the NAACP and Civil Rights-era activists with long careers and presence like Sharpton and Jackson, for Phillip Agnew, the killing of Martin Lee Anderson was his defining moment in becoming an activist (McGrory 2013).

Second, based on news coverage that activists presumably would not have had easy access to, the murder of Martin Lee Anderson *was* widely covered, both in the US and abroad. The facts of the case, especially the release of security camera video which caught the entire thirty minutes of guards kicking and kneeing Anderson while a nurse watched, sparked outrage that was widely felt and reported on. Indeed, in the Nexis Uni database, news transcripts from both television and radio far outnumbered newspaper and wire reports—1968 stories, vs, 388 and 519 respectively between 2006 and 2008. But this knowledge was probably not available to students and community protesters, who feared that without their actions, the criticisms over lack of investigations or charges might have been brushed off by state officials and no charges might ever have been brought.

Third, the students very consciously used Civil Rights-era protest tactics and references among their primary strategies. Tallahassee has a long history of civil rights activism, including its own bus boycott that was led by Black students at the city's Florida A&M University, one of the nation's largest Historically Black Colleges and Universities (HBCUs) (Smith 2006). Students including Agnew cited awareness of this history and of tactics used in that era (Waters 2006). When students protested the verdicts by stopping traffic in October 2007, they drew on tactics used in the earlier era of protests, including the March on Selma. In this way they overtly took on the mantle of that legacy of organizing and protest, as well as the legitimacy which it gained well after the fact.

Another very overt connection to prior Civil Rights activism came in February 2006. Those protesting the lack of indictments following Anderson's death held a forum on February 26, 2006. Leon County (FL) Commissioner Bill Proctor, who is Black, urged Anderson's family to move forward with an exhumation and second autopsy, saying he was "speaking to the crowd not as a politician, but as a father of three children" (Velazquez 2006). He said, "there are three examples of second autopsies that changed history: Medgar Evers, Emmett Till and Jesus." This is the first newspaper reference I was able to find where a speaker compared Martin Lee Anderson's killing to that of Emmett Till. On March 3, in advance of the exhumation, the family's lawyer Ben Crump announced that two autopsies would be performed on March 13 (Price 2006), nine weeks after his death. One would be by a Tampa-area medical examiner, and the other by the man who performed Medgar Evers' second autopsy in 1991. In his statement, Crump compared the decision to exhume Anderson's body to the decision made by Mamie Till-Mobley to place her son's mutilated body in an open casket "because she wanted the nation to see what racism had done." On March 11, speaking on behalf of Black Florida lawmakers, state Senator Frederica Wilson of Miami invoked the exhumations of Emmett Till and Medgar Evers, stating that such extreme measures should not have been necessary to achieve justice (Nelson 2006). By April 21, when over 2,000 protesters descended on the state capitol, student protesters among others wore black and white t-shirts imprinted with "The next Emmett Till?" (Hollis 2006).

There were also differences from activism of the Civil Rights era of the 1950s and 1960s. The students interviewed by various news outlets did not point to any one leader; nor did reporters seem to be seeking out one overall leader or even spokespeople per se. I observed that both women and men were asked for comments, and both women and men were quoted as leaders of various student organizations. This was not the case for the Civil Rights era, when the presence of women leaders in activist organizations was a fact only in the Black Panthers, the women's liberation movement and the lesbian liberation movements. Women activists like Ella Baker, Fannie Lou Hamer and others were not welcomed to the leadership ranks in the Civil Rights movement despite their organizational innovations, eloquence, and total commitment to the movement (Collier-Franklin and Thomas, 2001; Farmer 2017; Olson,2001; Ransby 2003). Forty-two years later, both young Black women and men were in the forefront. And Phillip Agnew, though an organizer, was not putting himself forth as *the spokesperson* for this group. The presence of many young voices in news reporting, both male and female, reflects what Astra Taylor (2016) referred to as a "leaderful" rather than "leaderless" approach to organizing.

Another difference was the beginnings of social media and cell phone use, both for specific organizing efforts and for sharing stories. We should recall that Martin Lee Anderson was killed in 2006, the year after Facebook was established. Twitter followed in 2006, and Instagram in 2010. Apple iPhones came out in 2011, with easy sharing of pictures and the ability to create videos. Even in early 2012, social media was still not being used to activate students at Bethune-Cookman University for the march to Sanford from their campus city of Daytona Beach to protest the murder of Trayvon Martin (Pulver 2012a). Physical fliers were still being used to alert Floridians to protests in 2012 (Milford Griner 2012). But new media and cell phones were beginning to enter the mix (De La Cruz 2006; Ensley 2006). Indeed, it had been the release of a video from the facility's own security camera of the thirty minutes of violence before Anderson's death which led to a review of the case, after the first autopsy claimed the death resulted from natural causes (Nelson 2006a). So, while this video was not from a "citizen camera," it once again demonstrated the power of such evidence to ignite public outrage.

2012: TRAYVON MARTIN, STAND YOUR GROUND, AND THE FORMATION OF DREAM DEFENDERS

Dream Defenders was formed after the murder of Trayvon Martin and the acquittal of George Zimmerman. The first newspaper reference to Dream Defenders that I found was on April 6, 2012, in the *Daytona News Journal* (Pulver 2012a).

Scores of college students from around Florida plan to convene in Daytona Beach today to begin a three-day, 41-mile march to Sanford, modeled after the historic 1965 civil rights march from Selma to Montgomery, Ala.

Students say they hope to promote racial equality in the wake of controversy related to the February shooting death of Trayvon Martin in Sanford.

... The marchers are calling themselves the Dream Defenders, organizing and promoting their campaign through social media such as Facebook and Twitter. (Pulver 2012a, A1)

Immediately the idea of a long march, from Daytona Beach to Sanford, Florida is linked to the historic Selma to Montgomery march, but in a very unique way: Gabriel Pendas, one of the march organizers, "and many others" had taken part in a "reenactment" of the Selma march one month prior (Pulver 2012a; Campbell 2012; Revived Voter ID 2012; Haines 2012; Gregg 2012). So Pendas, like Phillip Agnew, came to the Trayvon Martin cause with some significant activist experience already. In the present moment, student organizers were also thinking about the march "to promote racial equality" after the shooting of Trayvon Martin, in the face of "the extremes on both sides," according to Terray Rollins (Pulver 2012, A1).

Buses to the start of the march in Daytona would be leaving from Florida A&M and Florida State University in Tallahassee and Miami-Dade College (Pulver 2012). Students at local HBCU Bethune-Cookman University in Daytona said they had heard little about the march, except by word of mouth among friends. By the next day, news coverage had expanded to the *Orlando Sentinel* (Hernandez and Taylor 2012). When the grand jury decision not to charge George Zimmerman was announced on April 9, the Dream Defenders march also made the *Gainesville Sun* (Trayvon Martin 2012) and the *Ocala Banner* (Trayvon Martin 2012). On April 12, the *Orlando Sentinel* ran a timeline of the Trayvon Martin case, with April 6, 8 and 9 covering actions by Dream Defenders as they marched to Sanford and blocked the Sanford Police Department front doors for five hours (*Orlando Sentinel* 2012).

Governor Rick Scott in April 2012 responded to citizen, lawmaker and activist calls and created a "Task Force for Citizen Safety and Protection" (Fingeroot 2012). Its composition was criticized by FSU Dream Defender Michael Sampson for not representing people in their twenties. City officials in Sanford, FL, where Trayvon Martin was killed, also proposed a "community relations commission" (Comas 2012). Dream Defender Vanessa Baden called it "a good start," but "questioned 'how much teeth'" it would have. She said the role should be filled by a person selected by the community, to get outside of the "same good-old-boy system" (Comas 2012, A10).

Newspaper coverage then skips ahead to May 12, 2012, when Dream Defenders were present at the sentencing of Marissa Alexander, a Black woman from Jacksonville who was convicted of three counts of aggravated assault after shooting a warning shot when her husband was attacking her (Broward 2012). The activists burst into "Ella's Song," singing "we who believe in freedom cannot rest until it is won." This song was based on the words of Ella Baker during the Civil Rights era. The judge promptly threw them out of the courtroom.

In July 2012, Dream Defenders went to Polk County, just southwest of Orlando, to talk with residents who felt unjustly treated by law enforcement personnel (Malagon 2012). They held meetings at the Lakeland, FL campus of Polk State College and at the Polk County Jail in Bartow, FL. Dream Defenders are described as a "network of young adults and college students that focuses on criminal justice issues," quoting Gabriel Pendas, one of the group's organizers.

Pendas and Phillip Agnew reported that sixty Dream Defenders would hold workshops to educate county residents about their rights, listen to residents' experiences with police, and bring together the "large African American and Latino" communities that were feeling "disenfranchised." They vowed to return to the County again. The article also reported that in March 2012 the Southern Poverty Law Center had filed a "federal class action lawsuit in the US District Court at Tampa against the county sheriff over hostile conditions for incarcerated juveniles in the Polk County Jail."

An August 1, 2012 article in the *Tallahassee Democrat* profiled Ciara Taylor, Dream Defender and student at Florida A&M, as "the conscience of her class" (Blackburn 2012). She had participated in marches in February 2012 over the killing of Trayvon Martin and took part in the 40-mile march from Daytona to Sanford. In this article, Dream Defenders were described as "a coalition of students of color determined to see social justice become a reality." Ciara also had taken part in three days of protests in Bartow, FL the previous week over "corrupt criminalization practices by the Polk County sheriff." I found no coverage of those protests in either the ProQuest US Newsstream or Nexis Uni databases.

In August 2012, against the backdrop of Tropical Storm Isaac, Dream Defenders as part of the Coalition to March on the RNC staged a protest at the Republican National Convention in Tampa (Hastings 2012). Other groups taking part included "Students for a Democratic Society, the Uhuru Movement, the International Action Center, the Poor People's Economic Campaign, Code Pink, Freedom Road Socialist Organization, and others." At one point, protesters unfurled a 30-foot banner containing their demands. This article in a college news service was the only coverage I found of this protest.

The next mentions of Dream Defenders occur in October and November 2012, connected to the presidential election. On October 23, 2012, fifteen Dream Defenders were arrested for blocking a highway near Lynn University in Boca Raton, FL while a presidential debate was being held there (Seltzer 2012a). The article mentions chapters at seven public colleges and universities in Florida. It quotes the Dream Defenders' mission from its website which references the dream of Dr. Martin Luther King and describes the group as "a growing coalition of youth and students committed to replacing jails with schools, ending the illegal war on the undocumented, and dismantling the systems that criminalize our people." A statement from Ciara Taylor, who was one of the members arrested, cited the fact that Florida had the highest population of "youth" in prison serving life sentences, and connected this reality with the urgent need for candidates to address the criminalization of young people.

Of the Dream Defenders arrested, several remained active in the group and were cited in news stories in subsequent years, including Taylor, Gabriel Pendas, Lashanett Lorraine, Nahila (Nailah) Summers, Cecilia O'Brien, and Philip Agnew. Michael Sampson, also arrested, had already been quoted with respect to Governor Scott's safety task force (Fingeroot 2012). While the Fort Lauderdale *Sun Sentinel* characterized the arrests as without incident in the context of a smoothly-run presidential debate at Lynn University (Geggis 2012), the *Palm Beach Post* invoked the civil disobedience of the 1960s and protests at the 1968 Democratic National Convention in Chicago in its coverage (Seltzer 2012b). The *Tallahassee Democrat*, in a brief article on the protest and arrests, also gave substantial space to the group's issues: "the proliferation of for-profit prisons, funding cuts to education, and harsh sentences for juveniles . . . creating a 'school-to-prison pipeline'" (Pillow 2012a). In an updated version of the story the next day, Pillow (2012b) reported that Dream Defenders had put out a press release stating that "at least 120 students marched." In addition to quoting Dream Defender Lashanett Lorraine as in the previous day's article, Pillow quoted member Michael Sampson, who said that regardless of who won the presidential election, "'we're not going to stop . . . until our issues are discussed and solutions brought about.'"

The final 2012 mention of Dream Defenders listed them as providing rides to the polls for early voting (*Tallahassee Democrat* 2012). They were joined by the Tallahassee branches of the NAACP and Urban League, one state representative, one Leon County Commissioner, the Tallahassee Ministerial Alliance and the Got Power Coalition.

Before moving into subsequent years, I want to pause and note some important and enduring commitments and practices of Dream Defenders reported in Florida papers. First, their partners in a variety of coalitions represent a wide and deep range of issues facing communities of color and run the gamut from grassroots groups to more established advocacy organizations to traditional politicians. Socialist and Black Power organizations like the Uhuru Movement are partners, as well as the more mainstream Southern Poverty Law Center and Code Pink. In this and subsequent years, Dream Defenders would coalesce with the NAACP, Reverend Al Sharpton's National Action Network, the National Urban League and the ACLU, as well as voting rights and immigrant rights organizations. They also fully embraced #BLM.

These coalitions embody their commitment to working at the intersection of race and class issues. There was no distancing from groups advocating for the poor or for non-capitalist economic policies. This is consistent with a rejection of "respectability politics," one of the hallmarks of twentieth-century nonviolent activism. It also reflects that this new era of activism is happening after the end of the Cold War, McCarthyism and attempts by the FBI and others to discredit Martin Luther King, Jr. by tying him to communist backers and ideology. Civil rights and economic rights were largely separate struggles until near the end of King's life, in part because of the highly polarized ideological world of the Cold War era. Dream Defenders' commitment to the issues of Latinos as well as Blacks are apparent in Phillip Agnew's comments regarding their Polk County activities. By the same token, they also coalesced with lawmakers, and engaged in get out the vote efforts. They would protest to end for-profit prisons and political donations from such companies, and comment on state and local policing policies and commissions. So, there was also from the beginning an engagement with conventional politics, political processes and politicians, as well as with other activist organizations.

Second, although it would expand outward from colleges, initially Dream Defenders formed chapters at colleges and universities throughout Florida, including founder Phillip Agnew's alma mater and HBCU Florida A&M University, and schools in north, central and south Florida, all of which were public and had substantial percentages of Black and Latino students. Over time, as organizers graduate and some remain with the organization, Dream Defenders becomes less campus-centric. We begin to see references to "regional organizers" and Dream Defenders not identified in articles as associated with a particular college or university, though campus chapters also continue to be mentioned. By 2022, the Dream Defenders website listed seven "Squadds" of organizers in Florida: Miami, Broward, Orlando, Trill (Tallahassee), Goddsville (Gainesville), Bay Area (Tampa) and Pensacola (Dream Defenders, 2022). But it is fair to say that Dream Defenders begins as a campus-based organization.

Third, Dream Defenders in their very name and inspiration drew breath and strength from the Civil Rights movement: "We are dedicated to defending the dream etched in our memories by Dr. Martin Luther King" (Seltzer 2012b). We see references to Dream Defenders using nonviolent civil disobedience tactics from the Civil Rights era, including blocking roads, long marches, and protest rallies. For example, as they headed to Sanford,

The marchers, who plan to overnight in area churches, ended their first day with a prayer vigil at the Volusia Juvenile Detention Center, where they will start this morning. . . . On Easter Sunday, they will march to the Sanford City Hall and then attend a church service there. On Monday, they plan to engage in a campaign of nonviolent civil disobedience in Sanford and are encouraging others to participate in walkouts, strikes and sit-ins. (Pulver 2012a)

So we see both a nonviolence philosophy and tactical carryovers as well as connections to attending church, holding prayer vigils, and engagement with their spiritual humanity. At Marissa Alexander's sentencing, they sing a song called "Ella's Song" written by Bernice Johnson Reagon, SNCC Freedom Singer and founder of the musical group Sweet Honey in the Rock (Reagon 1993). It was written in honor of SNCC organizer Ella Baker's famous statement that "we who believe in freedom cannot rest until it is won." Awareness of this famous Sweet Honey song suggests a deeper generational transmission of movement knowledge and ideas. By the same token, Dream Defenders' commitment to ending the "school to prison pipeline" and private prisons are very contemporary concepts. They are central to ending the era of mass incarceration for Blacks which began in the 1990s, part of Michelle Alexander's (2010) concept of The New Jim Crow.

Fourth, both women and men are quoted by reporters speaking for Dream Defenders. They come from a variety of universities and locations. So it becomes clear that leadership is not the exclusive prerogative of men in this organization. I analyzed 685 articles in Florida newspapers between 2012 and 2022 including campus newspapers collected using the Proquest US Newstream and Nexis Uni databases, as well as online searches of the *Miami Herald* and *Sarasota Herald Tribune* archives at their websites. I found 409 persons identified as Dream Defenders quoted in those stories. Of these, there were 201 quoted females and 208 quoted males. Of quotes from male members, 95 or 45.7 percent were from Phillip Agnew, a founder and long-time executive director. The remaining quotes came from 39 other males in 1–15 stories each. For females quoted, Nailah Summers, a founder and long-time Defender, had the most quotes with mentions in 22 stories. Ciara Taylor was quoted in 20 stories; there were an additional 52 female Dream Defenders who were quoted in between one and 15 stories. This suggests that while Phillip Agnew was quoted in the greatest number of stories, the organization had 93 other members and leaders who were put forward to speak to the press or in some cases author or co-author columns. As the Dream Defenders have said of themselves, perhaps their most important achievement is the leaders they have developed.

And finally, we note references to the group's website and social media. Marchers tweeted and posted along the road to Sanford (Pulver 2012a).

Reporters were accessing timely posts as well as longstanding statements of principle to explain the group to the public. Notably, I was not able to determine when the group first published its core principles online, contained in its Freedom Papers (Dream Defenders 2023a). The only references to them that I found in Proquest US Newsstream and Nexis Uni are in 2018 in the context of the governor's race (for example Haas, 2018), the 2020 presidential race (Simone 2020), and a 2022 article entitled "Black Women Are Fueling the Rise of Democratic Socialism" (Ward 2022) in the *Sarasota Herald-Tribune*, penned by longtime Dream Defender Jessika Ward.

In sum, this group of young people, carrying forward the vision of Dr. Martin Luther King Jr., while also embracing women's leadership, social media, and a broad and intersectional agenda addressing the issues of all people of color, immigrants, the poor, and the school-to-prison pipeline, also upheld the importance of voting, the right to vote, and the need to change the agendas of government and policing as well as corporations and political donations. They had come together over the murder of the person they came to call the "Emmett Till of our generation," the young, unarmed Trayvon Martin (Edwards 2013; Tinker 2013). And they made it clear, over and over, that they were here to stay.

DREAM DEFENDERS AND FLORIDA GOVERNORS: ELECTION ISSUES AND THE RIGHT TO PROTEST

In a time when police and civilian killings of Black women, men and children have driven many protests, it is also important to explore the role played by activist organizations in other spheres of civic life, including electoral politics and law-making. Dream Defenders never eschewed electoral politics in their activism. Indeed, they staged protests at the site of a 2012 presidential debate in Boca Raton, worked for the election of Bernie Sanders, and in some cases even ran as candidates in Florida elections (Burlew 2022; Sheridan 2021). It was one of their commitments previously less discussed in the news, however, which played a large role in the 2018 gubernatorial election.

Andrew Gillum, the first Black mayor of Tallahassee and a Democrat, ran against Ron DeSantis, a two-term Republican US Representative from the 6th district in northeast Florida. Dream Defenders had sponsored a debate by four Democratic candidates before the primary in April (Mann 2018) and targeted Republican Attorney General Ashley Moody for taking campaign contributions from the Geo Group, a private prison company (March 2018). They also disrupted a speech by incumbent Republican Governor Rick Scott for taking Geo Group money at a GOP rally in July (Anderson 2018a, 2018b).

They continued their protests against the Geo Group in August, garnering a major article in the *South Florida Sun-Sentinel* (Ft Lauderdale) (Swisher and Chokey 2018). They made the clear connection between President Trump's crackdowns and detentions of immigrants and profits made by Geo Group for holding these detainees in inhumane and cruel conditions.

Andrew Gillum was an early supporter of Dream Defenders (Dobson 2014; Rossman 2013) and signed a pledge not to accept money from private prison companies in the 2018 gubernatorial race (Swisher and Chokey 2018). In a close race which Gillum lost by less than one-half a percent, it was Dream Defenders' solidarity with the Palestinian cause and their call for Boycott, Divestment and Sanctions against Israel which DeSantis called out in hopes of winning voters. In September when called out on racist remarks he had made during the campaign, he went on the offensive regarding Dream Defenders' associations with the Council on American-Islamic Relations (Lemongello 2018; Smith 2018). In several articles from September to Election Day, Dream Defenders were called out as anti-Semitic, in support of BDS, and/or anti-Israel (Carmona 2018; Koh, Smiley and Wilson 2018).

> DeSantis said Gillum "had a lot of explaining to do" regarding the Tallahassee mayor's support of what he described as anti-Israel groups, including the Dream Defenders, whose website says it stands in solidarity with Palestine and calls on ending U.S. aid to Israel.
> "In this race, we've never had a candidate who's been as hostile to Israel as Andrew Gillum has been," DeSantis said. (Lemongello 2018)

A fact-checking column found that "Dream Defenders and Black Lives Matter condemn Israel's treatment of Palestinians and do equate it with apartheid" (Schweers 2018). In response, Gillum affirmed that while he supported Dream Defenders, he did not share their commitment to Boycott, Divestment and Sanctions against Israel (Lemongello 2018).

Dream Defenders' solidarity with Palestine, discussed in some depth by participants including Phillip Agnew and Ahmad Abuznaid in a 2019 article on Black-Palestinian transnational solidarity delegations (Abuznaid et al. 2019), reflected their long-standing alignment with both Student Nonviolent Coordinating Committee (SNCC) and Black Panther Party positions on Palestine (Rickford, 2019). The Movement for Black Lives and Dream Defenders made a major statement supporting Palestine in 2016:

> Black activists quickly emerged as prominent advocates for Palestine. In August of 2016, the Movement for Black Lives (M4BL), a coalition of over sixty organizations, rolled out an ambitious policy statement aimed at dismantling racism, patriarchy, inequality, and militarism that included a forceful statement labeling

Israel an "apartheid state" and characterizing the ongoing situation in Gaza and the West Bank as "genocide." Predictably, conservatives and liberals attacked the statement—especially the charge of genocide—as misleading, incendiary, and anti-Semitic. But even faced with the potential loss of funding, M4BL never backed down. Dream Defenders' codirector Rachel Gilmer drafted much of the statement after she and other members of her organization visited Palestine in the spring of 2016. Her takeaway: "We are never going to get free in the U.S. if the rest of the world is in chains." (Kelley 2019, 70)

Although Michelle Alexander (2019) wrote compellingly of Martin Luther King's evolving and complex position on Israel and Palestine in the *New York Times*, it was mostly SNCC and other activist groups who had taken up the mantle of the shared struggle with Palestine at the time. In the Florida governor's race in 2018, its possible impacts on the election outcome were clear to both DeSantis and Gillum, as noted above, but also to Dream Defenders (Abuznaid et al. 2019).

There have been two major issues in which Dream Defenders has allied with other activist groups to fight in court. One was the need to extend online voter registration prior to the 2020 election when Covid made typical in-person voting dangerous (Schweers 2020). The other has been legal challengers to Governor DeSantis's attempts to throttle citizens' rights to protest in public spaces.

HB 1, currently titled "Combating Public Disorder," . . . seen by many as a response to the Black Lives Matter protests last year after the death of George Floyd, would subject Florida's protesters to some of the hardest punishments nationwide.

Its provisions include banning protesters from blocking roadways, increasing the severity of some offenses if they are committed during civil disturbances—like instituting a mandatory six-month minimum sentence for people convicted of battery on a police officer—and prohibiting people arrested under certain offenses from posting bail before their first court appearances. (Rice 2021)

In both efforts they have worked with groups like the Black Collective, Florida Immigrant Coalition, Chainless Change, New Florida Majority, the Public Rights Project, Community Justice Project, Black Lives Matter Alliance Broward, the Florida NAACP and the Southern Poverty Law Center (Rice 2021; Etters 2021). While they were unable to win an extension for voters to register in October 2020, the coalition has so far succeeded via court order to block the enforcement of the so-called anti-riot law, HB1, pending input from the Florida Supreme Court (Crowder 2023). This represents a major victory in protecting the right to protest in a state where Governor DeSantis has increasingly tried to silence opposing voices.

MEDIA COVERAGE IN FLORIDA: TONE AND FRAMES

There is ample research which has documented negative framing by main-stream media of protests and protesters, including for racial justice (Elmasry and el-Nawawy 2016; Entman and Rojecki 2001; Huspek 2004; Lee,2014; McLeod and Hertog 1992). Several media scholars have examined news framing of Black Lives Matter protests and related activism. Banks (2018) concluded that,

> Anti-racist struggles draw attention to and confront the historical structure of racism, sexism and State violence. This confrontation of negative societal aspects means that anti-racist movements like BLM have to be discursively and rhetorically delegitimized by those in power. The BLM group seeks to end the inequalities that confront Black people in their everyday lives, empower and create spaces in leadership for Black women, as well as queer and transgender Blacks, who are often omitted from the story of Black Civil Rights. However, Fox News, CNN, and New York Times' re-presentation of the BLM movement in a negative light means that the news media can ignore and delegitimize the movement's goals. (718)

Carney and Kelekay (2022) looked at news frames of the Black Lives Matter movement in five of the ten largest-circulation US newspapers for one-week periods in 2014 and 2020 following decisions by grand juries not to indict the police involved in the murders of Eric Garner, Breonna Taylor and George Floyd. They chose to examine the *New York Times, Washington Post, Los Angeles Times*, the *Minneapolis Star Tribune*, and *USA Today*. They found significant contextualizing of BLM within the history of earlier Black uprisings, but also identified the "erasure" of both Black women's leadership in BLM and of violence perpetrated against Black women. Cruz and Holman (2021) compared an ethnically diverse newsroom at the *Atlanta Journal and Constitution* to the predominantly White newsroom at the *Tampa Bay Times* in how they covered BLM and Deferred Action for Childhood Arrivals (DACA). They looked at word choice and framing, as well as the extent to which each newsroom adhered to best practices identified in prior research to "avoid perpetuating prejudices and stereotypes, such as using ethical news frames and providing context about the key issues" (9). They found that both papers performed better in using ethical frames after the murder of George Floyd, but both papers still printed readers' letters and politicians' rhetoric which did not align with AP guidelines for neutral language. Hailu and Sarubbi (2019) focused on media depictions of student protests within Black Lives Matter as covered in *The Chronicle of Higher Education*. In the 28 articles they analyzed, they found four themes: "(1) disparaging coverage of the BLM movement, (2) an emphasis on the methods of mobilization, (3) far reaching impacts of the BLM movement, and (4) an insistence on foregrounding the free speech debate" (113). Finally, Brown, Wilner and Masullo (2022) interviewed and surveyed over one thousand Black Americans regarding their satisfaction with media depictions of current protests and their communities. They concluded:

> Our work challenges blanket assumptions that negative protest coverage is delegitimizing and negatively affects public opinion. Here, we find that Black people critically read and challenge the master narratives of protest that are presented by the press. Instead, the coverage likely triggers more negative opinions about the press than about protests. Our research centers Black perspectives, illustrating the salient points that lead to their dissatisfaction in the coverage of protests and other issues. We find three key critiques of news coverage: it isn't comprehensive; it excessively utilizes stereotypes; and it erases important components of the story. (10–11)

I was therefore attentive in this study of the ways Dream Defenders were depicted in the newspaper stories I collected. A search of the Proquest US Newsstream database finds 22 articles mentioning both Dream Defenders and "radical." One article (Barszewski 2015) quotes from the Dream Defenders' Facebook page describing their mission to "develop the next generation of radical leaders to realize and exercise our independent collective power." In another article (Glidewell 2015) a defender of the Confederate flag calls Dream Defenders, Students for a Democratic Society and CHISPAS all "far left radical groups." In twelve articles surrounding the 2018 gubernatorial race, Democratic candidate Andrew Gillum is characterized as "too radical" for Florida, in part because of his support for Dream Defenders. Yet even in these articles, where journalists are describing Dream Defenders and not simply quoting Republican politicians, they are not delegitimated. Adam Smith (2018), referring to Ron DeSantis, wrote "He cited two groups, the Council on American–Islamic Relations (CAIR), a Muslim civil rights group, and Dream Defenders, a human rights group that has supported a boycott of Israel to protest the treatment of Palestinians." That is a factual description of Dream Defenders. Likewise, Koh, Smiley and Wilson (2018) refer to Republicans who have "highlighted Gillum's support from the Dream Defenders, a social justice organization that argues for a boycott of Israel." This is again an accurate portrayal of the group and one of its aims. Out of 685 articles this handful that used a trigger word for conservatives, namely "radical," when used by journalists (not quoting politicians) did not undermine the credibility of Dream Defenders or misrepresent their position.

I found seventy-nine characterizations of Dream Defenders as an organization in the 685 articles I collected. They included "civil rights organization," "human rights" group or organization, "social justice group," "voting rights group," "youth justice organization," "non-profit organization," "black feminist group" and "black student activist group." Almost one-fifth of the articles described them as having formed after the murder of unarmed Black teenager Trayvon Martin. Their monikers ran the gamut of their activities, from advocating for social justice for Black and Brown youth, to opposing private prisons and seeking to end the school-to-prison pipeline. The group was presented frequently as a state-wide organization, though just under 10 percent of the stories identified Dream Defenders as a Miami-based organization.

There were several designations of Dream Defenders by Ron DeSantis as "anti-law enforcement" because of their support for police abolition, a position which they state clearly and repeatedly on their website. One article out of 685 called them openly anti-Semitic and in support of terrorists for their consistent support of Palestine. By the same token, the state's largest newspaper, *The Tampa Bay Times*, called them a "human rights group that has supported a boycott of Israel to protest the treatment of Palestinians" (Smith 2018). In general, however, apart from remarks by Ron DeSantis, some sheriffs and Donald Trump, I did not find any pattern of either word choice or frames by journalists which would serve to delegitimate the mission and strategies of Dream Defenders. There were a wide variety of descriptions by journalists, all of which were accurate to the group and not defamatory or undermining. Journalists seemed to largely express respect for the group, its members, aims and actions. I find this a notable result, given the reputation of Florida politics in recent years to be bitter, divisive and extreme. One can cautiously conclude that newspaper coverage of Dream Defenders in Florida, whatever its incompleteness, does not on the whole seem to have been intent upon undermining the legitimacy of its mission or its actions.

It is beyond the scope of this chapter to delve more deeply into Dream Defender national press coverage, including television, or to compare it with social media posts and online exchanges. To the extent that media coverage impacts activist participation, such studies exploring its reception and the ways it has been framed on other media platforms will certainly add to our understanding of Dream Defenders, its effectiveness and its external challenges.

CONCLUSION

This chapter sought to track the first decade of Dream Defenders' presentation in Florida newspaper stories, including campus news. I began with looking at the preceding instance of activism by Phillip Agnew and two other future founders of Dream Defenders, namely their protests of the murder of

Martin Lee Anderson while being held in a Florida "boot camp." News coverage demonstrates a widely acknowledged aspect of this era of Black activism, namely its ties and connections to the previous great era of Civil Rights activism in the 1950s–1970s. Dream Defenders have functioned primarily as an on-the-ground, Florida-based organization with a modest presence on social media. In the years since its founding, it has played a vital role in protecting the right to vote and to protest in Florida. It has also been heavily involved in efforts to register voters and cancel student debt (Bacon 2023; Student Debt 2022). Its efforts to establish a safe responder unit for mental health emergencies in Miami have barely been covered, however.

One may conclude that while not disparaging Dream Defenders, often commending the activists and giving them both voice and visibility in Florida news coverage, Florida newspapers have somewhat shied away from focusing on Dream Defenders' self-identified commitments and non-Florida centric actions. These include their solidarity visits to occupied Palestine, their socialism, Black feminism, and their focus on abolishing police (Dream Defenders 2023b). Perry Bacon (2023) captures Dream Defenders looking ahead:

> (Nailah) Summers says Dream Defenders will start trying to expand outside Florida and build a national base of members in part to address these challenges. "Our movement would've been better off with some kind of organization that was having campaigns coming out of the protests of 2020 and having a membership base that was working together across networks to keep driving the work," she said. "We think a big national organization with more reach helps the movement grow."

Much remains to be done in Florida. I believe Dream Defenders will continue to find ways to develop Black leaders, mobilize more and more people, and continue to do the work in this era of Black activism which they sparked.

REFERENCES

Abuznaid, Ahmad, Phillip Agnew, Maytha Alhassen, Kristian Davis Bailey, and Nadya Tannous. 2019. "On Solidarity Delegations." *Journal of Palestine Studies* 48 (4): 92–102. https://www.jstor.org/stable/26873237.

Ackerman, Nicole, Melody Goodman, Keon Gilbert, Cassandra Arroyo-Johnson, and Marcello Pagano. 2015. "Race, Law, and Health: Examination of 'Stand Your Ground' and Defendant Convictions in Florida. *Social Science & Medicine*, no. 142, 194–201. https://doi-org.ezp.bentley.edu/10.1016/j.socscimed.2015.08.012.

Alexander, Michelle. 2010. *The New Jim Crow: Mass Incarceration in the Age of Color Blindness*. New York: The New Press.

———. 2019. "Time to Break the Silence on Palestine: Martin Luther King Jr. Spoke Bravely on Vietnam. We Must Do the Same to Meet This Moral Challenge." *New York Times*, January 20, 2019, 2. ProQuest U.S. Newsstream.

American Bar Association. 2015. "National Task Force on Stand Your Ground Laws: Final Report and Recommendations." Accessed March 3, 2023. https://search.issuelab.org/resource/national-task-force-on-stand-your-ground-laws-final-report-and-recommendations.html.

Anderson, Zac. 2018a. "Candidates Spar, Protesters Come Out at Sarasota GOP rally. *Sarasota Herald-Tribune*, July 28, 2018. *Sarasota Herald Tribune* Web Edition Articles.

———. 2018b. "Video: Protesters Disrupt Rick Scott Speech at Sarasota GOP rally." *Sarasota Herald-Tribune*, July 28, 2018. *Sarasota Herald Tribune* Web Edition Articles.

Anonymous. 2008. "TV Worth Watching: Reverend Al Sharpton and TV One's 'Murder in Black and White' Solving the Unresolved Civil Rights Cases." *Los Angeles Sentinel*, October 2, 2008. Proquest U.S. Newsstream.

Anonymous. 2012. "Revived Voter ID Laws Prompt NAN to Re-enact Voting Rights March of 1965." *Afro-American Red Star*, March 3, 2012, A.1. Proquest U.S. Newsstream.

Bacon, Perry. 2023. "The Civil Rights Movement Is So Different Now." *Philadelphia Tribune*, Mar 5, 2023. Proquest U.S. Newsstream.

Banks, Chloe. 2018. "Disciplining Black Activism: Post-Racial Rhetoric, Public Memory and Decorum in News Media Framing of the Black Lives Matter Movement." *Continuum: Journal of Media & Cultural Studies* 32 (6): 709–20. https:/doi:10.1080/10304312.2018.1525920/doi.org.

Barszewski, Larry. 2015. "Protesters Disrupt Lauderdale City Commission Meeting." *South Florida Sun–Sentinel*, February 4, 2015. Proquest U.S. Newsstream.

Blackburn, Doug. 2012. "Ciara Taylor: The Conscience of Her Class." *Tallahassee Democrat*, August 1, 2012. Proquest U.S. Newsstream.

Broward, Charles. 2012. "Woman's Sentence Brings Out Divisions." *Florida Times Union* May 12, 2012, A.1. Proquest U.S. Newsstream.

Brown, Danielle K., Tamar Wilner, and Gina M. Masullo. 2022. "'It's Just Not the Whole Story': Black Perspectives of Protest Portrayals." *Howard Journal of Communications* 33 (4): 382–95. https/doi:10.1080/10646175.2021.2012852/doi.org.

Bullard, Robert. 2000. *Dumping in Dixie: Race, Class, and Environmental Inequality*. Third edition. New York: Routledge.

Bullard, Robert, ed. 1993. *Confronting Environmental Racism: Voices from the Grassroots*. Boston: South End Press.

———.ed. 2005. *The Quest for Environmental Justice: Human Rights and the Politics of Pollution.* Berkeley: Counterpoint.

Burlew, Jeff. 2022. "Campaign Crunch Time: Will Doak Do It? Will Slates Succeed? 5 Things to Watch." *Tallahassee Democrat*, Aug 21, 2022. Proquest U.S. Newsstream.

Campbell, A. 2012. "New Selma-To-Montgomery March Is More Than Just A Reenactment." *St. Joseph News—Press,* March 6, 2012. Proquest U.S. Newsstream.

Carmona, Sergio. 2018. "Fla. Gubernatorial Candidates Court Jewish, Pro-Israel Voters." *Jewish Journal*, Oct 31, 2018. Proquest U.S. Newsstream.

Carney, Nikita and Jasmine Kelekay. 2022. "Framing the Black Lives Matter Movement: An Analysis of Shifting News Coverage in 2014 and 2020." *Social Currents*, 9(6): 558–572. https://doi.org/10.1177/23294965221092731.

Collier-Thomas, Betty and V. P. Franklin, eds. 2001. *Sisters in the Struggle: African American Women in the Civil Rights-Black Power Movement*. New York: NYU Press.

Comas, Martin. 2012. "Sanford Officials Propose Citizens Commission." *Orlando Sentinel*, April 20, 2012, A.10. Proquest U.S. Newsstream.

Crowder, Valerie, "Florida's Controversial Anti-riot Law Remains Temporarily Blocked," *Weekend All Things Considered*, National Public Radio. Tallahassee, FL:WFSU, January 24, 2023. https://news.wfsu.org/state-news/2023-01-24/controversial-anti-protest-bill-temporarily-blocked.

Cruz, Chamian Y. and Lynette Holman. 2022. "The Media and Race in the Trump Era: An Analysis of Two Racially Different Newsrooms' Coverage of BLM and DACA." *Howard Journal of Communications* 33 (2): 197–215. https/doi:10.1080/10646175.2021.2012853/doi.org.

Davis, Charles. 2019. *Rise Up!: Activism as Education*. East Lansing: Michigan State University Press.

De La Cruz, Ralph. 2006. "Taking a Stand at Sit-In." *South Florida Sun–Sentinel*, April 23, 2006. Proquest U.S. Newsstream.

Dobson, Byron. 2014. "Gillum's Slam-Dunk Win Was Years in the Making." *Tallahassee Democrat*, Aug 31, 2014. Proquest U.S. Newsstream.

Dream Defenders. 2022. "Squadds." Dreamdefenders.org. October 24, 2022. https://dreamdefenders.org/squadds/.

———.2023a. "The Freedom Papers." Dreamdefenders.org. April 1, 2023. https://www.dreamdefenders.org/freedom-papers.

———.2023b. "Our Ideology." Dreamdefenders.org. April 1, 2023. https://www.dreamdefenders.org/freedom-papers.

Edwards, Jonel. 2013. "Jonel Edwards: Trayvon Martin and the End of an Era." *Gainesville Sun*, March 4, 2013. Proquest U.S. Newsstream.

Elmasry, Mohamad and Mohammed el-Nawawy, M. 2016. "Do Black Lives Matter? *Journalism Practice*, 11 (7): 857–875. https://www.researchgate.net/deref/http%3A%2F%2Fdx.doi.org%2F10.1080%2F17512786.2016.1208058.

Ensley, Gerald. 2006. "Student Protesting Exudes Selflessness and Hope." *Tallahassee Democrat*, Apr 22, 2006. Proquest U.S. Newsstream.

———. 2007. "Hundreds Expected for NAACP March." *Tallahassee Democrat*, Oct 23, 2007. Proquest U.S. Newsstream.

Entman, Robert and Andrew Rojecki. 2001. *The Black Image in the White Mind: Media and Race in America*. Chicago, IL: University of Chicago Press.

Etters, Karl. 2021. "Tallahassee Commission Challenges 'Anti-Riot' Legislation." *Tallahassee Democrat*, October 15, 2021, A.1. Proquest U.S. Newsstream.

Farmer, Ashley. 2017. *Remaking Black Power: How Black Women Transformed an Era*. Chapel Hill: UNC Press.

Fingeroot, Lisa. 2012. "Students: Task Force Lacks Age Diversity." *Tallahassee Democrat,* April 20, 2012. ProQuest U.S. Newsstream.

Florida Today. 2007. "Guarding Basic Rights." *Florida Today*, October 16, 2007, A8. Proquest US Newsstream.

Francois, France. 2007. "Florida State U. Students Protest Verdict in Martin Lee Anderson Trial." *FSView & Florida Flambeau,* October 15, 2007. Nexis Uni.

Franks, Mary Anne. 2014. "Real Men Advance, Real Women Retreat: Stand Your Ground, Battered Women's Syndrome, and Violence as Male Privilege." *University of Miami Law Review*, 4 (68), 1099–1128. https://repository.law.miami.edu/umlr/vol68/iss4/7.

Gainesville Sun. 2012. "Trayvon Martin Death Won't Go to Fla. Grand Jury." *Gainesville Sun*, April 9, 2012. ProQuest U.S. Newsstream.

Geggis, Anne. 2012. "Boca's Basking in the Spotlight Euphoria Reigns After Debate Goes Off Without Any Problem." *South Florida Sun—Sentinel*, October 24, 2012, A.1. ProQuest U.S. Newsstream.

Glidewell, Danny. 2015. "Yes! the Flag is a Symbol of Our Shared Heritage." *Northwest Florida Daily News*, Jul 26, 2015. Proquest U.S. Newsstream.

Gregg, Michelle. 2012. "Walk Through Time." *Idaho Argonaut*: University of Idaho, 1. March 26, 2012. Nexis Uni.

Gainesville Sun. 2012. "Milford Griner: Gainesville Rallied for Justice for Trayvon Martin." *Gainesville Sun*, April 5, 2012. Proquest U.S. Newsstream.

Haas, Kyra. 2018. "DeSantis Puts Words in Gillum's Mouth That He Didn't Say in Florida Governor Race." *Politifact.com*, November 6, 2018. https://www.politifact.com/factchecks/2018/nov/06/ron-desantis/despite-desantis-anti-police-claims-gillums-record/.

Hailu, Meseret F. and Molly Sarubbi. 2019. "Student Resistance Movements in Higher Education: An Analysis of the Depiction of Black Lives Matter Student Protests in News Media." *International Journal of Qualitative Studies in Education* 32 (9): 1108–24. https:/doi:10.1080/09518398.2019.1645905/doi.org.

Haines, Errin. 2012. Rev. "Sharpton in Atlanta for Voting Rights Rally." *The Associated Press State & Local Wire*. February 24, 2012. Nexis Uni.

Hastings, Matt. 2012. "Hundreds March on the RNC Despite Threat of Isaac." *Uloop.com*. August 28, 2012 Tuesday. Nexis Uni.

Hernandez, Arelis and Gary Taylor. 2012. "College Students Protesting, Marching for 3 Days from Daytona Beach to Sanford." *Orlando Sentinel*, Apr 07. Proquest U.S. Newsstream.

Hill, Anita. 2021. *Believing: Our Thirty-Year Journey to End Gender Violence*. New York: Viking.

Hogan, Wesley. 2019. *On the Freedom Side: How Five Decades of Youth Activists Have Remixed American History*. Chapel Hill: UNC Press.

Hollis, Mark. 2006. "Students Protest Death of Teenager at Boot Camp." *South Florida Sun–Sentinel*, Apr 22, 2006. Proquest U.S. Newsstream.

Hordge, Christina. 2005. "Program Prepares Students for Florida Comprehensive Assessment Test." *University Wire*, December 21, 2005. Nexis Uni.

Huspek, Michael. 2004. "Black Press, White Press, and Their Opposition: The Case of the Police Killing of Tyisha Miller." *Social Justice* 31 (1): 217–241. http://www.jstor.org/stable/29768250.

Ijoma, Samone. 2018. "False Promises of Protection: Black Women, Trans People and the Struggle for Visibility as Victims of Intimate Partner and Gendered Violence." *University of Maryland Law Journal of Race, Religion, Gender and Class*, 18 (1): 255–296. https://digitalcommons.law.umaryland.edu/rrgc/vol18/iss1/24.

Johnson III, Ollie and Karin Stanford. 2002. "Introduction: The Relevance of Black Political Organizations in the Post-Civil Rights Era." In *Black Political Organizations in the Post-Civil Rights Era,* edited by Ollie Johnson III and Karin Stanford, 1–13. New Brunswick, NJ: Rutgers University Press.

Kam, Dara. 2006. "Black Lawmakers Call for Arrests, Firings in Boot Camp Death." *Palm Beach Post*, Mar 17, 2006. Proquest U.S. Newsstream.

Kelley, Robin. 2019. "From the River to the Sea to Every Mountain Top: Solidarity as Worldmaking." *Journal of Palestine Studies* 48 (4): 69–91. https://www.jstor.org/stable/26873236.

Khan-Cullors, Patrisse and Asha Bandele. 2017. *When They Call You a Terrorist: A Black Lives Matter Memoir*. New York: St. Martin's Griffin.

Kim, Eun Kyung. 2007. "Students March in Washington to Protest Bootcamp Verdict." *Gannett News Service*, November 19, 2007, 1. Proquest U.S. Newsstream.

Koh, Elizabeth, David Smiley, and Kirby Wilson. 2018 "DeSantis Gets Aggressive Against Gillum in Florida Governor's Race." *Tampa Bay Times*, October 5, 2018. Proquest U.S. Newsstream.

Krause, Thomas. "Acquitted on All Counts." *McClatchey-Tribune Business News*, October 13, 2007. Proquest U.S. Newsstream.

Lee, Francis. 2014. "Triggering the Protest Paradigm: Examining Factors Affecting News Coverage of Protests." *International Journal of Communication* (19328036) 8 (January): 2725–46. https://ijoc.org/index.php/ijoc/article/view/2873/1215.

Lemongello, Steven. 2018. "'I Think we'Re (sic) Good,' DeSantis Says of Standing with Trump." *Orlando Sentinel*, September 20, 2018. Proquest U.S. Newsstream.

Mack, LaKerri and Kristin Roberts-Lewis. 2016. "The Dangerous Intersection Between Race, Class and Stand Your Ground." *Journal of Public Management & Social Policy*, 23 (1): 47–60. https://digitalscholarship.tsu.edu/cgi/viewcontent.cgi?article=1044&context=jpmsp.

Malagon, Elvia. 2012. "Group Talks to Residents About Police Complaints. *The Ledger*, July 28, 2012. Proquest U.S. Newsstream.

Mallard, Aida. 2007. "Gillum Stays Busy at FAMU, in Capitol." *Gainesville Sun*, 13 Dec. 2007. Proquest U.S. Newsstream.

Man, Anthony. 2018. "Four Governor Debates Planned Before Primary." *South Florida Sun—Sentinel*, April 28, 2018, B.4. Proquest U.S. Newsstream.

March, William. 2018. "Video: Protesters Target Ashley Moody for Private Prison Contributions." *Tampa Bay Times*, July 10, 2018. Proquest U.S. Newsstream.

McGory, Kathleen. 2013. Activists Build on History With Sit-In. *The Ledger,* July 20, 2013. Proquest U.S. Newsstream.

McLeod, Douglas and James Hertog. 1992. "The Manufacture of Public Opinion by Reporters: Informal Cues for Public Perceptions of Protest Groups." *Discourse and Society* 3 (3): 259–275. http://www.jstor.org/stable/42887799.

Messerschmidt, Cristina. 2017. "A Victim of Abuse Should Still Have a Castle: The Applicability of the Castle Doctrine to Instances of Domestic Violence." *The Journal of Law and Criminology* 106 (3): 593–625. https://scholarlycommons.law .northwestern.edu/jclc/vol106/iss3/5

National Urban League. 2013. *Shoot First: Stand Your Ground Laws and Their Effect on Violent Crime and the Criminal Justice System.* Accessed November 17, 2023. https://s3.amazonaws.com/s3.mayorsagainstillegalguns.org/images/Shoot First_v4.pdf

Nelson, Melissa. 2006a. "2nd Autopsy Planned in Boot-Camp Death." *Orlando Sentinel*, February 25, 2006. Proquest U.S. Newsstream.

———. 2006b. "Body Exhumed in Boot-Camp Inquiry; Another Autopsy Will Be Done on a Teen Who Died After He Was Beaten by Guards." *Orlando Sentinel*, March 11, 2006. Proquest U.S. Newsstream.

Ocala Star-Banner. 2012. "Trayvon Martin Death Won't Go to Fla. Grand Jury." *Ocala Star-Banner*, April 9, 2012. Proquest U.S. Newsstream.

Olson, Lynne. 2001. *Freedom's Daughters: The Unsung Heroines of the Civil Rights Movement from 1830 to 1970.* New York: Scribner.

Orlando Sentinel. 2012. "Timeline: The Trayvon Martin Shooting." *Orlando Sentinel*, April 12, 2012. Proquest U.S. Newsstream.

Pecquet, Julian. 2006. "Teen's Death Inspires Students." *Tallahassee Democrat*, May 30, 2006, 1. Proquest U.S. Newsstream.

———. 2007. "Verdict: Not Guilty." Tallahassee Democrat, October 13, 2007. Proquest U.S. Newsstream.

Pillow, Travis. 2012a. October 24). "Tallahassee Students Arrested at Presidential Debate Protest." *Tallahassee Democrat,* October 24, 2012. Proquest U.S. Newsstream.

———. 2012b. Debate protest sparks arrests. *Tallahassee Democrat,* October 25, 2012. Proquest U.S. Newsstream.

Price, Stephen. 2006. "Students Protest Slow Justice in Beating Case." *Tallahassee Democrat*, October 20, 2006, A1. Proquest U.S. Newsstream.

———. 2008. "NAACP: Feds Dragging Heels on Anderson Probe." *Tallahassee Democrat*, May 14, 2008. Proquest U.S. Newsstream.

Pulver, Dinah. 2012. "Students Gathering to Begin Equality March." *The Daytona Beach News—Journal.* April 6, 2012, A.1. Proquest U.S. Newsstream.

Ransby, Barbara. 2003. *Ella Baker and the Black Freedom Movement: A Radical Democratic Vision.* Chapel Hill: UNC Press.

———. 2018. *Making All Black Lives Matter: Reimagining Freedom in the 21st Century.* Oakland: University of California Press.

Reagon, Bernice. 1993. *We Who Believe in Freedom: Sweet Honey in the Rock—Still on the Journey.* New York: Knopf Doubleday Publishing Group.

Rice, Katie. 2021. "'Rally to Save Protesting' Held After Anti-Riot Bill Passes Florida House." *Orlando Sentinel*, March 27, 2021, A.4. Proquest U.S. Newsstream.

Rickford, Russell. 2019. "'To Build a New World': Black American Internationalism and Palestine Solidarity." *Journal of Palestine Studies* 48 (4): 52–68. https://www.jstor.org/stable/26873235.

Rossman, Sean. 2013. "NAACP Stands Unified with Protesters, Encourages Others to Join." *Tallahassee Democrat*, July 19, 2013. Proquest U.S. Newsstream.

Schweers, Jeffrey. 2020. "Voter Registration Won't Be Extended: Judge Blasts State for History of Election Problems but Declines to Move Deadline After Website Crash." *The News Press*, October 10, 2020, A.6. Proquest U.S. Newsstream.

Seltzer, Alexandra. 2012a. "Deputies Arrest 15 Members of Youth Political Group in Lynn University Debate-Related Incident." *McClatchy–Tribune Business News*, October 23, 2012. Proquest U.S. Newsstream.

———. 2012b. 15 Sitting on Road Arrested; Youth Political Group Members Were in Middle of Yamato. *Palm Beach Post*, October 24, 2012, B.1. Proquest U.S. Newsstream.

Sheridan, Jake. 2012. "Four in Running for St. Petersburg Post: A Former Council Member, Teacher-Slash-Activist, Optometrist and Business Owner are Running to Replace Council Member Amy Foster." *Tampa Bay Times*, July 16, 2021. Proquest U.S. Newsstream.

Smith, Adam. 2018. "On Defense Over Racist and Extremist Backers, DeSantis levels His Own Charges Against Gillum. *Tampa Bay Times*, September 24, 2018. Proquest U.S. Newsstream.

Smith, Charles. 2006. "The Tallahassee Bus Boycott–Fifty Years Later." *Tallahassee Democrat,* May 21, 2006, X.16. Proquest U.S. Newsstream.

Smith, Robert. 2002. "The NAACP in the Twenty-First Century." In *Black Political Organizations in the Post-Civil Rights Era,* edited by Ollie Johnson III and Karin Stanford, 28–39. New Brunswick, NJ: Rutgers University Press.

Stanford, Karin. 2002. "Reverend Jesse Jackson and the Rainbow/PUSH Coalition: Institutionalizing Economic Opportunity." In *Black Political Organizations in the Post-Civil Rights Era,* edited by Ollie Johnson III and Karin Stanford, 150–169. New Brunswick, NJ: Rutgers University Press.

"Student Debt Day of Action in DC." 2022. *University Wire*, April 11, 2022. Proquest U.S. Newsstream.

Swisher, Skyler and Aric Chokey. 2016. "Prisons Firm's Cash Flows to GOP; Geo Group Under Fire for 2016 donation." *South Florida Sun-Sentinel,* August 19, 2018, A.1. Proquest U.S. Newsstream.

Tallahassee Democrat. 2005. Costly Campaigns Near End: There's No Limit on Candidate Spending. *Tallahassee Democrat,* February 19, 2005, B.1. Proquest U.S. Newsstream.

———. 2012. "Ride to the Polls to Early Vote Today." November 3, 2012. Proquest U.S. Newsstream.

Taylor, Astra. "Against Activism." *The Baffler*, no. 30 (2016): 123–31. http://www.jstor.org/stable/43959210.

Tinker, Cleveland. 2013. "In Trayvon's Name." *Gainesville Sun,* July 17, 2013. Proquest U.S. Newsstream.

Velazquez, Daniela. 2006. "NAACP Speaks on Boot-Camp Death." *Tallahassee Democrat*, February 26, 2006. Proquest U.S. Newsstream.

Ward, Jessika. 2022. "Black Women Are Fueling the Rise of Democratic Socialism." *Sarasota Herald-Tribune*, March 25, 2022. *Sarasota Herald-Tribune* Online Archive.

Waters, TaMaryn. 2006. "Boycott Events Wrap Up with Downtown March." *Tallahassee Democrat*, May 29, 2006. Proquest U.S. Newsstream.

Weaver, Zachary. 2008. "Note: Florida's 'Stand Your Ground' Law: The Actual Effects and the Need for Clarification." *University of Miami Law Review* 63 (October 2008): 395–430. https://repository.law.miami.edu/umlr/vol63/iss1/9.

Williams, Simone. 2020."Dream Defenders Endorses Bernie Sanders." *The Famuan: Florida Agricultural and Mechanical University,* February 22, 2020. Nexis Uni.

Chapter Three

Protecting Whom? Serving What?

Police Accountability in Ferguson Protests in 2014

Jozie Nummi and Amorette T. Young

In this chapter protest policing tactics and strategies are reviewed through comparison of Twitter data, an US Department of Justice Report[1] (2015) and news media coverage. The images of state officials attacking protesters with police canines, firing water hoses at protesters in the 1960s and the disappearances of activists in countries in repressive states are world renown. There is evidence of the disparities between the policing of right-wing and white racist movements compared to racial justice protests by communities of color. Less is known about the constructed nature of protest threats and how racialized assumptions impact police planning and actions (Bracey 2016; Correa 2011; Cunningham 2022; Cunningham, Ward, and Owens 2019; Davenport, Soule, and Armstrong 2011; Morris 1986). During this era of #BlackLivesMatter protests, images of police in riot gear and police mounted on top of military vehicles pointing rifles at protesters have joined these well-known examples of racialized state repression. This repression affects movement recruitment, legitimacy of protests, and movement mobilization. This chapter analyzes the state's role in infringing on the rights of protesters, news media, and other citizens (Della Porta and Reiter 1998; Skolnick 2000). The state's role in protests in Ferguson, Missouri in August 2014 after Wilson shot Michael Brown is as a form of repression. Specifically, the police can produce repressive and hard policing of protests, which can demobilize or radicalize protesters (Della Porta and Reiter 1998). Movement repression can be covert or overt depending on tactics and dynamics which depend on movement goals, state officials and available state resources. Previously elite-white-male dominance systems utilized repressive strategies against racial justice movements, such as the Brown Berets and American Indian Movement, reproducing systemic racism, classism, and sexism (Correa 2011; Cunningham 2022; Davis 1983; Earl

2003; Feagin 2020; Feagin and Ducey 2017; hooks 2000; Reynolds-Stenson 2018). To analyze this repression, this study documents protest policing strategy and tactics that construct the repressive strategies utilized by the over 50 law enforcement agencies responding to protests in Ferguson, Missouri between August 9 and August 31, 2014.

PROTEST POLICING STRATEGIES

There were numerous protest policing strategies utilized in Ferguson, Missouri between August 9 and August 31, 2014. The differing protest policing strategies deployed during Ferguson protests include the escalated force style of policing, negotiated management style, strategic incapacitation, and underenforcement of the law (Della Porta and Reiter 1998; Gillham, Edwards, and Noakes 2013). St. Louis County Police Department was responsible for police response from August 10 until August 14, 2014, and thus the escalated force style of policing was implemented by St. Louis County Police Department Chief Belmar. From August 14 until August 31, there were different strategies implemented, even within the same day. On August 14, 2014, Captain Johnson was appointed by Missouri Governor Jay Nixon and the Missouri State Highway Patrol to "command all operations necessary to ensure public safety and protect civil rights in the city of Ferguson and, as necessary, surrounding areas during this period of emergency" (Nixon 2014).

AUGUST 9 THROUGH 14:
ESCALATED FORCE STYLE OF POLICING

The first strategy documented through tweets, the U.S. DOJ Report (2015), and news media coverage was the escalated force model (Earl, Soule, and McCarthy, 2003; McCarthy and McPhail 1998). Previous studies document this strategy as containing "observable/overt coercion committed by national government actors includ(ing) military-based repression, national guard deployments, and public protest policing" (Earl 2011, 264–265). This strategy in Ferguson is exemplified through the plethora and variety of gear, armored vehicles, and repression tactics utilized by the over fifty law enforcement agencies, as categorized in Table 3.1 List of Tactical Equipment. Military vehicles and tactical equipment, such as automatic weapons on tactical vehicles, were used in situations when there was no danger posed to officers or citizens. This escalated force model is supported in the following excerpt: "Finding 16: During the first several days of the Ferguson demonstrations, law enforcement staged armored vehicles visibly in a way that was perceived to be threatening to the community and, at times, used them absent danger or peril to citizens or officers" (U.S. DOJ Report 2015, 60).

Media outlets like NBC and CNN criticized the rapid militarization of policing in Ferguson, Missouri in their protest coverage. The military gear, rifles, show of force, and other tactics contributed toward the dramaturgy that draws news media attention. NBC and CNN news coverage also summarized the escalated force style of policing through videos, images, and framing. The escalated force model is illustrated in this NBC news coverage language from August 14: "Last night's jarring images of police clad in military gear and firing tear gas and rubber bullets at protesters on the streets of an American suburb has reverberated across this country" (NBC 2014a). The military gear and crowd dispersal techniques contributed to the escalated force model and dramatic images that drew news media correspondents to Ferguson, at times from countries overseas. On August 15, 2014, the evidence of the escalated force was noted by news media correspondents and official sources. "As events unfold this week many couldn't help but think it was a military force and not a police force that was on the ground in Ferguson. Attorney General Eric Holder said he was deeply concerned about the deployment of military equipment and vehicles" (NBC 2014b). Attorney General Eric Holder's concerns were shared earlier by President Obama when he spoke on Thursday, August 14. This escalated force model also included arresting reporters covering the protests on Wednesday, August 13, 2014. The early show of force was summarized by the US DOJ Report (2015) but thoroughly documented through tweets, which included hyperlinks to Vine, YouTube, and other websites along with photographs uploaded to Twitter. Similar to police lines advancing on protesters, past studies describe police "as using 'fists and clubs'" and as marching "quickly in pairs" to subdue demonstrators (Burks 1971, 13; Earl, Soule, and McCarthy 2003, 590). This show of force to subdue demonstrators is illustrated by photographs, tweets, and news media coverage, particularly with rifles drawn and pointed at unarmed demonstrators. Figures 3.1 and 3.2 shows law enforcement officers in tactical gear firing tear gas at protesters. Table 3.1 lists the different types of tactical equipment and military gear worn. As only eight photographs in the US DOJ Report (2015) included examples of protest policing military style gear, tactics, and repression, Twitter, YouTube videos, and news media coverage were crucial to documenting protest policing tactics and answering the research question.

Figure 3.1.   A member of the St. Louis County Police tactical team fires tear gas into a crowd of people on August 18, 2014, in Ferguson, Missouri.
Courtesy of David Carson/St Louis Post Dispatch/Polaris. Used with permission.

Figure 3.2.   St. Louis County Police tactical officers firing tear gas in Ferguson, Missouri on August 11, 2014.
Courtesy of Robert Cohen/St. Louis Post Dispatch/Polaris. Used with permission.

Table 3.1.   List of Tactical Equipment

Military Gear Worn

- Kevlar Helmets
- Assault-Friendly Gas Masks
- Combat Gloves
- Knee Pads
- Woodland Marine Pattern Utility Trousers
- Marine Pattern (Marpat) Camouflage, aka Camouflage-Patterned Battle Dress
- Uniforms (BDU)
- Deltoid Armor
- Tactical Body Armor Vests
- Approximately 120 To 180 Rounds for Each Shooter
- Semiautomatic Pistols
- Disposable Handcuff Restraints Hanging from Their Vests
- Close-Quarter-Battle Receivers for Their M4 Carbine Rifles
- M4 Carbine (not listed in U.S. DOJ (2015))
- M16 Automatic Rifles
- Mega AR-15 Marksman Rifle
- Paintball Gun
- Advanced Combat Optical Gunsights
- Ka-Bar-Style Fighting Knife (not listed in U.S. DOJ (2015))
- Gerber Knife (not listed in U.S. DOJ (2015))
- Flare/Smoke/Tear Gas/Grenade Launcher
- Tactical Gas Mask
- Night-Vision Goggle Mount
- Camelback Straw
- Subdued Flag
- 12-Gauge Shotgun

Crowd Dispersal, Control, and Surveillance Tactics

- Rubber Bullets
- Tear Gas
- PepperBalls
- Wooden Baton Rounds
- Smoke Grenade and Smoke Bomb
- Stun Grenade
- Riot Gun
- Bean Bag Projectile
- Long Range Acoustic Device (LRAD)
- K-9
- Drones (not listed in U.S. DOJ (2015))
- Manfrotto Tripod
- Leupold Long-Range Scope

Vehicles

- BearCat (Mine Resistant Ambush Protected (MRAP) vehicle)
- Humvees
- MD Helicopter 500 Series

AUGUST 14–31 NEGOTIATED MANAGEMENT STYLE, STRATEGIC INCAPACITATION AND UNDERENFORCEMENT OF THE LAW

While escalated force style is defined as observable or overt coercion by national government or state actors, negotiated management style is characterized by state actors negotiating with protesters to signify cooperation from law enforcement (Della Porta and Reiter 1998). Strategic incapacitation is a repressive style of policing responding to a breakdown in communication and failure to deploy a negotiated management style (Gillham, Edwards, and Noakes 2013). This style of policing is characterized by spatial containment and limiting the capacity to see and record events or occurrences. Lastly, underenforcement is a response by state actors characterized by a lack of action in the face of looting, rioting, or other violent events (Della Porta and Reiter 1998).

NEGOTIATED MANAGEMENT STYLE

The escalated force style of policing transitioned to a negotiated management style on August 14, 2014. This negotiated management style was deployed by the Incident Commander and the unified command system established by the Missouri State Governor Jay Nixon. Strategic incapacitation and underenforcement of the law were deployed alongside negotiated management styles, often within the same day. These styles were inconsistently deployed as Incident Command and rank and file law enforcement personnel ascribed to different cultures, one being focused on negotiation with protesters and the other focused on social control and repression endemic to white racism and patriarchy.

First, Missouri State Governor Jay Nixon appointed Captain Ronald Jonson of the State Highway Patrol as Incident Commander. The transition to the negotiated management style of policing is attributed to Captain Johnson. On August 14, 2014, Governor Jay Nixon of the State of Missouri assigned Missouri State Highway Patrol as formal incident command agency for the protests and Captain Ronald S. Johnson as incident commander. Captain Johnson contacted a local pastor and walked with protesters on August 14. This change in leadership and negotiated management style was also noted by St. Louis Alderman Antonio French on August 14, 2014, in an interview with CNN.

> (Wolf Blitzer) Alderman French first you. Are you encouraged by the governor's decision to turn over security in Ferguson to the state highway patrol and effectively remove the Saint Louis County Police?

(Antonio French) I am. It is already a noticeable difference in tone. Really it has been the police presence. The heavy handed presence which has escalated the situation and I think lead to the violence each night and so it's good to see this new approach. Already there has been a different attitude and a different interaction between the crowd and police and I am very hopeful for a peaceful night. (CNN 2014a)

On August 16, NBC news coverage noted a shift in policing tactics from the escalated force style of policing to negotiated management style. "It (August 15 police tactics) was a far cry from what was seen earlier in the week when officers in riot gear clashed with demonstrators firing tear gas and rubber bullets, drawing national outrage that inspired a change in police tactics" (NBC 2014d). This change in tactics was noted again on August 20 and 21. On August 20 CNN news correspondent noted that "Instead of blocking the street. Instead of a huge, consolidated presence of police they are spread out throughout, up and down West Florissant. Which seems to be much more effective and less intimidating to the crowds. Last night, and we hope again tonight, Anderson. We saw really for the first-time last night" (CNN 2014d).

This lack of police presence in one spot illustrated a shift in intimidation tactics and shows of force. On August 21, 2014, this shift was observed again: "We just saw two tactical vehicles around the same time as we have the last two nights moving down into position. But the scene is drastically different than it has been in previous days. The number of people has gradually grown Polly since we've been on the air, maybe over the last hour, hour and a half" (CNN 2014e).

On August 21, Governor Nixon also ordered the National Guard to leave as tensions were easing (NBC 2014f). These tactics were attributed to Captain Johnson as he engaged in a negotiated management style with protesters. Captain Johnson's responsibilities as Incident Commander and actions are summarized in the following excerpt: "By August 16, Captain Johnson had become the public face of the police response while also serving as incident commander. The responsibilities taken on by Captain Johnson were diverse. Frequently he met with different community groups and leaders, provided media interviews, and was on the street among the demonstrators" (U.S. DOJ Report 2015, 25).

These tactical changes were also noted by law enforcement officers. "Even though officers commented that 'the strategy for managing the demonstrations was continually changing,' there were still patterns of behavior toward protesters that involved use of tear gas, the 'keep moving' order and arrests" (U.S. DOJ Report 2015, 25). Negotiated management is typified by meetings with protesters, usually ahead of time. These meetings indicate cooperation from law enforcement, resulting in protests benefiting from law enforcement agencies blocking off streets for marches and redirecting traffic. Captain Johnson's efforts and framing often went beyond what is expected of Incident Commanders. This is reflected in an invitation to speak at a Unity Rally on August 17, 2014, at which Michael Brown's family and attorneys also spoke. His actions were also recognized in the US DOJ Report (2015): "He proactively reached out to community members and groups. He spoke at a vigil for Mr. Brown and often allowed himself to be photographed with demonstrators" (20). Speaking at the vigil and with protesters reflects a different strategy than other incident commanders and law enforcement personnel. These actions not only differed from Ferguson Police Department's actions and attitudes with the community, but other police leaders as well. Community members reiterated the positive impact Captain Johnson had in the U.S. DOJ Report (2015): "Based on community interviews and the media, this seemed to have a positive impact on community relations. One community member interviewed stated, 'Things could have been worse if it had not been for the leadership of Captain Johnson'" (20).

In contrast, rank and file law enforcement personnel resisted Captain Johnson's negotiated management style. Rank and file law enforcement personnel's attitude toward Captain Johnson's negotiated management style was antagonistic, and their resistance to it reflected a culture of policing surrounding preceding protests based on an "us versus them" framing. This culture is illustrated by the behaviors and actions of the police such as show of force, arrests, infringement of free speech, and other tactics. These law enforcement officers' actions were also distinguished from Captain Johnson's negotiated management by the news media. On August 16, Jason Carroll, CNN news correspondent, identified organizational problems in protest policing strategies. He stated:

> The other reality on the ground here is the following, is that law enforcement itself may all have to get on the same page. Because what you have is, you have Captain Johnson's approach which is engage the people in the community, speak with them, back off a little bit. Let some people show a little bit of heat. What you also have is law enforcement here on the ground who are confused about when it is appropriate to make an arrest and when there's not. (CNN 2014b)

This excerpt solidifies Captain Johnson's actions as negotiated management and his public role as Incident Commander. Captain Johnson's efforts impacted officers negatively given the "us versus them" framing and policing culture steeped in systemic racism. "Over time, Captain Johnson's public appearances and perceived support for the demonstrators lowered morale among officers, including Missouri State Highway Patrol troopers, according to interviews with law enforcement" (U.S. DOJ Report 2015, 20–21). This "lowered morale" is likely because protest policing culture in the United States is based on systemic racism, classism, and sexism (Bolton and Feagin 2004; Feagin and Ducey 2017; Garza 2014; Kerner Commission 1968; Pacholok 2009; Worden 1996). Social movement studies find protest policing is harsher when the state is the target of protests, which is common in racial justice protests by people of color (Correa 2011; Correa and Thomas 2019; Davenport, Soule, and Armstrong 2011). Captain Johnson walked with protesters and emphasized his solidarity with protesters by stating "we're in this together" on August 15, 2014 (NBC 2014b). In fact, the tactics of Captain Johnson were embraced by citizens but criticized by officers according to the U.S. DOJ Report (2015): "However, based on interviews with officers from the four core agencies, they felt that his statements and actions were not always supportive of the officers involved" (20). At times Captain Johnson defended protest policing tactics and arrests officers made. He also emphasized officer safety as being central to decision making. In the end the negotiated management style and recognition of the humanity of Black men and the Ferguson community created divisions in leadership and with law enforcement personnel.

STRATEGIC INCAPACITATION

A second strategy deployed by rank-and-file officers and law enforcement personnel was strategic incapacitation. This strategy is deployed often in response to a breakdown in communication and lack of ability to deploy negotiated management style (Gillham, Edwards, and Noakes 2013). This protest policing strategy was characterized by spatial containment, arrests, and rendering recording and visual limitations. These strategies are aimed at controlling protesters' space, their ability to protest, and the ability to see and record events or occurrences by news media reporters, citizen journalists, and protesters alike.

Along with 236 arrests during the protest period there were violations to protesters' civil rights through the implementation of the "keep moving" order, orders to disperse, and interference with the news media through arrests and other repression tactics supporting the strategic incapacitation strategy. Repression tactics in this study went beyond traditional or documented techniques (see Table 3.2). There were numerous intimidation tactics documented in 847 tweets that included threatening arrest, infringement of Civil Rights, confiscating cell phones, and other behaviors. For examples of police lines and overwatch see Figures 3.2 and 3.3.

Figure 3.3.   Screenshot of Police Lines
Source: Screenshot from Blaze, Brown. 2014. "Ferguson Riot, Missouri, August 10, 2014." Posted August 12, 2014. Video, 7:47. https://youtu.be/EkACHGLugu8.

The "Keep Moving" order and requests to disperse were frequently mentioned by users. One incident involved an officer calling protesters 'rabid dogs' that needed to be put down. Despite the lack of documentation by U.S. DOJ Report (2015), there were 158 tweets documenting protester injuries or assaults by protest policing tactics. Two primary repression tactics, spatial containment and recording and visual limitations, are summarized below as part of strategic incapacitation of protests.

SPATIAL CONTAINMENT

Similar to Occupy Wall Street protests, free speech zones and press zones were established during the protests by police (Gillham, Edwards, and Noakes 2013). These zones were also facilitated by separating news media and protesters. This separation prevented news media from reporting on police actions and protesters. These arrests, separation, and containment were facilitated by an ad hoc rule, the "keeping moving" order, which was determined to be a violation of Missouri law after it was challenged by the ACLU in U.S. District Court on August 18. The court "determined that the operational impact of this unwritten ad hoc rule did not meet First Amendment constitutional standards protecting the freedom of assembly and free speech" (U.S.

DOJ Report 2015, 63). The "Keep Moving" order or five second rule was based on the failure to disperse statute (Missouri Revised Statute 574.060) but applies only to one who is "present at the scene of an unlawful assembly, or at the scene of a riot." The failure to disperse statute requires it to be a group of six or more people who agree to use force to violate criminal laws of the state or the United States. "The rule provided no notice to citizens of what conduct was unlawful, and its enforcement was entirely arbitrary and left to the unfettered discretion of the officers on the street" (U.S. DOJ Report 2015, 63). This ad hoc rule illustrates the interactive nature of protest policing as police respond to protests with new techniques, which protesters need to be prepared for and aware of as protest events unfold.

RECORDING AND VISUAL LIMITATION

A second strategy that is new to protest policing literature is the limitation of recording and visuals through the use of high beams, turning off streetlights, and flashing lights in people's eyes. The use of numerous police vehicles flashing their lights, often behind police lines, at protesters and cameras resulted in blinding people and preventing effective recording. Lights were turned off or on in various ways to repress protesters and news media as recorded by 83 tweets. These tactics included using a police car's high beams to blind protesters and prevent recording of police actions. On August 16, 2014, Mouse posted on Twitter, "We are being peaceful, and the cops are shining their high beams in our eyes. #Ferguson." This tweet exemplified the larger repression tactics and use of light during protests. On August 17, 2014, Pujols-Johnson posted, "Police turning off the streetlights and using night vision goggles against protesters is (fill in the blank). #Ferguson." Along with intimidation of protesters, media outlets were intimidated and controlled according to 351 tweets posted. Media outlets were told to disperse, evacuate, leave or to stop recording. At times their equipment was dismantled by police. Users also documented this repression using #mediablackout.

Protesters and Twitter users reacted to media intimidation tactics by retweeting and facilitating citizen journalists recording. As reporters were being arrested there was a need for citizen journalists to document repression tactics, which was carried out by Antonio French, a Saint Louis Alderman. There were 685 tweets in which he was mentioned, his photographs linked, or YouTube and Vine videos reposted. Additionally, Twitter reported police turning off streetlights, instituting a no-fly zone, and inciting riots.

Table 3.2.   Repression documented on Twitter

Coding Category	Tweets
Arrests of Protesters	2,450
Intimidation Tactics	847
Citizen Journalism	685
Media Intimidation and Control	351
Protester Injuries and Assaults	158
Other Repressive Tactics	83
Deployment of National Guard or State Troopers	62
Total	4,636

Source: Author tabulated data

Very similar to spatial containment, recording and visual limitation restricts the ability of protesters to exercise their First Amendment rights and for news media reporters to inform the public of protest events and police use of force during such protests.

UNDERENFORCEMENT OF THE LAW

In stark contrast to their escalated force model, law enforcement also underenforced the law in respect to looters. There are instances in which law enforcement agencies underenforce laws (Della Porta and Reiter 1998; Earl, Soule, and McCarthy 2003). This occurred during the protest period when looting occurred. The U.S. DOJ Report (2015) states officers did not go into areas or businesses for fear of their safety and that it would create "more conflict and violence," referred to as a "hands off" approach (37). This tactic was strategically deployed during looting, rioting, and other violent events. Although officer safety was framed as a justification for this lack of action. Reports of citizens, and even rival gang members, indicate they sought to prevent looting and violence and were recorded on news media and Twitter. On August 16, 2014, a news correspondent stated, "some people last night were arm in arm trying to stop the agitators from coming in and looting these stores" (CNN 2014b). This lack of enforcement was criticized by Tom Fuentes on CNN as a welcome message to bad people. This lack of action also occurred in regard to Canfield Apartments. "One interviewed officer stated, 'Canfield Apartments became a no-police zone. We were told we could not go into Canfield Apartments. We contained the area but did not go into the area, and by default the area became a safe haven for criminals.' Interestingly, Ferguson residents also complained that the police had 'abandoned' Canfield Green Apartments" (U.S. DOJ Report 2015, 15).

This underenforcement of law and lack of prevention of looting illustrates a strategic decision to allow protests to become centered on these violent, unrepresentative events. This dramaturgy was in turn fixated upon by news media coverage, as it was emphasized more than other protest events, tactics, or peaceful marches. Ironically few news media correspondents, police experts, or other sources characterized this as a failure of law enforcement agencies. This virtuousness of white supremacy was intact while blame was attributed to the Ferguson community, illustrating the flexibility and creativity of white racial framing of protest policing tactics. The lack of enforcement was also noted as citizens often tried to prevent looting. Tweets noted rival gangs were arm in arm and other citizen groups were in front of stores preventing looting. Despite calls for less violence by community leaders and Brown's family, the responsibility for the property damage was attributed to the community by news media experts and police sources.

PROTEST POLICING TACTICS AND EQUIPMENT

In addition to documenting protest policing strategies, this study details the various tactics and equipment deployed during Ferguson protests. By analyzing the tactics and equipment this study adds depth and detail to descriptions of the protest policing strategies. This analysis rejects more dichotomous models of classifications by analyzing six tactics, similar to Earl, et al. 2003. The model encompasses the greatest detail related to racialized state repression and tactics by documenting the use of the following six tactics each day: 1) use of weapons; 2) use of equipment (e.g., militarized vehicle); 3) use of arrests (protesters or journalists); 4) implementation of policies (e.g., "keep moving" order); 5) timing of police intervention and 6) number of agencies involved. These tactics comprise the elevated and repressive response to Ferguson protests by the more than fifty agencies involved. These tactics were used in concert to repress contentious collective action.

Twitter and news media coverage were crucial in documenting and summarizing protest policing strategies and tactics. Tactics were documented based on review of the U.S. DOJ Report (2015), 87 NBC and CNN news media coverage videos, and 13,280 tweets. Tactics were documented from August 9 until August 25, 2014, as this time period was covered by all three datasets. The U.S. DOJ Report (2015) did not provide consistent and transparent documentation regarding arrests, citizen injuries, protest size, number of officers, or other tactics. News media coverage and Twitter data also encompass actions outside of the four law enforcement agencies reviewed by the U.S. DOJ Report (2015). These were 1) the St. Louis County PD; 2) the

St. Louis Metropolitan PD; 3) the Missouri State Highway Patrol; and 4) the Ferguson Police Department (FPD). In total there were over forty agencies that responded to protests to provide support to these departments or protection to the Ferguson Police Department. Tables 3.2 and 3.3 below capture tweets about policing and tactical equipment used. The four law enforcement agencies' responses to the protests did not adhere to the National Incident Management Standards (NIMS), which are national standards developed for crowd control, emergency response to attacks and other events according to the U.S. DOJ Report (2015). NIMS call for less use of force and tactical equipment to be utilized early in protests. As the escalated force style of policing started on August 9 and continued for numerous days, it became harder to pull this strategy back and rebuild trust and negotiations with the community. Furthermore, use of tear gas was not properly announced, and protesters did not receive ample notification to ensure they could disperse. Police canine use is also not authorized to be used as a crowd control technique, which also occurred during Ferguson protests. Lastly the U.S. DOJ Report (2015) also noted that armored vehicles and tactical gear were used when there was no threat to the safety of officers, exacerbating the situation and increasing violence.

The weapons and use of tactics included Stingerballs, PepperBalls, bean bag rounds, baton rounds, police canines, tactical vehicles with overwatch, guns, and tear gas. Crowd dispersal techniques such as electronic control

Table 3.3. Protest Policing Tweet Themes

Coding Category	Percentage	Number of Tweets
Tactical Equipment and Show of Force	36%	4792
Repression of Media and Protesters	35%	4643
Framing of Police Actions	29%	3845
Total	100%	13280

Source: Author tabulated data

Table 3.4. Tweets about Tactical Equipment

Coding Category	Number of Tweets
Crowd Dispersal Techniques (tear gas, pepper spray, rubber bullets, etc.)	3484
SWAT	422
Bearcats or Armored Vehicles (tanks, armored vehicles, Humvees, etc.)	399
Police Canines	170
Military Gear	285
Rifles	16
Helicopter or drones	16
Total	4792

Source: Author tabulated data

weapons, also known as tasers, were used. Long-range acoustic devices (LRAD) were utilized for crowd dispersal as well. Armored vehicles were commonplace at protests as well; see figure 3.2 for examples of an armored vehicle and overwatch. There were numerous inconsistencies between reports by law enforcement agencies, videos in news media coverage and Twitter data on use of force, police canines' presence and threats of use of force by officers, which are explained below.

Crowd dispersal techniques that were used are considered "less-lethal weapons." These dispersal techniques were utilized on several days between August 9 and August 25, 2014. According to the U.S. DOJ Report (2015), "information received from law enforcement agencies indicated that less-lethal crowd dispersal projectiles—Stingerballs, PepperBalls, bean bag rounds, and baton rounds—were used on August 10–12 and 16–18" (48). Although there were many reports of rubber bullets being used, according to the report "none of the four agencies in this assessment had obtained or used rubber bullets" (U.S. DOJ Report 2015, 46). Crowd dispersal techniques were mentioned in 3,484 tweets, with rubber bullets mentioned in 194 tweets. Tweets mentioned tear gas and rubber bullets the most, illustrating the escalated force model of protest policing; see Figure 3.4, Tables 3.4 and 3.5.

Tweets and photographs showing various crowd dispersal techniques are demonstrated by Figure 3.2. Three different news media videos reference rubber bullets on August 14 and August 17, respectively (CNN 2014a; NBC 2014a, 2014e). Although tear gas is banned in warfare by the Chemical Weapons Convention of 1993, it was commonly used in Ferguson, Missouri. It should be noted the effects of tear gas are devastating. Rubin, a Marine who's

Figure 3.4. "Here is a collection of debris I found in #Ferguson yesterday there were tons more rubber bullets @mattdpearce [images uploaded]"
Tweet Debris in Ferguson QR Code *Note:* QR code takes you to: David Carson (@PDPJ). 2014.

experienced a gas chamber as part of training, described its effects as such: "Suffice it to say it sucks out your organs, hogs your oxygen and burns you inside and out. Interim blindness and extended coughing fits are common, as well as an overall sense that you are dying or dead. And they're dispersing this poison in people's backyards" (Rubin 2014).

These effects of tear gas were documented by U.S. DOJ Report (2015), tweets, and news media coverage, shown in Table 3.5. "Effects of exposure to CS gas range from an irritation of eyes and mucus membrane to vomiting, which are often over within an hour" (U.S. DOJ Report 2015, 49). Injuries from tear gas on individuals were not recorded by the U.S. DOJ Report (2015) and were categorically denied by police sources according to tweets. Reilly (2014) posted a YouTube video that documents injuries sustained by protesters.

Tear gas hitting protesters and news media was recorded on video on August 19. "Tear gas and stun grenades are fired into the crowds hitting both protesters and the news media" (CNN 2014c). See Table 3.6. Crowd Dispersal Technique Tweets for a full list of excerpts and tactics documented by news media. Crowd dispersal techniques such as tear gas were documented in 17 CNN excerpts and 7 NBC excerpts during news coverage. The U.S. DOJ Report (2015) concluded that "based on interviews with law enforcement and community members and review of video footage, evidence indicates that the deployment of tear gas was not always within policy guidelines, notably with respect to the notification requirement" (50). As tear gas was deployed and injured protesters, Ferguson residents, and news media correspondents, these injuries were treated with bottles of milk on hand as medical personnel were

Table 3.5. **Protest Policing Tactics on News Media**

Coding Category	CNN Excerpts	NBC Excerpts	Totals
Tactics	56	30	86
Armored vehicle/Overwatch	21	10	31
Crowd-dispersal Techniques	17	7	24
Officers in riot gear	13	10	23
Tear gas	10	10	20
Precision Rifle	12	4	16
Curfew	10	3	13
Arrests	8	4	12
SWAT Team	8	3	11
Police not going into a business, pulling back	2	1	3
Arrest of media	3	0	3
Keep Moving order	3	0	3
Soft repression	1	1	2
Police Dogs	1	1	2

Source: Author's Tabulations from News Media Videos

Table 3.6.   Crowd Dispersal Technique Tweets

Coding Category	Number of Tweets
Tear gas	3095
Rubber bullets	194
Tweets mentioning firing on protests	81
Pepper spray	67
Bean bag rounds	31
Wooden pellets	10
Protesters wearing gas mask	3
Flash grenades	2
Chemical weapons	1
Total	3484

Source: Author tabulated data

restricted from entering the protest area at times. This use of tear gas and resulting injuries support police use of the escalated force model.

In addition to tear gas, PepperBalls, bean bag projectiles, Stingerballs and other projectiles were fired at protesters. PepperBalls are defined in the following way: "similar in design to recreational paintballs, this projectile disperses pepper spray when it is broken. The PepperBall is intended to be shot at a wall or the ground to break the ball so the spray can escape into the air near targeted individuals" (U.S. DOJ Report 2015, 46). Although the U.S. DOJ Report (2015) describes PepperBalls as non-lethal, their use was banned by the Boston Police Department after a woman was killed by one (Slack and Smalley 2005). Similar to PepperBalls, bean bag projectiles were fired at protesters throughout the time period studied. Bean bag projectiles are defined as follows: "this low-velocity ammunition for a 12-gauge shotgun expands to approximately 1 square inch after being fired" (U.S. DOJ Report 2015, 46). This projectile is also considered a "less-lethal" force by police sources. Despite this classification, they "are capable of causing serious injury or death if they hit a relatively sensitive area of the body such as the eyes, throat, temple, or groin" (U.S. DOJ Report 2015, 46). Figures 3.5, 3.6, and 3.7 all illustrate images to protesters from tear gas, which were all injuries left out of the U.S. DOJ Report (2015).

Similar to Stingerballs and PepperBalls, wooden baton rounds were used and attributed to injuries by Twitter users. Additionally, wooden baton rounds are intended to "provide 'pain compliance' to disperse people who are resisting dispersal orders" (U.S. DOJ Report 2015, 47). These wide-ranging crowd dispersal techniques were often used without warning, and tear gas and smoke drifted into residential homes.

The use of police canines during the protests illustrated a show of force to protesters that echoed earlier eras of protest policing in the 1960s, as

Figure 3.5.   Cassandra Roberts has milk poured over her eyes on August 17, 2014. Milk is used to alleviate exposure to tear gas.
Courtesy of Robert Cohen/St. Louis Post Dispatch/Polaris. Used with permission.

Figure 3.6.   Injury to Protester Tweet
QR Code Note: QR Codes takes you to: Antonio French (@Antonio-French). 2014. "This woman who was helping to calm the crowd last night got shot by a rubber bullet later on. #Ferguson. [images uploaded]" Twitter, August 14, 2014, 3:48 pm. https://twitter.com/AntonioFrench/status/500021221392936961.

Figure 3.7.   Injury to Protester from Tear Gas
QR Code Note: QR Codes takes you to: Joel D. Anderson (@byjoelanderson). 2014. "This is what happens to a hand that grabs a tear gas canister. #Ferguson [image uploaded]" Twitter, August 20, 2014, 4:34 p.m., https://twitter.com/byjoelanderson/status/502207124454137859.

documented on Twitter. This show of force is common in the escalated force style of policing and strategic incapacitation. Use of canines can be requested but decisions to use them are often left up to the handler: "According to interviews with personnel from the four core agencies, only one crowd-control deployment of canines was authorized during the assessment period. On August 9, immediately after the officer-involved shooting and before the homicide scene was secured, a crowd was growing and encroaching on the evidence scene" (U.S. DOJ Report 2015, 44). Instances of canine use went undocumented by the U.S. DOJ Report (2015) as they noted "the actual deployment of a dog is most commonly left up to the decision of the handler based on factors at the scene and the dog's capabilities" (U.S. DOJ Report 2015, 43). The U.S. DOJ Report (2015) discussed police canines as largely symbolic and only "perceived" to be a threat. "The symbolism of using canines appeared to have a profound effect on community members that law enforcement did not seem to appreciate" (U.S. DOJ Report 2015, 44). This framing of police canines justified the virtuousness of law enforcement agencies, while denying the reality that police canines used by the FPD only bite African Americans and did cause injury to protesters. The assertion they were used to "back up" officers was in sharp contrast to the photographs shared on Twitter and news media websites showing dogs lunging at protesters a foot away or less, displaying their teeth and growling (St. Louis Post-Dispatch 2014). There were 170 mentions of canine use in tweets. Police

Figure 3.8. Police officers stand to confront a crowd with a canine unit on August 9, 2014, in Ferguson, Missouri.
Courtesy of David Carson/St. Louis Post Dispatch/Polaris. Used with permission.

dogs were mentioned or photographed every day between August 9 and 31 except for August 29. Brown Blaze documented the use of force and police canine use on August 10, 2014, indicating protesters could encounter police canines often without warning (Blaze 2014).

Police canine use was only approved to protect the crime scene on August 9, 2014, according to law enforcement personnel. However, none of the four agencies as part of the U.S. DOJ Report (2015) forbid the use of canines for crowd control, which is not consistent with national standards for policing practices. Deployment of police canines are usually left up to the dog's handler. Despite police reports that canines were only approved on August 9, numerous news media reports and tweets documented their use during protests, with photographs of dogs lunging at protesters. Police officers also stated canines were available as "back-up" other days. In the investigation of Ferguson Police Department police canines bit people of color 90 percent of the time when biting non-police.

ORGANIZATIONAL PROBLEMS

The over 50 law enforcement agencies led by the unified command under Captain Johnson and Saint Louis County Police Chief Belmar had numerous organizational problems throughout the protests. These problems were similar to the problems described in the National Advisory Commission on Civil Disorders report, commonly known as the Kerner Commission Report (1968). The report contained an assessment that numerous organizational planning, logistical decisions, and reactions to protests resulted in an increase in violence at protest events. Although the four law enforcement agencies reviewed in the U.S. DOJ Report (2015) were in compliance with all required trainings, the NIMS were not followed. Similar to Correa's (2010) findings regarding the East Los Angeles Brown Berets movement between 1967 and 1973, police officers used harassment and brutality to repress and discourage protests. Rifles were pointed at Brown Beret members' heads, and they were called racial slurs (Correa 2010). In Ferguson rifles were commonly pointed at protesters' heads and Overwatch, a sniper monitoring groups from a higher position, such as on top of an armored vehicle. This tactic was used to surveil peaceful crowds. Police lines and intimidation tactics were common as police officers actively resisted the negotiated management style of Captain Johnson. See Figure 3.3 (above) for examples of police lines and Figure 3.2 (above) for an example of overwatch. Self-deployment of officers was also noted as a problem throughout the protests, despite their mental and physical concerns over working long hours during intense conditions. Officers also stopped wearing name badges, as they were targeted for identity theft attacks online.

This distinction between Captain Johnson and rank and file officers illustrates the limited power people of color have within a white supremacist system. The white racism and hegemonic masculinity principles associated with superiority and social control of people of color clashed with the negotiated management style of Captain Johnson. It impacted command negatively; rank and file officers cited his actions as "lowering morale." An "us" versus "them" mentality is clear as this attitude by rank-and-file officers demonstrated resistance to the negotiated management protest policing style taken by Captain Johnson. This illustrates the relative lack of power people of color have in white systems as they try to make modest changes to institutional cultures and structures; as they attempt to challenge racial inequality they are demoted, intimidated, or fired because of the covert and overt cultural racism produced through police departments and other predominantly white institutions (Davis 2002; Feagin 2020).

The range of behaviors documented by Twitter, news media, and the U.S. DOJ Report (2015) indicate First Amendment rights were infringed upon throughout the protests. One key finding of the U.S. DOJ Report (2015) and federal courts was the violation of freedom of assembly by the "keep moving" order, known colloquially as the "five second rule." In enforcing this rule, peaceful protesters were arrested, and this pattern was communicated to unified command policymakers. Second, tear gas was administered ineffectively during the protests. First it was deployed without warning and "deployment was intuitive rather than tactical" (U.S. DOJ Report 2015, 50). Police officers did not consider environmental conditions, safe exit for protesters and news media, or weather conditions, to name a few. The use of lights to blind protesters and news media cameras illustrates another violation of First Amendment Rights. Furthermore, the arrests of 19 journalists indicate another violation of freedom of press (Sandvik 2022). Despite the violations of First Amendment rights, there were no grievances filed against police officers, likely given the structural barriers and lack of an online system to do so.

Despite claims of "outside agitators" at the protests and professional activists, only 32 of the 236 arrests were of people from outside Missouri. The U.S. DOJ Report (2015) report estimates 300 arrests took place, but they did not document them as not all agencies were included in their report. These arrests constitute approximately 13.5 percent of arrests. In total, 36 arrests were for felonies and 200 were for misdemeanor crimes. The vast majority of arrests were failure-to-disperse arrests (U.S. DOJ Report 2015). It should be noted that this number of arrests is less than what occurred. Law enforcement agencies were underreporting total arrests and not charging individuals after holding them for between 9 and 15 hours. These arrests are a form of state repression of protests. They raise the stakes in which protesters operate and increase the risks of engaging in protests.

INCONSISTENCIES BETWEEN DATASETS

Documenting significant issues with transparency and protest policing strategy and tactics within official government reports has gone unrecognized by previous social movement literature. This study finds repression tactics similar to past protests and new tactics unique to Ferguson protests documented on Twitter (Earl 2003; Earl, Soule, and McCarthy 2003; Gillham and Marx 2018). There were numerous repression tactics documented on Twitter that were not included in the U.S. DOJ Report (2015) as listed in Table 3.2. This study finds the perceived objectivity, completeness, and factuality of official police reports are severe limitations in social movement protest policing literature by Gillham, Marx, Della Porta, and others. There were numerous inconsistencies between reports by law enforcement agencies, videos in news media coverage and Twitter data on use of force, police canines' presence and threats of use of force by officers as summarized in Table 3.7.

MISSING INFORMATION OR INCONSISTENCIES BETWEEN DATASETS

In contrast to the lack of documentation, transparency, and information provided by the U.S. DOJ Report (2015), 13,280 tweets documented tactics and protest policing strategies. Although there were many reports of rubber bullets being used, according to the report "none of the four agencies in this assessment had obtained or used rubber bullets" (U.S. DOJ Report 2015, 46). Despite these inconsistencies there were no complaints filed against officers during and following the protests. This is likely because 1) officers stopped wearing name tags; 2) each organization had their own complaint system, some of which were online; 3) protesters and media members felt a lack of trust in law enforcement agencies. There were numerous repression tactics, such as police canines, arrests, and injuries to protesters that were "unknown" to authors of the U.S. DOJ Report (2015).

This "unknown" data shows a lack of democratic process and adherence to accountability of law enforcement agencies. Grievance procedures were unclear for protesters who did try to go to different law enforcement agencies. As there were four lawsuits filed after the protests citing intimidation tactics,

Table 3.7. Missing Information or Inconsistencies Between Datasets

Police Canine Units		
Institute for Intergovernmental Research (2015) and Official Sources	*News Media Coverage*	*Twitter Data*
K-9 units were only authorized to protect crime scene on August 9. They were deployed to back up officers facing protesters (U.S. DOJ Report 2015, 13). Handlers got to decide to deploy them or not. According to the U.S. DOJ Report "the practice of canine officers to self-deploy for backup, the numbers of instances when canines may have directly or peripherally had contact with protesters is simply not known" (2015, 45).	Two news media coverage videos on August 13 document police use of canines.	170 mentions of canine use. Police dogs were mentioned or photographed every day between August 9 and 31 except for August 29. Brown Blaze (2018) documented the use of force and police canine use on August 10, 2014, on YouTube.
Rubber Bullets		
Rubber bullets were not used on protesters according to U.S. DOJ Report(2015).	Two news media coverage referenced rubber bullets being used on August 14 (CNN 2014a; NBC 2014a). August 17 rubber bullets were referenced in an NBC news coverage video (NBC 2014e).	194 mentions of rubber bullets. Rubber bullets were mentioned in tweets posted everyday between August 12 and August 21. Users also posted about them on August 24 and 28, 2014.
Injuries to Protesters		
Injuries of protesters were not recorded by U.S. DOJ Report except for when police assisted a person shot because ambulances were not allowed into protest area. 14 tweets reference that police reported no injuries to protesters. Specifically, Tweet 4641 "#FergusonPolice Chief on @SeanHannity: "Not a single protester has been injured. The only injuries have been to police officers" #Ferguson" (Right is Wrong 2014).	News media coverage discussed militarization, use of crowd dispersal techniques and other tactical equipment use generally. Injuries were not found or documented through news media coverage.	75 tweets mention injuries to protesters. Tweets were posted from August 11 through 15, August 17 through 22, August 24, August 25, August 26 and August 27. Of the 75 tweets, 34 tweets include hyperlinks, and 16 tweets have a photograph attached.

arrests, injuries, and numerous criticisms of law enforcement personnel, it is disturbing to discover no grievances were filed. This reflects a deep distrust in law enforcement agencies. There was also a lack of time, as some protesters were held for over twelve hours. Other structural barriers to filing grievances include required time for family care, work schedules, and transportation needs. As such, this calls for an online and accessible process for police departments across the country and the need for closer monitoring of protest policing tactics. This lack of transparency, documentation and information illustrates processes that ultimately shield white supremacist institutions from accountability processes that are crucial to maintaining liberty, freedom, and justice for all United States citizens, especially in communities of color.

Protest policing strategies, tactics and equipment deployed severely constrained protesters, prevented reporters from covering police actions and protests, and infringed upon First Amendment rights. Thus, protest control by the more than 50 law enforcement agencies involved directly affected citizens' and news media's capacity to exercise their First Amendment rights. It affects the broader society's access to information and ability to make informed decisions in a democratic society.

CONCLUSION

The vast number of photographs, hashtags related to repression, and counter-framing of police repression suggests Twitter users are crucial to protest movements. Twitter users simultaneously critique protest policing strategies and tactics while documenting their abuse. Lack of standardization of accepted policing practices reflects the nature of white supremacy and capitalism within democracies. The decentralized nature of police departments is responsible for the intentional continuation and reproduction of racial oppression in police departments, even departments that are meant to serve predominantly black communities and communities of color, such as Ferguson. This study corroborates findings from the Kerner Commission, that police departments continue to struggle with both planning and execution of plans. Specifically, the organizational problems with the over 50 law enforcement agencies involved included self-deployment by officers, implementation of an illegal keep moving order, arrests, and show of force tactics during peaceful daytime protests.

Even though canine unit use for crowd control is not part of the National Incident Management system, it did not violate the policies of the four core agencies evaluated as part of the U.S. DOJ Report (2015). The use of canine units further alienated protesters, given the history of canine bites Ferguson residents have with FPD. Specifically, police canines have been used against Ferguson residents as a type of force and exclusively bite African Americans (DOJ 2016).

The four agencies' policies and behaviors consistent with those policies documented within the U.S. DOJ Report (2015) illuminate how these exploitative processes continue to dispossess protesters of their freedoms. They continue to cause mental and physical trauma as part of the triple helix of oppression implemented and produced by the elite-white-male dominance system. This system is upheld through bureaucratic and legal policies of the four agencies through colorblind language, which espouses to protect liberty but in reality protects property and state institutions.

Similar to law enforcement agencies, news media coverage had a negative effect on Ferguson protests. Because of the reliance on official sources, episodic focus on investigation and protest events, simplification and delegitimizing frame devices, Ferguson protests did not receive symbolic rewards from traditional news sources (Gitlin 2003; Lipsky 1968; Morgan 2010). The editing decisions and news coverage impacted the framing of the events to support the white racial framing of police brutality protests. The protesters are not framed as having legitimate concerns because of this coverage. These choices lessen the chances of future #BlackLivesMatter protests to gain legitimacy and attract new followers. These findings illustrate how the decisions of elites in positions of media leadership avoid addressing systemic oppression in the United States and thus support the mythology of racial equality in the post-Civil Rights era.

Twitter facilitated counter-framing and documentation of police abuse of force throughout the protest. This framing resulted in diffusion of critiques of police officers, documentation of police use of force, and other framing crucial to social movement success. Thus, this framing illustrates resistance against white racial framing and delegitimization by official state sources and news media coverage.

No leaders or protesters on news media coverage produced diagnostic framing. This demonstrates the need for Twitter and the symbolic rewards available to information and communication technologies (ICTs). These findings confirm Fleming and Morris (2015) that "blacks' political engagement on social media both extends and diverges from prior forms of mobilization" (115). This engagement creates political pressure on different social institutions (Fleming and Morris 2015; Nummi, Jennings and Feagin 2019). In the case of Ferguson, two reports were produced by the U.S. Department of Justice (2016, 2015) documenting the abuses by the Ferguson Police department and violations of civil liberties during Ferguson protests. Therefore, fines and fees were levied in Ferguson because of the DOJ's investigation. This demonstrates material rewards were gained as the target opponents, FPD, responded to some of the protester's injustice claims. This political pressure is possible because of the large number of users, aka, producers of content on social media. This phenomenon of having more producers differs from past decades without the internet and ICTs when alternative news sources had relatively few producers and limited means of distribution. Previously there was top-down diffusion of information in contrast to contemporary social media. Now as Ito (2018) argues, there are "peer-to-peer" and "many-to-many" informal connections between users across ICTs and around the world. This facilitates a broader diffusion of information. As Nummi, Jennings and Feagin (2019), found, "the #BLM online presence—including millions of social media tweets and other posts—has forced civil rights and other key social values from the edges of society into the white-controlled center, and thereby has resulted in new political pressures on that center's powerful white figures" (15). This study confirms these findings given the themes illustrated through the Twitter data. Furthermore, the technosocial practices shed light on the interactions and relationships between state authorities, news media coverage, and social movement participants. Outside of traditional news coverage, protests garner attention, facilitate framing, and encourage participation online through the technological affordances of ICTs.

But this pattern of racial oppression existed long before the Ferguson protests and formed the impetus for many of the protests. Emails, interviews, and statistical data on use of force document a pattern of Civil Rights violations. Moreover, the community reported that FPD remained in their cars while in the neighborhood. Michael Brown's death at the hands of former Officer Wilson was like many protests of the Civil Rights Movement. It was the spark that lit the fuse after but including a long pattern of racist police violence. This spark in turn evolved into the #BlackLivesMatter movement, which has grown into the largest social movement in US history (Buchanan, Bui, and Patel, 2020).

NOTE

1. hereafter referred to as the U.S. DOJ Report (2015)

REFERENCES

Blaze, Brown. 2014. "Ferguson Riot, Missouri, August 10, 2014." Posted August 12, 2014. Video, 7:47. https://youtu.be/EkACHGLugu8.

Bracey, Glenn E. 2016. "Black Movements Need Black Theorizing: Exposing Implicit Whiteness in Political Process Theory." *Sociological Focus* 49 (1): 11–27.

Bolton, Kenneth, and Joe Feagin. 2004. *Black in Blue: African-American Police Officers and Racism*. Routledge.

Buchanan, Larry, Quoctrung Bui and Jugal K. Patel. 2020. "Black Lives Matter May Be the Largest Movement in U.S. History." *New York Times,* July 3, 2020. https://www.nytimes.com/interactive/2020/07/03/us/george-floyd-protests-crowd-size.html.

Burks, Edward C. 1971. "Protest Mars Start of Final City Hall Budget Hearing." *New York Times*, May 28, 1971, 13.

CNN (Cable News Network). 2014a. "Missouri / Police Shooting / Interviews." Vanderbilt Television News Archive. 07:00:20 pm–07:11:00 pm. Aired August 14, 2014. https://tvnews.vanderbilt.edu/broadcasts/1070204?.

———.2014b. "Ferguson / Karen Conti / Michael Brown / Captain Ron Johnson." Vanderbilt Television News Archive. 12:00:52 am–12:09:20 am. Aired August 16, 2014. https://tvnews.vanderbilt.edu/broadcasts/1297701?.

———.2014c. "Missouri / Police Shooting / Johnson, French Interviews." Vanderbilt Television News Archive. 07:00:20 pm–07:13:20 pm. Aired August 19, 2014. https://tvnews.vanderbilt.edu/broadcasts/1070468.

———.2014d. "Missouri / Police Schooling." Vanderbilt Television News Archive, 07:56:30 pm–07:58:10 pm. Aired August 20, 2014. https://tvnews.vanderbilt.edu/programs/1070537.

———.2014e. "Missouri / Police Shooting / Mayor, Pastor Interviews." Vanderbilt Television News Archive, 07:31:30 pm–07:40:00 pm. Aired August 21, 2014. https://tvnews.vanderbilt.edu/programs/1070501.

Correa, Jennifer G. 2011. "The Targeting of the East Los Angeles Brown Berets by a Racial Patriarchal Capitalist State: Merging Intersectionality and Social Movement Research." *Critical Sociology* 37 (1): 83–101. https://doi.org/10.1177/0896920510378766.

Correa, Jennifer G., and James M. Thomas. 2019. "From the Border to the Core: A Thickening Military-Police Assemblage." *Critical Sociology* 45 (7–8): 1133–1147. https://doi.org/10.1177/0896920518794269.

Cunningham, David. 2022. "Policing White Supremacy: Asymmetry and Inequality in Protest Control." *Social Problems* spac010, February 23, 2022. https://doi.org/10.1093/socpro/spac010.

Cunningham, David, Geoff Ward, and Peter B. Owens. 2019. "Configuring Political Repression: Anti-Civil Rights Enforcement in Mississippi." *Mobilization: An International Quarterly* 24 (3): 319–343. https://doi.org/10.17813/1086-671X-24-3-319.

Davenport, Christian, Sarah A. Soule, and David A. Armstrong. 2011. "Protesting While Black? The Differential Policing of American Activism, 1960 to 1990." *American Sociological Review* 76 (1): 152–178. https://doi.org/10.1177/0003122410395370.

Davis, Angela Y. 1983. *Women, Race and Class*. New York: Vintage.

———.2002. "Chapter 5: Masked Racism." In *Race and Resistance: African Americans in the Twenty-First Century*, edited by Herb Boyd, 53–59 Cambridge, MA: South End Press.

Della Porta, Donatella, and Herbert Reiter Reiter, eds. 1998. *Policing Protest: The Control of Mass Demonstrations in Western Democracies*. Vol. 6. Minneapolis: University of Minnesota Press.

Earl, Jennifer. 2003. "Tanks, Tear Gas, and Taxes: Toward a Theory of Movement Repression." *Sociological Theory* 21 (1): 44–68. https://doi.org/10.1111/1467 -9558.00.

———.2011. "Political Repression: Iron Fists, Velvet Gloves, and Diffuse Control." *Annual Review of Sociology*, no. 37, 261–284. https://doi.org/10.1146/annurev .soc.012809.102609.

Earl, Jennifer, Sarah A. Soule, and John D. McCarthy. 2003. "Protest Under Fire? Explaining the Policing of Protest." *American Sociological Review* 68 (4): 581–606. https://doi.org/10.2307/1519740.

Feagin, Joe R. 2020. *The White Racial Frame: Centuries of Racial Framing and Counter-Framing*. Third edition. New York: Routledge.

Feagin, Joe R., and Kimberley Ducey. 2017. *Elite White Men Ruling: Who, What, When, Where, and How*. London: Taylor & Francis.

Fleming, Crystal M., and Aldon Morris. 2015. "Theorizing Ethnic and Racial Movements in the Global Age: Lessons from the Civil Rights Movement." *Sociology of Race and Ethnicity* 1 (1): 105–126. https://doi.org/10.1177/2332649214562473.

Garza, Alicia. 2014. "A Herstory of the #BlackLivesMatter Movement." The Feminist Wire, October 7, 2014. Accessed April 22, 2023. https://thefeministwire .com/2014/10/blacklivesmatter-2/.

Gillham, Patrick F., and Gary T. Marx. 2018. "Changes in the Policing of Civil Disorders Since the Kerner Report: The Police Response to Ferguson, August 2014, and Some Implications for the Twenty-First Century." *RSF: The Russell Sage Foundation Journal of the Social Sciences* 4 (6): 122–143. doi: 10.7758/RSF.2018.4.6.06.

Gillham, Patrick F., Bob Edwards, and John A. Noakes. 2013. "Strategic Incapacitation and the Policing of Occupy Wall Street Protests in New York City, 2011." *Policing and Society* 23 (1): 81–102. https://doi.org/10.1080/10439463.2012.727607.

Gitlin, Todd. 2003. *The Whole World is Watching: Mass Media in the Making and Unmaking of the New Left*. Berkeley: University of California Press.

hooks, bell. 2000. *Feminist Theory: From Margin to Center*. London: Pluto Press.

Ito, Mizuko. 2018. "Introduction." In *Networked Publics*, edited by Kazys Varnelis, 1–14 Cambridge, MA: MIT Press.

Kerner Commission. 1968. *Report of the National Advisory Commission on Civil Disorders*. Washington: US Government Printing Office.

Lipsky, Michael. 1968. *Protest in City Politics: Rent Strikes, Housing, and the Power of the Poor*. Chicago: Rand McNally.

McCarthy, John D., and Clark McPhail. 1998. "The Institutionalization of Protest in the United States." In *The Social Movement Society: Contentious Politics for a New Century*, edited by David Meyer and Sidney Tarrow, 83–110. Lanham, MD: Rowman & Littlefield.

Morgan, Edward P. 2010. *What Really Happened to the 1960s: How Mass Media Culture Failed American Democracy*. Lawrence: University Press of Kansas.

Morris, Aldon D. 1986. *The Origins of the Civil Rights Movement.* New York: Simon and Schuster.

NBC (National Broadcasting Company). 2014a. "Ferguson / Michael Brown / Missouri Highway Patrol / Ferguson Police Department." Vanderbilt Television News Archive. 12:01:13 am–12:04:47 am. Aired August 14, 2014. https://tvnews.vander bilt.edu/broadcasts/1297450.

———.2014b. "Ferguson / Missouri State Highway Patrol / St. Louis County Police / Ron Johnson." Vanderbilt Television News Archive. 12:05:00 am–12:006:27 am. Aired August 15, 2014. https://tvnews.vanderbilt.edu/broadcasts/1307785.

———.2014c. "Ferguson / Steve Luce / John Kirby / Jeff Bernice." Vanderbilt Television News Archive. 12:06:27 am–12:08:44 am. Aired August 15, 2014. https:// tvnews.vanderbilt.edu/broadcasts/1307786.

———.2014d. "Missouri / Police Shooting." Vanderbilt Television News Archive, 05:31:10 pm–05:37:10 pm. Aired August 16, 2014. https://tvnews.vanderbilt.edu /programs/1070349.

———.2014e. "Missouri / Police Shooting." Vanderbilt Television News Archive. 05:31:10 pm–05:42:00 pm. Aired August 18, 2014. https://tvnews.vanderbilt.edu /broadcasts/1071932.

———.2014f. "Ferguson / Michael Brown / McCullough / Darren Wilson." Aired August 21, 2014. Vanderbilt Television News Archive, 12:09:53 am–12:12:18 am. https://tvnews.vanderbilt.edu/programs/1309490.

Nixon, Jeremiah W. 2014. *Executive Order 14–08.* Retrieved May 18, 2022. https:// www.sos.mo.gov/CMSImages/library/reference/orders/2014/eo14_08.pdf.

Nummi, Jozie, Carly Jennings, and Joe Feagin. 2019 "# BlackLivesMatter: Innovative Black Resistance." In *Sociological Forum* 34 (S1): 1042–1064. DOI: 10.1111 /socf.12540.

Pacholok, Shelley. 2009. "Gendered Strategies of Self: Navigating Hierarchy and Contesting Masculinities." *Gender, Work and Organization* 16 (4): 471–500. https://doi.org/10.1111/j.1468-0432.2009.00452.x.

Reilly, Ryan J. (@ryanjreilly). 2014. "St. Louis Resident Describes Being Injured By Police In Fer." Posted August 21, 2014. Video, 1:57. https://www.youtube.com /watch?v=7H83xQA0ztY.

Reynolds-Stenson, Heidi. 2018. "Protesting the Police: Anti-Police Brutality Claims as a Predictor of Police Repression of Protest." *Social Movement Studies* 17 (1): 48–63. https://doi.org/10.1080/14742837.2017.1381592.

Right is Wrong, The (@therightiswrong). 2014. "#FergusonPolice Chief on @SeanHannity: 'Not a single protester has been injured. The only injuries have been to police officers' #Ferguson." Twitter, August 14, 2014, 9:24 pm. http://twitter.com /therightswrong/statuses/500105606058229761.

Sandvik, Runa A. 2022. "Documenting the Arrests of Journalists in Ferguson." *Freedom of the Press Foundation,* Aug 19, 2014. Accessed May 19, 2022. https:// freedom.press/news/documenting-the-arrests-of-journalists-in-ferguson/.

Skolnick, Jerome H. 2000. *The Politics of Protest.* New York: Simon and Schuster.

Slack, Donovan, and Suzanne Smalley. 2005. "Police Leader Shakes Up Top Ranks." *Boston Globe,* February 11, 2005. http://archive.boston.com/news/local /articles/2005/02/11/police_leader_shakes_up_top_ranks?pg=full.

St. Louis Post-Dispatch. 2014. "Tear Gas Used to Clear Crowd Gathered Near Qui-kTrip." *St. Louis Post-Dispatch*, Aug 11, 2014. https://www.stltoday.com/news /local/crime-and-courts/tear-gas-used-to-clear-crowd-gathered-near-quiktrip /article_588ca269-0299-583f-b047-702a4268314b.html.

U.S. Department of Justice Office of Community Oriented Policing Services, and Institute for Intergovernmental Research (US). 2015. "After-Action Assessment of the Police Response to the August 2014 Demonstrations in Ferguson, Missouri. Department of Justice, Office of Community Oriented Policing Services." Accessed March 1, 2023. https://cops.usdoj.gov/ric/Publications/cops-p317-pub.pdf.

U.S. Department of Justice. 2016. "Justice Department Files Lawsuit to Bring Constitutional Policing to Ferguson, Missouri." Accessed April 29, 2016. https://www .justice.gov/opa/pr/justice-department-files-lawsuit-bring-constitutional-policing -ferguson-missouri.

Washington Post. 2014. "What Weapons Are Police Using in Ferguson?." *Washington Post*, August 17, 2014. Video, 1:10. https://www.youtube.com /watch?v=rQZglVP4EyM.

Worden, Robert E. 1996. "The 'Causes' of Police Brutality: Theory and Evidence on Police Use of Force." In *Police Violence: Understanding and Controlling Police Abuse of Force,* edited by William A Geller and Hans Toch, 23–51. New Haven, CT: Yale University Press.

Chapter Four

The Camera as "Moral Agent" and Testimonial for Black Reparative Justice

Testimonial for Black Reparative Justice

Joyce Hope Scott

The camera in the hands of the Black photographer has posed a counter-narrative of Black life which contested that presented by the dominant media. It has held the power to redress injustice, distortion, erasure, selective memory, and dispossession suffered by the Black community. It has made the marginalized visible by withdrawing the veil which W.E.B. Du Bois identified as the line of demarcation between African Americans and the promise of full citizenship in the twenty-first century. From its appropriation by nineteenth century Black camera men, who used their devices and photography studios as sites of liberation on the Underground Railroad, to today's camera phone and its ability to empower anyone to become a storyteller in the cause of social justice, the camera has created the penetrating narrative of truth in images impossible to deny.

This is all rightly called "Citizen camera-witnessing," an unmediated recording and capturing of history as it happens. In essence, there is no "history." There is just "the story" (Andén-Papadopoulos 2014). Over the past several years, the Black Lives Matter movement has engaged in activism and resistance which the individual cell phone camera recorded immediately and uploaded to the world. This citizens' use of the cell phone provides an alternative to traditional written history, a deconstructive reportage, an "instant primary source," that allows for liberation of the resisting narrative ever present at the margins of monologic official discourse. The power of this reporting of unfolding history is evident in that often, even the mainstream media takes down its stories from Facebook and Twitter.

The citizen-camera as a reportorial device signifies on and acknowledges the historical genre of the slave narrative which imposed personal testimony of the formerly enslaved onto the body of discourse of apologists for slavery.

The claim here is that the camera/phone creates what I have called "a dialogic of perspectives between the filmic 'eye' of the camera" (Scott 2016) and the master-narrative of mainstream media's reporting of events. The power of such images of violence against Black bodies disrupts the public's ability to passively consume events unfolding on the television screen.

This chapter critiques the role of the camera from a nineteenth century device enabling the imagistic remaking of the enslaved African American to the present "emerging modes of civic engagement for justice connected to the mobile camera phone, and the ways in which they require us to rethink" (Andén-Papadopoulos 2014, 753) and bear witness to injustice and brutality. The cell phone with its built-in camera has become an objective, infallible witness, permitting entirely new performative rituals of testifying, using wireless global communication networks and video as graphic evidence in efforts to engage in acts of advocacy for restorative justice and political solidarity.

Critically, the performance of "citizen camera-witnessing" (Andén-Papadopoulos 2014) is exemplified in the ways it makes distinct claims to truth in the name of oppressed people who put their bodies on the line in an effort to redress injustice and claim restitution for violations of Black human and civil rights. The chapter interrogates the "mediatization of camera witnessing" as an agent of our moral awareness, of our seeing/looking which imposes an "ethical imperative . . . on those that witness" and closes "the veracity gap between events and their meanings" (Scott 2017, 1). The citizen camera "functions as a witness, similar to a curious personage, both insensible and concrete at the same time . . . the camera admits no disguises and divulges everything" (Scott, 2016) without partiality or deference to anyone. In the hands of the Black photographer/videographer, it becomes a "culture resistance reader . . . culture that is used to resist and/or change the dominant political, economic and/or social structure. . . ." (Duncombe 2002, 5).

PHOTO-LIBERATION OF THE BLACK BODY

Beginning in the nineteenth century, the camera became a potential weapon of redress of anti-Black racism and violent aggression against African Americans. By most accounts, Frederick Douglass was the most photographed person of the nineteenth century. Frederick Douglass himself seized the new visual device (the daguerreotype) as a weapon of racial uplift. In his famous essay, "Pictures and Progress," Douglass noted that, "The process by which man is able to posit his own subjective nature outside of himself . . . is at (the) bottom of all effort and the germinating principles of all reform and all progress" (Guterl 2015). Indeed, he maintained that the new camera device wielded a force that could be transformative in the cause of anti-slavery and justice for Black people as well as serve as a powerful new medium of democracy. As he wrote in his narrative about the important role of education to the slave's freedom, he felt also that seizing control of representations of the Black man was a powerful force of liberation. The "picture-making faculty," he said, "is a mighty power" (Guterl 2015).

Renee Graham (2016) echoes this observation about Douglass' belief in the power of the camera; she notes that "In posing for dozens of portraits, he showed what Black freedom and dignity looked like." Thus, the camera as a "technological weapon," for Douglass, provoked a confrontation with the nation's anti-Black racism. Douglass' many photographs served to revalorize the Black male image, challenging society's negative portrayals by showing "what Black freedom and dignity (really) looked like." However, despite Douglass' optimism about the power of the camera to change conditions of Black life, in the hands of whites, it continued its destructive role of defamation of African Americans. Nowhere is this more profoundly obvious than in the seminal work of D.W. Griffith, *Birth of a Nation*. The film not only projected the Black man as a brutal beast; it had the effect of further mobilizing White terrorism against Black communities.

After the Civil War, Black Codes and terror lynchings were implemented against African Americans for being homeless and jobless and facilitated a return of many Black people to a state of forced labor resembling a new kind of slavery, as Douglas Blackmon suggests in *Slavery by Another Name* (2008). Lynchings became a brutal extra-judicial practice as whites took the law into their own hands in murdering Black men, women, and children to keep the African American community terrorized. The camera archived these horrors as it became a device for distributing images of Black lynchings through post cards. At great risks to themselves, Black journalists like Ida B. Wells and others of the NAACP began their own collections of images and stories describing lynchings in their newspapers. Journalists like Wells weaponized the camera to challenge the accounts of lynchings provided in mainstream White newspapers. At the same time, it took "putting their Black Skin in front of harm—and the camera—to do so" (Ramirez 2020). It was a powerful picture that changed the conscience of a nation and fostered the rise of the Civil Rights Movement of the 1960s. "A Black mother . . . redirected the use of (the camera) as an attack, wielding it against the attackers" (Ramirez 2020). By insisting that the brutalized body of her son Emmett Till be exposed in an open casket for the world to see, Mamie Till challenged America to confront its conscience.

Thus, the camera became a moral device in the hands of Black photographers. It centered Blacks as subjects who gained a new agency through the visibility of posed bodies like those of Martin Delany, Richard Allen, William Wells Brown, Frederick Douglass and other Black leaders during Reconstruction. It is during this era that Black photographers as well as subjects began to seize control of the Black image through a carefully crafted, positive iconography.

> African Americans' engagement with photography in the nineteenth century began a tradition promoting social change through the camera. As a result, African Americans, whether they are in front of or behind the camera, create empowering images that define the beauty, resilience, and resistance contained within the Black experience. (The Conversation 2021)

While racist caricatures distorted the Black body and mocked Black society, artist-activists weaponized the camera to impose the dignity of Black life.

Jessica D. Brier, curator of the "Visible Bodies" collection at Vassar, said of these images that they illuminate "how and why Black artists have deliberately chosen photography as a tool to combat erasure and violence. . . . The ongoing struggle to make Black experiences more visible connects some of the earliest photography to important work made by Black artists today" (Hendrie 2021). Examining the works of James Van Der Zee, whose photographs are among the most enduring portraits of prominent figures and everyday life during the Harlem Renaissance, we see further affirmation of the role of the Black photographer nearly a century later. Van Der Zee's materials, images, and references create a portrait of Black agency, of positive Black American resistance to brutality and injustice through his mastery of the reconstructive power of camera technology. His works follow a seminal period of African American history—the Harlem or New Negro Renaissance. This was not only the high point of the Great Black Migration from the South to northern and western port cities, but also a transformative moment where the brutality of the "Red Summer," WWI and Jim Crow jurisprudence facilitated the containment of African Americans in a vicious cycle of injustice: of share-cropping, convict-leasing, and dispossession.

CITIZENS CAMERA: EMBODIMENT OF BLACK AGENCY & STRUGGLES FOR SOCIAL JUSTICE

In her text *Black Looks* (1992), bell hooks refers to "(t)he Oppositional Gaze," and suggests that "it is a site of resistance; it is deconstructive, political and powerful for dispossessed people around the world" (115–116). hooks argues that the dispossessed in such power relations "learn experientially that there is a critical gaze, one that 'looks' to document, one that is oppositional" (116).

This is what happens with the mediatization of the camera-phone. Hooks notes that in resistance struggles, those who are oppressed acquire the ability to cultivate a resistance or looking (117). The witnessing of the citizen's camera is an act of willful agency that results in hooks' contentious/oppositional looks or looking. The claim here is that the recorded document is an agential character, a confrontational weapon of subversion that holds both the power to confront inequity and violations of civil and human rights and the power to advance the cause of reparations, atonement, and restorative justice.

With respect to captive Africans, the initial "re-spatialization of Blackness was accompanied by a myriad of architectures of confinement, policing and surveillance. In the public imagination, the enslaved African was rendered hopelessly barbarous, and the enslaved body became an unable and unwilling mass of flesh for use and abuse" (Scott 2022, 270–271). The Black body became real estate, commerce, sexual object, or workhorse.

> This denial of personhood is evident, for example, in the advertisements for runaway slaves, especially the early ones which have only the barest outline of a human form. This nondescript imagery is associated with the captive's socio-political, economic, and legal status as a piece of property. This placed the enslaved African in between racial being and nothingness. (Scott, 2022, 271)

The Black body became a figure, in fact, of remaking, a product of the White imagination.

However, one might claim that the citizen camera begins as an agent of resistance, of revalorization and contesting dialogue with visual narratives of the White racist camera in the early historical period of African enslavement. In 1775, Black Free Masonry, spearheaded by Prince Hall, offered a visual model of Black masculine perfectibility through the mechanical means of reproduction realized in the portraits of Hall, Martin Delany and others as "models of Black exceptionalism to be emulated by other Black masons and respectable African American men" (Wallace 2000, 183). Hall was a tireless abolitionist committed to the idea of carving out a place for free men of color in colonial American culture. "Freemasonry and the military . . . offered the social and cultural technologies for 'the making men,'" as Maurice Wallace (2002, 56) writes. These leaders aimed to create a Black male respectable identity, one that offered a counter-narrative to the mainstream negating representations of apologists for slavery. In so doing, they were associating themselves with the honorable trade of craftsman, and thus as co-builders of American society.

After slavery, for the newly freed African American, the camera became a new weapon against erasure and image manipulation. It had been instrumental in the abolitionist movement, revising the Black subject in full-framed bodies, clothed and comfortable, in essence, visible during Reconstruction. In fact, one could argue that Hall's, Delany's and others' appropriation of this iconographic identity seemed credible in light of the fact that the exiled European man had "transformed himself from White male subjects into republican citizen (Wallace 2020, 182). In opposition to the nondescript rendering of Black men in photographic representations as commodities for sale or as runaways in the 1700s, the self-fabricated images of these free men had the effect of resituating the Black man in the new text of America being reformulated by the White male power structure.

THE CAMERA AS A WEAPON AGAINST ERASURE OF BLACK MANHOOD

The Post-Civil War Reconstruction era also necessitated a reformulation of the Black male. "At the same time, the expansion of communications and the development of photography in the late nineteenth and early twentieth centuries gave reporting a vividness it had never had before" (Hall 1983, 330). It is during this period that another central negative image for the Black man emerged onto the stage of American popular culture. Southern whites' uneasiness with the new freedman during the period of Reconstruction prompted the image of Blacks as a dependent dysfunctional race and of the Black man in particular as the dangerous, over-sexualized buck in opposition to the White man as racially superior. While there were traits characterized as masculine ideals for the White man, such traits when associated with the former Black slave rendered the Buck the White man's worst nightmare.

While Douglass and Jacobs (among others) demonstrated Black resistance and pioneered the process of restitution of the Black image, nineteenth century photographers like William Goodridge launched a business which included both sales of goods and services and clandestine support for escapees on the Underground Railroad (Jezierski 2000). Goodridge was one of the most successful African American businessmen of his time. As such, he was able to apply knowledge he gained as a barber to additional investments like real estate, photography and other enterprises. Amazingly, he was also a key figure on the Underground Railroad going back to the 1851 Christiana Riots. He used his photo and barber shops to hide runaways and aid them in their flight to liberty on the Underground Railroad

Christiana, Lancaster County, Pennsylvania, sits 20 miles north of the Maryland border. In the decades before the Civil War it was a refuge both for free Blacks and fugitive slaves (Anderson 2013). The Christiana Riot resulted from the passage of the Fugitive Slave Law in 1850, which empowered slave owners to enter free states to capture escaped slaves. The Christiana Resistance was carried out by free Blacks, former slaves and abolitionists, and successfully stopped the attempted recovery of escaped slaves by the slaveowner Edward Gorsuch and federal marshals. William Goodridge's involvement with the Underground Railroad is documented and places him at the center of the Christiana Riots (Weir, 2004). Some fugitives who were involved in the riot were smuggled across Pennsylvania to Canada on Goodridge's railroad cars. Glenalvin Goodridge, "son of former-slave-turned entrepreneur William C. Goodridge and his wife, Evalina," followed suit and also became prominent actors at the center of slave liberation and abolitionist activities (McClure 2022). Glenalvin "opened his first photo studio at the age of 18 in 1847, in one of his father's businesses, and later operated his studio out of the Goodridge residence on East Philadelphia Street" in York, PA (McClure 2022). "That house, now the Goodridge Freedom Center, served as the intersection of early photography" for leisure and for social justice and the Underground Railroad. "Glenalvin worked with the various kinds of photographic technology of the day. . . . Customers found all kinds of uses for their new likenesses" (McClure 2022). Glenalvin had a commitment to social justice and saw how his camera could facilitate the democratic potential of photography.

In addition to the use of the camera and photography by Black families and others, there was a faction of African Americans who saw an opportunity to use the camera for political purposes. For instance, in the nineteenth century, the most photographed man in the world was Frederick Douglass (Guterl 2015). He was famous as an orator and an abolitionist, "known for using his eloquent voice to expose the brutality and inhumanity of slavery, which he had experienced firsthand. He traveled all over the country, speaking to large crowds" (Ramirez 2020) and arguing against the enslavement of Black people. Douglass' images offered the "public a positive view of a Black person to oppose the negative caricatures that were commonplace in newspapers (Ramirez 2020).

Douglass' portraits became weapons against malicious, denigrating Black images, and thus, his pictures had some effect on public perception of Black men (Graham 2016). Douglass re-commodified himself in the cause of justice and moral commitment to his people in promoting a well-known notion with us today—Black images/Black lives mattered. When Douglass had his pictures taken, positive images of Black people were surely subversive, but his photos were a claim to equality nevertheless. Picture-taking became a big business and a radical expression of Black agency in the nineteenth century. W.E.B. Du Bois also embraced what he saw as the great potential of the camera and hoped that it would serve the cause of racial justice. DuBois knew the power of image-control and believed that positive black images could influence the American mind. He used pictures to showcase Black achievement and introduced positive black images in his Exhibit of American Negroes at the 1900 World's Fair in Paris (Smith 2000).

CAMERAS OF DESTRUCTION

DuBois' collection offered an exposé of African American agency and creativity which centered black people as positive subjects in their own visual narrative. However, in 1915, D. W. Griffith released his film *The Birth of a Nation* (Facing History and Ourselves 2022). The movie created all sorts of false narratives of the Civil War and Blacks and portrayed the actions of the Ku Klux Klan as positive. Griffith's film promoted White supremacist secret societies as heroic, as saviors of White women and the American nation. More damaging was the fact that the actors who really portrayed Blacks as brutal and ignorant were really White men dressed up in Blackface. The film was an instant hit, and even President Woodrow Wilson did a White House film screening and remarked on Griffith's skill as a movie-maker.

The movie helped to further contaminate the country's perception of Black people—demonstrating that D.W. Griffith, like DuBois and Douglass, knew the power of the camera in the hands of the citizen. Lynchings and White terrorist campaigns became the order of the day after the Reconstruction and cameras became weapons of importance for both Blacks and whites. Cameras in the hands of White spectators at lynchings captured the gruesome scenes and made them into post cards to share around the country (Ramirez 2020). Black journalists and reporters filmed in their turn and brought their stories back to Black newspapers like the *Pittsburgh Courier*, *New York Age*, *The Chicago Defender*, and others which recounted the event from the black perspective (Potter et al. 1999). While many reports explain African Americans' exodus to the North as a search for jobs, a truer reason was that they were fleeing the South to save their lives (Ramirez 2020).

Even in the North, terrorizing Black people was a widely accepted practice. Robert Lewis was lynched on June 2, 1892 in Port Jervis, New York (Spivey 2021).

For many of these murders, cameras were ringside, capturing burned and broken Black bodies. These photographs were often sold and distributed (as souvenirs). Unlike Douglass' portraits, they were not rendered to make African Americans more human but less.

. . . As lynchings increased, many spoke up against them, but their voices were largely ignored. The Herculean efforts of Black journalist Ida B. Wells, starting in the 1890s, brought these atrocities to national attention. While Black people knew of them, what the mainstream world needed was proof . . . Wells collected statistics and wrote up depictions of lynchings in her newspaper. . . . Wells and the NAACP used technology to provide hard evidence, and they filled the national consciousness with images and newspaper articles, and flagpole alerts in an effort to create change. (Ramirez 2021)

This visual campaign for justice is what filmic warriors like James Van Der Zee and Gordon Parks continued into the twentieth century. Van Der Zee produced the most comprehensive documentation of the period of the New Negro (or Harlem) Renaissance (Bertrand 2023). His camera recorded a counter-story of Black life during the Harlem Renaissance; he was able to create a contentious dialogue about Black people through capturing them in families, as professionally well-dressed men and women and children living like many other Americans. The artist used photography as a means not only to celebrate Black culture but also provided his subjects with a feeling of pride. Further, Van Der Zee's camera captured the Black political fervor of the period through images of the revolutionary movement of Marcus Garvey, in the famous 1924 march through Harlem.

Gordon Parks, an artistic son of Van Der Zee, "was one of the most groundbreaking figures in twentieth century photography. His photojournalism . . . reveals important aspects of American culture, and he became known for focusing on issues of civil rights, poverty, race relations and urban life" (Fulleylove n.d.). His works created a counter-narrative, a challenge to the treatment of African Americans by highlighting inequality in images that came to symbolize Black life in pre-civil-rights America. His seminal film "The Learning Tree" is a case of centering the camera in the nature of African American experience of Black manhood in terms of its ephemeral nature (The Gordon Parks Foundation n. d). A simple day of swimming at a pond can end in the murder of a Black boy by whites—very much the same for Michael Brown, walking down the street, George Floyd, Tamir Rice, playing in the park, and so many others whose lives were snuffed out on the whim of a White police officer.

Like Douglass, William and Glenalvin Coodridge and other black photographers, Parks found a soulful mission with the camera: " I saw that the camera could be a weapon against poverty, against racism, against all sorts of social wrongs. I knew at that point that I had to have a camera" (The Gordon Parks Foundation n.d.). He goes on to locate the camera as a central device of social justice for Black people of the future:

People in millenniums ahead will know what we were like in the 1930s and the thing that, the important major things that shaped our history at that time. This is as important for historic reasons as any other. There's another horizon out there, one more horizon that you have to make for yourself and let other people discover it, and someone else will take it further on, you know. (The Gordon Parks Foundation n.d.)

In *Bearing Witness While Black*, Allissa Richardson (2020) looks at the camera as a powerful device testifying to injustice in the age of a new "digital journalism." She calls Black witnessing or "bearing witness while Black," an act in the tradition of Black resistance, "an innovative style of protest journalism" where regular "people of color put their bodies on the line to capture . . . untimely and unjust deaths with little more than a cell phone" (45). Richardson maintains that these are testimonies from the margins of society, witnesses that create a contestatorial dialogue with mainstream journalism, voicing Black memory and amplifying accounts muffled by White terrorism (153).

Richardson (2020) elaborates further defining Black witnessing as "carrying moral, legal and spiritual weight" (5). It is a positioning that delivers a counter-narrative about Black deaths and other events of injustice that impact Black life. Like bell hooks' "Black looking," Richardson calls Black Witnessing a unique gaze where looking becomes a weapon in Black hands. In an interview with Zoë Corbyn (2020), Richardson explains that the camera as a device of Black witnessing captures a picture of "defiance, self-defense, and self-preservation" contrary to the official account of events archived in "police body cameras (and) dash cameras." Black witnessing, on the other hand, is truth-telling; it is the authentication of details of the story that contest the official version as read through images and voice-over news accounts. Richardson maintains that the heroism of African Americans who used their smartphones and filmed and tweeted accounts of White police murders of Black people had an impact on activists around the world. She argues convincingly that the new technology of smartphones continues the testimonial legacies of the Black experience begun by authors of slave narratives, Black journalists, and activists of the Civil Rights Movement. This is all in a lineage that she refers to as "witnessing while Black."

Siva Vaidhyanathan (2020) also supports the power of Black witnessing in his study of the ubiquitous video. He notes of the camera video of George Floyd's death that "The footage . . . punctuated illusions, ignited (our frustrations), forced the issue with its length: dreadful and transfixing." Vaidhyanathan underscores the moral agency of the footage as Floyd's death was "captured by raw video. Its truths were impossible to deny. The officer's voice was clear. Floyd's voice was clear. The bystanders' voices were clear. The image was clear." This visual testimony from a camera held in the hand of an unprofessional teenager rivaled the power of "any video of police brutality that came before, and yet it also built upon them all." The lineage of the images extends back from nineteenth century journalistic reporting of lynchings to twentieth century newspaper accounts of terrorist acts of racial cleansing, like that of Tulsa's Black Wall Street to the filmed murders of Michael Brown and Philando Castile.

THE CAMERA AS A TOOL OF REMATRIATION, RESTITUTION, AND CULTURAL REVALORIZATION

As a device enabling retrievals of stories that have been silenced by the oppressions of enslavement and colonization, the cell phone and video platforms affirm their power as prophetic purveyors of Black agency. They are particularly powerful in memorialization and "re-memory" efforts designed to capture the whole Black experience—including that which remains in the common consciousness of African-descended people. From nineteenth century Black camera men who disguised their sites on the underground railroad to today's video cameras, these righteous tools have advocated for not only the importance of Black lives but also functioned as an agent of cultural rematriation and psychological repair. The idea of rematriation is used to reference the historical and cultural restitution needed for repair of violations suffered by descendants of captive Africans forcibly removed from Africa (INOSAAR 2021). Rematriation in this regard is seen as the method by which people of the African diaspora can reclaim—culturally and spiritually—indigenous knowledge archives. This notion acknowledges that chattel slavery was not only theft of the body and its (pro)creations but also, and equally important, the severing of the African captive from the cosmological and metaphysical knowledge that informs the very foundation of his/her human identity.

Anna Reading's assessment of the impact of mobile devices like the camera on communication today (2009) confirms that it is cultural and social as well as technological, as "the mobile camera phone is extending and modifying media languages, practices, and forms" (Koliska and Roberts 2015, 1675) while also "traversing binaries such as the private and the public . . . the journalist and the citizen" (Reading 2009, 63). Reading specifies that images taken via mobile devices are "mobile witnessing" because "mobile phones allow us to capture, circulate, and engage with data on the move" (72). Mobile witnessing means exchanging data "through global networks" that can be understood as "performances and speech acts between different parties" (73). "After all, mobile phone images are often taken to be shared to evoke emotional reactions or to serve an informational purpose" (Koliska and Roberts 2015, 1674).

The Prophetic Lens by Phil Allen (2022) supports Reading's assessment of the selfie. Both scholars maintain that the cell phone and video camera are righteous tools advocating for not only the importance of Black lives but also functioning as agents of cultural revalorization and restorative justice. Allen's study argues that the camera can be a catalyst for cultural change. While his and Reading's analyses focus on manifestations in the United States, clearly the cell phone and video camera have traversed the globe and made their impact in every location. One important group of storytellers and cultural archivists affected by these techno-devices are to be found in West Africa. I speak specifically of the spiritual leaders, practitioners, performers, and scholars in the Republic of Bénin.

I became especially interested in the intersection of the cell phone, video camera and performance—whether music videos (filmed typically from a simple video camera or good-quality cell phone) during my tenure as a Fulbright Professor at the Université d'Abomey-Calavi from 2001–2003. During that time, I began to notice the proliferation of inexpensive VHS video camcorders and cell phones used to produce music videos and local films based on spiritual traditions. To understand the importance of this phenomenon, it must be remembered that film or video productions in most African countries originated primarily as a result of external assistance rather than truly indigenous efforts. Also, in most African countries, particularly West Africa, at that time, there were no localized televisions stations. What one found in most cases were television stations that served as relay posts for films produced elsewhere (Goldfarb 1995). There was little to no production capability and basically no funds with which to purchase or co-produce feature films or television series. Local recording artists and performers especially caught my attention because of their dedication to infusing productions featuring the backdrop of some of their pre-colonial spiritual and religious traditions of Vodou. They were using selfies and other techniques of representations of self and community as counter-narrative to dogmatic intrusions from outside religious and political ideologues (Koliska and Roberts 2015).

I became acquainted with international recording star, Angelique Kidjo, whose musical repertoire almost exclusively featured images and vocal references to the ancestors and Vodou gods of Bénin. She, like many of the other contemporary performers, emphasized her dedication to the ancient tradition. One example that is useful here to show the counter-hegemonic focus of her music is Kidjo's seminal selection, "Ilé Ifé." The song draws on yet revises and inverts the discursive power of western video narratives through an imposition of images of beautiful women and men who are representations of adepts of Vodou gods and goddesses. Kidjo's didactic voice-over becomes a signaling device for adoration of the sacred texts of IFA/FA scriptures of the Orisha and Vodou religions, through her technological showcasing of this West African spiritualty.

Indeed, as the video opens, Kidjo's image is superimposed on the circular image of a serpent, depicting the classic mythology of the Dahomean Vodou cosmos—where the Great creator God/Goddess, MAWU is encircled by her son, the serpent divinity, Dahn (or Aiydo Houédo/Aido Hewdo, the Rainbow Serpent). Aiydo Houédo supports the goddess as well as holds up the universe (Leeming and Leeming 1994). The dancers are representations of various other Orisha/Vodoun and Spiritual forces, also featured in other videos by her and other musical colleagues of Bénin. The camera gives very clear billing to the gods Shango, Sakpata and Ogun (god of the forge/metal and by implication, video technology). Her aural-over sounds/lyrics become a praise song to the founding gods of Ilé-Ifé and to the ancestral honored dead founders of Dahomey, now known as Bénin, land of the Vodoun (Olupona 2011).

This video is simply one example of the many in her repertoire, as well as other artists of Bénin and neighboring countries. We now see Nollywood (Nigerian version of Hollywood) and Gollywood (Ghana's "Hollywood"), industries that began with the cell phone and simple video camera. It is important to acknowledge the pan-Africanist agenda that the use by Blacks in the USA and those in West Africa have put these devices to, principally as a witness to their creativity, power and humanity so long masked by discourses of Black erasure. Often in their use in Africa, we clearly see pedagogic narratives of the camera foregrounded as a didactic technique employed to position the viewer in a receptive mode. The presentations confirm the reality of indigenous communal agency, for despite the brutalization of the slave trade and subsequent European colonization, the fact is that these local productions by citizen cameras reaffirm and revalorize their original epistemology as popular artists engage in a renaissance of cultural values, advocate for restitution, and promote a strong agenda of decolonization of the mind and spirit.

The recuperation and preservation of tradition in Africa speaks to the power of the enduring narratives of their cosmologies, ancestral beliefs and practices and their skill in technological adaptation to reject the yoke of European socio-cultural hegemony and neo-colonial dogmas, all of which have the objective of denigration and mis-representation of African-descended people and their cultural productions to the world. Brian Goldfarb points out in his essay "Pedagogical Cinema: Development Theory, Colonialism and Post-Liberation African Film" (1995) that "This pedagogical tactic operates as an important means of intervention in dismantling and re-configuring colonialist cultural forms."

CONCLUSION

In essence, the people's embrace of western technologies of the cell phone and video camera to record and preserve their own collections are testimonies to Black agency and validation of the Black-self, their culture and their spiritual traditions. Further preservation is assured through appropriation of ancestral masks and spiritual figures in their music videos. This all becomes a way of underscoring the culture's importance and ensuring its continuity in a rapidly-transforming contemporary society. The moral impact of the camera in the hands of average Black citizens has proven to be an act of willful agency that results in contentious or oppositional looks or looking in the name of justice. In this sense, then, as Richardson and other scholars have suggested, the camera is a storyteller, a moral weapon whose testimony is ultimate truth-telling. Its power confronts both inequity, violations of civil rights, and crimes against humanity. The camera's long history of Black agency-making creates an archive of justifications for reparative justice for African Americans and other people of African-descent, emanating from the violations of enslavement, anti-Black racism, and ongoing Black dispossession.

REFERENCES

Allen, Phil. 2022. *The Prophetic Lens: The Camera and Black Moral Agency from MLK to Darnella Frazier*. Minneapolis: Fortress Press, 2022.

Andén-Papadopoulos, Kari. 2014. "Citizen Camera-Witnessing: Embodied Political Dissent in the Age of 'Mediated Mass Self-Communication." *New Media & Society* 16 (5): 753–769. https://doi.org/10.1177/1461444813489863.

Anderson, John. 2013. "Christiana Riot of 1851." *Blackpast.* November 19, 2013. https://www.blackpast.org/african-american-history/christiana-riot-1851/.

Bertrand, Sandra. 2023. "James Van Der Zee: A Portrait of the Harlem Renaissance." *Highbrow Magazine*. April 13, 2023. https://www.highbrowmagazine.com/19770-james-van-der-zee-portrait-harlem-renaissance.

Blackmon, Douglas. 2008. *Slavery by Another Name: The Re-Enslavement of Black Americans from the Civil War to World War II*. New York: Doubleday.

Corbyn, Zoë. 2020. "Interview With Allissa Richardson: It's Telling That We're OK With Showing Black People Dying." *The Guardian*, August 16, 2020. https://www.theguardian.com/world/2020/aug/16/allissa-richardson-its-telling-that-were-ok-with-showing-Black-people-dying.

Duncombe, Stephen. 2002. *Cultural Resistance Reader*. Brooklyn: Verso.

Facing History and Ourselves. 2002. "The Influence of "The Birth of a Nation." Facing History and Ourselves. January 5, 2022. https://www.facinghistory.org/resource-library/influence-birth-nation.

Fulleylove, Rebecca. n. d. "Seven Gordon Parks Images That Changed American Attitudes." Google Arts & Culture. Accessed April 28, 2023. https://www.gordonparksfoundation.org/gordon-parks/biography.

Goldfarb, Brian. 1995. "Pedagogical Cinema: Development Theory, Colonialism and Post Liberation African Film." *Iris*, No. 18, 7–24.

Graham, Renee. 2016. "Frederick Douglass Used Photographs to Force the Nation to Begin Addressing Racism." WBUR. July 21, 2016. https://www.wbur.org/news/2016/07/21/picturing-frederick-douglass.

Guterl, Matthew Pratt. 2015. "Frederick Douglass's Faith in Photography: How the Former Slave and Abolitionist Became the Most Photographed Man in America." *The New Republic*. November 2, 2015. https://newrepublic.com/article/123191/frederick-douglasss-faith-in-photography.

Hall, Jacquelyn Dowd. 1983. "The Mind that Burns in Each Body: Women, Rape and Racial Violence." In *Powers of Desire: The Politics of Sexuality*, edited by Ann Snitow, Christine Stansell, and Sharon Thompson, 328–349. New York: Monthly Review Press.

Hendrie, Alison. 2021. "Visible Bodies: Representing Blackness." Vassar College. January 28, 2021. https://www.vassar.edu/stories/2021/visible-bodies-representing-Blackness-celebrates-Black-visibility-through-photography.html).

hooks, bell. 1992. *Black Looks: Race and Representation*. Boston: South End Press.

International Network of Scholars & Activists for Afrikan Reparations (INOSAAR). 2021. "Rethinking Reparations for Afrikan Enslavement as Rematriation." University of Edinburgh. Accessed April 23, 2023. https://www.inosaar.llc.ed.ac.uk/en/blog/rethinking-reparations-afrikan-enslavement-rematriation-0.

Jezierski, John. 2000. *Enterprising Images: The Goodridge Brothers, African American Photographers, 1847–2022*. Detroit: Wayne State University Press.

Koliska, Michael and Jessica Roberts. 2015. "Selfies: Witnessing and Participatory Journalism with a Point of View." *International Journal of Communication*, no. 9, 1672–1685. https://ijoc.org/index.php/ijoc/article/viewFile/3149/1392.

Leeming, David Adams and Margaret Adams Leeming. 1994. *A Dictionary of Creation Myths*. Oxford: Oxford University Press.

McClure, Jim. 2022. "The Tale of William C. Goodridge of York, PA Would Make a Good Movie." *York Daily Record*, February 8, 2022. https://www.ydr.com/story/opinion/2022/02/08/tale-william-c-goodridge-york-pa-would-make-good-movie/6710489001/.

Olupona, Jacob. 2011. *City of 201 Gods: Ilé-Ifè in Time, Space, and the Imagination*. Berkley: University of California Press.

Potter, Lou, Jill Nelson, Stanley Nelson, and Marcia Smith. 1999. *The Black Press: Soldiers Without Swords*. Stanley Nelson, producer and director. Chicago: Half Nelson Production. 83 minutes.

Ramirez, Ainissa G. 2020. "Black Images Matter: How Cameras Helped—and Sometimes Harmed—Black People." *Scientific American*, July 8, 2020. https://www.scientificamerican.com/article/Black-images-matter-how-cameras-helped-mdash-and-sometimes-harmed-mdash-Black-people/.

Reading, Anna. 2009. "Mobile Witnessing: Ethics and the Camera Phone in the 'War on Terror.'" *Globalizations* 6 (1): 61–76. https://www.tandfonline.com/doi/abs/10.1080/14747730802692435.

Richardson, Allissa. 2020. *Bearing Witness While Black: African Americans, Smartphones, and the New Protest #Journalism*. New York: Oxford University Press.

Scott, Joyce Hope. 2016. "New Griottes of the African Sahel: Intersectionalities and Women's Narrative Authority in Sanou Bernadette Dao's *La Dernière èpouse* and Aïcha Fofona's *Mariage on Copie.*" *Advances in Literary Study* 4 (4): 54–66. doi: 10.4236/als.2016.44010.

Scott, Sasha A. Q. 1017. "Mediatized Witnessing and the Ethical Imperative of Capture." *International Journal of E-Politics* 8 (1): 1–13. DOI: 10.4018/IJEP .2017010101.

———. 2022. "Reparations, Restitution, and Transitional Justice: American Chattel Slavery & Its Aftermath, a Moral Debate Whose Time Has Come." *Wisconsin International Law Journal* 39 (2): 269–99. https://search-ebscohost-com.ezp.bentley .edu/login.aspx?direct=true&db=a9h&AN=159342946&site=ehost-live.

Smith, Shawn Michelle. 2000. "'Looking at One's Self Through the Eyes of Others': W. E. B. Du Bois's Photographs for the 1900 Paris Exposition." *African American Review* 34 (4): 581–599. https://doi.org/10.2307/2901420.

Spivey, William. 2021. "A Man Was Lynched Yesterday: The Story behind the Flag." An Injustice. September 2, 2021. https://aninjusticemag.com/a-man-was-lynched -yesterday-2c4256a0de6.

The Conversation. 2021. "How Black people in the 19th century used photography as a tool for social change." The Conversation. Last updated February 26, 2021. https://theconversation.com/how-Black-people-in-the-19th-century-used-photog raphy-as-a-tool-for-social-change-154721).

The Gordon Parks Foundation. n. d. "Gordon Parks." The Gordon Parks Foundation. Accessed April 15, 2023. https://www.gordonparksfoundation.org/gordon-parks /biography.

Vaidhyanathan, Siva. 2020. "The Dangers of Seeing the World Through Ubiquitous Video." *Wired.* August 18, 2020. https://www.wired.com/story/dangers-ubiquitous -video-propaganda/.

Wallace, Maurice. 2000. "'Are We Men?': Prince Hall, Martin Delaney, and the Masculine Ideal in Black Freemasonry, 1775–1865." In *The Cultural Work of American Iconography*, edited by Larry J. Reynolds and Gordon Hunter, 182–210. Princeton: Princeton University Press.

———. 2002. *Constructing the Black Masculine: Identity and Ideality in African American Men's Literature and Culture, 1775–1995.* Durham: Duke University Press.

Weir, Sue Hunter. 2004. "Early African American Barbers in Minneapolis." The Alley Newspaper, February 2004. Accessed April 29, 2023. https://alleynews.org /2021/01/tales-from-pioneers-and-soldiers-memorial-cemetery-4/.

Chapter Five

Community and Communal Coping

The Role of Social Media as a Resource for Black Activism and Black Refuge

David Stamps

Steps toward racial progress for Black communities are often countered by groups who encourage anti-Blackness and racism (Steele 2018). The Civil Rights Movement of the 1960s is lauded as a substantial accomplishment toward racial progress. However, Dr. Martin Luther King Jr., who is often framed as a dreamer and assimilative activist, acknowledged that his "dream" had become a nightmare as equality would not be realized due to the grievance, intolerance, and antipathy from White people (King 1986). Social movements and efforts within activism spaces that aim to achieve racial equality can seem intangible for Black communities. However, the call for Black communities to march, fight, and forge toward inclusion and fair representation has not been conceded. The need for continued advocacy is necessary—yet scholarship that has explored mediated spaces for Black audiences to increase knowledge about social issues relevant to the group, build community among like-minded others, and seek refuge amid the contentious struggle remains underexplored.

Contemporary illustrations of Black-centered social movements include the Black Lives Matter movement, which provoked its counter, the January 6th insurrection, and a concerted effort by the majority of White conservatives who have attacked racial justice efforts, including the vilification of critical race theory (Asare 2021). In response to increased anti-Blackness, Black folks engaged in activism and sought out communal coping to combat the exhaustion from advocacy work. Such actions, including engagement with social media, have provided novel opportunities to recognize discrimination and racial exclusion (e.g., #OscarsSoWhite) and create community focused collations (Negrete and Hurd, 2020). The Black Lives Matter movement and pivotal moments, such as the murder of George Floyd, have highlighted the Black community's alignment to promote racial justice when White supremacists espouse anti-Black rhetoric and promote white nationalists' policies. Fittingly, Black audiences' social media use and the role of Black social media influencers' thought-provoking engagement to promote advocacy, increase engagement in collective action, and provide refuge as a coping mechanism are essential.

The current work draws upon media dependency theory (Ball-Rokeach and Defleur 1976) and communal coping (Afifi, Basinger, and Kam 2020) to explore, via case studies, Black activists–social media influencers' content centered on Black liberation, activism, and racial equity. The chapter assessed social media content from Black activists–social media influencers Conscious Lee and Lynae Vanee. The salient themes found with the analysis illustrated how social media content produced forms of refuge among Black audiences who often confront white backlash (i.e., disparagement by predominately White, heterosexual, cis-gender, conservative individuals toward non-White groups). The findings exemplified the role of social media as a means of coping under the lens of media dependency theory, which denotes how audiences rely on media amid crises (e.g., anti-Blackness and racism) for knowledge-seeking and comfort (Ball-Rokeach and Defleur 1976).

BLACK AUDIENCES AND SOCIAL MEDIA USE

Ownership of smartphones and computers has approached saturation in the U.S. and has suggested that many individuals have some type of access to social and digital media (Pew Research Center 2021b). Compared to other racial groups, Black individuals are increasingly active on social media platforms such as YouTube and Twitter (Tynes et al. 2012; Stamps 2023). Black audiences use social media and achieve gratifications that support a range of favorable outcomes that include affective (e.g., building self-confidence), cognitive (e.g., knowledge seeking), and social (e.g., increasing relationships) needs (Cho et al. 2003). Researchers have supported the finding that the digital media landscape, which includes social media sites (e.g., Facebook Watch), digital platforms (e.g., YouTube), and streaming services (e.g., Hulu), offer a plethora of favorable options for Black viewers (Sobande, Fearfull, and Brownlie 2020). Black audiences benefit from the numerous possibilities for social media engagement with their racial peers, and outcomes range from increased advocacy to vocational aspirations (Brooms and Davis 2017; Stamps 2022). In summary, Black audiences are avid social media users and content creators, and their reasons for social media consumption are often associated with community building, advocacy work, and celebrating culture (Mesch 2012; Stamps, Mandell, and Lucas 2021).

Social media use can contribute to Black audiences' well-being amid the racial backlash and encounters with white supremacy (Leach and Teixiera 2021). Additionally, social media is an outlet for Black individuals and organizations to engage in activism and build coalitions (Carney 2016). Conversely, traditional media outlets, such as broadcast television, are no longer strongholds for momentum-building toward collective action (Lee 2017). Media gatekeepers (e.g., newspaper editors), to an extent, are not the sole arbiters of access to knowledge-seeking. The confines of traditional media (e.g., newspapers) and publication timelines are no longer a hindrance to disseminating content (Juris 2016; Mundt, Ross, and Burnett 2018). Black audiences can build legitimacy outside of whiteness, draw attention to needs directly related to group members, and promote the efforts directly to spectators using social media platforms. Black media consumers and content creators are afforded the opportunity to increase awareness and advocate for racial and social issues that are salient to Black communities (Blevins et al 2019; Brock 2012; Lee 2017; Maragh-Lloyd 2020).

Research that has investigated Black individuals' experience with identity-related social media use is of keen interest as scholars call for specific theory applications and data that underscore group identity (Salter and Adams 2013). Identity often motivates racial audiences to seek out social media (Chan 2014). Scholars have noted that in Black US households, the consumption of media, including scrolling, posting, and commenting on social media channels (i.e., Instagram and Facebook), may exceed the time dedicated to face-to-face socialization (Tynes and Ward 2009). Black individuals utilize the Internet (i.e., surfing the web, creating content) for roughly five hours per day, which outpaces the average of two hours spent by non-Black internet users (Tynes et al. 2012). Undoubtedly, Black people are watching, engaging in, and creating digital media. However, Black audiences' use of social and digital media is not wholly disparaging, as social media use may be a socializing tool, a community build apparatus, and the impetus for advocacy among Black consumers (Negrete and Hurd 2020). "There is potential for Black audiences to curate an affirmative social media diet through engagement with social media influencers" (Stamps 2022, 662). Often Black influencers purposefully limit negative imagery and demeaning narratives and promote group-conscious themes. The use of social media amid the crisis of anti-Blackness, the backlash from White conservatives directed at Black communities, and the continued efforts of collective action steeped in racial justice in the twenty-first century call attention to audiences and media dependency.

MEDIA DEPENDENCY THEORY

Media dependency theory recognizes that audiences who face a crisis (e.g., racial discrimination and discrimination) often rely on media as a source of information and comfort (Ball-Rokeach and Defleur 1976). Consumers seek media to inform, educate, and reduce uncertainty during hardship as knowledge seeking is often key to alleviating stress (Gearhart, Trumbly-Lamsam, and Adegbola 2017). The consumption of social media content may allow Black audiences to navigate discrimination, address issues through advocacy, and obtain knowledge about resources during social unrest (Jacobs et al. 2006). Group-based concerns or adversity, such as racism and anti-Blackness, often lead to heightened media use as audiences may rely on information to better understand their social environment and navigate turmoil (Kim and Ball-Rokeach 2006, Lowrey 2004). Kim and colleagues (2004) noted that audiences relied on media after the September 11 terrorist attacks to cope with the tragedy and stay informed about subsequent events post the attack. Media dependency is also correlated with crises among consumers who seek mental and physical health resources to manage the turmoil from such crises (Tai and Sun 2007).

Despite the widespread application of media dependency theory, the framework has not been explored regarding Black audiences' social media use and their navigation of racism and discrimination. Although this chapter does not aim to test media dependency, I argue that crises may create an environment where Black audiences' dependency on media, and in this case, social media is necessary. Numerous crises include continued racism, anti-Blackness, and racial-centric conflict, including countless examples of police brutality, the attacks on critical race theory, and a general anti-Black sentiment from social structures (e.g., right-wing politics). A concentrated effort to minimize racial issues, including criminal justice reform and the redistribution of law enforcement funds toward restorative justice, housing security, and mental health services, are additional illustrations of what Black individuals seek amid turmoil. Due to Black audiences' heavy usage of social media, the group may likely exercise trust in social media content that addresses pertinent crises related to Black individuals. In turn, relying on social media content to minimize uncertainty amid multiple race-based crises may result in communal coping efforts.

COMMUNAL COPING

Communal coping is a relational process whereby individuals work interdependently and rely on certain mechanisms, such as media consumption, to navigate traumatic events (Afifi, Hutchinson, and Kam 2006). Likewise, individuals navigate stressful life circumstances using action-oriented behaviors, including social media consumption, to seek communal coping (Afifi, Basinger, and Kam 2020; Richardson and Maninger 2016). Communal coping acknowledges that a group collectively recognizes an issue and responds to reduce uncertainty and increase knowledge to handle or minimize outcomes related to a predicament (Lyons et al. 1998). Communal coping involves a fluid exchange of ideas and dialogues among people instead of a process with a fixed start or end (Afifi, Hutchinson, and Kam 2006). Communal coping compels individuals to shoulder mutual responsibility and respond to a situation or stressor cooperatively.

The communal coping efforts among Black individuals and their use of social media are often underexplored, which may limit the acknowledgment of diverse experiences among the population (cf. Terhune 2008). Social media influencers are individuals who take on the responsibility to inform, entertain, and educate audiences with topics that are salient to consumers (Arthur 2021). Concepts such as coalition building and collectivist tendencies are considered integral to communal coping, and social media influencers are influential in championing these actions (Afifi, Basinger, and Kam 2020). Black communities have historically demonstrated an ability to act as agents of change by engaging in coping efforts that combat inequalities and injustices and use social media as a communication and organizational tool to accomplish this task (Florini 2019). Black individuals are embedded in community-based activities, and these objectives are at the core of their coping efforts. The use of social media as a resource for encouraging collective action (Stamps 2022), constructing identity (Ince, Rojas, and Davis 2017), and confronting misrepresentation and enacting social change (Garcia, Fernández, and Okonkwo 2020) is real.

Black individuals are collectivist, racially centered, and look to community members to navigate turmoil and may use social media as a tool to connect with others who have similar goals (Mercier, Abbott, and Ternes 2022). Collective responses to crises often prompt community members to help one another rather than employ individualistic actions (Drury 2018). The collective responses can be seen anecdotally with the inception of the Black Lives Matter movement, the creation of hashtags such as #Blackintheivory, and among journalists and activists who use social media to raise funds for families who have lost loved ones to police violence (Subbaraman 2020). Biddlestone and colleagues (2020) found that collectivistic thinking is a better predictor of mitigating negative outcomes. Collective groups often express community support, solidarity, and coping through group cooperation and communication (Drury, Cocking, and Reicher 2009).

BLACK ACTIVISTS–SOCIAL MEDIA INFLUENCERS: CONSCIOUS LEE AND LYNAE VANEE

As part of the analysis, it is necessary to situate the social media content creators and their alignment with Black audiences. Under the social media moniker Conscious Lee, George Lee is a social media influencer and educator who covers areas of diversity, equity, inclusion, and racial justice. Conscious Lee, as of the publication of this book chapter, has amassed over 2 million followers across his social media platforms and was named a 2022 YouTube Black Voice Creator (theconsciouslee.com, n.d.). Conscious Lee's content is a mixture of Black culture, including hip-hop dance and rap artistry. However, his signature and most shared content is the intellectual debate often cited as thought-provoking, culturally relevant, and intersectional, blending themes of Black feminist thought and progressive standpoints (DeYoung 2022). Conscious Lee showcases the role of unapologetic Blackness and intellectual curiosity, and his content is noted as absent of respectability politics (DeYoung 2022).

Conscious Lee's educational background includes a bachelor's degree in African and African American Studies, a master's degree in Human Relations and Adult Higher Education, and graduate certificates from the University of Oklahoma in Women and Gendered Studies and Human Resource and Diversity Development. Conscious Lee has appeared in *Forbes* and *Essence Magazines*, *The New York Times*, the *Washington Post*, *The Atlantic*, and *Yahoo Life* (theconsciouslee.com, n.d.).

Lynae Vanee Bogues, under the social media moniker Lynae Vanee, is a multiple NAACP Image Award nominee for outstanding social media personality. Her social media following has garnered over 20 million views across social media sites Instagram, TikTok, and YouTube. Lynae Vanee has featured Democratic gubernatorial candidate Stacey Abrams and actress Gail Bean in her weekly social media show, "Parking Lot Pimpin." The show has averaged 300,000 views, likes, and comments per episode and is centered on politics, intersectional inclusivity, race, and feminism. Lynae Vanee, via her signature proclamation, aims to "keep it Black, but keep it brief" (lynaevanee.com, n.d.).

Lynae Vanee is a graduate of Spelman College and received a master's degree in African American Studies from Boston University. Lynae Vanee's critical and insightful coverage of Black culture, themes, and social issues have brought her to mainstream audiences via the Microsoft/National Broadcast Company's (MSNBC) show, *The Cross Connection with Tiffany Cross*, the *L.A. Times*, and *Bustle*. Her work has brought attention and garnered partnerships with several brands, including Netflix, Target, Revolt, Meta, and Tommy Hilfiger (lynaevanee.com, n.d.).

ANALYZING BLACK ACTIVISM
IN SOCIAL MEDIA CONTENT

I collected Instagram "posts," which included videos, stills, and threads from the Black activists–social media influencers, Conscious Lee and Lynae Vanee's Instagram pages. Due to the content cross-posted on several social media platforms, including Facebook and TikTok, the singular focus on Instagram provided robust content for data collection. The content was collected in two rounds, March 2022 and August 2022, and I analyzed posts that were dated between January 1, 2020, and August 1, 2022. The initial number of posts for analysis was 8,460. Posts that did not include conversation, text, or promotional material (e.g., highlighting cultural topics) were not included in the analysis.

I focused on the verbal exchanges, visual representations, and storylines displayed in the social media posts using thematic analysis. Scholars often seek to employ thematic analysis to understand the complex expressions and relationships regarding the social construction of identities and systems in the content (Lynn and Lea 2005). However, the examination of images and dialogue does not suggest that data has only one meaning. Lexical ambiguity exists, and thus, my reading of the social media posts is *one* of the data's multiple possible interpretations (Fiske 1991). I viewed each social media post with repetition to assess each influencer's visual and verbal discourse, paying attention to the latent and manifest messages and markers related to Black activism, education, and refuge (Lynn and Lea 2005). The analysis yielded several themes: the recognition of Anti-Blackness, the reduction of respectability politics, and the promotion of advocacy on behalf of intersectional Blackness.

The analysis focused solely on social media videos and imagery, as Black audiences create, view, comment, and share social media content at a higher rate than their racial counterparts (Pew Research Center 2021a). Black individuals are more active on social media platforms such as YouTube and Twitter than their peers. The lexicon of Black social media has even rendered terminology including Black Twitter (Lu and Steele 2019). Below I provide examples of social media posts and topics to support the themes that surfaced within the analysis.

THE RECOGNITION OF ANTI-BLACKNESS

Anti-Blackness is defined as the actions of the state and, by extension, civil society in the continued dehumanization of Black people (Bledsoe and Wright 2019). Anti-Blackness became a formal marker and reality in our global society at the onslaught of the chattel enslavement of African people. However, anti-Blackness includes the implicit and explicit forms of racism, dehumanization, and numerous inequitable policies and programs, such as restricting voting rights, redlining, and policies such as "stop and frisk." The goal of anti-Blackness aims to impede advancement in Black social and civil life. The content from Conscious Lee and Lynae Vanee called attention to and criticized the systems and individuals who often exercised anti-Blackness.

Social media, similar to other technological advancements, has highlighted how civilization is living through a moment in which hyper-visualized anti-Black violence has prompted discourse. Moreover, the discourse has become unapologetic as the role of media gatekeepers is somewhat constrained in social media settings (Bledsoe and Wright 2019). Conscious Lee and Lynae Vanee consistently across their social media content discussed numerous topics related to anti-Blackness enacted by the state. For example, Vanee (2021) discussed the anniversary of the January 6th insurrection. She highlighted the circumvented and minimized ways in which criminals, the individuals who broke multiple laws, including breaching the Capitol Building, attacking law enforcement, and attempting to attack, kidnap, or affront public servants, have been glossed over by mainstream media and society. More importantly, Vanee discussed that if the majority of the mob at the Capitol were not White people, the outcome and subsequent conversation about the topic would be different. Vanee asked in her I.G. post, "How do you think the rest of 2021 would have turned out had this mob been filled with Black and brown people aggressively demanding changes from their government while armed and equipped (with weapons)?" With over 30,000 likes and 900+ comments, audiences discussed the way anti-Blackness has been manifested and a white supremacist perspective was uplifted as "patriotic." When White people commit a crime, and the actions are documented and lambasted across media platforms, the actions are excused, or prosecution is delayed as justice "needs to be pursued." The same responses to incredulousness are often not extended to non-White communities. Anti-Blackness provided the lens to view how Black individuals are not afforded the same privileges. One such example is the actions and subsequent outcomes related to the January 6th insurrection.

Conscious Lee, in the same vein as their social media influencer counterpart, also highlighted numerous examples of anti-Blackness in various social settings and institutions. Conscious Lee (2020) unpacked the claims that Northern US White people were progressive and one of the first "groups" to free enslaved people. This notion aimed to distinguish bad Southern White individuals from good, progressive White people. White people's claim to compartmentalize themselves is a form of social creativity, where individuals shift identities to preserve esteem and favorable group comparison (Tajfel and

Turner 1979). In the Instagram post, Lee (2020) discussed the idea of the separation of good and bad White people and the rationale is a decision that US White people apply among themselves. The reality is that anti-Blackness was persuasive throughout the United States, took on different forms and policies throughout the country, and was upheld by White people across geographic locations. Lee highlighted policies such as escaped enslaved individuals who had to be returned to their owners, no matter which state they resided in or traveled to, and that enslaved individuals were only counted as 3/5th of a human being across the United States (Lee 2020). Lee also posted content that discussed anti-Blackness in higher education, the healthcare system, and between groups, particularly among White individuals who often promote anti-Blackness to justify group differences, inequity, and unequal access and representation. Lee and Vanee discussed how institutions and individuals, absent of race, openly and explicitly promoted anti-Blackness. Both influencers used their platforms to draw attention to the fallacies and misnomers often presented by White individuals or power structures (e.g., media and government) that have been historically anti-Black, but aim to save face.

INTERSECTIONAL BLACKNESS

The pervasive impact of anti-Black racism, which manifests in various types of explicit and implicit prejudice, stereotyping, and discrimination, is reflected by individuals and systems that position people of African descent as inferior to non-Black individuals. Concurrently, Black people hold intersectional identities related to nationality, class, sexuality, ability, gender, and other characteristics. The overlapping identities are not independent of one another. Black folks exist at the intersection of race, and additional salient characteristics and the interlocking systems of oppression target each identity and results in forms of racism, sexism, xenophobia, homophobia, and bias (Crenshaw 2013). To illustrate, Black, gay immigrants may confront racism, sexism, and xenophobia, which places a person in the crosshairs of diverse forms of oppression.

Conscious Lee (2021) in an Instagram post on August 16th highlighted the intersection of weight, gender, and anti-Blackness. Lee drew focus to a clip of Kathy Hilton, of the Hilton Hotel empire and *Real Housewives of Beverly Hills* fame, who mistakenly stated that Lizzo, a multi-award-winning songwriter and performer, was Gabourey Sidibe, an award-winning actress, on the Bravo talk show, *Watch What Happens Live*. The post recognized the intersection of anti-Blackness, fatphobia, and misogynoir (Bailey and Trudy 2018). In the discussion, Conscious Lee recognized the role of attacking

Black women, particularly regarding their weight, and how anti-Blackness, fatphobia and weight discrimination is persuasive. Conscious Lee stated the difference in bias between self-identified Black men and women and noted how misogynoir, or the contempt or disregard of Black women, permeates society. The post garnered over 150 comments and unpacked how the layered identities of Black women including weight, class, and ability status, are either ignored or disrespected in media. Conscious Lee defined fatphobia and argued that weight discrimination is often normalized, framed comically, and are routine for women in general and Black women specifically (Beauboeuf-Lafontant 2003). Equally important, the post brought to light the insult, stigma, and discrimination Black women face as one form of sexism, fatphobia, and anti-Blackness (Patterson-Faye 2016).

Vanee (2020) discussed the history of reparations, the conflict between the term and social status or class, and the extension of compensation given to Indigenous and Japanese individuals as reparations for Black Americans remain inadequate. In Vanee's Instagram post, they introduced and championed the role of House Resolution 40, a commission to study reparations for Black Americans and the absent conversation regarding the racial wage gap between White and Black individuals. The absence of conversation remains in lieu of 250 years of wealth created by Black enslaved individuals that has primarily benefited White Americans. The Instagram reel discussed redlining, housing discrimination, the lagging federal minimal wage, and the multitude of programs and policies that continued to harm Black people, particularly Black folks who are impacted by class. Vanee presented the history of enslavement and its continued economic impact that benefited non-Black groups and continued to neglect Black Americans. She ended a critical conversation with the evidence that America has extended reparations to 175 Indigenous tribes and Japanese individuals, in the amounts of $1.3 billion dollars for seized land and $20,000 per person for mistreatment that included imprisonment in internment camps (Barth 1998; U.S. Commission of Civil Rights 2018). Vanee ends the post with several suggestions for reparations for Black Americans, including stimulus checks, student loan forgiveness, land, and tax exemptions. The post, one of many, drew attention to the lived experiences of Black people and particularly those impacted economically and who have missed the opportunity to build wealth and shift their class status.

RESPECTABILITY POLITICS

Respectability politics refers to individuals, systems, and the actions that attempt to champion social change but only in a way deemed acceptable by mainstream, dominant groups and social structures. When offered to the Black masses, respectability is said to protect vulnerable persons (e.g., marginalized groups) from prejudices and systemic injustices by adhering to nonthreatening actions and behaviors. On the surface, respectability would seem like a palatable remedy to decrease group conflict and discrimination. However, the assimilation to majority (i.e., white) standards and practices has yet to reduce the harm directed at Black people. The structures that uphold white supremacy and racial hierarchy, which privileges White people, do not accommodate Black individuals in the same way as Black people are directed to acclimate to White ideas regarding dress, behavior, and group-level engagement (Bunyasi and Smith 2019, 180). From a macro perspective "To what extent does respectability politics serve to hinder a broader embrace of Blacks who face different sets of interlocking systems of oppression, such as Black women, formerly incarcerated Blacks, undocumented Black people, and Black members of LBGTQ communities in an era marked by Black social movements?" (180). Commentaries by Lee and Vanee aimed to tackle such topics, and their Instagram posts highlighted the nuanced spectrum of issues that hindered progress due to the expectations of respectability and the performance of respectability politics.

The role of respectability was interwoven throughout the social media content featured on Lee and Vanee's Instagram accounts. For example, on Lee's website and social media posts, he highlighted how assimilation to mainstream or white norms does not allow for acceptance and agency for most Black individuals. Lee denoted how he aimed to debunk respectability politics and stated on his website that knowledge does not equate to respectability. Scholars have noted that freedom and liberation are rarely associated with respect for Black folks and Blackness. Blackness, including skin hue, demeanor, and sheer presence, cannot visibly accommodate white supremacy and is often a hindrance to social and economic autonomy for Black individuals in a racist society (Aziz 2015). The overarching issue with respectability politics is that it "relies on policing Black individual behavior and attitudes rather than directly addressing the structural forces that perpetuate racial inequalities, agency, and policies" (Lopez Bunyasi and Watts Smith, 2019, 186).

The social media influencers discussed the seemingly explicit issues with how White and Black people are treated differently. Lee and Vanee discussed the difference in scrutiny by mainstream media between Colin Kaepernick, a bi-racial individual and at one point, the quarterback for the San Francisco 49ers, who knelt during National Football League games in protest of anti-Blackness and Aaron Rodgers, a White Green Bay Packers quarterback, who lied about being tested for COVID-19. The two athletes were treated differently by mainstream media and White audiences. However, Rodgers was not lambasted, nor did he suffer dire consequences for his actions as Kaepernick, who took a stand against racial injustice and inequity, experienced. Rodgers continues to play football for the National Football League (NFL). Kaepernick, as a quarterback, an upstanding American football player, and at one time, a beloved athlete, was not shielded from being belittled, blackballed, and ostracized by the NFL. Rodgers actions were selfish, his choice to not be vaccinated is one issue, but his lies and disregard for others health and wellness would speak to his character. The notion that their skin color is absent from comparing both individuals' actions and their subsequent treatment by media and society would be misleading. Kaepernick's' adherence to respectability to uphold White people's notion of acceptable behavior did not shield him from criticism and the actions would mean minimizing the racial issues and experience of being Black in an anti-Black society.

Additional topics in Lee and Vanee's social media commentary included Black sexuality and mainstream musical artists Cardi B and Megan Thee Stallion. Both artists released music that celebrated sexuality, bodily autonomy, personal agency, and sexual behaviors. Both artists were criticized because their music lyrics did not conform to behaviors that would be seen as acceptable to the dominant (i.e., white) culture. Multiple posts by both influencers, throughout 2020 and 2021, posited that rap lyrics have always historically challenged the status quo, celebrated urban culture, and promoted unapologetic Blackness. However, the critique, which came from multiple groups, including Black audiences, was that this example of rap music went too far. Higginbotham (1994), as one example, addressed the concept of politics of respectability and recognized how Black middle-class women aimed to dismantle the negative stereotypes associated with their race and gender by exercising distance from other Black individuals who did not embody traits or characteristics that were deemed honorable. Topics the group was mostly concerned with included exercising self-restraint, respectful manners, language, and promoting a formal style of dress and sexual purity. As seen here, the contradiction of respectability is stark in comparison to the lyrics from Cardi B and Megan Thee Stallion's single *WAP* (2020), which explicitly negate these attributes:

> Your honor, I'm a freak b***h, handcuffs, leashes. Switch my wig, make him feel like he cheatin'. Put him on his knees, give him something to believe in.

Lee and Vanee make the case that the success of the song and the unapologetic lyrics are not meant to conform to white norms, appease White audiences, or uphold a Black respectable politic. Moreover, the criticism that Black artists should embrace respectability would negate the reality that performing for the status quo does not render liberation for Black folks. The United States, as a 400-year-old capitalist, white society, has only seen Black bodies as something to be owned or controlled, and for profit.

The social media commentary from Lee and Vanee aimed to dismantle the idea that respectability politics are associated with freedom or liberty. The social media content that addressed areas of anti-Blackness, respectability, and other timely issues used salient topics and subjects relevant to Black audiences and that engage a Black populace, absent the needs and consideration of non-Black individuals. Themes such as misogynoir, the discrimination directed at Black women, and colorism, bias driven by skin tone and hue discrimination, are intended to shed light on the Black experience unapologetically.

CONCLUSION

Black activism requires Black refuge, a space where Black individuals can express frustration and position themselves to engage in advocacy. Across social media outlets, Black influencers provide content that confronted America's racist past in explicit detail and explored the often forgotten and descriptive history that textbooks tend to miss or whitewash. The social media material added much-needed context to the Black experience and framed Black issues through a lens that spoke to the realities of how Black folks navigate anti-Blackness, intersectional Blackness, and respectability politics. Lee and Vanee richly explored lesser-known figures, salient issues, and timely topics that matter to Black audiences, and did so in a medium (i.e., social media) that may reach young, tech-savvy, and ambitious Black consumers. Black audiences, as an active social media consumer group, and their dependency on media, arguably demonstrates the unique opportunity for learning, growth, and coping during crises, particularly via social media consumption.

In summary, social media has become a refuge for Black individuals to create digital spaces (e.g., Black Twitter) and digital content that celebrates Black culture, identity, and collectivistic tendencies (Steele 2018). For centuries Black folks have engaged in activism and continually sought communal coping amid the misinformation and the vilification of Black communities. Social media, within the past few decades, has become one of many spaces for these activities and positions Black community members to survive and thrive, despite ongoing subjugation and discrimination. The work of activists, on the ground and within digital spaces, who continue to create community, inform the Black populace, and encourage advocacy is no small matter. Black lives matter, and how Black people cope, use social media, and fight for liberation matters.

REFERENCES

Afifi, Tamara, Erin Basinger, and Jennifer Kam. 2020. "The Extended Theoretical Model of Communal Coping: Understanding the Properties and Functionality of Communal Coping." *Journal of Communication* 70 (3): 424–446. https://doi .org/10.1093/joc/jqaa006.

Afifi, Tamara, Susan Hutchinson, and Stephanie Krouse. 2006. "Toward a Theoretical Model of Communal Coping in Post-Divorce Families and Other Naturally Occurring Groups." *Communication Theory* 16 (3): 378–409. https://doi.org/10.1111 /j.1468-2885.2006.00275.x.

Arthur, Tori. 2021. "#Catchmeinashithole: Black Travel Influencers and the Contestation of Racialized Place Myths." *Howard Journal of Communications* 32 (4): 382–393. https://doi.org/10.1080/10646175.2020.1819481.

Asare, Janice. 2019. "The War on Critical Race Theory Continues as Some Call It Anti-White." *Forbes Magazine,* May 9, 2021. https://www.forbes.com/sites /janicegassam/2021/05/09/the-war-on-critical-race-theory-continues-as-some-call -it-anti-white/?sh=46a32f6c73a7.

Aziz, Sahar. 2015. "Irreconcilable Contradiction in 'Respectability Politics.'" *Racism Review*. October 20, 2015. http://www.racismreview.com/blog/2015/10/20 /irreconcilable-contradiction-in-respectability-politics/.

Bailey, Moya, and Trudy Stone. 2018. "On Misogynoir: Citation, Erasure, and Plagiarism." *Feminist Media Studies* 18 (4): 762–768. https://doi.org/10.1080/14680 777.2018.1447395.

Ball-Rokeach, Sandra. 1998. "A Theory of Media Power and a Theory of Media Use: Different Stories, Questions, and Ways of Thinking." *Mass Communication and Society* 1 (1–2): 5–40. https://doi.org/10.1080/15205436.1998.9676398.

Ball-Rokeach, Sandra, and Melvin DeFleur. 1976. "A Dependency Model of Mass-Media Effects." *Communication Research* 3 (1): 3–21. https://doi.org/10 .1177/009365027600300101.

Barth, G. (1998). "Japanese Americans." In *The New Encyclopedia of the American West*, edited by Howard Lamar, 1118–1119. New Haven: Yale University Press.

Beauboeuf-Lafontant, Tamara. 2003. "Strong and Large Black Women? Exploring Relationships Between Deviant Womanhood and Weight." *Gender & Society* 17 (1): 111–121. https://psycnet.apa.org/doi/10.1177/0891243202238981.

Bledsoe, Adam, and Willie Wright. 2019. "The Anti-Blackness of Global Capital." *Environment and Planning D: Society and Space* 37 (1): 8–26. https://doi .org/10.1177/0263775818805102.

Biddlestone, Mikey, Ricky Green, and Karen Douglas. 2020. "Cultural Orientation, Power, Belief in Conspiracy Theories, and Intentions to Reduce the Spread of COVID-19." *British Journal of Social Psychology* 59 (3): 663–673. DOI:10.1111 /bjso.12397.

Blevins, Jeffrey, James Jaehoon, Erin McCabe, and Ezra Edgerton. 2019. "Tweeting for Social Justice in #Ferguson: Affective Discourse in Twitter Hashtags." *New Media & Society* 21 (7): 1636–1653. https://doi.org/10.1177/1461444819827030.

Brock, André. 2012. "From the Blackhand Side: Twitter as a Cultural Conversation." *Journal of Broadcasting & Electronic Media* 56 (4): 529–549. https://doi.org/10 .1080/08838151.2012.732147.

Brooms, Derrick, and Arthur Davis. 2017. "Exploring Black Males' Community Cultural Wealth and College Aspirations." *Spectrum: A Journal on Black Men* 6 (1): 33–58. https://doi.org/10.2979/spectrum.6.1.02.

Bunyasi, Tehama Lopez, and Candis Smith. 2019. "Do All Black Lives Matter Equally to Black People? Respectability Politics and the Limitations of Linked Fate." *Journal of Race, Ethnicity, and Politics* 4 (4): 180–215. doi:10.1017 /rep.2018.33.

Cardi B and Megan Thee Stallion. 2020. *WAP.* Atlantic Records, digital single.

Carney, Nikita. 2016. "All Lives Matter, but So Does Race: Black Lives Matter and the Evolving Role of Social Media." *Humanity & Society* 40 (2): 180–199. https:// doi.org/10.1177/0160597616643868.

Carter, Dorinda. 2007. "Why the Black Kids Sit Together at the Stairs: The Role of Identity-Affirming Counter-Spaces in a Predominantly White High School." *The Journal of Negro Education* 76 (4): 542–554.

Chan, Michael. 2014. "Social Identity Gratifications of Social Network Sites and Their Impact on Collective Action Participation." *Asian Journal of Social Psychology* 17 (3): 229–235. https://psycnet.apa.org/doi/10.1111/ajsp.12068.

Cho, Jaeho, Gil De Zuniga, Hernando Rojas, and Dhavan Shah. 2003. "Beyond Access: The Digital Divide and Internet Uses and Gratifications." *IT & Society* 1 (3): 46–72. https://www.researchgate.net/deref/http%3A%2F%2Fwww.itandsociety .org%2F.

Crenshaw, Kimberlé. 2013. "Demarginalizing the Intersection of Race and Sex: A Black Feminist Critique of Antidiscrimination Doctrine, Feminist Theory and Antiracist Politics." In *Feminist Legal Theories*, edited by Karen Maschke, 23–51. New York: Routledge.

DeYoung, Amy. 2022. "George Lee of The Conscious Lee on Education and Empowerment Online." Net Influencer. https://www.netinfluencer.com/george-lee/.

Drury, John, Chris Cocking, and Steve Reicher. 2009. "The Nature of Collective Resilience: Survivor Reactions to the 2005 London Bombings." *International Journal of Mass Emergencies & Disasters* 27 (1): 66–95.

Drury, John. 2018. "The Role of Social Identity Processes in Mass Emergency Behaviour: An Integrative Review." *European Review of Social Psychology* 29 (1): 38–81. https://psycnet.apa.org/doi/10.1080/10463283.2018.1471948.

Ellen, Ingrid Gould. 1997. "Welcome Neighbors? New Evidence on the Possibility of Stable Racial Integration." *Brookings Review* 15 (1): 18–22. https://www.brook ings.edu/articles/welcome-neighbors-new-evidence-on-the-possibility-of-stable -racial-integration/.

Fiske, John. 1991. "For Cultural Interpretation: A Study of the Culture of Homelessness." *Critical Studies in Media Communication* 8 (4): 455–474. https://doi. org/10.1080/15295039109366809.

Florini, Sarah. 2019. *Beyond Hashtags: Racial Politics and Black Digital Networks.* New York: NYU Press.

Garcia, Patricia, Cecilia Fernández, and Holly Okonkwo. 2020. "Leveraging Technology: How Black Girls Enact Critical Digital Literacies for Social Change." *Learning, Media and Technology* 45 (4): 345–362. https://doi.org/10.1080/17439 884.2020.1773851.

Gearhart, Sherice, Teresa Trumbly-Lamsam, and Oluseyi Adegbola. 2018. "Why Isn't Health a Priority? A Survey of Journalists Serving Native American News Media." *Journalism Practice* 12 (9): 1183–1200. https://doi.org/10.1080/17512786.2017 .1363658.

Gibson, William. 2010. "The Group Ethic in the Improvising Jazz Ensemble: A Symbolic Interactionist Analysis of Music, Identity, and Social Context." In *Studies in Symbolic Interaction*, edited by Norman Denzin and Michael Ryan, 11–28. Bingley, UK: Emerald Group Publishing Limited.

Harris, Fredrick. 2014. "The Rise of Respectability Politics." *Dissent* 61 (1): 33–37.

Higginbotham, Evelyn. 1994. *Righteous Discontent: The Women's Movement in the Black Baptist Church, 1880–1920*. Cambridge, MA: Harvard University Press.

Hindman, Douglas. 2004. "Media System Dependency and Public Support for the Press and President." *Mass Communication & Society* 7 (1): 29–42. https://doi .org/10.1207/s15327825mcs0701_3.

Ince, Jelani, Fabio Rojas, and Clayton Davis. 2017. "The Social Media Response to Black Lives Matter: How Twitter Users Interact with Black Lives Matter through Hashtag Use." *Ethnic and Racial Studies* 40 (11): 1814–1830. https://doi.org/10 .1080/01419870.2017.1334931.

Jacobs, Elizabeth, Italia Rolle, Carol Ferrans, Eric Whitaker, and Richard Warnecke. 2006. "Understanding African Americans' Views of the Trustworthiness of Physicians." *Journal of General Internal Medicine* 21: 642–647. https://doi .org/10.1111%2Fj.1525-1497.2006.00485.x.

Juris, Jeffrey. 2016. "Reflections on #Occupy Everywhere: Social Media, Public Space, and Emerging Logics of Aggregation." In *Youth, Space and Time*, edited by Pamela Abbott, Claire Wallace, and Paul Hodkinson, 385–414. Leiden: Brill.

Kim, Yong-Chan, and Sandra Ball-Rokeach. 2006. "Civic Engagement from a Communication Infrastructure Perspective." *Communication Theory* 16 (2): 173–197. https://doi.org/10.1111/j.1468-2885.2006.00267.x.

Kim, Yong-Chan, Joo-Young Jung, Elisia Cohen, and Sandra Ball-Rokeach. 2004. "Internet Connectedness Before and After September 11 2001." *New Media & Society* 6 (5): 611–631. https://doi.org/10.1177/146144804047083.

King Jr, Martin Luther. 2010. *The Trumpet of Conscience*. Boston: Beacon Press.

Leach, Colin Wayne, and Cátia Teixeira. 2021. "Some Psychological Implications of Black Struggle." *Contention* 9 (1): 149–154. https://doi.org/10.3167/cont.2021 .090108.

Lee, Conscious. (n.d.). The Conscious Lee. Accessed October 3, 2021. http://thecon sciouslee.com/.

Lee, George. 2020. *My Granny Would Call This "Dense," What About Yours??*. Instagram Reel, video, July 18, 2020. https://www.instagram.com/reel/CgKFhTCDz wA/?igshid=NmNmNjAwNzg=.

———. 2021. *Exploring Weight and Race Discrimination.* Instagram Reel, video, August 16, 2021. https://www.instagram.com/reel/ChVBuxBDKFT/?igshid=Nm NmNjAwNzg=.

Lee, Latoya. 2017. "Black Twitter: A Response to Bias in Mainstream Media." *Social Sciences* 6 (1): 26. https://doi.org/10.3390/socsci6010026.

Lu, Jia, and Steele, Catherine. 2019. "'Joy is Resistance': Resilience and (Re)Invention of Black Oral Culture across Platforms Online." *Information, Communication & Society* 22 (6): 823–837. https://doi.org/10.1080/1369118X.2019.1575449.

Lynn, Nick, and Susan Lea. 2005. "Through the Looking Glass: Considering the Challenges Visual Methodologies Raise for Qualitative Research." *Qualitative Research in Psychology* 2 (3): 213–225. https://doi.org/10.1191/1478088705qp039oa.

Lyons, Renee, Kristin Mickelson, Michael Sullivan, and James Coyne. 1998. "Coping as a Communal Process." *Journal of Social and Personal Relationships* 15 (5): 579–605. https://doi.org/10.1177/0265407598155001.

Maragh-Lloyd, Raven. 2020. "A Digital Post-Racial Parity? Black Women's Everyday Resistance and Rethinking Online Media Culture." *Communication, Culture & Critique* 13 (1): 17–35. https://doi.org/doi.org/10.1093/ccc/tcz046.

Mastro, Dana and David Stamps. 2018. "Race/Ethnicity and Media" In *Mediated Communication*, edited by Philip Napoli, 341–358. Berlin, Boston: De Gruyter Mouton.

McLuhan, Marshall. 1964. *Understanding Media: The Extensions of Man.* New York: New American Library.

Mercier, Caitlin, Dena Abbott, and Michael Ternes. 2022. "Coping Matters: An Examination of Coping among Black Americans During COVID-19." *The Counseling Psychologist* 50 (3): 384–414. https://doi.org/10.1177/00110000211069598.

Mundt, Marcia, Karen Ross and Charla Burnett. 2018. "Scaling Social Movements Through Social Media: The Case of Black Lives Matter." *Social Media + Society* 4 (4): 2056305118807911. https://doi.org/10.1177/2056305118807911.

Negrete, Andrea, and Noelle Hurd. 2021. "System-Justifying Beliefs and Trajectories of Global Self-Worth Among Black and Latinx College Students." *Cultural Diversity and Ethnic Minority Psychology* 27 (2): 227. https://doi.org/10.1037/cdp0000334.

Patterson-Faye, Courtney. 2016. "'I Like the Way You Move': Theorizing Fat, Black and Sexy." *Sexualities* 19 (8): 926–944. https://doi.org/10.1177/1363460716640731.

Pew Research Center. 2021a. "Social Media Fact Sheet." Accessed April 7, 2021. https://www.pewresearch.org/internet/fact-sheet/social-media/?menuItem=2fc5fff9-9899-4317-b786-9e0b60934bcf.

Pew Research Center. 2021b. "Mobile Fact Sheet." Accessed April 7, 2021. https://www.pewresearch.org/internet/fact-sheet/mobile/.

Ramasubramanian, Srividya, Asha Winfield, and Emily Riewestahl. 2020. "Positive Stereotypes and Counter-Stereotypes: Examining Their Effects on Prejudice Reduction and Favorable Intergroup Relations." *In Media Stereotypes: From Ageism to Xenophobia,* edited by A. C. Billings and S. Parrot, 257–276. Bern: Peter Lang.

Richardson, Brian, and Laura Maninger. 2016. "'We Were All in the Same Boat': An Exploratory Study of Communal Coping in Disaster Recovery." *Southern Communication Journal* 81 (2): 107–122. https://psycnet.apa.org/doi/10.1080/1041794X.2015.1111407.

Riles, Julius Matthew, Srividya Ramasubramanian, and Elizabeth Behm-Morawitz. 2022. "Theory Development and Evaluation Within a Critical Media Effects Framework." *Journal of Media Psychology* 34 (2): 1–12. https://psycnet.apa.org/doi/10.1027/1864-1105/a000339.

Salter, Phia, and Glenn Adams. 2013. "Toward a Critical Race Psychology." *Social and Personality Psychology Compass* 7 (11): 781–793. https://doi.org/10.1111/spc3.12068.

Sobande, Francesca, Anne Fearfull, and Douglas Brownlie. 2020. "Resisting Media Marginalisation: Black Women's Digital Content and Collectivity." *Consumption Markets & Culture* 23 (5): 413–428. https://doi.org/10.1080/10253866.2019.1571491.

Stamps, David. 2022. "Black Audiences' Identity-Focused Social Media Use, Group Vitality, and Consideration of Collective Action." *Journalism and Mass Communication Quarterly* 99 (3): 660–675. https://doi.org/10.1177/107769902211041.

———. 2023. "The Nexus Between Black Media Consumers' Racial Identity, Critical and Digital Media Literacy Skills, and Psychological Well-being." *Information, Communication, and Society*. https://doi.org/10.1080/1369118X.2023.2174789.

Stamps, David, Lyric Mandell, and Renee Lucas. 2021. "Relational Maintenance, Collectivism, and Coping Strategies Among Black Populations During COVID-19." *Journal of Social and Personal Relationships* 38 (8): 2376–2396. https://doi.org/10.1177/02654075211025093.

Steele, Catherine. 2018. "Black Bloggers and Their Varied Publics: The Everyday Politics of Black Discourse Online." *Television & New Media* 19 (2): 112–127. https://doi.org/10.1177/1527476417709535.

Stevenson, Clifford, Juliet Wakefield, Isabelle Felsner, John Drury, and Sebastiano Costa. 2021. "Collectively Coping with Coronavirus: Local Community Identification Predicts Giving Support and Lockdown Adherence During the COVID-19 Pandemic." *British Journal of Social Psychology* 60 (4): 1403–1418. https://doi.org/10.1111/bjso.12457.

Subbaraman, Nidhi. 2020. "How #BlackInTheIvory Put a Spotlight on Racism in Academia." *Nature* 582 (7812): 327–328. https://doi.org/10.1038/d41586-020-01741-7.

Sullivan, Jas, and Gheni Platenburg. 2017. "From Blackish to Blackness: An Analysis of Black Information Sources' Influence on Black Identity Development." *Journal of Black Studies* 48 (3): 215–234. DOI:10.1177/0021934716685845.

Tai, Zixue, and Tao Sun. 2007. "Media Dependencies in a Changing Media Environment: The Case of the 2003 SARS Epidemic in China." *New Media & Society* 9 (6): 987–1009. https://doi.org/10.1177/1461444807082691.

Tajfel, Henri, John Turner, William Austin, and Stephen Worchel. 1979. "An Integrative Theory of Intergroup Conflict." *Organizational Identity: A Reader* 56 (6): 978020350598416.

Tatum, Beverly. 2017. *Why Are All the Black Kids Sitting Together in the Cafeteria? And Other Conversations about Race.* New York: Hachette Books.

Terhune, Carol. 2008. "Coping in Isolation: The Experiences of Black Women in White Communities." *Journal of Black Studies* 38 (4): 547–564. https://doi .org/10.1177/0021934706288144.

Tynes, Brendesha, Adriana Umana-Taylor, Chad Rose, Johnny Lin, and Carolyn Anderson. 2012. "Online Racial Discrimination and the Protective Function of Ethnic Identity and Self-Esteem for African American Adolescents." *Developmental Psychology* 48 (2): 343–55. https://doi.org/10.1037/a0027032.

Tynes, Brendesha, and Monique Ward. 2009. "The Role of Media Use and Portrayals in African Americans' Psychosocial Development." In *Handbook of African American Psychology*, edited by Helen Neville, Brandesha Tynes, and Shawn Utsey, 143–158. Thousand Oaks: Sage.

United States Commission on Civil Rights. 2018. *Broken Promises: Continuing Federal Funding Shortfall for Native Americans: Briefing Before the United States Commission on Civil Rights.* Washington, DC: United States Commission on Civil Rights.

Vanee, Lynae. (n.d.). Lynae Vanee. Accessed June 25, 2022. https://www.lynaevanee .com/.

———. 2020. *A Brief Overview on Reparations . . . Cut the Check . . . Period.* Instagram Reel, video, February 26, 2020. https://www.instagram.com/tv/CLxBizHh QjE/?igshid=NmNmNjAwNzg=.

———. 2021. *Parking Lot Pimpin On the One Year Anniversary of the Capitol Insurrection.* Instagram Reel, video, January 6, 2021. https://www.instagram.com/tv /CYcVGHTj4uH/?igshid=NmNmNjAwNzg=.

Williams, Sherri. 2016. "#SayHerName: Using Digital Activism to Document Violence against Black Women." *Feminist Media Studies* 16 (5): 922–925.

Chapter Six

From Protests to Pride and Back Again

New York Pride's Origins and the Modern BIPOC Queer Movement to Reclaim It

Moussa Hassoun

For tens of millions of people in the United States and around the world, a Pride parade represents an opportunity to celebrate and affirm the visibility of lesbian, gay, bisexual, transgender, and Queer people (collectively referred to in this chapter as "Queer" people) and their diverse and unique identities from sexual orientation to gender expression. In much of the United States, Pride parades have achieved mainstream popular acceptance and attract significant government and corporate sponsorships.

The mainstream appeal of Pride parades in much of the United States is a significant departure from the origins of the parades: the Christopher Street Liberation Day March in New York City. In 1970, Queer activists organized the march at the one-year anniversary of a violent uprising by Queer people against police brutality and persecution at the Stonewall Inn in New York City. But after years of activism, marches aimed at equality and reforms gave way to Pride parades driven by respectability politics, white policy priorities, and celebration.

To many, including Queer Black, Indigenous, and people of color ("BI-POC"), modern Queer advocacy organizations and Pride organizers have focused on the priorities of white Queer people at the cost of the most marginalized members of society. This chapter seeks to: (1) review the origins of New York City Pride throughout the 1970s and the chasm between White and Queer BIPOC activists' priorities, (2) compare the 1970s chasm to the contemporary policy priorities of Queer advocacy organizations and NYC Pride organizers, and (3) describe the modern organizing of BIPOC activists to redefine the modern Queer rights movement's priorities, in part galvanized by the rise of the Black Lives Matter movement.

THE STONEWALL UPRISING

On June 28, 1969, the New York City Police Department ("NYPD") raided the Stonewall Inn ("Stonewall) in what would become the most well-known violent uprising in response to police brutality against Queer people in modern US history. Raids against Queer bars were commonplace in New York City throughout the 1960s. Raids were often conducted against bars who did not have a license to serve liquor (American Experience 2019). In New York state, the state liquor license agency had broad authority in granting or denying liquor licenses for businesses that risked becoming "disorderly." Stonewall, a gay bar created by a New York crime family, not only served alcohol to Queer people but also allowed them to dance together; as a result, it did not carry a liquor license.

During the raid, patrons refused to comply with police efforts to enforce the state's gender-appropriate clothing requirements. Like many states at the time, New York had no express statute prohibiting cross-dressing, but the police used unrelated laws to enforce their views on gender-appropriate dress which were known as "masquerade laws" (Ryan 2019). One of New York's oldest law dating back to 1845 prohibited "face painted, discolored, covered, or concealed, or otherwise disguised . . . (while) in a road or public highway." Originally intended to prohibit farmers from dressing up as Native Americans to attack tax collectors, police interpreted masquerading and various morality laws broadly and used them to harass and abuse Queer people. To Queer people, police discretion became known as the "Three Article Rule," whereby a person could be arrested for wearing three or fewer articles of clothing matching their supposed gender (Lucero 2019).

At Stonewall, patrons refused police demands to identify themselves or go to the bathroom to expose their genitalia to confirm their sex (Carter 2004). The brazen harassment by police, long an issue before the Stonewall raid, had simmered to a spontaneous breaking point. As the police moved Stonewall employees and patrons into police vehicles, Stormé DeLarverie, a biracial butch patron, resisted arrest. DeLarverie escaped multiple times as a large crowd of Queer people looked on outside Stonewall. Police struck DeLarverie against her head causing her to bleed. In the scuffle she yelled "Why don't you guys do something?" to the onlookers (152). After being placed inside the police vehicle, the crowd exploded in rebellion against the NYPD's harassment and brutality. Zazu Nova, a Black trans sex worker reportedly threw the first brick at police in response to Delaverie's call for action and witnesses recalled seeing her fighting with police officers throughout the night.

Over the course of the next 45 minutes hundreds of Queer people, including Black and Latina Queer activists, fought police, resisted and escaped arrest, and threw bricks, bottles, and pennies at officers outside on Christopher Street (Carter 2004). The crowd sang "We Shall Overcome" and called out for "Gay Power." The crowd was composed of gay men, lesbians, gender non-conforming people such as trans people and drag queens, and the local homeless Queer people who stayed in the park across the street. One night's clashes turned into six as protesters and police traded volleys at each other night after night. Marsha P. Johnson, a Black self-identified drag queen and activist, was a fixture in the Queer New York City scene by the time she got involved with the Stonewall Uprising. During the first two nights, witnesses reported Johnson threw objects at police officers and climbed a lamppost where a brick she threw shattered a police car's windshield.[2]

The events of those nights are most commonly described as the "Stonewall Riots," however the resistance of Queer people on Christopher Street in 1970 is better understood as the "Stonewall Uprising." One witness described the events this way: "The word is out. Christopher Street shall be liberated. The fags have had it with oppression." Stormé DeLarverie described the events that night as "a rebellion, it was an uprising, it was a civil rights disobedi-ence—it wasn't no damn riot" (Chu 2022). Michael Fader, a Stonewall Inn patron, described the events in those days in the following way:

> "It was the police who were doing most of the destruction. We were really trying to get back in and break free. And we felt that we had freedom at last, or freedom to at least show that we demanded freedom. We weren't going to be walking meekly in the night and letting them shove us around—it's like standing your ground for the first time and in a really strong way and that's what caught the police by surprise. There was something in the air, freedom a long time overdue and we're going to fight for it. It took different forms, but the bottom line was, we weren't going to go away. And we didn't." (Carter 2004, 160)

Although there was no organization or preconceived protest when the NYPD raided Stonewall, Queer people's spontaneous anger triggered a col-lective rage that culminated in civil disobedience with NYPD directives. This civil disobedience reflected both the anti-establishment and anti-police brutality sentiment throughout the Queer community in New York City and the Black civil rights movement in 1969.

One year after the Stonewall Riots, on June 28th, 1970, activists organized the Christopher Street Liberation March, a protest march from Stonewall to Central Park to speak out against the unequal treatment of Queer people at the hands of the police and local, state, and federal governments (Carter 2004). To the surprise of activists, the march proceeded without interruption by the police and ended in Central Park with a "Gay Be In" to display their Queerness proudly.

POST-STONEWALL INTERSECTIONAL QUEER ACTIVISM

Shortly after the Stonewall Uprising, Queer activists formed a number of organizations to channel collective frustration into advocacy and activism. The Gay Liberation Front ("GLF") was created by activists who were frustrated by the reform-minded approach of older activists (Branson n.d.). Zazu Nova and Marsha P. Johnson were some of the original members. The GLF rejected traditional organizational structure for a consensus-driven open forum approach. Through consensus with all its members, GLF took on a whole host of issues including anti-war activism against the Vietnam War, support for the demands of the Black Panthers regarding racism, and women's rights advocacy.

The GLF believed in a left wing anti-capitalist ideology and spoke out against the "capitalist conspiracy" that was responsible for the collective oppression of Queer and non-Queer people alike.[3] The GLF described itself in the following way:

> "GLF differs from other gay groups because we realize that homosexual oppression is part of all oppression. The current system denies us our basic humanity in much the same way as it is denied to blacks, women and other oppressed minorities, and the grounds are just as irrational. Therefore, our liberation is tied to the liberation of all peoples." (Branson n.d., 3)

Ultimately, the GLF's decentralized and consensus driven structure led to its demise two years after its founding (Branson n.d.). However, many of its members carried out its radical intersectional advocacy through separate organizations.

Marsha P. Johnson co-founded the Street Transvestite Action Revolutionaries ("STAR") with her close friend, activist, and fellow drag queen, Sylvia Rivera (Cohen 2007). Rivera, born to Puerto Rican and Venezuelan parents, came up with the idea for the organization during a sit-in protest against discrimination by NYU (Cohen 2007, 80–163). Other Black Queer activists joined, including Zazu Nova. Over several years, STAR provided housing for homeless queer youth and advocated for "gay power," respect for "transvestites," and Queer freedom. At the time, Rivera said "STAR was for the street gay people, the street homeless people and anybody that needed help at that time. Marsha and I had always sneaked people into our hotel rooms. Marsha and I decided to get a building. We were trying to get away from the Mafia's control at the bars" (Feinberg 2006).

STAR released a manifesto describing their worldview including condemnation of racism, police harassment, and a lack of protection for gender nonconforming people in prison, among a slew of other issues (Zagria 2017).[4]

STAR demanded free social services, healthcare, and education and, like the GLF, linked individual freedom to collective freedom for all people. Their focus on a range of issues, and most prominently, on homeless Queer youth, set STAR apart in those early days, largely inspired by the experiences of its founders. Both Johnson and Rivera lived without shelter for significant portions of their lives and their efforts primarily benefited Queer BIPOC people. Johnson and Rivera organized fundraisers to fund STAR efforts but primarily raised money through their sex work (Feinberg 2006). Both had been sex workers through their adult lives; in Rivera's case that work had begun when she was not yet eleven years old.

POST-STONEWALL ACTIVISM CHASM

The broad intersectional advocacy of these organizations, including GLF in particular, divided activists (Marotta 1981). What was the appropriate approach to organize the movement for Queer equality? Who should be included and what issues should be prioritized? These questions led to a remarkable split in the GLF just six months after the Stonewall Uprising. Members of the GLF who believed that gay and lesbian advocacy organizations should only focus on gay and lesbian rights and equality left to form the Gay Activists Alliance ("GAA"). These activists, who were all white, considered themselves politically neutral and sought change within existing political, legal, and business structures. Their organization would not organize in support of racial equality, against police brutality not aimed at gay and lesbian people, or against the Vietnam War. They were not interested in revolution. According to the GAA's constitution, it was a single-issue organization that eschewed "all ideologies, whether political or social" and demanded dignity and freedom for gay people" (Gay Activist Alliance 1969). The GAA pursued these goals through public embarrassment of public office holders and acts of civil disobedience aimed at getting favorable media attention for the cause of gay and lesbian equality (Marotta, 1981).

The departure of dissatisfied members of the GLF to form the GAA reflected a broader debate among Queer people about how to achieve their desired results and to whose benefit (Marotta 1981). Sylvia Rivera, Marsha P. Johnson, and Zazu Nova believed in the liberation of all people with a particular emphasis on gender nonconforming BIPOC Queer people and homeless Queer youth. The GAA was focused on outlawing gay and lesbian job discrimination, resisting police oppression against gay and lesbian people, and creating social events in which gay and lesbian people could act freely without prejudice, such as dances. To activists in the GAA leadership, police oppression was an issue because they were subjected to it due to their sexuality; they had not experienced a lifetime of police abuse and criminality in the same way as so many BIPOC Queer activists.

Over time, the GAA was successful in its efforts to convince the gay and lesbian community in and around New York City to adopt an assimilationist approach intended to convince the rest of the country that gay and lesbian people were normal and just like straight people (Marcus 2002). This approach spread across the country and became the primary tactic used by White-led Queer advocacy organizations to achieve gay and lesbian equality from the 1970s until today. It was reflected on by Randy Wicker, one of the most active organizers in New York City's gay and lesbian scene in an interview with Eric Marcus in 1989:

> I had spent ten years of my life going around telling people homosexuals looked just like everybody else. We didn't all wear makeup and wear dresses and have falsetto voices and molest kids and were Communists and all this. . . . I mean, the last thing to me that I thought at the time we're setting back the gay liberation movement twenty years, because I mean all these TV shows and all this work that we had done to try to establish legitimacy of the gay movement that we were nice middle-class people like everybody else and, you know, adjusted and all that. And suddenly there was all this, what I considered, riffraff. (Marcus 2018)

As a result of this sentiment, the activism and demands of Johnson, Rivera, Nova and other Queer BIPOC people[5] were ignored. The sidelining of their demands occurred just a few years after the Stonewall Uprising. White gay and lesbian middle-class organizers viewed the demands of BIPOC trans and gender non-conforming people as distractions to their cause. The concerns which most animated Black Queer advocates such as racism, homelessness, and criminality of sex work were passed over for more respectable causes such as job discrimination.

In fairness, the demands and activist strategies of the GAA were distinct and much more controversial than the methods that preceded the Stonewall Uprising. Protests for gay equality, such as the Annual Reminder organized since the 1960s in Philadelphia by the Mattachine Society, were typically quiet stand-ins with no displays of homosexuality or gender non-conformity (Marcus 2002). Post-Stonewall, GAA protests included marches, loud chants and even organized public displays of affection among gay and lesbian people, such as the Gay Be-In in Central Park at the end of the first Christopher Street Liberation Day March. Further, the GAA's demands for an end to job discrimination and police abuse toward gay and lesbians were much needed at the time and not popular among the general New York City or United States populations. Despite the GAA's forward-looking demands, they represented a strategic and intentional disregard for the plight of Queer BIPOC people who had long been subject to police brutality, homelessness, and other forms of discrimination. GAA activists were simply not interested in the concerns of BIPOC people beyond their sexuality.

This sidelining led to confrontations between Queer BIPOC activists (most prominently Rivera) and White activists. During the 1973 Christopher Street Liberation Day Parade, STAR members (typically BIPOC gender nonconforming Queer people) were asked to march at the end of the parade (LoveTapes Collective 2019). In response, Rivera interrupted a speech being given by a lesbian activist at Washington Square Park and called out the gay and lesbian assimilationist approach, including their ignorance of issues affecting incarcerated and homeless Queer people. She called attention to her contributions to the gay rights movement by saying: "I have been beaten, I have had my nose broken, I have been thrown in jail, I have lost my job for gay liberation. And you all treat me this way!" Finally, she called out White gay and lesbian activism for not focusing on solutions for Queer BIPOC people saying: "The (activists working in STAR) are trying to do something for all of us and not men and women who belong to a white middle class white club. And that's what you all belong to."

Rivera's public scolding of the movement has also been recognized by academics who agree with her observations. In a 2006 article in the *American Sociological Review*, scholars Elizabeth Armstrong and Suzanne Crage conclude: "As the movement took shape, it centered the experience of middle-class white gay men and marginalized the concerns of less privileged individuals" (744).

Furthermore, Zazu, Rivera, and Johnson's work was sidelined by White gay and lesbian advocates not only because of the priorities for which they advocated but due to their complex histories and personalities (Carter 2002). All three were cross dressing drag queens or trans women who had worked as sex workers for years. All had served time in prison, and Johnson and Rivera struggled with severe mental health issues and substance abuse. Their lives on and off the streets made them unpalatable for gay and lesbian campaigns aimed at convincing the populace at large that gay and lesbian people deserved dignity and respect before the law. In a remarkable case of white-washing the Stonewall Uprising, Johnson's lived experience and struggles were so unvalued that some witnesses refused to include Johnson in their telling of the Stonewall Uprisings out of fear that her mental state and drag presentation "could have been used effectively by the movement's opponents" (Carter 2002, 298).

MAINSTREAM QUEER MOVEMENT
AND ITS FOCUS ON WHITE PRIORITIES

The Language Shift from Gay Power to Gay Pride

The Christopher Street Liberation Day march has transformed into major "Pride" parades that attract millions of people in New York City and parades throughout the United States and around the world. Corporations, government officials, and police have participated in Pride marches and events, transforming the once revolutionary anti-police brutality Queer movement into a pageantry of excess with a focus on feel-good pride.

The shift in purpose and language surrounding the Christopher Street Liberation Day march has been noted by academics. During the Stonewall Uprising and in protests after it, protesters typically shouted "Gay Power" chants. These chants were akin to the "Black Power" chants heard throughout the 1960s (Armstrong and Crage 2006, 736). Sylvia Rivera's now-famous speech at the 1973 Christopher Street Liberation march focusing on the concerns of the marginalized included her leading the crowd in a chant for "Gay Power" (LoveTapesCollective 2019). Media coverage of Queer marches and protests chanting "Gay Power," often protected by police officers after organizers applied for local government permits, created an important record of the movement's legitimacy. Academics note that this approach "borrowed liberally from the civil rights, black power, women's, and New Left movements" (Armstrong and Crage 2006, 736). However, as the movement continued to build on its progress, "Gay Power" made way for "Gay Pride," likely as a result of the assimilationist movement, moderating White gay male activist leadership, and the dissolution of the more radical Queer organizations.

Progress for White Gay and Lesbian People

The priorities of assimilationist White middle class gay and lesbian activists of the 1970s continued to dominate national and regional activists' campaigns in the United States. Although Queer BIPOC activists continued to organize in the coming decades, with a focus on their communities and priorities, they failed to gain state-level or national attention comparable to White gay and lesbian organizations. For example, during the AIDS epidemic starting in the 1980s, White gay men founded AIDS activist organizations such as Gay Men's Health Crisis and ACTUP, the latter of which was 80 percent white in its New York chapter. However, white-led organizations were also ill equipped, and rarely tried, to reach out to BIPOC Queer people who were greatly affected by the same disease (Royles 2017). When white-led organizations eventually rolled out outreach programs targeted toward BIPOC people, they were rarely organizational priorities and, in some cases, inspired opposition by White gay men. By example, in response to BIPOC demands that Philadelphia AIDS Task Force provide greater resources for outreach to the Black community, "one volunteer wrote in an angry letter to the *Philadelphia Gay News,* 'When was the last time that half of the monies and efforts by any Black organization were used to further the health and welfare of Whites?'" (Whiting 1986, 9).

BIPOC Queer organizations however persisted. Organizations such as Salsa Soul Sisters, (the first Black lesbian organization and currently known as African Ancestral Lesbians United for Societal Change), "Black and White Gay Men Together (BWGMT), the National Coalition of Black Lesbians and Gays, Dykes Against Racism Everywhere (DARE), and Combahee River Collective" (Taylor, 2014) (a Black lesbian and feminist group) all formed by 1980 and tackled race issues. BWGMT held workshops to train attendees on fighting racism (D'Emilio 2017). DARE and the New York chapter of BWGMT organized anti-police protests in response to police raids in the early 1980s, including the infamous Blues raid (Lewis 2010). The Combahee River Collective were thought leaders in organizing Queer Black feminists and advanced Black feminist ideas, projects and issues (The Combahee River Collective 2019). These and other groups also carried out protests but did not receive the same attention as did White gay and lesbian organizations.

Fast forward over fifty years from the Stonewall Uprising, gay and lesbian people in the U.S. have made significant progress in their fight for equality and dignity. Marriage equality, a goal of gay and lesbian activists, scholars, and writers, became legal in all fifty states in 2015 after a favorable U.S. Supreme Court decision in *Obergefell vs. Hodges* struck down state laws denying such marriages (Chappell 2015). Further, about thirty states include laws prohibiting discrimination for housing or public accommodations based on sexual orientation (Movement Advancement Project 2023). In addition, the US Supreme Court ruled that an existing federal anti-discrimination statute protected people from discrimination based on sexual orientation and gender identity (Legault et al. 2020).

United States popular opinion has also moved in favor of gay and lesbian people over the years. Approval of marriage between same sex couples has increased steadily. A 2021 Gallup poll showed 70 percent of US adults support same sex marriage; in 1996, the first year the poll was taken, only 27 percent supported legal recognition of such unions (McCarthy 2021). Similar polling by Gallup has shown that in 2021, 71 percent of US adults believed that same sex relationships were morally acceptable, compared to 45 percent in 2001 (Gallup 2023).

Corporations Buy Pride and Pride Reflects Their Priorities

As the priorities of White middle class gay and lesbian activists defined the national progress made for Queer people to the present, corporations began to sponsor Pride events. Starting in the 1990s, NYC Pride found their first corporate sponsors and the number has increased significantly since. In 2017, NYC Pride had sixty-one corporate sponsors and thirty-one media sponsors (Passy 2017). This type of sponsorship has become so prominent in current Pride parades and events that it has been described as "rainbow capitalism." Rainbow capitalism refers to the shallow attempt by corporations to leverage public support for Queer people and their human rights causes into positive media coverage and brand loyalty through their sales of Queer -themed merchandise or sponsorship of Queer events such as parades. Mark Ng, an LGBT segment manager at Wells Fargo, shared that the company's sponsorship of Pride events "most certainly" drew customers (Kurtzleben 2012). Pride organizers such as Amy Drayer, who works for GLBT Community Center of Colorado, the producer of Denver PrideFest, have indicated that companies expect a return on investment when they sponsor Pride events: "Nobody sinks multiple thousands of dollars into a festival on an investment without an expectation on return" (Kurtzleben 2012).

This temporary annual investment typically occurs in the month of June and is rarely seen at any other time of year. In recent years however, these sponsorships have come under increasing fire (Abad-Santos 2018). While corporations seek to portray support for Queer people and their causes, they continue to support elected representatives who push anti-Queer legislation. Data For Progress, a think tank and advocacy group, analyzed the political contributions of some of the largest sponsors of Pride events in the United States It found that Pride sponsors such as Toyota, Comcast, Amazon, and General Motors were among 30 Pride sponsors that donated about $1.6 million to anti-Queer elected representatives (Data For Progress 2022). A 2021 investigation by other another publication, *Popular Information*, found that twenty-five corporations, including CVS Health, Verizon, and Walmart, who engage in Queer-friendly marketing campaigns during Pride month have donated as much as $10 millions since 2019 to Congressional representatives with a poor record on Queer human rights issues (Legum and Zekeria 2021).

Importantly, corporations have rarely aligned themselves with the causes championed by Queer BIPOC people such as the criminalization of sex work, police brutality against communities of color, mistreatment in the prison system, homelessness, and the need for broad challenge to what activists have long called an unjust capitalist system. To many, corporate involvement in Pride represents a self-serving investment in white-led Pride celebrations with an expected financial return; a far cry from the calls for anti-capitalist revolution by BIPOC Stonewall Uprising activists.

PRIDE AND POLICE

Like corporate partnerships, White-led Pride parade and event organizers have sought permits from local governments authorizing their parades or events, often to comply with local laws (NYPD, n. d.). They also often request local police escorts to be present at the celebrations. The inclusion of police in modern Pride events reflects the decision made by White middle class gay and lesbian activists to pursue an assimilationist approach in the 1970s and 1980s. Unlike BIPOC Queer people, white middle class people today do not view the police as a force that might threaten their safety. In addition, Queer people who are undocumented immigrants don't trust police and are not willing to risk arrest and deportation if questioned on their immigration status. As a result, they avoid police interactions in most cases. Finally, Queer sex workers, the formerly incarcerated, and the homeless all have relationships with police that are grounded in trauma, violence, and discomfort. These groups are exactly the populations that BIPOC Queer activists have focused their efforts since the Stonewall Uprising, but who have been largely ignored by White middle class gay and lesbian organizers. As a result, mainstream US Pride events effectively exclude these individuals and create an environment they often feel is unsafe.

BIPOC QUEER ACTIVISTS REDEFINE THE MODERN QUEER RIGHTS MOVEMENT

Black Lives Matter and the Reassessment of White Pride and White-Led Organizations

In 2013, three Black women, Patrisse Cullors, Alicia Garza, and Opal Tometi, created the Black Lives Matter movement in response to the acquittal of George Zimmerman in the shooting and death of Trayvon Martin. Since then, the decentralized movement has organized in response to the unjustified death of Black lives at the hands of state and police actors throughout the country. In particular, the death of George Floyd in 2020 at the hands of police officers galvanized both Black Lives Matter activists and lay people to protest the treatment of Black people. The movement, however, continued to expand its scope to include broader causes such as the systemic oppression of Black people, often called "systemic racism" or "institutional racism" (Harmon et al. 2020).

Garza and Tometi, both Black Queer women, have been outspoken about the need to elevate the concerns of Black Queer people including criminalization of sex work, police abuse, and the increased risk of death suffered by trans women of color (Garza, 2019). Simultaneously, BIPOC Queer advocates have organized for years to force a shift in the focus and priorities of Pride parades and mainstream gay and lesbian advocacy organizations. This struggle harkens back to the activism of Marsha P. Johnson and Sylvia Rivera in the early 1970s against the mainstreaming of white middle class gay and lesbian priorities.

BIPOC Queer activists have demanded White-led gay and lesbian advocacy organizations shift their focus on issues that concern BIPOC communities and a wide range of potential solutions. These demands vary and have included everything from calls for an abolition to police and prisons to specific policing reforms to improve police interactions with BIPOC Queer people. However, two demands stand out among those pushed by BIPOC Queer activists:

1. Focus advocacy and awareness efforts on the distinct challenges and threats trans people of color face, in particular Black trans women; and
2. End police presence at Pride parades and events.

Jonovia Chase, who serves as co-lead organizer of House Lives Matter, a community organization lead by Queer BIPOC people, described the plight of Black trans people: "We are a prime target because of our Blackness, and our intersectionality of being trans adds an extra target on our backs" (Salzman 2020). In fact, in 2019 the American Medical Association has declared the deaths of Black trans women an "epidemic" (Rojas and Swales 2019).

The work of BIPOC Queer advocates have pressured major white-led Queer organizations to develop a renewed focus on the threats and challenges facing BIPOC trans people. In a change from its earlier disavowal of trans people, the Human Rights Campaign, the country's largest advocacy organization for Queer people, has an initiative focused on the rights and freedoms of trans people and regularly recognizes that most victims of anti-trans violence are BIPOC trans people (Human Rights Campaign n.d.). PFLAG, the first and largest organization dedicated to supporting Queer people and their families, has publicly declared a "commitment to inclusion, anti-racism, and ending white supremacy" (PFLAG n. d.). As part of its efforts, it has committed to investing in minority-owned depository institutions, starting Board diversity initiatives, and "Creating intentional partnerships with Black, Indigenous, and People of Color (BIPOC)-led and centered organizations" (PFLAG n. d.).

Pride organizers have also become aware of and responsive to the concerns of BIPOC Queer activists. People of color, Black Queer people, immigrants, and other disenfranchised Queer people have often voiced that they feel unsafe around police officers. This important long-standing criticism of police involvement at Pride parades is finally being recognized and addressed. After organizing its largest Pride parade in history in 2019, Heritage Pride, the Queer organization responsible for New York City's Pride parade and related events, received a slew of calls for change (Leland 2021). Feedback from the BIPOC Queer community called New York City's Pride parade disconnected to the grassroots movement it claimed to represent. Organizations such as the New York City Anti-Violence Project called for Pride to end all relationships with the NYPD and replace them with private security. Other activists, including the Strategic Transgender Alliance for Radical Reform ("STARR"), a group of trans activists inspired by Sylvia Rivera's STAR, called on Heritage of Pride to turn over Pride organizing to people of color.

As a result, in 2021 Heritage of Pride announced that it would bar uniformed police officers from marching in the parade until at least 2025 (Leland 2021). Heritage of Pride's decision stated: "The sense of safety that law enforcement is meant to provide can instead be threatening, and at times dangerous, to those in our community who are most often targeted with excessive force and/or without reason." The organization also committed to increase "community-based" security and distance on-duty officers at least one block away from the parade. While the move was hailed by BIPOC Queer activists, it triggered significant backlash within the organization, the media, and government officials.

Bill DeBlasio, the New York City Mayor when the decision was made, called the decision discriminatory, and the Editorial Board of the *New York Times* described it as a "misstep" by the organization (Editorial Board 2021). Shortly after the announcement, members of Heritage of Pride voted to reverse the Board's decision (Leland 2021). That same night however, the Board met once more to invalidate the membership's vote. The backlash was so intense that one of the organization's co-chairs, Andre Thomas, a Black activist, declared his resignation. However, Thomas later reversed his decision and publicly rededicated himself to helping educate those who disagreed on the causes and impacts of systemic racism. Eric Adams, New York City's second Black Mayor and a former police officer, has denounced the organization's continued exclusion of police officers from the parade (Riley 2022).

Whether these White-led national Queer advocacy organizations and Pride organizers maintain a sustained effort to address the issues facing BIPOC

Queer people remains an open question. Public commitments by such organizations to focus on issues facing BIPOC Queer people are promising. But the political and media pressure, coupled with the corporate investment in modern Pride celebrations, raise concerns about their ability to sustain such efforts.

Alternative Marches and Protests

The effort to focus existing White-led Queer advocacy organizations on BIPOC issues, has not, however, deterred BIPOC Queer activists from organizing on their own terms; much in the same way Johnson and Rivera organized in the 1970s.

In response to a failure by mainstream White-led Queer organizations to advocate for the lives of trans people of color, Queer BIPOC activists organized The Black Trans Lives Matter rally, one of the largest trans rights protests in history, where nearly 15,000 attendees gathered in Brooklyn in June of 2020 (Madani 2020). The protest focused on the severe discrimination faced by Black trans people, including trans women, and the systemic racism to which they are subjected. Organizers neither sought local government permits for the event nor requested police presence.

Activists have also organized Pride protests in an effort to shift attention away from the celebratory Pride parades to the issues facing BIPOC Queer people. The Reclaim Pride Coalition formed in 2018 in response to the corporatization of NYC Pride and its focus on celebration rather than protest (Leland 2021). Starting in 2019, the Coalition marched "in our communities' tradition of resistance against police, state, and societal oppression, a tradition that is epitomized and symbolized by the 1969 Stonewall Rebellion" (Reclaim Pride Coalition n.d.). It explicitly rejects corporate sponsorship of its march and grounds itself in an intersectional Queer history of protest. It specifically cites the work of Black and Latina Queer activists such as Marsha P. Johnson and Sylvia Rivera, and organizations such as the GLF and STAR among many others as inspirations for its work.

Unsurprisingly therefore, the Coalition lists its opposition to all forms of discrimination including racism and xenophobia, among many others (Leland 2021). The breadth of its scope recalls the GLF's ideology to achieve Queer liberation. The Reclaim Pride Coalition calls for an end to "institutional expressions of hate and violence as well as government policies that deny us our rights and our very lives, from the NYPD to ICE, from the prison industrial complex to state repression worldwide" (Reclaim Pride Coalition n.d.).

In 2020, the Reclaim Pride Coalition titled its march "Queer Liberation March for Black Lives and Against Police Brutality" and attracted over 50,000 protesters (Leland 2021). Unsurprisingly, many members of the

Reclaim Pride Coalition marched in many of the Black Lives Matter protests that took place in 2020 in response to George Floyd's death by police. However, the march was interrupted by the NYPD who were trying to arrest a marcher. Police rushed the crowd and pepper sprayed multiple individuals in Central Park. In response to the incident, one of the organizers thanked the NYPD "for continuing to show us why you should be abolished" (Stahl 2020). In 2022, the Coalition declared its Queer Liberation March for Trans and BIPOC Freedom, Reproductive Justice, and Bodily Autonomy in response to the Supreme Court's reversal of long-standing abortion rights (Reclaim Pride Coalition n.d.).

BIPOC Queer Activists continue their efforts to re-align the modern Queer rights movement to issues long highlighted by Queer BIPOC activists since the Stonewall Uprising. In part due to the killing of George Floyd and the rise of the Black Lives Matter Movement, they may yet be more successful than their predecessors.

CONCLUSION

For decades, Queer advocacy and Pride parades have concentrated on the concerns of White middle and upper class gay and lesbian people at the expense of BIPOC, lower income, marginalized individuals. While the Stonewall Uprising was led by BIPOC Queer activists, their causes and concerns were disregarded because they were sex workers, were sentenced to prison throughout their lives, and experienced homelessness, mental institutionalization, and substance abuse. They were deemed distractions to the White Queer cause as were the issues they sought to address: Racist police brutality, inhumane conditions for incarcerated Queer people, and homelessness to name but a few.

White gay and lesbian campaigns and organizations changed public opinion using an assimilationist strategy to convince the US populace that gay and lesbian people are no different than straight people. As a result, popular opinion has swung in support of same sex unions and gay and lesbian people while Pride protests shifted from a focus on "Gay Power" to "Gay Pride." Significant progress has been made in their struggles for marriage equality, job discrimination protection, and freedom to serve in the military. In addition, with a change in popular opinion, corporations have invested heavily in PRIDE parades in a shallow attempt to get a return on investment in niche marketing campaigns while supporting campaigns, candidates, and agendas that ignore the demands of BIPOC Queer activists.

In response to decades of organizing in the shadows of national White-led Queer organizations, BIPOC Queer activists have led a multi-decade fight to

154 Moussa Hassoun

bring attention to issues most affecting their communities. These efforts were turbocharged under a changing political and social environment spurred by the formation of the Black Lives Matter movement. Where those white-led organizations have failed to move swiftly enough, BIPOC Queer activists, and their allies have organized their own alternative organizations to reclaim the spirit of the original Christopher Street Liberation Day march and the Stonewall Uprising.

Their efforts have already influenced White-led Queer organizations to shift resources and priorities to address the epidemic of trans deaths (including BIPOC trans deaths) across the United States and "systemic racism." While there is no guarantee such organizations will maintain those commitments if the political or social winds change yet again, BIPOC Queer activists have seized the shift in society triggered by the Black Lives Matter movement to reinvigorate the spirit of Marsha P. Johnson, Sylvia Rivera, Zazu Nova, Stormé DeLarverie, and so many other Queer BIPOC activists during the Stonewall Uprisings.

NOTES

1. At the time, Nova and other trans people typically identified as "transvestites" although the term has fallen out of favor today.

2. Johnson has also been described as throwing a shot glass on the first night and screaming, "I got my civil rights," although that account is disputed.

3. The GLF also believed that a fundamental shift in Queer culture was required. Members of the GLF wanted to change the way people thought about relationships. They developed "egalitarian," mutual," and non-monogamous relationships within their communes and organization. The GLF's expansive agenda covered many areas, not all of which are relevant to this chapter but are nonetheless noteworthy in their breadth and ambition. Branson, n.d., 1.

4. Notably, the Manifesto included: "An end to exploitation and discrimination against transvestites within the homosexual world."

5. This chapter cannot and does not attempt to chronicle all the efforts by Queer BIPOC activists arising out of the Stonewall Uprising. For example, two other notable activists, Lani Ka'ahumanu and Miss Major Griffin-Gracy, were present during the Stonewall Uprisings and went on to become active in the Bay Area Queer movement.

REFERENCES

Abad-Santos, Alex. 2018. "How LGBTQ Pride Month Became a Branded Holiday." *Vox*, June 25, 2018. https://www.vox.com/2018/6/25/17476850/pride-month-lgbtq-corporate-explained.

American Experience. 2019. "Stonewall Uprising: Why Did the Mafia Own the Bar?" American Experience. *Public Broadcasting Service.* Accessed October 4, 2022. https://www.pbs.org/wgbh/americanexperience/features/stonewall-why-did-mafia -own-bar/.

Armstrong, Elizabeth, and Suzanna Crage. 2006. "Movements and Memory: The Making of the Stonewall Myth." *American Sociological Review* 71 (5): 724–743. https://web.ics.purdue.edu/~hoganr/Soc%20525/Armstrong_and_Crage_2006 _Stonewall.pdf.

Branson, Lindsay. (n.d.). "Gay Liberation in New York City, 1969–1973." *OutHistory.* Accessed December 2, 2022. https://outhistory.org/exhibits/show/gay-libera tion-in-new-york-cit/glf.

Carter, David. 2004. *Stonewall: The Riots That Sparked the Gay Revolution.* New York: St. Martin's Press.

Chappell, Bill. 2015. "Supreme Court Declares Same-Sex Marriage Legal in All 50 States." *NPR,* June 26, 2015. https://www.npr.org/sections/thetwo-way /2015/06/26/417717613/supreme-court-rules-all-states-must-allow-same-sex -marriages.

Chu, Grace. 2022. "From the Archives: An Interview with Lesbian Stonewall Veteran Stormé Delarverie." *AfterEllen.* August 15, 2022. https://afterellen.com/an-inter view-with-lesbian-stonewall-veteran-storm-delarverie/.

Cohen, Stephan. 2007. *Gay Liberation Youth Movement in New York: "An Army of Lovers Cannot Fail."* New York: Routledge.

Combahee River Collective. 2019. "(1977) The Combahee River Collective State-ment." *Black Past,* August 29, 2019. https://www.blackpast.org/african-american -history/combahee-river-collective-statement-1977/.

Data for Progress. 2022. "Accountable Allies: DFP's Corporate Accountability Proj-ect." Accessed November 8, 2022. https://www.dataforprogress.org/accountable -allies.

D'Emilio, John. 2017. "In the Archives: Black and White Men Together." *OutHistory,* May 18, 2017. https://outhistory.org/blog/black-and-white-men-together/.

Editorial Board. 2021. "A Misstep by the Organizers of Pride." *The New York Times,* May 18, 2021. https://www.nytimes.com/2021/05/18/opinion/nyc-pride-police -parade.html.

Feinberg, Leslie. 2006. "Street Transvestite Action Revolutionaries Lavender & Red, Part 73." *Worker's World.* September 24, 2006. https://www.workers.org/2006/us /lavender-red-73/.

Gallup. 2023. "LGBT Rights." *Gallup.com,* February 16, 2023. https://news.gallup .com/poll/1651/gay-lesbian-rights.aspx.

Garza, Alicia. 2019. "What's Happening to Black Trans Women Isn't Just a Moral Issue—It's an Economic Issue, a Political Issue, and a Social and Cultural Issue. I, and We, Are Committed to Standing with Black Trans Women to Build Power and Transform It. Black Trans Women Deserve to LIVE Full Lives." *Twitter,* June 15, 2019. https://twitter.com/aliciagarza/status/1140015686510620674.

Gay Activists Alliance. 1969. "Constitution and Bylaws of the Gay Activists Alliance." New York Gay Activists Alliance. Accessed April 27, 2023. chrome-extension://

efaidnbmnnnibpcajpcglclefindmkaj/https://paganpressbooks.com/jpl/GAACONST
.PDF.

Harmon, Amy, Apoorva Mandavalli, Sapna Maheshwari, and Jodi Kantor. 2020.
"From Cosmetics to NASCAR, Calls for Racial Justice Are Spreading." *The New
York Times*, June 13, 2020. https://www.nytimes.com/2020/06/13/us/george-floyd
-racism-america.html.

Human Rights Campaign. (n.d.). "Fatal Violence against the Transgender and
Gender Non-Conforming Community in 2022." Accessed 2022. https://www.hrc
.org/resources/fatal-violence-against-the-transgender-and-gender-non-conforming
-community-in-2022.

Kurtzleben, Danielle. 2012. "How Corporations Are Profiting from Gay Pride."
U.S. News & World Report, June 11, 2012. https://www.usnews.com/news/ar
ticles/2012/06/11/how-corporations-are-profiting-from-gay-pride.

Legault, Melissa, Daniel Pasternak, Laura Lawless and Lew Clark. 2020. "Landmark
U.S. Supreme Court Ruling Prohibits Sexual Orientation and Gender Identity-
Based Discrimination in Employment (US)." *Employment Law Worldview*,
June 15, 2020. https://www.employmentlawworldview.com/landmark-u-s-supreme
-court-ruling-prohibits-sexual-orientation-and-gender-identity-based-discrimina
tion-in-employment-us/.

Legum, Judd, and Tesnim Zekeria. 2021. "These 25 Rainbow Flag-Waving Corporations Donated More than $10 Million to Anti-Gay Politicians in the Last Two
Years." *Popular Information*, June 14, 2021. https://popular.info/p/corporate-pride
-political-donations.

Leland, John. 2021. "Pride Said Gay Cops Aren't Welcome. Then Came the Backlash." *The New York Times*, May 28, 2021. https://www.nytimes.com/2021/05/28
/nyregion/lgbtq-pride-parade-reclaim-heritage.html.

Lewis, Abram. 2010. "'Within the Ashes of Our Survival' Lesbian and Gay Antiracist
Organizing in New York City, 1980–1984." In *Within the Ashes of Our Survival:
Lesbian and Gay Antiracist Organizing in New York City, 1980–1984*, edited
by Kevin McGruder, 139–160. Berkeley: University of California Press. https://
escholarship.org/uc/item/4zr1v4bq#main.

LoveTapesCollective. 2019. "L020A Sylvia Rivera, 'Y'all Better Quiet Down'
Original Authorized Video, 1973 Gay Pride Rally NYC." YouTube video,
5:28. May 23, 2019. https://www.youtube.com/watch?v=Jb-Jl0WUw1o&ab
_channel=LoveTapesCollective.

Lucero, Louis. 2019. "Memories of That Night at the Stonewall Inn, from Those
Who Were There." *The New York Times*, June 16, 2019. https://www.nytimes
.com/2019/06/16/us/revisiting-stonewall-memories-history.html.

Madani, Doha. 2020. "Rally for Black Trans Lives Draws Enormous Crowd in
Brooklyn." *NBC News*, June 14, 2020. https://www.nbcnews.com/feature/nbc-out
/rally-black-trans-lives-draws-packed-crowd-brooklyn-museum-plaza-n1231040.

Marcus, Eric. 2002. *Making Gay History: The Half-Century Fight for Lesbian and
Gay Equal Rights*. New York: HarperCollins.

————. 2018. ""Marsha P. Johnson and Randy Wicker." *Making Gay History: The Podcast*. Last revised May 2018. https://makinggayhistory.com/podcast/episode-11-johnson-wicker/.

Marotta, Toby. 1981. *The Politics of Homosexuality*. Boston: Houghton Mifflin. https://archive.org/details/politicsofhomose00maro/mode/2up.

McCarthy, Justin. 2021. "Record-High 70% in U.S. Support Same-Sex Marriage." *Gallup.com*, November 20, 2021. https://news.gallup.com/poll/350486/record-high-support-same-sex-marriage.aspx.

Movement Advancement Project. 2023. "Nondiscrimination Laws." Movement Advancement Project. Accessed October 4, 2022. https://www.lgbtmap.org/equality-maps/non_discrimination_laws.

New York Police Department (NYPD). n d. "Parade and Sound Permits, Permits & Licenses." New York Police Department. Accessed April 25, 2023. https://www.nyc.gov/site/nypd/services/law-enforcement/permits-licenses-permits.page.

Passy, Jacob. 2017. "Why LGBT Pride Festivals Have Become Increasingly Corporate." MarketWatch, June 26, 2017. https://www.marketwatch.com/story/why-lgbt-pride-festivals-have-become-increasingly-corporate-2017-06-23.

Parents and Friends of Lesbians and Gays (PFLAG). (n.d.). "Our Commitment to Inclusion, Anti-Racism Work, and Ending White Supremacy." Accessed October 4, 2022. https://web.archive.org/web/20200902220740/https://pflag.org/our-commitment-inclusion-anti-racism-work-and-ending-white-supremacy.

Reclaim Pride Coalition. (n.d.). "Reclaim Pride Coalition ~ NYC." Reclaim Pride Coalition. Accessed April 23, 2023. https://reclaimpridenyc.org/.

Riley, John. 2022. "Mayor Condemns NYC Pride Parade's Ban on Uniformed Police Officers." *MetroWeekly*, May 31, 2022. https://www.metroweekly.com/2022/05/mayor-condemns-nyc-pride-parades-ban-on-uniformed-police-officers/.

Rojas, Rick, and Vanessa Swales. 2019. "18 Transgender Killings This Year Raise Fears of an 'Epidemic.'" *The New York Times*, September 27, 2019. https://www.nytimes.com/2019/09/27/us/transgender-women-deaths.html.

Royles, Dan. 2017. "Race, Homosexuality, and the AIDS Epidemic." *Black Perspectives*, July 6, 2017. Accessed April 26, 2023. https://www.aaihs.org/race-homosexuality-and-the-aids-epidemic/?utm_campaign=buffer&utm_medium=social&utm_source=twitter.com.

Ryan, Hugh. 2019. "When Dressing in Drag Was Labeled a Crime." *History.com*, June 19, 2019. https://www.history.com/news/stonewall-riots-lgbtq-drag-three-article-rule.

Salzman, Sony. 2020. "From the Start, Black Lives Matter Has Been about LGBTQ Lives." ABC News, June 21, 2020. https://abcnews.go.com/US/start-black-lives-matter-lgbtq-lives/story?id=71320450.

Stahl, Aviva. 2020. "Queer Liberation March Draws Massive Crowd: 'No Barricades, No Cops, and Keeping Black Trans People Safe.'" *Gothamist*, June 29, 2020. https://gothamist.com/news/photos-queer-liberation-march-2020.

Taylor, Eleanor. 2014. "What Does the 'Q' Stand For Anyway?: Queerness and Agency Competence." Masters Thesis, Smith College, 2014. https://scholarworks .smith.edu/theses/1762.

The Combahee River Collective. 2019. "(1977) The Combahee River Collective Statement." *Black Past*, August 29, 2019. https://www.blackpast.org/african-amer ican-history/combahee-river-collective-statement-1977/.

The Editorial Board. 2021. "A Misstep by the Organizers of Pride." *The New York Times*, May 18, 2021. https://www.nytimes.com/2021/05/18/opinion/nyc-pride-pol ice-parade.html.

Whiting, Bill. "Divisive Events Hurt Everyone." *Philadelphia Gay News*, October 3–10, 1986.

Zagria. 2017. "Sylvia Rivera Part III: Street Transvestite Action Revolutionaries." *Blogspot*, September 9, 2017. https://zagria.blogspot.com/2017/09/sylvia-rivera -part-iii-street.html#.YxlaLuzMJQI.

Chapter Seven

Challenging "Taken-for-Granted" Assumptions in Academia

Scholarship as Activism

Anne Rawls

Taken-for-granted assumptions about the relative contributions of White and Black[1] Americans and Indigenous peoples to the success of the US and "Western" society more generally, that are false and racist, are damaging the social cohesion of our country and our ability to educate. Assumptions about the *sui generis* character of the Individual and symbolic meaning that are taken-for-granted by many academic disciplines import false "Eurocentric" ideas that damage the academy.[2] In sociology the culprit has been a Eurocentric Individualism that not only stripped the discipline of its founding theories—its reason d'être—but prevented recognition of important revivals of those foundations by twentieth century Black and Jewish scholars (Duck and Rawls 2023). Many have unfortunately been taught a version of social history that not only undervalues the importance of social interaction but encourages the prioritization of policies grounded in Individualism that have never been successful. Challenging taken-for-granted assumptions that privilege myths about the contributions of White Europeans over the social/historical record is both a work of intellectual activism and a work of science. Like the quest for freedom and equality, however, the goal of educating people "to discern facts from fiction" is currently under attack. As Martin Luther King said in 1947 in an article for his school newspaper, "On the Purpose of Education":

> I too often find . . . a misconception of the purpose of education. Most . . . think that education should equip them with the proper instruments of exploitation so that they can forever trample over the masses. . . . We are prone to let our mental life become invaded by legions of half truths, prejudices, and propaganda . . . the classroom . . . and the pulpit in many instances do not give us objective and unbiased truths. To save man from the morass of propaganda. . . . Education

must enable one to sift and weigh evidence, to discern the true from the false, the real from the unreal, and the facts from the fiction.

The assault on the study of Black History, Racialized Slavery, and Critical Race Theory, across the US today—with many states passing laws against teaching these subjects—is a reminder both of how far we have come and how little has changed since 1968, when student protests first called attention to the lack of academic focus on Black Americans across college campuses. Proponents of the current repression claim that Black Studies have nothing to add to the curriculum: That they are mere exercises in "ideology," and/or "identity politics" designed as an assault on "White civilization"—which they claim is the "real" academic subject of merit.

In many respects, current efforts to outlaw teaching these subjects echo responses to the original demands for Black Studies programs in 1968–1971. The assumption then as now being that "legitimate" academic disciplines have nothing to learn from Black Studies; that Black history is not American history; and that established Eurocentric approaches are "factual" while teaching Black and African history is somehow "ideological." To top it all off, now Black Studies are also being called racist, because the history of slavery and racism make White people uncomfortable.

However, there is one big difference this time around. Black and African History and the study of Racialized Slavery and its contribution to the development of Western Society, have become well-entrenched academic subjects at prestigious universities. Scholars inspired by the first push for Black Studies have been documenting in detail the classic arguments about the importance of Racialized Slavery of the famous Black scholars, W. E. B. Du Bois, Eric Williams and Oliver Cromwell Cox. Indeed, Aldon Morris's *The Scholar Denied: W. E. B. Du Bois and the Birth of Modern Sociology* (2015) has received many awards and Morris was elected the 2021 President of the American Sociological Association (see also Bobo 2000; Briggs 2005; Deegan 1988; England and Warner 2013; Gabbidon 2007; Hancock 2005; Hunter 2013a, 2013b; Morris and Ghaziani 2005; Wright 2002a, 2002b, 2002c, 2006; Zuckerman 2004).

Much that was taken-for-granted as factual in 1968 has since been exposed as Eurocentric and ideological. We now know not only that Black history is American history, but that European and US History have vastly undervalued the indebtedness of the "rise of Western society" to the Racialization of Slavery by 16th century colonial European Empires (Allen 1994, 1996; Beckert 2010; Cox 1948; Du Bois 1946; Williams 1944).

When academic subjects do not take Racialized Slavery and the experience of Black and Indigenous people into account, they tell a false story. It was not the hard labor, alleged "superior" reason, or personal sacrifice of White men and women that created the wealth that bankrolled the Industrial Revolution. It was their willingness to steal labor they tortured out of Black and Indigenous people; kidnapped, forcibly enslaved, purchased on credit, and working on stolen land, which created that wealth (Baptist 2014; Beckert 2010; Beckert and Rockman 2016; Du Bois 1946; Jenkins and Leroy 2021; Kiser 2017; Reséndez 2016; Rosenthal 2018; Williams 1944). Eurocentric assumptions, it turns out, are not only one-sided, but also fundamentally incorrect.

Whereas in 1968–1971, the widespread reluctance to accept the "legitimacy" of Black Studies—often even by "sympathetic" academics—was grounded in a general ignorance of the relevance of Race and Racialization and supported by unexamined assumptions about the alleged superiority of European culture and the "objectivity" of existing disciplines, *today many scholars know better*. It took the work of many intellectual activists across many disciplines six decades to get us to this point. In 1968 even "sympathetic" academics were not sure what research might reveal. We now know a great deal about Black, Africana, and Diaspora Studies, and how integral they are to understanding the "rise" of Europe, Britain, and the US (see Beckert 2010; Beckles 2013). We know that Black Americans are poorer than other Americans because their wealth has been repeatedly stolen from them (Madigan 2001), and that government programs, rather than favoring Black Americans, have consistently penalized them (Baradaran 2017; Brown 2021; Flitter 2022; Oliver and Shapiro 2006; Roediger 2007; Slater 2021; Taylor 2019). We also know about mass incarceration and the new Jim Crow (Alexander 2010; Butler 2018; Hinton 2016; Kim, Losen, and Hewitt 2010; Messenger 2021).

Essential classic research by marginalized scholars which had been generally disregarded, has been rediscovered (e.g., W.E.B. Du Bois, Oliver Cromwell Cox, and Eric Williams). Important classic arguments that had been misinterpreted in ways that made them appear to support Eurocentric assumptions about Individualism which they had explicitly criticized are being reexamined. This reappraisal is focusing on Emile Durkheim (Rawls 2019) as well as Erving Goffman, Harold Garfinkel, and Harvey Sacks (Rawls 2022a, 2022b). The task as it turned out, was not only to do new research, but also to recover, reintegrate, and build on the voices of those Black, Jewish and other marginalized scholars who had already given us the benefit of their heightened awareness and been ignored (Duck and Rawls 2023).

Suppressing Black Studies in the US today would require stifling some of the most prestigious scholars at elite universities like Harvard, Princeton, Chicago, Columbia, Yale, UC Santa Barbara, UC Berkeley and Stanford. Black Studies are here to stay and have been joined on college campuses by Women's and Gender Studies, Asian American Studies, Semitic Studies, Chicano/a and Latinx Studies, and Native American Studies as valued interdisciplinary programs that challenge the unexamined assumptions of established disciplines.

Consequently, current efforts at suppression have become overtly political. Informed by the explicit purpose of keeping American citizens ignorant and undermining the Black vote (along with the civil rights of women, LGBTQ+ persons, the young and the marginalized). Such efforts are running up against the well-grounded work of prominent academics who are insisting on the general relevance of Black Studies.

This current era of Black activism and racialized politics marks the first period of general racial awareness since the decade of the Civil Rights Movement—1955–1965—and the initial push for Black Studies it ushered in. After over 60 years of *not noticing*, the public has once again become aware of Race as an issue. But as Carol Anderson (2016) notes, such periods of awareness have appeared before and been wasted. They do not last long. This is a moment for intellectual activism to *eliminate taken-for-granted Eurocentric assumptions* from the academy.

This chapter considers the transition from 1968 to the present, and the role of community activists, student protests, and academics as activists in bringing it about. As I have been one of those intellectual activists, my journey is situated within this history, centering the challenge marginalized scholars brought to taken-for-granted assumptions in sociology.[3] While community activism is essential, without intellectual activists challenging false assumptions embedded in academic disciplines, the position in education today would still be much what it was in 1968, and we would be even more vulnerable to political manipulation.

ACADEMIC SCHOLARSHIP AS ACTIVISM: RECONSTRUCTING DISCIPLINARY PRACTICE

Working to reconstruct a discipline built on Eurocentric assumptions and practices that were originally purposed to support colonization and Racialized Slavery is a work of activism that disciplinary leaders often resist. Nevertheless, the number of scholars successfully doing this work across many disciplines is multiplying.[4] Although US sociology in the 20th century began by embracing taken-for-granted assumptions about Individualism, causality, rationality, determinism, and the importance of durable concepts, that supported the development of heroic narratives of White European male superiority, the discipline was founded in the 19th century by five marginalized scholars whose explicit objective was to contest the mythology of Individualism and its accompanying fallacies. Three of these founders were Jewish:

Emile Durkheim, Karl Marx, and Georg Simmel. The fourth, W.E.B. Du Bois was a Black American, and the fifth, Max Weber, experienced stigma because of his mental illness.

Recovering the foundational arguments that set sociology apart as the study of social fact making and its preconditions requires substantial reconstruction, including a rereading of classic texts to disentangle the original arguments from a century of misinterpretation. Preliminary work toward that end shows that Durkheim's critique of individualism (Rawls 2009, 2019) would eviscerate most current sociology. It also shows that Du Bois was taking a similar position against individualism (Morris 2015, Wright 2002a). A long lineage of research on social fact making in interaction and in ritual and formal organizational settings, running from Durkheim and Du Bois through Talcott Parsons to Harold Garfinkel, Erving Goffman and Harvey Sacks, has begun to achieve recognition. This lineage puts the experience of marginality and research on social facts back at the center of sociology where they belong (Rawls 2019, Rawls and Turowetz 2021, Duck and Rawls 2023).

Durkheim's argument for the social construction of the Individual and "Reason" is of particular importance (Rawls 2009, 2019). But, without discoveries by Garfinkel and Sacks (1970) of the detailed order properties of interaction and its taken-for-granted assumptions, Durkheim's argument that justice—as a guarantee of freedom and equality—is required to successfully use the self-organizing "constitutive" practices of modernity, was misunderstood. Interpreted as an argument about concepts and ideas, rather than about the constitutive practices for making them, Durkheim's position was turned into a circular and conservative functionalism.

In the hands of majority thinkers, the revolutionary ideas of marginalized founders have repeatedly been transposed into their opposites—making them appear compatible with the very same Eurocentric positions these marginalized scholars had contested. The Protestant Ethic and the benefit of hard work and frugality it is alleged to have bequeathed to Western civilization—along with capitalism itself—have in the canonical narrative become quintessential Western accomplishments. The "rational individual" and "free markets" are credited with securing the superiority of what is often called Western Civilization and sometimes even White Civilization.

However, no person who "belonged" to the social order in Europe when capitalism first developed was "free" in the sense we mean it today. Those who did not belong; principally Jews, Arabs, and Roma (Travelers), posed a problem. Guild members (made "free" of society by guild membership, beginning around 1200 CE), who lived in towns and cities (in England designated as "free" towns to make commerce, artisan work, and trade possible) also did not "belong" to the local social order. Such persons lived in enclaves.

Between periods of persecution, they operated without regard to the laws/ customs of the societies by which they were surrounded.

That no one who belonged to the social order of European society was free until much later raises the question where the idea of freedom in Europe came from. The classic answer is that it came from the Protestant Ethic and the European Enlightenment, fueled by science and the emergence of "free" trade in the late 1700s. This idea, in combination with the belief that the rise of capitalism in Europe set people free, grounds a powerful conservative movement.

However, new research building on the classic work of Du Bois, Williams, and Cox confirms that it was Racialized Slavery as it developed in various colonies in the 1600s, not free labor (in Europe, or elsewhere) that generated the capital necessary to kick off the industrial revolution and create a "free" middle class in England, France, and the colonies (Baptist 2014; Beckert 2010; Beckert and Rockman 2016; Jenkins and Leroy 2021; Kiser 2017; Reséndez 2016; Rosenthal 2018). The Enlightenment that followed set free only those we now call White and then only men. For centuries before this, it was principally craft guilds that used the terminology "made free" to denote acceptance into guild membership—and guilds were inventions of the ancient Middle East, not Europe.

The Enlightenment that resulted from Racialized Slavery did not set Africans free, or Jewish, Chinese, Japanese, or Indigenous men. Nor did it set any women free, although the industrial boost did lead to a greater acceptance of women into guilds (particularly the prestigious silversmith guild in the 1600s and 1700s). This origin of the freedom of White middle and working-class men in Racialized Slavery may partially explain the attachment to fantasies of Whiteness among so many White men today.[5]

Disentangling people's fears from the myths and stereotypes that fan those fears, and challenging taken-for-granted assumptions grounded in a colonial history of Racialized Slavery is important work. This work is going on across many disciplines inspired by the classic works of Black and other marginalized scholars—whose efforts were ignored until Black Studies emerged from the student protests of 1968–1971.

THE PROTEST MOVEMENT FOR BLACK STUDIES: 1968–1971

When the Black Student Alliance at Yale convened a symposium on the campus in spring 1968 to debate the issues and demand programs, departments, and courses in Black American and African studies, the general response of the academics with whom they met—although sympathetic enough to show up—was that there might not be enough known about the subject(s) to comprise a "legitimate" academic discipline (Robinson, Foster, and Ogilvie1969; Hall 1999,18).[6] Even Black scholars like Martin Kilson,[7] who was teaching African politics at the time, were unsure whether there was adequate scholarship to populate the needed courses—or even what those courses might be. As Kilson explained to the gathering, each academic is an expert in their own small area, and they were being asked questions about the general curriculum they could not answer. Three years later Kilson was teaching Black Politics based on his essay "Black Politics: A New Power*" in *Dissent* August 1971), which he mentioned at Yale as new research that might result in a course (Robinson, Foster and Ogilvie 1969, 31).[8] Fortunately, a sense of urgency overcame the hesitation.

It was all happening so fast. *The whole world was in crisis in 1968*: the Vietnam War was still raging, President Lyndon B. Johnson had announced that he would not run for a second term as president, student protests and teach-ins on college campuses were ongoing not only in the United States but worldwide, universities in Berlin and Paris were shut down, the seven-week Paris protests stopping the entire French economy in May; a series of assassinations of Black and White leaders, culminating in the death of Martin Luther King that April, shook the world.

Debate at the Yale symposium was reflective of discussions and protests at universities all over the US, standing out from the others mainly because the organizers published a relatively complete account of the event (Robinson et al. 1969). According to Robinson (one of the student organizers), the discussion responded both to a general ignorance of the "Afro-American experience" and an unwillingness to grant the possibility that anything about the Black experience met the "rigorous" standards of the university:

"Our symposium originated as a response to the resistance in educational circles to pressures for Afro-American studies, this resistance, in turn, flows from two major concerns. First, many educators question the moral responsibility involved in complying with public pressures for curriculum reforms; they worry lest they might be deserting their obligation to maintain high standards of excellence in curricular offerings by responding favorably to insistent protest from local groups. Second, many educators seriously question the assertion that the experience of Black people in Africa and the new world is a subject of sufficient amplitude and depth to justify general study and instruction on all educational levels." (Robinson et al.1969, viii)

This hesitancy to accept the "legitimacy" of Black Studies, according to Robinson (and others who participated in such efforts) could be explained in terms of ignorance—but that ignorance had racist origins. Academics did not know much about what Black Studies might discover because the subject had been suppressed. Few who were making the argument for its inclusion in the university curriculum knew enough to make the kind of intellectual argument that established academics were asking for. Many felt the requirement itself was racist. As Robinson put it:

> Undoubtedly much of the hesitancy with which educators have met demands for inclusion of such materials in their curricular offerings arises from a perfectly understandable ignorance of the Afro-American experience. Yet, the rhetoric of almost all such reservations is phrased in intellectual terms—questions about matters of "academic responsibility," and the "intellectual defensibility" of using black issues and themes as a basis for instruction—rather than granting the possibility that there are things worth teaching of which even most academicians may be unaware. (Robinson, Foster, and Ogilvie 1969, viii)

They might have added that the need to earn tenure often kept scholars from pursuing subjects that would not be viewed in a positive light by senior colleagues—another way topics of interest to Black Americans had been suppressed. In contesting these objections, the arguments of the students often became political and personal—backed by a conviction that if universities would only allow the research and teaching to begin, important things would be discovered. As Perry Hall, first Director of the Black Studies Center at Wayne State University, put it, he knew from personal experience that his own Black experience was being misconstrued by the so-called "academic" approach:

> The need for a "relevant" education so insistently demanded by blacks on American campuses then, when our strongest guide was the authority of our own experience, seems even more pressing in retrospect. Before discovering a language to express it, we objected to the bias, the chauvinism, the cultural imperialism inherent in concepts like "cultural deprivation," under which some liberal minds proposed to address the needs of "disadvantaged" blacks. "*I'm* not culturally deprived," I remember amiably telling some whites on my undergraduate campus "*you* are." (Hall 1999, 3)

Perry would have said that with both a smile on his face and the absolute certainty that he was correct. The established academic approach at the time assumed that anything which differed from White middle-class expectations in the United States was deficient. The possibility that an alternative social experience could or should be considered valid—and even important—was unthinkable to most scholars at the time. But Perry and other Black student protesters and activists were just as sure that the established position was racist and that Black Studies research would eventually prove them right—as it has.

The first department to emerge from the student protests in 1968 was headed by Nathan Hale at San Francisco State University, now known as the

Africana Studies Department. By the spring of 1971 (when I entered the picture) "more than 500 programs, departments, and institutes had been founded on four-year college campuses" around the US (Brooks 2006). They included the Institute of African Studies at Columbia University, started in 1971, with Hollis Lynch as its first Director.[9]

Having secured the establishment of programs and departments, researchers began to do the work of discovering the richness of African and Black American history and culture while rediscovering existing scholarship on these issues that had been largely erased. Since 1968, scholarship in Black Studies and reappraisals of the debt that the rise of "western society" owes to Racialized Capitalism have enjoyed something of a renaissance, generating both a wealth of new knowledge and the rediscovery of the classic Black scholarship of W. E. B. Du Bois, Eric Williams, Oliver Cromwell Cox, and C.L.R. James.

After the protests Cedric Robinson (1983), Patricia Hill-Collins (1986, 1990), Aldon Morris (1986), Mansbridge and Morris (2001), Kimberlé Crenshaw et al. (1996), Derek Bell (1987, 1992), Elijah Anderson (1979, 1992) and others kicked off a new generation of scholarship. After an early period during which Black Studies sometimes mirrored the biases of Eurocentrism with counter-biases of its own, scholars began to build solid foundations. Their discoveries now challenge the taken-for-granted Eurocentric assumptions of many disciplines. That academic work done within universities can restructure understanding in ways that support community activism matters. That this new knowledge and the contributions of Black and African Studies to scientific understanding, can also restructure disciplines within universities, also matters.

THE ROLE OF A WHITE SCHOLAR IN BLACK STUDIES

Although I attended protests in response to articles by Arthur Jensen and Richard Herrnstein on Race and IQ at Harvard in fall 1971 (where I was taking night courses), *joining the protest movement was not to be my role*. The meetings coincided with ongoing Black student protests aimed at getting the administration to agree to establish a Black Studies department at Harvard. Like the founding of the BlackLivesMatter movement many decades later, the protests for Black Studies were led by Black students and scholars. I understood this. But I also realized that White scholars would eventually have an important role to play.

The most obvious role would be to support Black colleagues and students who are often misunderstood and marginalized. But there is also a role for scholar activism in challenging disciplines to eliminate taken-for-granted

Eurocentric assumptions. Many such assumptions are involved in the way White society perpetuates racism, and although White academics have paid little attention and have almost no awareness of this problem, a White scholar could have unique access to how this works. They would also have access to how taken-for-granted social processes between White Americans work, as well as to how White people think they work—which is not at all the same thing. Understanding the White side of racism could be an important missing piece of the puzzle.

However, it would first be necessary to stop taking those social processes for granted and develop a heightened awareness of how racism works in interaction, which, inspired by Du Bois, Waverly Duck and I have called "White Double Consciousness" (Rawls and Duck 2020). White and privileged, I would always lack the experience that DuBois called "double consciousness," although I would be shocked into acquiring some "heightened awareness" and "second sight." The years I spent living with Black Americans in parts of the world generally identified as Black spaces gave me very little self-awareness. But I did come to realize my presence was not "helping" anybody but myself, and that I needed to use what I had learned to pay back the community for my education. However, it was the virulent response to my egalitarianism by other White people, some of whom I had known much of my life—not relationships with Black Americans—that finally shocked me into direct action and heightened awareness.

My first experience with this White response came after Richard Herrnstein published an article on IQ and Race in 1971 which reverberated across college campuses and rekindled the debate over Arthur Jensen's article (1969) on the same topic two years earlier. Herrnstein was stirring the pot—in the "best" tradition of academic racism, claiming that he was *merely reporting "the facts"*—and a neighbor of mine was loving it. Confronted with his assertion that Black Americans were genetically inferior, accompanied by his "gift" of Herrnstein's article, I was stunned to realize I did not know how to respond except with anger. I knew he was wrong and that I was on the receiving end of a profoundly racist action. But I didn't have "the facts."

I was not unread in matters of Black American culture and politics. In fact, I had read a great deal from 1968–1971, during which time much new literature was being published. But my knowledge of Black American history was slim, and I did not know anything about studies of Black IQ testing. Were there any studies of Black IQ testing at the time?[10] Why did I not know anything about these things? Why did I not even know that intelligence tests had been invented in the first place to justify the exclusion of Polish and Eastern European immigrants after WWI?

I remember telling the neighbor what he could do with himself (in unprintable terms) and then heading for the local library to check out books on African and Black American history. This was spring 1971 and there were not many, but I read what was in that library and then went to another. Shortly thereafter I discovered I could take courses at Harvard's Extension program, which offers courses taught by Harvard professors to the public at night for low tuition and university credit. This enabled me to study Black Politics with Martin Kilson, African Religions and Philosophy with Ephraim Isaac, and the Development of Language in Early Childhood (with lectures on language development among Black children) with Courtney Cazden.

Most of my students today experience this same wonder that there is so much known about such important things—and yet none of it has been taught to them. They soon realize that their teachers—like me in 1971—did not know much about it either.

TRANSITIONING FROM CHALLENGE TO DISCOVERY

Perry Hall was the first Director of the Black Studies Center at Wayne State University, where I taught from 1989 to 2001. In his book *In the Vineyard: Working in African American Studies* (1999), he gives a personal account of early attempts to get Black Studies programs started, a movement in which he was an active participant. He describes the push-back, as White scholars not only criticized the effort to establish Black and Africana Studies for not being academic in standard disciplinary terms, but also criticized the efforts of Black scholars to position themselves in ways that challenged the Eurocentric assumptions of White scholars and established academic disciplines.

From my own perspective it seemed obvious that the standard academic approaches were getting it wrong—so remaining within their boundaries even in opposition was a problem. Sure, they were Eurocentric—but the problem was much larger than that. It was not just that they were privileging a White Eurocentric perspective. They were privileging a perspective that obscured the way things worked even among White people. In other words, Eurocentrism was not only leaving Black people/society out—it was leaving White people/society out too.

Because of that, it was impossible to explain the basic social processes and relationships that are foundational to sociology. The theories of society were incorrect because the taken-for-granted assumptions they were built on were false, and this, in a rather circular way, perpetuated the false/racist assumptions which had led to the problem in the first place.

When one year after taking courses in Black and African Studies I was admitted to a small teaching college, I remember sitting in classes being struck repeatedly by the many ways in which what I was being taught conflicted with what I had already learned about Black and African History, as well as what I knew about Black Americans and the Black community from living in it. In sociology classes I ran into the same problem at first: assumptions about reified structures and how they constrained the generic individual in ways that reproduced the status quo. Curiously, in spite of the inherent Individualism of the approach *there were no people* in this version of sociology, which focused on ideas, concepts, and structures of various sorts. The introduction of an opposition between agency and structure by Anthony Giddens in 1982 only exacerbated the problem. The person had become an epiphenomenon.

Then I encountered Francis Chaput Waksler (2010), a gifted scholar who was teaching courses on the social Self in the work of Goffman and Garfinkel. Fran, who had studied social interaction at Boston University with George Psathas, taught an interactionism that carried the implication that the shifting social categories of Race and Gender, and the conflicting social expectations of Black and White Americans and competing social classes were being created every day in social interaction—and therefore that studies of interaction were the key to understanding how it was all being done.

Most sociologists were taking interaction for granted and building on unexamined assumptions. By contrast, Goffman (1959, 1963) and Garfinkel (1967) were doing research with the purpose of exposing taken-for-granted social practices and assumptions. This promised to lead to new discoveries challenging taken-for-granted disciplinary thinking. Transferring to Boston University to study with Psathas and Jeff Coulter, the next summer I arrived in time to take a seminar with Garfinkel, and to meet Harvey Sacks and John O'Neal. That was 1975.

THE APPEAL OF THE DISCOVERY ORIENTATION IN SOCIAL INTERACTIONISM

Without realizing it, I had aligned myself with Jewish scholars of social interaction who were often criticized—although I did not then recognize that their being Jewish had anything to do with how and why their arguments were being dismissed.[11] That awareness would come only later (Duck and Rawls 2023). I did realize they were paying a high price for challenging the established theories and methods of sociology and that the attacks were quite vicious and personal. But since challenging taken-for-granted assumptions was my objective, I jumped onboard.

The task as I saw it was to reinterpret the classics and repair the breach developing in the 1970s between established scholars who claimed to be working in "the" classic tradition, and influential younger (mostly Jewish and Black) scholars, who were challenging the Eurocentric position taken by those established scholars. Goffman, Garfinkel and Sacks in particular were developing an alternate lineage that focused on *discovery* to challenge the mainstream position. As early as 1948 Garfinkel had written about the need to study what was happening in social interaction to avoid a taken-for-granted Eurocentrism in Parsons' social theory. He would go on to make the work of exposing the taken-for-granted the foundation of his overall approach (Eisenmann and Rawls 2023).

Because, as I understood it, taken-for-granted assumptions were the heart of the problem, this approach seemed promising. As Gerald A. McWorter (as he was known in 1969, now Abdul Alkalimat) put it at the Yale symposium, taken-for-granted assumptions not only sit at the center of much academic work, but Black (and other marginalized scholars) are expected to adopt the taken-for-granted assumptions of White people as the price of admission to academic legitimacy.

> In the beginning, it is important to understand that as black intellectuals think on these issues more and more, things are becoming very clear. Basically this clarity has to do with a set of assumptions that black people have made for a long period of time. We rationalize our various positions on the basis of these assumptions. I find here that people have different sets of assumptions and are asking black intellectuals rather than to rationalize positions on basic assumptions *black* people hold, you're asking that black people make rationalizations of positions based on the assumptions that *white* people hold . . . debate that white people carry on about "science" and "ideology" is something that we feel, basically, is a closed question. Whatever you do, the *fact* is that this is a racist country and that the scientists who have operated in this country, by and large, have been racists. Intentionally or unintentionally, the fact is that they have functioned as such and so have their theories. (Robinson 1969, 56)

To make progress it would be necessary to closely examine those taken-for-granted assumptions, particularly the ones that arose in service of Racialized Slavery and White Supremacy. Similarly, to achieve an understanding of when, how, and why societies need justice/equality to work well in modernity (Durkheim's 1893 argument), assumptions whose purpose had been to support the inequality of Racialized Slavery would need to be abandoned.

Many people advised me to stop aligning with this line of research—or at least to stop referring to it in print if I continued doing the work. Some very nice people who hoped to hire me said to "at least stop putting the word ethnomethodology on your resume." This is one of the reasons why it takes intellectual scholarship so long to self-correct. I could see there would be a price to pay for writing about Garfinkel and that it was probably not a winning move—at least in the short run. But I did not see much purpose or honor in pretending to embrace ideas that were fundamentally racist and needed to be challenged. An intellectual career is very personal and a great privilege. One needs to find something worth doing and to find others willing to share the labor even if it turns out to be difficult.

Continuing to pursue studies in social interaction and ethnomethodology, I managed to kick up something of a ruckus, until in 1987 William Julius (Bill) Wilson, the famous Black sociologist, and then president of the American Sociological Association, challenged me. If the point of my studying social interaction was in the first place to discover a new approach to Race, racism, and social justice—as I claimed—wasn't it about time to do something about it? I had been following this course for over a decade, earning a PhD and getting published. Bill had tried to get me a job in the sociology department at Chicago while he was chair, although it became clear that my arguments had ruffled the feathers of several prominent members of the department, including James Coleman, who it turned out would be its next chair. While I was disappointed not to get that or any other major job for several years, I took it as a good sign that even unemployed, I had become notorious for challenging taken-for-granted disciplinary assumptions, and a six-part sequence of replies and responses to one of my articles on the importance of Interaction Orders began appearing in *Sociological Theory*. I considered that I was making what John Lewis called "good trouble." My first article on Durkheim in 1996 was similarly controversial and secured another opportunity to publish a reply, this time in the prestigious *American Journal of Sociology* in 1998.

WHITE PEOPLE ARE NOSEY—BLACK PEOPLE ARE RUDE

But, back to Bill Wilson's challenge. How to find the Race in social interaction that I was convinced was there. I wandered around for several years talking about this and pestering friends and colleagues, particularly Black friends and colleagues. Perry Hall, who has featured repeatedly in this narrative, had stepped down from his position as Director of the Black Studies Center at Wayne State University and was now my colleague in the Sociology Department (until 1993 when he left to take up a position in African, African American and Diaspora Studies at the University of North Carolina—Chapel Hill). Perry was one of those to whom I frequently pitched questions about Race in interaction. One afternoon in 1992, I got lucky and his almost inexhaustible tolerance for what I now recognize as my typical and irritating White behavior finally ran out.

Perry and I had gone to the student center for coffee and I was asking more questions. He looked at me in exasperation and said, "You are just like every other White person. You are so nosey." I suppose I should have been chastened by this. But instead, I got excited. Here was something about Race in interaction. I said, "Oh oh! Perry. What does it mean White people are nosey?" He said something like "Oh my god! It means what I said" and got up and we walked back to the department. He went to his office. I went to the main office where there were two Black secretaries and asked them if White people were nosey.

They laughed. Over the following weeks I found that when I asked Black Americans this question they laughed. But when I asked White people, they just got puzzled looks on their faces. This was my first big break and I have Perry to thank for it. It took me many years to follow the thread, but by 2000 I had published my first article (Rawls 2000) laying out how Race manifests in social interaction as tacit taken-for-granted racialized preferences, and how they reflect the orientation of White Americans toward Individualism and Individual competition versus the orientation of Black Americans toward what came out in the Yale symposium as an orientation toward "survival" that tends to be quite democratic in its interactional affordances. The difference traces back to DuBois, who noted the extreme interactional separation between Races in his 1903 *Souls of Black Folk,* and the strong preference among Black Americans for a commitment to "the good of the whole" over the "strong man" Individualism of White Americans in his 1890 Harvard commencement address. It all tied in with the development of "Double Consciousness" among Black Americans and its lack among White people.

As I did this research, Black students were amazed to hear that White people asked each other the series of questions I had identified as a typical White introductory sequence (e.g., exchanging names, then asking: "What do you do? Where do you work/live? Where did you go to school? etc.). They had been sure White people were asking them these questions—often called an "interrogation"—because they were Black. It was inconceivable to them that White people would "subject each other" to questions they found so offensive. It became apparent that things that are "normal" for White people, violate Black American interactional expectations.

White Americans make similar mistakes in interpreting their interactions with Black Americans—often experiencing a lack of questioning and answering by Black Americans as "rude." The heightened awareness of Race and inequality among Black Americans—a double consciousness that comes from experiencing racism that White Americans know little about—plays an important role in shaping these interactional differences. Black Americans have developed social practices that minimize inequality, whereas White American practices maximize inequality. It is ironic that White Americans often experience the reticence of Black people they speak with as rude, when that reticence actually increases equality among speakers and maximizes survival under unfair conditions.

While White people say and do many racist things intentionally, the problem quite often is that racism and segregation have forced Black and White Americans to live in separate worlds for so long that they are strangers to each other and consequently have developed separate and clashing Interaction Orders—conceived as sets of taken-for-granted assumptions that are used to make sense of interaction (Goffman 1983; Rawls 1987, 2000; Rawls and Duck 2020). Consequently, many ordinary things White Americans do and say are strange and offensive to Black Americans. This is in effect *what many of the Black student activists were saying at Yale.*

The *assumption* that Black and White Americans live in the same social world leads to an expectation that Black Americans live according to White expectations. Whereas we expect people from other countries to act differently, and often make allowances for those differences, White Americans expect Black Americans to act like White Americans. When they do not there is a tendency to blame Black Americans for any differences (attributing a deficiency to them).

While White people are often not aware that any of this is going on, Black Americans are typically acutely aware of such differences and find it hard to believe that White people are not aware. Black Americans talk about the need to "code-switch" when interacting with White people. Differences that are ultimately the result of racism and segregation have burrowed so deeply into our tacit taken-for-granted expectations that they can produce racial troubles independently of any intentional racism, a form of taken-for-granted practice that my co-author Waverly Duck and I call *Tacit Racism* (2020).

Although the majority of White people are not aware of most of this, we also know from research in Black Studies and Critical Race Theory that most of the legal and political changes that began in 1968 (the war on drugs, mass incarceration, attempts to end welfare and social security), had the explicit purpose of disenfranchising Black Americans. Research on *The Long Southern Strategy* (Maxwell and Shields 2019), the War on Crime (Hinton 2016) and *The New Jim Crow* (Alexander 2010) have shown this beyond the shadow of a doubt. While most White Americans acting out these policies are still apparently not aware of the racism embedded in them, those in charge of designing the laws and policies have been well aware of what they were doing (Anderson 2016; Bell 1987, 1992).

Black scholars have insisted for over a century that the focus should be on institutional racism and not on individual racists. But a taken-for-granted Eurocentric bias in favor of Individualism led White scholars to reject this plea—and scholarship on institutional racism has mostly come from Black scholars until recently. While they have done impressive work examining the racism that is institutionalized in various important social organizations and institutions, however, a strong bias toward *formal institutions* (the flip side of the Eurocentric emphasis on the Individual) has ironically resulted in a general disregard for aspects of racism that are *institutionalized in social interaction* independently from any formal social institutions.

SOCIAL INTERACTIONISM EXPOSES THE TAKEN-FOR-GRANTED IN SOCIAL LIFE

What initially drew me to the work of Garfinkel and Goffman was that their arguments did not violate my sense of the way the world worked the way other approaches did. I soon realized that this was because they were challenging the assumptions that had seemed wrong by observing interactional processes in detail to discover how things actually work. This paralleled the trend toward careful groundwork that was emerging in Black Studies. The task was to cut beneath the taken-for-granted to an awareness of what is actually going on—how social facts are being made. This it turned out was a way of doing something entirely new. In the end the problematic assumptions are overturned, and what you have in their place are the social processes for making social facts, stripped of the false explanations previously given to them.

The trick is to resist the spaces where the displaced assumptions are asking to be replaced with new assumptions. Garfinkel called this resistance "ethnomethodological indifference." Endlessly misunderstood, it means ignoring the old questions/assumptions and developing new ones based on an understanding of how social interaction works. What needs to be discovered is how people are making meaning and social order together—and what is actually going on turns out *not to fit any of the old assumptions*. It is entirely counter-intuitive. Which is kind of nice.

In trying to discover what was being "taken-for-granted" in ordinary interaction, it turned out that Garfinkel and Goffman had been doing research on something similar to Double Consciousness, and that their preoccupation in 1962–1963 with what they called "passing" involved this question (Rawls 2023). Garfinkel had already focused on aspects of self-presentation and decision-making related to passing in his dissertation (Turowetz and Rawls 2021). The question is what happens when those who are excluded try to pass.

The answer is that such persons develop the heightened awareness needed to pass but not double consciousness.

Garfinkel (1967) built this argument on his study of Agnes (a transwoman) referring to her as a "natural experiment" who could describe her own work of passing. Those like Agnes who pass must acquire heightened awareness, and can even talk about it, which makes them a good source of data. But the act of passing also has negative effects that can result in something like what Frantz Fanon (1952) called "The Colonial Mentality." Because persons who pass must align with those who oppress them (using their awareness to join their oppressors), persons who "pass" *cannot trust their own judgment* and do not develop the group solidarity that characterizes Black American Double Consciousness. They are aware of playing a part and often feel "fake," a situation that, according to Garfinkel, results in an extreme toleration of contradiction. Goffman also described this in his 1963 book *Stigma* (Rawls 2023).

Garfinkel developed exercises to help his students get beyond the taken-for-granted (Eisenmann and Rawls 2023), while also producing research on interactional "doings" that challenged conventional theory and methods. He was not the first to contribute to this new approach, however. A similar focus on actual practices in Durkheim's work had been overlooked (Rawls 1996, 1997, 2009, 2019). Durkheim's foundation for arguing that justice becomes necessary in a diverse and differentiated (modern) society rested on the "constitutive" character of what he called "self-regulating" practices. In modernity, durable objects maintained by cultural consensus would be largely replaced by fragile objects created using "self-regulating" constitutive practices (Rawls 2019, 2021). The argument could be traced forward to some extent into the work of Parsons, to appear again in Garfinkel, Parsons' student (Rawls and Turowetz 2021).

W.E.B. Du Bois, while not usually recognized as an interactionist, also described interactional differences and separations—especially the all-important first moment of experiencing Double-Consciousness. His insights align with Garfinkel's discussion of the "heightened awareness" that came from the constant experience of being othered, which the latter developed in his (1967) discussion of "Agnes" (Duck and Rawls 2023). The practice of ethnomethodology in fact rests on the premise that people take for granted their practices for doing things until they experience trouble. Most majority people do not experience serious trouble often enough to gain the heightened awareness needed to stop taking their practices and commitments to them for granted. Garfinkel understood that if awareness of the taken-for-granted could be raised by making people experience trouble, their practices for making social facts could be revealed and documented.

Starting from either Eurocentric or Afrocentric assumptions results in an endless regress. The solution is to discover how people are making social facts in the first place. If meaning, social objects, and social cohesion are being made right in front of us—by us together with others—endless conceptual regress can be avoided by studying how that work is done. If things are being done differently by place—or by differently identified people—what they are doing differently and how that results in different meanings and expectations can be made evident.

Academic disciplines could then be based on understanding how the social world is being accomplished by people cooperating together, instead of on taken-for-granted assumptions. Young scholars studying processes of "racialization" are often doing just that. Historians working with archival materials are doing it as well. Scholars of communications and media looking at the cooperative uses of new technologies are also exposing the taken-for-granted. The job is to reconstruct a theoretical lineage compatible with these discoveries. It turns out to be a venerable lineage comprised of marginalized scholars for the most part. Clarifying this lineage makes it clear that the research in Race and marginality which majority scholars have located at the margins of sociology belongs at the center of the discipline and always has.

INTERACTION ORDERS AND THE SO-CALLED "CULTURE WARS" DIVIDING THE UNITED STATES

According to this sociological lineage, we should understand current divisions in the United States—popularly referred to as "Culture Wars"—as reflecting a serious failure of our society to change with the times (Rawls 2021). Taken-for-granted assumptions grounded in Individualism have gotten in the way of understanding important classic arguments about the situation we now face. The current state of division in the United States involves two very different ways of making culture—social facts—that Durkheim issued warnings about in his 1983 *Division du Travail Sociale*.

Typically interpreted as if he had made an argument about the industrial division of labor, Durkheim was explaining that the increasing differentiation of social roles throughout society in modernity had changed the prerequisites for social coherence—for making social facts—which he called "the implicit conditions of social contract" and equated with justice. In making this argument Durkheim distinguished between two ways of achieving social coherence. The first, a traditional form, produces durable social facts, clings to the past, resists change, and does not require justice. The second, a modern form that embraces change and diversity, produces fragile social facts that support invention, growth, and new technology, and does require justice.

Not recognizing that society was moving into the modern phase in which justice becomes a requirement for the coherence of the whole society; justice had been treated as an ideal rather than a necessity. The consequences are dire. The parts of the United States that cling to the traditional form of social fact making are no longer economically viable, whereas those that have embraced change, diversity, and justice, are the economic, technological, and social engine of the nation.

What we are experiencing is not merely a clash between two cultures. It is a clash between two ways of making social order, sense, and self together. One relies on a consensus of durable beliefs and ideas (descended from Racialized Slavery and fueled by stereotypes of the other) that are no longer viable, while the other operates without consensus, embracing diversity, change and technology. Durkheim warned that without sufficient equality in society, increasing diversity would bring modernity to this point.

The argument makes a difference both to how we understand the current crisis and how we approach its solution. The consequences for politics and democracy are obvious. But the difference between the two forms of social organization and its effect on increasing divisions in the US has been misunderstood. This is the case even for most Durkheim scholars because they typically still treat social consensus as a requirement—as if consensus *could still work* in a diverse modern context (and as if that would be a good thing).

Having made the mistake of thinking that what we are confronting is merely a clash of cultures—rather than a conflict between two different ways of making the social facts of a culture, one of which is compatible with diversity and social change and one that is not—has us looking in the wrong places both for racism and for the theoretical grounding needed to explain current divisions. The various strands of Eurocentric thinking have gotten in the way. If, in diverse modern social contexts that cannot support consensus we need constantly to make social facts together in situ—as Durkheim (and Parsons, Goffman, Garfinkel and Sacks) argued, then we need to cooperate to make that happen. This in turn requires sufficient freedom and equality to enable reciprocity and the justice to guarantee them. It requires what Garfinkel (1963) called "Trust Conditions."

Ironically, this justice requirement—or Trust Condition—of modernity threatens any consensus-based order grounded in a racial hierarchy. So, it is not surprising that racists feel threatened. It is, however, economic and technological progress that threatens their way of making culture, not civil rights for Black Americans (or women). And, if they do not embrace civil rights for all—they will also need to do without economic and scientific progress.

CONCLUSION

The hope as reflected in the MLK quote in the introduction to this chapter is that education can get us to a bright new future wherein racism and inequality are overcome. However, this cannot happen if academic disciplines embed tacit cultural and racialized assumptions that prevent them from recognizing the forms of social order that diversity and progress require.

Marginalizing studies of Race and inequality, and the Black, Jewish, and other marginalized scholars who have produced them, has impoverished social and political theory and prevented the new discoveries that are coming from Black and African American Studies from having the impact they should. Majority scholars often have a culturally biased understanding of how society works that is reinforced by embedded Eurocentric assumptions—while the excluded ironically are more likely to see behind the taken-for-granted and achieve greater understanding both of how society works and of what the majority take-for-granted (Duck and Rawls 2023).

As more marginalized scholars gain recognition, research that builds on their work is producing results that are being built on in turn by activists inside and outside academia to create social change. Among other things, these results challenge assumptions about what "order," "identity" and "rational" mean. They challenge economic theory, turn the understanding of racism (and other "isms") toward the structure of societies and how they embed Race and other inequalities—and away from the focus on individual racists that has so hampered understanding.

Scholars are rediscovering and documenting the history of Racialized Slavery and its contribution to the rise of Western Capitalism. Following up the early scholarship of Eric Williams (1944), Oliver Cromwell Cox (1952), W.E.B. Du Bois (1903), and C.L.R. James (1938) with detailed studies of historical archives, they are showing the importance of racialized slavery in almost unimaginable detail. They have combed through diaries from the 1700s to document the contributions of Racialized Slavery to the development of accounting, management, marketing, finance, banking, credit, mortgages, etc. (Beckert and Rockman 2016; Rosenthal 2018; Rothman 2014). Beckert traces global trade networks back 5,000 years to China, India and Africa. Rather than crediting England with generating modern global trade through hard work and innovation, Beckert (2010) argues that in a period of what he calls "war capitalism" the English managed to destroy thousands of years of skill and manufacturing knowledge, in an effort to force world markets to accept their inferior products.

Cedric Robinson's (1983) emphasis on "Racial Capitalism." which also builds on Williams and Cox, is finally having an impact. There was always capitalism and slavery. As Beckert and others are demonstrating, capitalism and world trade go back 5,000 years. But the racialization of slavery and capitalism was new. Beginning in the American colonies in the 1600s, the process of racialization progressed over the course of that century to transform the world after 1700, primarily through a colonialization so thorough that no part of the world was left untouched. This process of racialization finally gave rise in the late 1800s to new "scientific" ideologies of permanent biologically-based racial divisions that have proved difficult to exorcise.

In sociology, W.E.B Du Bois provided a wealth of early argument on which scholars are now building new and better approaches. Overlooked for a century, his monumental works are finally being taken seriously by scholars who are also being taken seriously (Morris, 2015). Du Bois' (1890) challenge to Individualism, which he formulated in terms of an "Individual Strong Man" is particularly relevant today. How the worship of an Individual who does not care about the good of the whole—an ideal that is inimical to democracy— could have captured the popular imagination and become one of the pillars of belief in those parts of the United States that still cling to tradition and consensus, stands as one of the most salient contradictions in the United States today.

Studies of how social interaction is cooperatively organized to create meaningful social facts play a central role in addressing these questions. However, because questioning taken-for-granted disciplinary assumptions is risky, and disciplinary leaders have emphasized the "objectivity" of numbers since WWII (Rawls 2018), it should not be surprising that studies of interaction have been discouraged in sociology for decades.

Taking these arguments seriously and reading them in the light of new detailed studies of how social categories are achieved in interaction, promises to bring minority insights to the center of disciplinary research where they belong. The recognition that people do not need to be personally racist to act out structural racism and that racism is structured into the expectations of interaction is important. Rather than singling out Individual racists, the system, its Individualism and its Interaction Orders are now being examined for the racism in which all of us participate.[12]

NOTES

1. Preferred terms for Race categories change over the years and vary between groups. The practice of many Black scholars of alternating between Black and African American, while using the terminology of the time where appropriate (e.g., Afro-American in 1968) has been adopted. The first letter of social facts like Race and Gender that are typically treated as if they were biological facts are also capitalized in this chapter and other publications to call attention to their social fact status.

It is a possibly irritating reminder that societies make up these categories—which as such are entirely arbitrary.

2. Throughout this chapter I use the term Eurocentric rather than Western-centric. "Western" sets up a west/east dichotomy that is distracting if not outright racist. The point at issue is that the history of the rise of the United States and Europe as dominant capitalist nations has been told in ways that credit European colonists, merchants, industrialists, and politicians with achievements that in fact relied on the stolen labor of others, not an east/west contrast.

3. These taken-for-granted assumptions concern the primacy of the Individual and Individualism, the durability of concepts and categories, the need for social consensus, the scientific nature of numbers/statistics, and the belief that studies of social interaction, particularly detailed studies, are subjective and trivial (Rawls 2018).

4. In addition to research activism, I have also pursued a kind of teaching activism by having students in my classes write observations of racism in their lives. Other scholars are also doing this. It is an important kind of activism that gets students directly involved in interrogating their own lives—and the context in which they learned and did not learn about racism.

5. There is excellent recent scholarship on how poor Whites in the antebellum South were not accorded the same rights or protections as wealthier White slaveowners. Keri Leigh Merritt's *Masterless Men: Poor Whites and Slavery in the Antebellum South* (2017) is a careful and powerful history. Wayne Flynt's *Dixie's Forgotten People: The South's Poor Whites (*1979), Matt Wray's *Not Quite White: White Trash and the Boundaries of Whiteness* (2006) and Nancy Isenberg's *White Trash: The 400-Year Untold History of Class in America* (2017) all disambiguate the class lines within the White population, with particular attention to poor southern Whites.

6. The symposium was recorded, and a transcript published in Robinson et. al. (1969). An extended analysis and discussion of this text appears in Hall (1999).

7. Martin Kilson became the first Black Professor to be tenured at Harvard in 1969, the year after the Yale symposium.

8. I remember questions challenging Kilson from Black students in that class, the tone of which I did not understand at the time. The transcript of the Yale symposium helps make sense of what was going on. Kilson had worked quickly after 1968, which created a disjuncture between the concerns he expressed in 1968 about the ability to staff Black Studies courses, and his own contribution to Black Studies three years later.

9. Having secured a position in summer 1971 as a nanny for the Lynch family and their two girls, Hollis Lynch made his books and his students available to me. That was the year Lynch managed to save the African institute (which had been scheduled for elimination), enabling it to survive and become the African American and Africa Diaspora Studies Department at Columbia University.

10. Many such studies did quickly appear.

11. By the following year I had taken courses with Kurt Wolff, Gila Hayim, and Emmanuel (Manny) Schegloff.

12. see Waring, Hansun and Nadja Tadic, forthcoming, and Rawls, Whitehead, and Duck (2020).

REFERENCES

Alexander, Michele. 2010. *The New Jim Crow: Mass Incarceration in the Age of Colorblindness*. The New Press: New York.

Allen, Theodore. 1994. *The Invention of the White Race, Volume I*. New York: Verso.

———. 1996. *The Invention of the White Race, Volume II*. New York: Verso.

Anderson, Carol. 2016. *White Rage*. New York: Bloomsbury Publishing.

Anderson, Elijah. 1979. *A Place on the Corner*. Chicago: University of Chicago Press.

———. 1992. *Code of the Street*. New York: W.W. Norton.

Baptist, Edward. 2014. *The Half Has Never Been Told: Slavery and the Making of American Capitalism*. New York: Basic Books.

Baradaran, Mehrsa. 2017. *The Color of Money and the Racial Wealth Gap*. Cambridge, MA: Belknap Press.

Beckert, Sven. 2010. *Empire of Cotton: A Global History*. New York: Vintage.

Beckert, Sven, and Seth Rockman, eds. 2016. *Slavery's Capitalism: A New History of American Economic Development*. Philadelphia: University of Pennsylvania Press.

Beckles, Hilary. 2013. *Britain's Black Debt: Reparations for Caribbean Slavery and Native Genocide*. Kingston, Jamaica: University of the West Indies Press.

Bell, Derek. 1987. *And We Are Not Saved: The Elusive Quest for Racial Justice*. New York: Basic Books.

———. 1992. *Faces at the Bottom of the Well: The Permanence of Racism*. New York: Basic Books.

Bobo, Lawrence. 2000. "Reclaiming a DuBoisian Perspective on Racial Attitudes." *Annals of the American Academy of Political and Social Science* 568(1): 186–202.

Briggs, Charles L. 2005. "Genealogies of Race and Culture and the Failure of Vernacular Cosmopolitanisms: Rereading Franz Boas and W. E. B. Du Bois." *Public Culture* 17(1): 75–100. https://doi.org/10.1215/08992363-17-1-75.

Brooks, Noliwe. 2006. "The Beginnings of Black Studies." *The Chronicle of Higher Education*, February 10, 2006. https://www.chronicle.com/article/the-beginnings -of-black-studies/?cid=gen_sign_in&cid2=gen_login_refresh.

Brown, Dorothy. 2021. *The Whiteness of Wealth: How the Tax System Impoverishes Black Americans—And How We Can Fix It*. New York: Random House.

Butler, Paul. 2018. *Chokehold: Policing the Black Man*. New York: The New Press.

Cox, Oliver Cromwell. 1948. *Caste, Class and Race: A Study in Social Dynamics*. New Jersey: Doubleday.

Crenshaw, Kimberlé, Neil T. Gotanda, Gary Peller and Kendall Thomas, eds. 1996. *Critical Race Theory: The Key Writings that Formed the Movement*. New York: The New Press.

Deegan, Mary Jo. 1988. "W.E.B. Du Bois and the Women of Hull-House, 1895–1899." *American Sociologist* 19 (4): 301–11. doi:10.1007/BF02691827.

Du Bois, W.E.B. (1890) 1996. "Jefferson Davis as a Representative of Civilization." In *The Oxford W. E. B. Du Bois Reader*, edited by Eric J. Sundquist, 243–245. New York: Oxford University Press.

———.1903. *The Souls of Black Folk*. London: Longmans, Green & Co.

————.1946. *The World and Africa*. New York: International Publishers.

Duck, Waverly and Anne Rawls. 2023. "Black and Jewish: Double Consciousness Inspired a Qualitative Interactional Approach that Centers Race, Marginality and Justice." *Qualitative Sociology*. https://doi.org/10.1007/s11133-023-09535-9.

Durkheim, Emile. (1893) 1933. *The Division of Labor in Society*, translated by George Simpson. New York: Free Press.

Eisenmann, Clemens and Anne Rawls. 2023 (in press). "The Continuity of Garfinkel's Approach: Seeking Ways of 'Making the Phenomenon Available Again' Through the Experience and Usefulness of 'Trouble.'" In *The Anthem Companion to Harold Garfinkel*. London/New York, edited by Phillipe Sormani and Dirk von Lem: Anthem Press.

England, Lynn, and Keith W. Warner. 2013. "W.E.B. Du Bois: Reform, Will, and the Veil." *Social Forces* 91(3): 955–73. doi:10.1093/sf/sos188.

Fanon, Frantz. 1952. *Black Skin, White Masks*. New York: Grove Press.

Flitter, Emily. 2022. *The White Wall: How Big Finance Bankrupts Black America*. New York: One Signal Publishers.

Flynt, Wayne. (1974) 2004. *Dixie's Forgotten People: The South's Poor Whites*. Bloomington: Indiana University Press.

Gabbidon, Shaun L. 2007. *W.E.B. Du Bois on Crime and Justice: Laying the Foundations of Sociological Criminology*. Aldershot: Ashgate.

Garfinkel, Harold. 1963. "A Conception of and Experiments with Trust as a Condition of Stable Social Actions." In *Motivation and Social Interaction: Cognitive Determinants*, edited by O. J. Harvey, 187–238. New York: Ronald Press.

————. 1967. *Studies in Ethnomethodology*. New Jersey: Prentice-Hall.

Garfinkel, Harold and Harvey Sacks. 1970. "On Formal Structures of Practical Action." In *Theoretical Sociology: Perspectives and Developments*, edited by John McKinney and Edward Tiryakian, 338–366. New York: Appleton Century-Crofts.

Goffman, Erving. 1959. *The Presentation of Self in Everyday Life*. Chicago: Free Press.

————. 1963. *Stigma: Notes on the Management of Spoiled Identity*. Chicago: Free Press.

————. 1983. "The Interaction Order." *American Sociological Review* 48 (1): 1–17.

Hall, Perry. 1999. *In the Vineyard: Working in African American Studies*. University of Tennessee Press: Knoxville.

Hancock, Ange-Marie. 2005. "W.E.B. Du Bois: Intellectual Father of Intersectionality?" *Souls: A Critical Journal of Black Politics, Culture, and Society* 7(3): 74–84. https://doi-org.ezp.bentley.edu/10.1080/10999940500265508.

Hill-Collins, Patricia. 1986. "Learning from the Outsider Within: The Sociological Significance of Black Feminist Thought." *Social Problems* 33 (6): 14–32. https://doi.org/10.2307/800672.

————. 1990. *Black Feminist Thought: Knowledge, Consciousness, and the Politics of Empowerment*. Boston: Unwin Hyman.

Hinton, Elizabeth. 2016. *From the War on Poverty to the War on Crime: The Making of Mass Incarceration in America*. Cambridge, MA: Harvard University Press.

Hunter, Marcus Anthony. 2013a. *Black City Makers: How the Philadelphia Negro Changed Urban America*. Oxford: Oxford University Press.

———. 2013b. "A Bridge Over Troubled Urban Waters: W.E.B. Du Bois's *The Philadelphia Negro* and the Ecological Conundrum." *DuBois Review* 10 (1): 7–27. https://doi.org/10.1017/S1742058X13000015.

Herrnstein, Richard. 1971. "IQ." *The Atlantic*, September 1971, 43–64. Accessed April 25, 2023. https://cdn.theatlantic.com/assets/media/files/sept_1971_-_herrnstein_-_i.q..pdf.

Isenberg, Nancy. 2016. *White Trash: The 400–Year Untold History of Class in America*. New York: Penguin Books.

James, C. L. R. 1938. *The Black Jacobins: Toussaint L'Ouverture and the San Domingo Revolution.* London: Penguin.

Jenkins, Destin and Justin Leroy, eds. 2021. *Histories of Racial Capitalism*. New York: Columbia University Press.

Jensen, Arthur. 1969. "How Much Can We Boost IQ and Scholastic Achievement?" *Harvard Educational Review*, 39 (1): 1–123. https://arthurjensen.net/wp-content/uploads/2014/06/How-Much-Can-We-Boost-IQ-and-Scholastic-Achievement-OCR.pdf.

Kilson, Martin. 1971. "Black Politics: A New Power." *Dissent*, August 1971.

Kim, Catherine, Daniel Losen and Damon Hewitt. 2010. *The School-to-Prison Pipeline: Structuring Legal Reform*. New York: NYU Press.

King, Jr., Martin Luther. 1947. "The Purpose of Education." *The Maroon Tiger*, January/February, 10. Accessed April 25, 2023. https://kinginstitute.stanford.edu/king-papers/documents/purpose-education.

Kiser, William. 2017. *Borderlands of Slavery: The Struggle over Captivity and Peonage in the American Southwest*. Philadelphia: University of Pennsylvania Press.

Madigan, Tim. 2001. *The Burning: Massacre, Destruction and the Tulsa Race Riot of 1921*. New York: St. Martin's Press.

Mansbridge, Jane and Aldon Morris, eds. 2001. *Oppositional Consciousness*. Chicago: University of Chicago Press.

Maxwell, Angie and Todd Shields. 2019. *The Long Southern Strategy*. Oxford: Oxford University Press.

Merritt, Keri. 2017. *Masterless Men: Poor Whites and Slavery in the Antebellum South*. Cambridge: Cambridge University Press.

Messenger, Tony. 2021. *Profit and Punishment: How America Criminalizes the Poor in the Name of Justice*. New York: St. Martin's Press.

Morris, Aldon. 1986. *The Origins of the Civil Rights Movement*. Free Press.

———. 2015. *The Scholar Denied: W.E B. DuBois and the Birth of Modern Sociology*. Berkeley: University of California Press.

Morris, Aldon D., and Amin Ghaziani. 2005. "DuBoisian Sociology: A Watershed of Professional and Public Sociology." *Souls: A Critical Journal of Black Politics, Culture, and Society* 7(3–4): 47–54. https://doi-org.ezp.bentley.edu/10.1080/109999405265425.

Oliver, Melvin and Shapiro, Thomas. 2006. *Black Wealth/White Wealth: A New Perspective on Racial Inequality*. New York: Routledge.

Rawls, Anne. 1987. "Interaction Order Sui Generis: Goffman's Contribution to Sociological Theory." *Sociological Theory* 5(2): 136–149. doi:10.2307/201935.

———. 1996. "Durkheim's Epistemology: The Neglected Argument." *American Journal of Sociology* 102 (2): 430–482. doi:10.1163/24683949-12340103.

———. 1997. "Durkheim and Pragmatism: An Old Twist on a Contemporary Debate." *Sociological Theory* 15 (21): 5–29. http://www.jstor.org/stable/202133.

———. 2000. "'Race' as an Interaction Order Phenomenon: W.E.B. Du Bois's 'Double Consciousness' Thesis Revisited." *Sociological Theory* 18(2): 241–274. doi:10.1111/0735-2751.00097.

———. (2004) 2009. *Epistemology and Practice: Durkheim's The Elementary Forms of Religious Life*. Cambridge: Cambridge University Press.

———. 2009. "An Essay on Two Conceptions of Social Order: Constitutive Orders of Action, Objects and Identities vs Aggregate Orders of Individual Action." *The Journal of Classical Sociology* 9 (4): 500–520. https://doi-org.ezp.bentley.edu/10.1177/1468795X09344376.

———. 2018. "The Wartime Narrative in US Sociology, 1940–1947: Stigmatizing Qualitative Sociology in the Name of 'Science.'" European Journal of Social Theory 21 (4): 526–546.

———. 2019. *La Division du Travail Revisited: Vers une Théorie Sociologique de la Justice*. Translated by Francesco Callegaro and Philip Chanial. Paris: Le Bord de l'Eau.

———. 2021. "Durkheim's Self-Regulating 'Constitutive' Practices: An Unexplored Critical Relevance to Racial Justice, Consensus Thinking, and the Covid-19 Pandemic." In *Durkheim and Critique*, edited by Nicola Marcucci, 227–263. London: Palgrave Macmillan.

———. 2022a. "Harold Garfinkel's Focus on Racism, Inequality, and Social Justice: The Early Years 1939–1952." In *The Ethnomethodology Program: Legacies and Prospects*, edited by John Heritage and Doug Maynard, 90–113. Oxford: Oxford University Press.

———. 2022b. "Situating Goffman's "Interaction Orders" in Durkheim's Social Fact Lineage: Grounding an Alternate Sociology of Modernity in Heightened Awareness of Interaction." *Etnografia e Ricerca Qualitativa*, no.1 (Jan.–April), 27–62. DOI: 10.3240/103744.

———. 2023 (in press). "The Goffman-Garfinkel Correspondence: Planning 'On Passing." *Etnografia e Ricerca Qualitativa*.

Rawls, Anne and Waverly Duck. 2020. *Tacit Racism*. Chicago: University of Chicago Press.

Rawls, Anne and Jason Turowetz. 2021. "Garfinkel's Politics: Collaborating with Parsons to Document Taken-for-Granted Practices for Assembling Cultural Objects and Their Grounding in Implicit Social Contract." *The American Sociologist* 52 (1): 131–158.

Rawls, Anne, Kevin Whitehead and Waverly Duck, eds. 2020. *Black Lives Matter: Ethnomethodological and Conversation Analytic Studies of Race and Systemic Racism in Everyday Interaction*. New York: Routledge.

Reséndez, Andrés. 2016. *The Other Slavery: The Uncovered Story of Indian Enslavement in America*. New York: Houghton Mifflin Harcourt.

Robinson, Armstead, Craig C. Foster, and Donald Ogilvie. 1969. *Black Studies in the University: A Symposium*. New Haven: Yale University Press.

Robinson, Cedric. 1983. *Black Marxism: The Making of the Black Radical Tradition*. London: Zed Press.

Roediger, David. 2007. *The Wages of Whiteness: Race and the Making of the American Working Classes*. New York: Verso.

Rosenthal, Caitlin. 2018. *Accounting for Slavery: Masters and Management*. Cambridge, MA: Harvard University Press.

Rothman, Joshua. 2014. *Flush Times and Fever Dreams*. Athens: University of Georgia Press.

Slater, Gene. 2021. *Freedom to Discriminate: How Realtors Conspired to Segregate Housing and Divide America*. Berkeley: Heyday Books.

Taylor, Keeanga-Yamahtta. 2019. *Race for Profit: How Banks and the Real Estate Industry Undermined Black Homeownership*. Chapel Hill: UNC Press.

Turowetz, Jason and Anne Rawls. 2021. "The Development of Garfinkel's 'Trust' Argument From 1947 to 1967: Demonstrating How Inequality Disrupts Sense and Self-Making." *Journal of Classical Sociology* (21)1: 3–37. doi:10.1177/1468795X19894423.

Waksler, Francis Chaput. 2010. *The New Orleans Sniper: A Phenomenological Study of Constituting the Other*. New York: University Press of America.

Waring, Hansun and Nadja Tadic. Forthcoming. *Critical Conversation Analysis*.

Williams, Eric. 1944. *Capitalism and Slavery*. Chapel-Hill: University of North Carolina Press.

Wray, Matt. 2006. *Not Quite White: White Trash and the Boundaries of Whiteness*. Durham: Duke University Press.

Wright, Earl, II. 2002a. "The Atlanta Sociological Laboratory, 1896–1924: A Historical Account of the First American School of Sociology." *Western Journal of Black Studies* 26 (3): 165–74. https://search-ebscohost-com.ezp.bentley.edu/login.aspx ?direct=true&db=a9h&AN=8771906&site=ehost-live.

———. 2002b. "Using the Master's Tools: Atlanta University and American Sociology, 1896–1924." *Sociological Spectrum* 22(1): 15–39.

———. 2002c. "Why Black People Tend to Shout! An Earnest Attempt to Explain the Sociological Negation of the Atlanta Sociological Laboratory Despite Its Possible Unpleasantness." *Sociological Spectrum* 22(3): 325–61.

———. 2006. W. E. B. Du Bois and the Atlanta University Studies on the Negro, revisited. *Journal of African American Studies* 9(4): 3–17. doi:10.1007/s12111 -006-1015-2.

Zuckerman, Phil, ed. 2004. *The Social Theory of W.E B. Du Bois*. Thousand Oaks, CA: Pine Forge Press.

Chapter Eight

The Black Professor

Utz McKnight and Greg Austin

"How do you say your name, Utz?" After years of talking to one another, Cornel West wanted to make sure he said it correctly in a public talk he was to give in the next hour. "Do you care about students?" Cornel looked me steadily in the eyes as he said this. We were having coffee at a conference and had managed to find a quiet corner to talk about professional problems as Black academics. He was insistent and serious as he continued, "Caring about students is the only thing that matters." More than two decades later I still remember hesitating a little before saying that yes, students were what made me an academic. "They are the reason I am an academic." As though reassured about something, Cornel West relaxed and continued talking about the profession and our role as Black professors, his own writing and research interests. Student wellbeing and learning still matter the most to me in describing my vocation as a Black professor.

My hesitation in the moment, however slight, was important. A few years before, my enthusiasm for teaching as my vocation had been untarnished. I said to any and all of those interested in hiring me that teaching was the reason for wanting a tenure track job, without understanding that their concern about me as a potential Black hire was whether I could publish, not if I would appeal to students and build a reputation as someone approachable and generous with my time. Would I do too much service? Their concerns made an additional criterion for assessing the importance of the Black professor—can I help myself—can Black people help themselves, and still get research done? They could not see that the need for Black professors to meet student demand was because of the racism the students experienced in classes and on the campus, not some aspect of shared experience that only Black people needed to affirm between themselves—a double burden unique to the few Black professors at universities. Walking with students on campus while discussing ideas and listening to them, valuing their conversation in the classroom and in the office, this wasn't the concern of a potential hiring committee.

Could I, Utz McKnight, because of the very description of Blackness that I possessed for others, write about race and political theory such that book publishers and journal editors could find a sufficiently large audience? It was not enough to say the academic conversation about race in my discipline was not considered important or that too few people had read the sources I was using in an argument or that the questions I was asking in my research were not germane to other areas of research. For example, was there a space to publish for a Black political theorist who wrote about race? What mattered to those I spoke to was the understanding about race as an idea for political theorizing by an audience that included almost no Black academics. In fact, one political theorist friend of mine described how after being hired, one of the search committee members had said to her that one criterion for her selection was that she wasn't Black. She told me how the person had said that even though the committee wanted someone who specialized in race as a topic of research, Black people can't be objective about race. For most university departments the best outcome of a search to address the needs of Black students is someone who is not Black but cares, someone who understands the supposed plight and pathos of Black life such that they can comfort those who suffer under the burden of this assignment and identify those who are willing to accept their captivity in this description and yet still excel.

Why exactly, the search committee asks the Department, the Dean, do we need to hire a Black professor, except that Black students want it? A White professor is after all not merely White, but also and pertinent to the situation desired by students, still a professor. The inconvenience of Black students, that they are not merely Black. But in this moment of calculated indecision and indeterminacy of this further challenge to the conditions that still describe the absence of Black professors at universities, the activism inherent in the establishing the role of the Black professor, of those who advocate for the hiring of the Black professor, becomes apparent to everyone as well. To ask why we need to hire Black professors rather than to go about the work of hiring them, is to potentially accept the ontology of a Blackness that requires that we motivate the inclusion of Black people on the faculty, by meeting the standards of a Whiteness that in turn refuses implication in the argument.

The very Blackness being offered up by the committee was defined as in tension with the objective criteria by which scientific research is propagated, being confirmed instead by a strange subjective essence that was defined by racial inferiority instead of something else. The idea of hiring someone Black in an environment where the demands of the moment required that their Blackness appeal to students, while assuming that this very idea of affirming students, supporting them in their quest for knowledge in a university rife with unexamined racism, was antithetical or at best in contrast with the demands to publish research, created a situation that is impossible for the individual Black professor to successfully fulfill. Impossible unless that person was able to in their work address what race means at the university.

How do our ideas as a society change with regard to race, what it means for each of us, and as a topic for research? The description of the Black academic as activist and scholar is wrapped up in the answer to this question. One answer concerning the role of the Black professor is therefore that it is dependent on the state of the public conversation about race in the society, rather than complexly a dilemma solely for the Black individual. Who is more provocative or dangerous in society than Socrates, after all? What if instead of being killed, Socrates was encouraged to teach in the public space for ideas about what was just and good? This is the philosophical context for the answer I needed to give to Cornel. To what extent was my own definition of the professor tied up in this idea of vocation?

In the traditional conversation between Ralph Ellison and James Baldwin about the responsibility of the Black writer toward the political aspirations and needs of a collective Black community, the distinction between the vocation of the writer and that of the Black writer depends on the state of race, how it matters in the society, for everyone. To say with Walter Benn Michaels that there is no need today for the Black writer, in contrast to someone who is a writer and also Black, is to reduce the work of the Black writer to that of simply reproducing the conditions of their own inferiority as writers, to always being assessed as Black in ways that affirm that something else is desirable, if only they would stop writing, stop asking to be included. In this description of the writer, there is no place any longer for race to matter, and anyone who describes race as important except as legacy of past inequalities, uncorrected proofs so to speak of a society trying to establish racial equality, is conflating personal ascription with public claims for justice. This perspective confuses the political aspiration of a raceless world, with the actual description of race in society that does not meet that criteria. Race still matters, as much as it did in 1962 when I was born. More than sixty years later, race still matters. There is not any singular public definition of race, in law or in social relationships, between persons such that we could identify a specific Blackness to which a writer should aspire with finality as a condition of writing.

Race is a conversation that is never finished, complete, but rather the purview of the individual's description of how Blackness matters to them. The description of race is also at the same time conventional, not contingent. It is the responsibility of the researcher to explore the different conventions such that solutions can be found to improve how we can live together. One solution erroneously offered, is to describe Blackness narrowly, as an idea about phenotype and beliefs held by individuals about inferiority and difference, as the limit condition to the otherwise ongoing determination by people to define what racial equality requires of the society.

PUBLISH OR PERISH

"Utz, what do you think of the book?" Charles Henry asked me quietly in the office. Charles was then the chair of African American studies at UC Berkeley. My answer was tentative. "I wonder if it is too critical. Will people find it too threatening?" At the time I was insecure about my own approach to writing about race, democracy, and politics, and it showed. In 2000, I was only a few years from having completed my own PhD. We were talking about the book *The Racial Contract*, which was written by a mutual acquaintance Charles Mills, and had just been published a couple of years before. Courageous and potentially provocative because it asked questions of the social contract tradition in political philosophy, it challenged the conventions by which several academic disciplines described the importance of race as a subject for thought. Charles Henry and I agreed on the value of the work, but he was understandably less timid than I, in finding solace in the very challenge the book posed for traditions that sought to minimize the importance of race for theories of democracy and society.

Charles Henry had published important work and was an established political scientist, but as he said at the time, "I have never been able to consistently be published in mainstream literature. You have to find Black publishers." Charles explained that I couldn't expect to be published in mainstream journals and with traditional book publishers, as there was no interest in the questions that Black people were asking about equality and justice, except as this was associated with the current conventions defining the public conversation of civil rights. But the charge for the Black professor is not limited to speaking for the race as a critic of contemporary politics, as an advocate for equality and against injustice. They must publish.

The exasperation was evident in his voice as Charles Mills complained to me, "As much as people are reading *The Racial Contract*, I haven't had a job offer. I am still at XX. And people aren't buying the book." A decade later he would complain to me that no one read his later work where he answered some of the criticisms by other scholars of *The Racial Contract*, and Charles continued to talk of his disappointment with the job market and the reception of the book's argument. What I heard was the message that a particular appeal to an audience was no guarantee that one's argument was understood or valued beyond the narrow frame of acceptable discourse. Without a larger conversation about the role of the Black professor, without a space for research about race that wasn't immediately appealing to an audience that didn't do the research themselves or attended uncritically to the conventions of a discipline that defined limits on the importance of racial equality, the number of successful Black professors was unlikely to increase in number.

In the twenty years or so since these conversations, this observation has been proven true. Taken across generations of scholars there seem to be Black professors in abundance, but if you consider yearly cohorts, when people have received their PhDs and by discipline, rather than the numbers as a whole, there are too few still today in any one academic discipline to sustain more than a small conference social gathering. The problem for the Black professor isn't how few there are for the purpose of social community, but how the description of race in society limits their number. The lack of Black professorial representation in the academy is a reflection of how race remains an important distinction at universities. Why should the universities be unique in this regard, after all they reflect the priorities of the society in their training of the next generation.

WHAT IS AN ACTIVIST?

In *Anything We Love Can be Saved*, Alice Walker suggests that progress and social change are measured by the activity of everyone—both by those whose activism results in their being beaten, imprisoned, or killed and by the individual acts of the writer (xxii, xxv). She shows that while it is tempting to allow the changes that occur because of grand gestures or public activism by others to cause us to question the value of our own protests and refusals to accept injustice, those of us who write and teach for the living should not be dissuaded. As Walker explains, while others publicly protested and risked their lives and personal freedom in the late 1960s and early 1970s when she lived in Mississippi, she taught at two local Black colleges, created history booklets for school children to have access to African American history, and wrote books that centered the Black experience. These activities were enough then to affirm her and others, despite the constant news of disaster and death. The Black writer, and even more so the professor, must not only hold their time in thought but acknowledge the vocation in which they have a shared purpose with others.

To speak as we will here of the Black professor and activism is therefore to accept the distinction that Baldwin makes in the essay "Everybody's Protest

Novel" (1985) between confirming the tropes of Black inferiority and exploring the possibilities of life outside of the structures of inequality—an
equality of purpose and condition that obviates the necessity of testing the
environment for proof of one's humanity (43). Instead of seeking recognition, sympathy, consolation, acceptance, through limning the concepts that
confirm subjugation, the Black professor seeks to avoid being as Baldwin
writes in the essay "The Discovery of What It Means To Be An American,"
"merely Black" within the confines of the definition of inferiority that otherwise seeks to make them an inferior opaque captive, even as they must
also avoid being merely a Black professor to the world around them and to
themselves (1985, 179).

In railing against the conditions of a description of inferiority, the activist
accepts the stage set by others upon which they are to perform; they concede
the description of inferiority for themselves as well as to the world. The individual (the writer, the professor) must instead ask how these descriptions of
difference came about. In so doing, they find that who they are, what they can
do, is not fully contained within the definition of Blackness, nor that of the
professor, the writer, that is marked solely by the difference Baldwin makes
between literature and sociology. In this sense of what it means to be Black,
as a value and not a role, to rail against one's condition is to reify the terms
of one's captivity. This distinction between a desire not for mere social equality but for political equality is as old as chattel slavery in America, and it is
good to be reminded of the possibilities inherent in the latter, even as many
mistakenly bemoan the absence of the former.

The activist must instead hold their sense of the possibility of their actions
foremost, as Walker reminds us, even as they also toil within the everyday
requirements of a life. As Baldwin asks in the essay "They Can't Turn Back"
(1985, 222), do we want to merely be a story or to write one? The meta-
physics of watching oneself perform an act, continuously and permanently,
should not become the measure by which we assess value to ourselves and
others. As Walker describes in the essay, "This That I Offer You" (1997),
those of us who desire to change the world, must constantly critique the assumption of our centeredness (183). The measure of our activism must be
rather to nurture and engage in a series of actions with others that will remain
incomplete and yet enough.

A BLACK PROFESSOR

But the university is also the space where the research work to change how
race is described is potentially developed, where its societal description is

brought into question. With this perspective we return to the claim by Baldwin of the place of the Black writer in society, echoed by Toni Morrison as well in *Playing in The Dark* (1993), that the Black person must write themselves, their importance as thinkers in society, into existence. The need to constantly justify their presence at the university against the background of the current description of race in the society is matched by the need to describe Black life without reference to a claim to equality, but instead as a necessary call to action. This use of the academy to develop what it means to have a Black life, along with their work addressing the professional development in their respective disciplines, and their attention to students, this is the vocation.

Kiese Laymon explicitly states that he writes for us, for Black people. Without reducing the experience of Black life to a table of values, instead leaving open the possibility of what being Black might come to mean, the idea of writing for Black people, rather than about Black people for others, allows for the freedom to create outside the narrow confines of seeking social acceptance and equality. The pursuit of recognition within the description of a racial difference that is a slippery signifier, with a meaning that while fungible is always also still immutable as a category, is by definition an exercise in disappointment and futility. In *Long Division* (2013), Laymon offers the reader a refusal to engage with the proscribed limits of a Black life and instead provides his audience with the possibility of another future, one that exists through the reimagined history of the Black experience.

Citoyen, the eponymous Black child in *Long Division*, discovers in his traveling through time, a technique for asking which history we are defining as our own. This is reminiscent to the plot found also in Octavia Butler's *Kindred*, that the too easy theoretical claim of the finality of a description of Black life as social death can be exceeded. To live beyond the limit provided for Black life in society requires both a return to the problem of what history we use to define ourselves and centrally to the idea of race in theory that we associate with our political possibilities in the society. What is the competition in which we are participating? What race are you in, and what is a good enough outcome for you?

In the opening pages of *Heavy* (2018), Laymon returns to the political potential of a reimagined Black life by examining a history of sexual assault and the description of community from his childhood. A return to the site of trauma, as a witness and participant, provides us with a new history. We reflect on our own experiences and consider what it would be like if these events were no longer described solely by what was important to know in the moment, but also given by how we might today see our past anew. If we considered what the lies of history have cost us, how our complicity in these stories has deformed our possible futures, what might be possible (Laymon,

103)? Can we stop lying to others and therefore ourselves, about what happened, what we do every day, and how we imagine Black life?

The end of the novel *Corregidora* by Gayl Jones (1975), when Dora re-embraces Mutt, reads differently in this phrasing, a concession not to the wounds of the past but instead a desire to avoid the trauma in the future. Jones suggests that only by returning to the site, the source of loss, and figuring its erasure, can Dora find a way forward for herself. The story isn't about Mutt, but her own possible future. Similarly, in *Heavy* (2018), Laymon asks of his childhood to produce the potential for release from a potentially stultifying traumatic past, he finds in a complex revision of his life, the source material for the vindication to search for improvement, new directions to explore in his own future—to revise his own life. Stop lying about race, as though we know definitively the solutions to injustice and inequality in society, and allow for revision, change. But this only occurs if we stop engaging the conceptual contours of racial inequality as an idea, and instead work creatively to develop our own lives.

In this context the question by Cornel, "Do you care about students?" resonates in our ears differently. The student is always still ourselves, the limit of our imagination for what might be possible. To not engage in defining their lives is to also refuse to question the limitations that race creates for everyone in society. This was how I heard Cornel, did I understand that the professor was another version of the student, someone whose vocation was to engage in a constant reassessment of the conditions and conventions by which I lived? How did I see myself, as a Black professor?

To answer this question, but as a collective description of the requirements of the vocation, I turn to the writing of Regina Bradley. In her study of Outkast, Bradley (2021) asks what the freedom to create outside the expectations of established values allow us to accomplish. In the introduction to the *Outkast Reader* (2021), she goes through a list of categories, eschewing each as an explanation, as a limit for what the group Outkast established in the rural/urban southern space, in the juxtaposition between West and East coast hiphop, and in the idea of a Black mecca in Atlanta in the music production of the group and the Dungeon Family. For Bradley the constant signifying over and against the limits of place and discourse by the group establishes the potential for music to engage in worldbuilding similar to that offered by the concept of revision in the work of Laymon. Her writing about Outkast makes available to us the possibilities of music to challenge conventions, to as she puts it, engage in a "willing alienation," from the description of the same (10).

In her popular and well-regarded podcast series *Bottom of the Map* (2019, 2020) Bradley explores the potential for the study of Hip Hop in the South to engage with the problems of contemporary society. Addressing topics across

The Black Professor   195

the range of concerns for Black people in the United States, but principally focused on the potential of creative work in music to provide new ideas about how to live, by reexamining the conventions that we use to describe the good, justice, and the place of music in our lives, Regina Bradley, with her co-host Christina Lee, provide a trenchant and critical interpretation of society. Bradley and her co-host offer a way to bring the study of Southern Hip Hop from the relative margins of the disciplinary study of music and society to the center, and in doing so describe an understanding of the potential in a Black life that isn't defined by the constant need to justify its terms as given by the idea of captivity and the subsequent demand for social equality.

In *Chronicling Stankonia* (2021), Regina Bradley develops on these themes of a necessary alienation and description of creativity as integral to Black life, without reifying its contours as categorical and defined by an inherent inequality. Addressing the assumption concerning the place and description of trauma that is thought in certain theoretical conventions to underlie Black life, Bradley collapses time, suggesting that the way forward is to think with Black writers and musicians about the multiplicities of Southern Blackness existing simultaneously in the past, present, and future (59). That specific creative insight found in Hip Hop allows us to work through our ideas of trauma and loss, while refiguring how we think of young Black men in the South, as well as allowing for their visibility in spite of conventions that suggest young Black men are both expendable and opaque. A coming to terms with Black masculinity through the lyrics and beats of the music is explicit, challenging the racist assumptions of Black male difference, and also in that moment asking about its terms, what masculinity should require of Black men in grief and in life (Bradley, 84–85).

As a Black professor, Regina Bradley makes possible an analysis of the nuances of Black life, as both human as Baldwin would claim, but also as available to predation and captivity. She explores what we are to make of our condition, both simultaneously available to the constant recovering and reclaiming of racial definitions of difference, and always developing our human capacity to describe ourselves and others in spite of these conventions of inferiority. Bradley provides a description of how specific Black music and writing allow for a richer definition of Black life than that given by racism. Her work is a form of activism that isn't reducible to protest and agitation in its traditional collective forms, but instead is available through the intellectual work of the professor as a vocation.

In *Come Kingdom* (2022) Derrick Harriell, currently chair of African American Studies at the University of Mississippi, first gives us a study of the obduracy of pretention as a definition of male confidence and its inevitable collapse into the human condition of humility and reconciliation. Cast as a story of complicity and shame, Harriell asks us to consider how both misogyny and racial descriptions lurk uncontested in our perceptions of the world, and how this description of inviolate masculinity plays a part in how we think of fertility, family, and sex. Over several poems, he explores the process of coming to terms with the difference between the idea of the game and the rules by which it has to be played. Harriell offers the reader a way to reconsider how to see ourselves in a world where fallibility and responsibility are descriptions for Black male gender politics. Need, desire, and failed expectations provide the nuance and generosity to define a culpable and self-aware Black male persona, one that sees the ineluctable loss for men that accompanies the grift of proffered conventional descriptions of masculinity.

Harriell then provides in "Talking Dirty to the Kingdom" (2022) a meditation on our contemporary social condition, writ in the lives of props and publicity seekers, the actions of a child and of adults. The description of Black life, as every life, is redemptive and restorative. Giving racism its due, which is at the same time both overdetermined and a bit part, Harriell demonstrates that to describe a life within the confines of race is to truncate and diminish the capacity to live. Race cannot encompass everything, all desires and needs. Race isn't even, is not merely, a role to occupy but instead something that happens in the midst of the rest of a life. And what a life. Harriell in "Mandrake Bouquet" (2022) continues the description of how intimacy and expectations should allow us to ask questions of our community, uncomfortable and awkward, about what it is that we do with one another, and to ourselves.

But it is in the turn in Come Kingdom toward a meditation on the relationship between father and son in the poem "Anno Domini" (2022) that requires a redescription of our lives, the families we imagine we come from, and our relationships to sons and fathers—a profound and difficult journey into the needs and failures of human beings trying to provide something valuable, and even love, to others as a description of a life, its fulfillment. The final poem, "Kingdom Come" (2022) reads as a paean or offering to sanctify this life as we wish it, and as it finally is. A poignant journey.

The Black Professor isn't a thing, it is a vocation. One that requires an activist heart, a desire to educate oneself and others about new ideas, and in doing so to come together with others and make a better world.

CHANGING THE UNIVERSITY

For many the idea of activism in the academy is predicated on the capacity for change in the university as an institution. The ability to advocate for change in a particular university, to create new ways of thinking as a function of research and course development, to establish new concentrations and programs, and to have an impact on the direction of education at the institution is an important part of the work of every professor. This is evident in the creation of relatively new disciplines such as African American Studies and Women's Studies, now both more than fifty years old, and many more programs which address new technologies and approaches to traditional research areas such as Cultural Studies and Digital Media Studies. The university as an institution is also slow to change, a function in part of the role of higher education in the society, where traditions and a continuity of purpose and content ensure the stability of societal structures, as well as the research methods that are popular at these institutions.

While the university is a place for the development of new ideas it is slow to change how it delivers the education for the next generation of student. Universities create for generations of students a social commitment, developing traditions and rituals that attach to particular schools. These artifacts of student attendance reflect also the history of the institution, how it has formed over time and what values it has inculcated in its classrooms, the hallways and social spaces in its buildings, the relationships between faculty and students, and living arrangements. Administrators, professors, and staff have a role in the development of the institution in these capacities as well.

Universities that up until the 1960s were attended predominantly by White students today continue to both reflect the ongoing larger societal politics of race and contribute their own institutional responses to the issue. This is the case for the University of Alabama, where both of us work. In the context of this external pressure of ideas about race and the actual processes that define the university's approach to race, the Black professor has to ask what the possibilities are for change in the use of race at their institution. It is valuable to distinguish between three areas of interest, the first being the university as a place of work, the second being the processes that allow the university to fulfill its mission of education, and the third being the classroom.

THE WORKPLACE

For the Black professor the workplace is characterized by the structuring of the university into at least three semiautonomous parts, generalizable in terms of the academic departments, student affairs, and human resources. Though tenure protects the research and teaching mission in some respects, the process of achieving tenure also creates its own challenges for the individual faculty member, and the environment in a Department reflects the people and social traditions that exist, as well as the history of race in the workplace. For example, a department that has had issues hiring more Black faculty members, or has never done so before, or has had several generations of Black faculty achieve tenure and successfully train doctoral students, and maybe even have chaired the Department have different policies and practices with regard to addressing the presence of a Black faculty member. This does not eliminate the importance of the individual behaviors of coworkers, the activity in formal meetings necessary to complete the work of the Department, and the administrative support for research and teaching.

But a department has to develop processes through which to both provide support unique to the position of being a Black professor, however this particular status develops within the department and in their time at the university, and also allow for the professor to produce original research and be a successful teacher. Often the lack of awareness of the conditions that determine the description of race in the department becomes the source of dissatisfaction and conflict between the needs of the Black faculty member and the workplace. This has for many Black faculty members been the primary source of their activism, the need to advocate for themselves and other Black faculty in their department. The success of these initiatives largely depends on being able to institute practices that respond to the effects of race generally, even as the Black faculty represent a particular case for the workplace. This can be a daunting experience, particularly in a department where the idea of race as an issue to address is thought to begin and end with the often complex process of hiring the Black professor. Because of the importance of race in the society, much more is required of a department to retain and provide the opportunity for the Black professor to be successful.

Often the need for personal professional advocacy is daunting enough that the faculty member should be encouraged by the department chair to seek the support and assistance of other resources, including faculty outside the department, the Dean's office, and the university Black Faculty and Staff Association or similar organization on the campus. But within a department, the other faculty and the chair should be developing ways to improve the workplace for the Black professor, if necessary, asking advice from those in departments that have developed successful retention processes and positive work environments for Black faculty members. The successful inclusion of Black faculty in the mission of the department isn't the sole responsibility of Black faculty, because the description of race isn't caused by their presence in the Department, but already a part of how the workplace defines its operations with respect to supporting research and providing an education to students.

The faculty and chair in the department should communicate with their Black faculty members to create a workplace that allows for their professional success. Often this means that the faculty need to create inclusive research writing groups, make sure opportunities for the Black faculty member to collaborate exist in the department, and ensure that sufficient lab and research space exists to complete their research. The faculty in a department should be willing and able to share the service burdens that accompany the role of the Black professor as still an uncommon resource at most universities for students and others. Professional assistance by the chair and faculty should be provided to assist the faculty member in developing a successful publishing network for their research.

THE INSTITUTION

The Black professor at a university is part of an institution with a history and ongoing pattern of practices with regard to race. If they choose to, all professors can engage with this history and try to address problems that exist today at their universities. For many this becomes how they define their activism. Examples of professor activist work would include joining organizations that advocate for changing the names on campus buildings, providing alternative campus tours to address the otherwise invisible history of the work and presence of Black people and others on the campus, working together with students to change recruitment policies with regard to race for student organizations, changing the membership rosters of faculty organizations to reflect the presence of Black faculty on the campus, creating new opportunities through awards and financial incentives to publicly acknowledge the work of those on campus that improve its record with regard to its racial history and contemporary practices, building strong faculty and staff advocacy organizations to improve the services and support for Black faculty and staff on the campus, advising student advocacy organizations, mentoring Black students, and serving on thesis committees for Black students across the campus.

These efforts are important, and the list above is by no means exhaustive of the work that faculty, and Black faculty are encouraged to do beyond their regular obligations while working at a university. However, the more difficult task of creating equity in the incentive structure for Black faculty and the success of Black students at the university often requires a significant investment in time as well as the mobilization of professional networks and resources external to the university. Persistent problems exist at most universities with respect to Black student graduation rates, financial award levels, recruitment and retention, and career success for graduates. Black faculty often experience difficulty in finding venues for publication, receiving financial support for their research, acquiring affordable housing and security of employment, as well as the affirmation of their peers in their regional and national professional associations. To address these problems requires more than campus advocacy.

There are many Black professors who devote considerable attention to the national conversation of how race continues to describe the provision of higher education in the society. Among the many descriptions of activism that are otherwise invisible to most working at a university, but define much of the work by Black professors, are examples of those who regularly serve as external reviewers of African American Studies programs and other Departments, join Department leadership boards at universities across the country, assist Black PhD students and faculty in finding employment, join the executive committees of regional, national, and international professional associations, nominate exceptional research publications and careers for national awards, serve as reviewers for foundations and fellowship committees, join editorial boards of journals, volunteer to review manuscripts written by Black authors for journals and book publishers, create journals and presses that accept innovative and creative work not acceptable elsewhere, and mentor Black faculty, providing for the professional success of the next generation. For many, this is an activism only available to those who have achieved a level of professional success that is difficult to attain as a Black scholar.

For this reason, it is important to acknowledge this work, for example by Dianne Pinderhughes, a member of the National Academy, and past President of the American Political Science Association, who has in the discipline of Political Science been a constant source of support and institution building outside of her duties and professorship at Notre Dame. Nominating scholars for awards, serving on countless boards, writing and publishing work with other Black professors, being an external reviewer for tenure cases, department programs, manuscripts, as well as doing the work of changing how a discipline supports Black faculty through her participation on the executive councils of national and international professional associations, Dianne is an example of a Black professor who mentors numerous Black professors outside of her obligations of her own university with the express purpose of building a better university for both Black faculty and students at the national level. While this activity would be laudatory for any professor, Dianne represents by her example here the many Black professors who see an important part of their professional work as integral to addressing institutional barriers to racial equality within the national academy.

IN THE CLASSROOM

The last category of activism by the Black professor is the classroom. While the classroom is often the centerpiece of much of the attention given to hiring Black faculty, because it occurs directly with students, the work of addressing race in the classroom is usually invisible labor. In the framework of the current discussion about the responsibilities and description of the Black professor, the challenge is to develop material and lessons for students that critically engage with race in ways that are not conventional, not given by the existing norms through which inequality is fostered and abetted. The classroom must be a location for developing new ideas to resolve the problem of racial injustice, where pedagogical practices are informed by the fact that race is considered a still unsettled and contested concept. These requirements form part of how the Black professor addresses race in class. The other part is to provide a structure for learning through discussion, readings, and assignments that develop a space for productive engagement by everyone.

The Black professor must negotiate the discussion between students to create an environment that serves the needs of each individual. For first-year students in an Introduction to African American studies course, the material is most often quite new to the students, regardless of race. The role of the professor, along with simply introducing the material, is to make the material available, to make relevant the pages from the readings so that all students make connections to their own thinking. The centering of Blackness, of Black experiences, in the curriculum makes sense in this context as a corrective to the exclusion of Black voices in the students' education in other disciplines.

The inclusion of new material doesn't mean that students need to share the experiences of other students to make sense of an idea expressed by others or to contribute effectively to a discussion about a topic in the classroom. Students are assigned to lead class discussion on race topics that they have no personal facility with; it is the responsibility of the professor to remind all the students that they are there to discuss the material and that all the students who read the material can participate. The understanding in class is that first they discuss the material, and then answer the professor's questions. After this, students can add their personal experiences to liven up the material, to give it fuller meaning. It is at this point that the representational role for the Black professor can be important, as the professor can speak from their own experience to nuance how students are considering topics. The authority of the professor in the classroom changes the potential for legitimizing specific perspectives and addressing the problem of a necessary reticence and hesitation by students to discuss race in front of others. Able to finally participate with others in a conversation about what race means for everyone is enlivening. The capacity to encourage this active engagement reminds all students that this material is important for all of us to learn.

The creation of nuanced, sustained critical analysis is facilitated by nontraditional forms of analyzing course readings. Students' arguments need to be understood and valued beyond the narrow frame of the standards of a discourse that either elides the importance of race as an idea in society or suggests that the definition of race in our everyday lives is too fraught, rather than an obvious part of the societal description of Black life through generations of the struggle for civil rights. The erasure of race from conversation in effect can be thought to mirror the desire to stifle and limit the claims by Black people for equality and justice in the society. Kiese Laymon reflects on the complexity of this issue when he recounts in *How to Slowly Kill Yourself and Others in America* (2020) that he "loved knowing that Faulkner's literary virtuosity was inflected by his real and imagined experiences with Black Mississippians. Somewhere around eleventh grade, though, my body tired of imitating white writers who simply could not see, hear, love, or imagine Black folk as part of, or central to, their audience" (23). Part of the role of the Black professor in the classroom is to challenge the approach to what is important and how students learn; we do not want Black students alienated from a critical approach to race and racism, especially if it must be couched in the format of language designed to alienate or exclude, what Laymon calls "the kind of voice that (sits) with its legs crossed, reading the *New York Times*" (2020, 34).

The acknowledgement of the contributions of African Americans to the society, and continuing the political conversation about race, through careful study and reflection, is of great value to students. They are the next generation of activists and have to be able to frame the questions about what they desire collectively in the future. In African American Studies courses, when the topic of race is more explicit in the readings, Black students create a space within which to define a contingent epistemic community primarily by examining the course material and through sharing related life experiences. Anyone can join this process through the sharing of concepts and conversation about these experiences. The African American Studies classroom is often a site where students can disrupt traditional modes of inquiry and expound upon how we all inevitably interact with racial concepts in our lives, both inside and outside the classroom. My experience as a teacher has been that as long as we have centered the readings and built our discussion around these, students can be respectful of one another, and enjoy the opportunity provided by a new type of classroom. The students are reminded that not everyone starts the course with the same level of familiarity with the material, and that knowledge is then used as a way to build a classroom where everyone explicitly agrees that they are there to learn from one another and from the material.

For many students at PWIs, their Black professor in a given class will be the only Black professor they will have while a student. Consequently, for that professor there is a special burden of representation, of the person and profession, that exists and should not be ignored. In this context the Black professor in the classroom has a singular role in teaching and student learning, and the representative character of the Black professor is often evident in the classroom. A few semesters ago, Greg Austin taught an upper-division undergraduate seminar on Black Politics and a few White students were enrolled. One particular day in class, the week before Thanksgiving Break when many students take early vacation days, it just so happened that the only students in class were Black. We went ahead with the schedule and discussed whatever was on the syllabus. The discussion was plodding along normally when one of the young women said she was glad she had an opportunity to speak freely in class that day because there were no White students.

She was careful to mention that she had no ill-will toward White students, but that she felt there was an impediment to her being able to express her relationship to the material in front of White students. When I pressed further as to why, she recounted the familiar justifiable complaint of being tired of shouldering the responsibility of explaining race and racism to other people. While she was comfortable in our particular course, with the material centered on race, she explained that sometimes she felt the burning gaze of White students pressuring her to explain to them why she feels how she does, or why she said what she did, or why she interprets the material in the manner she does. In such a moment, the Black professor can both commiserate, support the students with additional conversation and problems to study, and further explain the purpose behind the larger politics of enjoining others to a conversation about race.

Students often feel pressure to perform racial representation in class. We must recognize that discussions of race in class can bring with it a kind of requirement to perform: to be on task—to be responsible for interpreting for others all things racial. Just as with the Black professor this presents a unique challenge to students in these courses. On the one hand, it is important for Black students to represent otherwise silent voices, underrepresented views, and neglected perspectives in order to ensure classroom conversations are complex and nuanced. This often brings with it an obligation to always represent the Black life as a product of absence, conflict, and loss. What is then created is a classroom space where certain students become arbiters of the interpretations of the course readings on race, rather than equal participants in the discourse. Even as students often expect a certain amount of graciousness when discussing matters of race, students are not permitted to become angry, at the risk of being denounced at once as biased.

The resulting requirement of the conversation about race to exist in a space where generosity is expressed and negative judgments are muted takes its toll on all the students. Often students decide to abdicate from the conversation when it becomes too difficult to maintain the equality of insight in the conversation space with regard to specific materials or ideas. The refusal of representation, the strategic mobilization of differences to problematize the certainty of position and conviction have to persist as a value in the classroom. Only this way is it possible to maintain a classroom where race does not encompass everything that we do as persons, but its study is an exercise in classroom learning. In the same way the Black professor doesn't fully represent anything, but can use the fact of racial representation to provide examples and promote conversation.

It is important that course assignments also reflect a commitment to active discussions in the larger society. The impact of social media as a space for Black activism to engage beyond traditional settings marks a transformative moment in organizing and collective action. Feminista Jones (2019) discusses how digital spaces are not only a tool for activists, but an important site for being heard and supported beyond what had already been commonplace in hair salons and churches (5, 6). Much like the traditional classroom space, "social media networks provide platforms for conversations that we have long been having in our hair salons and our churches" (Jones 2019, 6). The content creation that is happening online by Black people has begun to work its way into the traditional classroom space where Black voices can be centered as they have always been in traditionally Black social spaces.

Allowing the students to engage with social media in the classroom narrows any distinction they feel exists between our specific university space and the outside world. A project for upper-division seminars requires students to take a topic related to their course material, but not covered in the syllabus, and conduct research. They must gather the relevant scholarly sources and contextualize their topics, but they must also include a Twitter thread or TikTok video that speaks to their topic in some way. Engagement with social media is crucial in getting students to see that the political issues they're interested in online can be and are the same things we are talking about in class; it is important that we, as a community of learners, understand the value of popular culture's role in helping to shape people's perceptions of themselves and other people (Dates and Ramirez 2018, 13).

Each classroom, each semester, each iteration of a course forges a new epistemic community, something outside the description of race otherwise available to students, a shared understanding of how they have common values in a determination to address racial inequality and injustice. It is this confidence in the classroom and the professor that allows them to consider the way that we together occupy the world. The question asked by Cornel resonates differently after considering the possibilities in providing a place for the Black professor in the classroom. How can we not support students and what is possible in the classroom, as the purpose and vocation of the professor, and a particular calling for the Black professor?

MEASURE FOR MEASURE

In the book *The Richer, The Poorer* (1995) Dorothy West describes how her father was a slave when young and then over the course of his life became a successful grocery wholesaler to the Boston market. As a newly freed young slave he saved money and paid someone to teach him to read, write, and do arithmetic. Instead of seeing his Blackness as a hindrance, West describes his attitude toward his success as one of necessary enterprise and work. This in spite of the inferior attributes ascribed to him by others. That West shared with her father this characterization of what the world had to offer her, writing and publishing, accepting the support and admiration of others as her due is what we try to teach students. If only it was this easy.

Instead, the call to activism for the Black professor begins with their first job, in the difficult task of creating a space where often none exists in which they can do the work they are ostensibly hired to do. Some are then called to administration and service to the university in this effort, and they work to change the campus itself in their time there. Others work to secure a better future for Black professors across a region and the country, in a given discipline, focused on that which remains undone to support the research that is possible. The Black professor writes and produces work that asks all of us to think differently about the world, even as they model what it means to be Black, and a professor, in the classroom and care for their students.

REFERENCES

Baldwin, James. 1985. "Everybody's Protest Novel." In *The Price of the Ticket: Collected Nonfiction 1948–1985*, 38–45. Boston: Beacon Press.

———. 1985. "The Discovery of What It Means to Be an American." In *The Price of the Ticket: Collected Nonfiction 1948–1985*, 179–184. Boston: Beacon Press.

———. 1985. "They Can't Turn Back." In *The Price of the Ticket: Collected Nonfiction 1948–1985*, 221–235. Boston: Beacon Press.

Bradley, Regina. Host. 2019–2020. *Bottom of the Map*. (Audio Podcast.) BOTM Media. www.bottomofthemap.media.

Bradley, Regina, ed. 2021. *An Outkast Reader: Essays on Race, Gender, and the Postmodern South*. Athens, GA: The University of Georgia Press.

Bradley, Regina. 2021. *Chronicling Stankonia: The Rise of the Hip-Hop South*. Chapel Hill, NC: The University of North Carolina Press.

Butler, Octavia. 1994. *Kindred*. Boston: Beacon Press.

Dates, Jannette, and Mia Ramirez. 2018. *From Blackface to Black Twitter: Reflections on Black Humor, Race, Politics, & Gender*. New York: Peter Lang Publishing.

Harriell, Derrick. 2022. *Come Kingdom: Poems*. Baton Rouge, LA: Louisiana State University Press.

Jones, Feminista. 2019. *Reclaiming Our Space: How Black Feminists Are Changing the World From the Tweets to the Streets.* Boston: Beacon Press.

Jones, Gayl. 1975. *Corregidora.* New York: Random House.

Laymon, Kiese. 2013. *Long Division.* New York: Scribner.

———. 2018. *Heavy.* New York: Scribner.

———. 2020. *How to Slowly Kill Yourself and Others in America.* New York: Scribner.

Mills, Charles. 1997. *The Racial Contract.* Ithaca, NY: Cornell University Press.

Morrison, Toni. 1993. *Playing in the Dark: Whiteness and the Literary Imagination.* New York: Vintage Books.

Walker, Alice. 1997. *Anything We Love Can Be Saved: A Writer's Activism.* New York: Ballentine Books.

West, Dorothy. 1995. *The Richer, The Poorer: Stories, Sketches, and Remembrances.* New York: Anchor Books.

Part 2

THE EFFECTS OF BLACK ACTIVISM
ON INSTITUTIONS

Chapter Nine

An Investigation of Fortune 100 Companies' Responses to the 2020 BLM Movement

Ziyuan Zhou

The BLM movement after the murder of George Floyd in 2020 marked one of the biggest social movements in US history (Buchanan, Bui, and Patel 2020). Changing the status quo of racial injustice requires efforts from various entities. As corporations gain increasing influence and power in society, one cannot ignore the role of corporations in leading and facilitating a social movement. Indeed, from a corporation's perspective, being profitable nowadays could only meet the most basic expectation of stakeholders. To satisfy stakeholders, corporations need to shoulder more social responsibilities. Furthermore, besides safe topics like environmental protection and labor rights, corporations have become vocal on more controversial issues. From Levi's support for gun control (Bhattarai 2018) to Disney's investment in LGBTQ+ communities (Cohen 2022), corporations are not hesitant to show their advocacy.

Corporate social advocacy (CSA) refers to corporations publicly taking "a stance on controversial sociopolitical issues" (Dodd and Supa 2014, 15). In the public relations literature, CSA is documented to help corporations build strong relationships with publics including increased public-company identification (Park and Jiang 2020), greater willingness to share positive word-of-mouth (Li, Kim, and Alharbi 2022), and improved reputation (Lim and Young 2021). In addition, big corporations' CSA could also shape publics' opinions on certain issues (Parcha and Westerman 2020). Despite the various benefits, it remains a challenging issue how to make advocacy more authentic and curb publics' feelings of skepticism (Austin, Gaither, and Gaither 2019; Park 2021).

After the death of George Floyd on May 25, 2020, many corporations immediately joined the discussion of racial justice and showed support for the BLM movement (Tarin, Upton, and Hernández 2021; Purtell and Kang 2022). However, besides words, it is unclear what specific action the corporations have taken to address the issue and if the action is enough to satisfy publics' expectations. If a corporation only verbally supports the movement without mentioning action, it may well be regarded as trendjacking the movement. Through a content analysis of Fortune 100 companies' statements and news releases after the death of George Floyd, this study examined what action was taken by these companies. In addition, this study also investigated if certain industries were more likely to speak up and take action for the movement. Practically, this study provides insight into managing CSA programs and communication. Theoretically, it encourages researchers to explore more CSA programs that could facilitate a movement and build positive relationships with publics.

LITERATURE REVIEW

Black Lives Matter (BLM) Movement and Corporations

The start of the BLM movement dates to 2013 when George Zimmerman, a man who murdered a teenage Black boy, Trayvon Martin, in Sanford, Florida, was acquitted. The case generated wide discussion about racial injustice. In response to the event, three Black activists, Alicia Garza, Patrisse Cullors, and Opal Tometi, started the political movement called Black Lives Matter. Since then, numerous people expressed their anger and frustration over the court's decision on Twitter using the hashtag #BlackLivesMatter (Black Lives Matter Movement n.d.). The outcry facilitated the establishment of a nonprofit organization, Black Lives Matter Global Network Foundation, with a mission to "eradicate white supremacy and build local power to intervene in violence inflicted on Black communities by the state and vigilantes" (Black Lives Matter n.d.). The death of Michael Brown who was shot by a police officer, Darren Wilson, in Ferguson, Missouri, further propelled the movement in 2014 (Mourão, Brown, and Sylvie 2021). Most recently in 2020, footage released online indicated that a police officer, Derek Chauvin, held his knee on a Black man, George Floyd, for over nine minutes until his death (Levenson 2021). The event drove massive protests not only nationally but also internationally. According to Crowd Sourcing Consortium, an estimated 15 to 26 million people participated in the 2020 BLM movement in the United States, making it possibly the largest social movement in US history (Buchanan, Bui, and Patel 2020).

Right after the death of George Floyd, many corporations took action to support the movement including making donations (Livingston 2020). Corporations, an integral part of modern society, have been playing an increasingly important role in social issues. Compared to government and media, people generally have a higher level of trust in corporations (Edelman Trust Barometer 2022). Chen, Dechow, and Tan (2021) disclosed that some corporations voluntarily supported the movement because the practice serves the interest of stakeholders and as a result the organization will face less risk. Johnson (2021) argued that the Securities and Exchange Commission (SEC) should require public companies to put more effort into diversity and inclusion when nominating board members. In addition, corporations should ensure that big decisions about antiracism from the top could be implemented in their daily practices. As people are increasingly aware of the role of corporations in tackling racism, from the corporations' perspective, it is important to understand people's expectations and what to do to meet these expectations. From the perspective of corporate communication and public relations, corporations must understand how to implement strategies for racial justice and communicate their efforts.

Corporate Social Advocacy

Modern management not only requires corporations to be profitable but also emphasizes social obligations (Jones 1980). Carroll (1991) proposed that corporations need to shoulder "four kinds of social responsibilities (that) constitute total CSR: economic, legal, ethical, and philanthropic" (40). Similarly, Dahlsrud (2008) identified five dimensions of CSR: environmental, social, economic, stakeholder, and voluntariness (4). As social issues like racial justice, climate change, gun control, and abortion generate division in society, corporations need to be more cautious and strategic when addressing these issues. However, some corporations like Nike, Ben & Jerry, and Levi's are willing to take a stand on these controversial issues. These practices have attracted increasing research attention in recent years, and the term is coined corporate social advocacy (CSA) (Dodd and Supa 2014, 2015).

CSA is defined as "the taking of a public stance on a controversial social-political issue by corporations, most often in the form of a CEO statement" (Dodd and Supa 2015, 287). CSA differs from CSR in three ways. First, the issue the corporation addresses does not have a direct link to the corporation's business. Second, the issue is controversial, which might isolate some stakeholders. Third, financial outcomes are not stressed by the corporation (Dodd and Supa 2014). As corporations increasingly get involved in CSA practices, various CSA issues have been explored in the public relations literature including gun control (Gaither, Austin, and Collins 2018; Austin, Guidry, and Meyer 2020), racial justice (Heffron and Dodd 2021; Li, Kim, and Alharbi

2021; Overton et al. 2020; Waymer and Logan 2021), LGBTQ+ (Dodd and Supa 2015; Lim and Young 2021; Yim 2021), and climate change (Zhou and Dong 2021). Due to the controversial nature of CSA practices, researchers attempted to discover both its positive and negative consequences. In early research, Dodd and Supa (2015) revealed that CSA practices could boost consumers' purchase intentions. Later research also reinforced that CSA practices could also increase positive word-of-mouth (Li, Kim, and Alharbi 2021; Overton et al. 2020) and loyalty (Park and Jiang 2020). In addition, besides changing people's attitudes toward the corporation, Parcha and Westerman (2020) even found that a corporation's stance on a controversial issue could alter people's attitudes toward the issue under certain circumstances, indicating the strong power of corporations in shaping public perceptions.

As a global event, the BLM movement attracted special research attention from the perspective of corporate communication. Through a critical analysis of Nike's statements, actions, and campaigns (Colin Kaepernick), Waymer and Logan (2021) argued that Nike's CSA practices on racial justice were able to drive engagement, and further empowered marginalized groups. Ciszek and Logan (2018) analyzed Ben & Jerry's support for the BLM movement and advocated for embracing dissensus in the context of digital communication. They contended that Ben & Jerry's failed to engage in meaningful dialogue because the comment thread was full of contentious interactions, which violated the nature of trust, reciprocity, and responsiveness for a dialogue (Ciszek and Logan 2018). Through an analysis of fifty statements released by outdoor and recreation companies, Tarin, Upton, and Hernández (2021) concluded that simply releasing a statement is not enough to address systematic racism and white supremacy. Purtell and Kang (2022) investigated Fortune 500 companies' motives to respond to the BLM and revealed that the motives include "risk management, organizational functioning, market positioning, civic positioning, moral positioning, and social reform" (120). Although many studies demonstrated the value of CSA, it does not go without risk. Zhou and Dong (2022) examined the dark side of CSA and indicated that negative word-of-mouth and boycott intention might be generated if a corporation fails to take action, showing the importance of matching actions with promises. As the conventional saying goes, "actions speak louder than words." Regarding CSA, what a corporation does to contribute to a social issue is more important than a simple statement (Tarin, Upton, and Hernández 2021; Zhou and Dong 2022). In addition, research has shown skepticism and authenticity play important roles in people's perceptions of CSA (Lim and Young 2021; Park 2021; Yim 2021). Taking specific action to address racial issues may be able to lower people's skepticism than verbal support. Therefore, what corporations did after the 2020 BLM deserves more research attention.

Public Relations and Race

Race is a frequently discussed topic in public relations literature. Munshi and Edwards (2011) argued race in the public relations context is socially constructed that goes beyond simply dealing with people from different countries and backgrounds. It is different in different contexts, at different times, and with different people. To theorize race in public relations, public relations scholars need to acknowledge the complex contexts (Munshi and Edwards 2011). Waymer (2010) advocated for emphasizing race in public relations theory building because it informs public relations practices including CSR, internal communication, and crisis management. However, compared to other research topics, race has attracted only limited attention (see Edwards 2013; Logan 2011, 2016; Waymer and Street 2015). Pompper (2005) demonstrated the failure to integrate race into public relations theory building was due to paradigm limitations, underrepresented datasets, a lack of ethnic variables, and few minority public relations researchers.

In response to the call for more theory-building efforts in public relations, Logan (2021) introduced the theory of corporate responsibility to race (CRR) based on three premises.

Corporations have a responsibility to support racial justice by communicating in ways that improve race relations because (b) corporations are organizational forms that have emerged through processes of racism and racialization, and (c) corporations have directly and indirectly perpetuated—and benefited from—racial discrimination and oppression, which has contributed significantly to racial strife and social instability. Put simply, because the institution of corporate America has capitalized on racial discrimination and perpetuated racial oppression, the institution as well as the organizations that comprise it have a responsibility to work toward achieving a more racially just and harmonious society. (Logan 2021, 13)

Public relations, as the channel to demonstrate a corporation's values, plays a central role in communicating CRR. Corporations should use their resources to raise awareness of racism and advocate for racial justice. The communication effort should be guided by five principles. First, CRR communication must raise awareness of racism. Second, CRR communication must reflect the influence of racism. Third, CRR communication must support racial justice. Fourth, CRR communication must improve race relations to build a harmonious society. Fifth, CRR communication must emphasize the need of society rather than financial outcomes (Logan 2021). Different from most public relations theories that build on theories from other disciplines. CRR emerges from public relations and has a deep root in corporate communication.

Based on the previous discussion, corporations not only have the responsibility to speak up on racism but also take action to improve race relations. Purtell and Kang (2022) investigated Fortune 500 companies' Instagram responses and Tarin, Upton, and Hernández (2021) examined the statements of outdoor sporting and recreation companies after the 2020 BLM movement. Since social media is good for short content, it is difficult to examine a corporation's complete action through social media content. It is still unknown what specific action companies have taken regarding the 2020 BLM movement and if the action has reached its target. Therefore, the following research question was proposed:

RQ1: What specific action do Fortune 100 corporations take in response to the 2020 BLM movement?

Different industries bear varying levels of pressure to implement CSR programs and use diverse strategies to approach social issues. Agudelo, Johannsdottir, and Davdsdottir (2020) found that companies with production processes such as energy companies are forced to shoulder more social responsibilities like labor rights and environmental production. In comparison, technology companies in California are criticized for gentrification and increasing the living cost of the local community. To address the social impact, tech giants need to adopt a different strategy from the energy sector (Okafor, Adeleye, and Adusei 2021). Through analyzing the annual CSR reports of companies in different industries, Sweeney and Coughlan (2008) noted that companies reported CSR efforts in significantly different ways, mainly to satisfy their main stakeholders. Since CSR practices are different across industries, different industries may have different levels of CSA involvement. However, it is unknown if certain industries paid more attention to the BLM movement and if industries used unique strategies to approach the issue. Therefore, the following research questions were proposed:

RQ2: What industries are more willing to speak up for the BLM movement?
RQ3: What industries are more willing to take action for the BLM movement?

METHOD

This study investigates how Fortune 100 corporations responded to the death of George Floyd in 2020. In detail, this study interrogates which specific actions corporations took that were mentioned in their statements or news releases. In addition, this study also questions if different industries favor different strategies to approach the issue. To answer the research question, a content analysis was carried out. Lacy et al. (2015) contended that content analysis is appropriate to systematically and quantitatively examine large amounts of messages and communication materials.

Sampling

This study focused on Fortune 100 corporations' responses to the BLM movement because large corporations have more power and influence on social issues. The 100 companies were captured using the 2022 list of Fortune 500 companies (Fortune n.d.). After confirming the companies, the researcher visited the official website of each company. Most companies had a designated section called "newsroom," "press center," or "media center." All news releases, statements, and corporate blogs about the BLM movement from the section were documented. The researcher focused on the materials published after May 25, 2020, the day of George Floyd's death, till July 25, 2020, a period of two months. Any materials using words such as "Black Lives Matter," "George Floyd," "race," "racial justice," or "racism" were included in the sample. The researcher focused on the print content and excluded pictures, captions, and videos. Out of the 100 companies, 65 companies published news releases, statements, or corporate blogs related to the movement on their website. The 65 corporations published 84 news releases, statements, and corporate blogs in total.

Coding Scheme

The researcher first coded the basics of each item including 1) company, 2) company sector, 3) date of publication, and 4) tone (corporate vs. personal). The company sector was coded based on the S&P 500 sectors "including information technology, health care, financials, consumer discretionary, communication services, industrials, consumer staples, energy, utilities, real estate, and materials" (CFI Team 2022). The sector categorization of S&P 500 companies was consulted when the coders encountered problems. If the corporation used an open letter or email from the CEO or other C-suite members, it was coded as a personal tone. If the corporation issued a news release or statement purely from the corporation's perspective, it was coded as a corporate tone. To answer the first research question, the researcher used the grounded theory building approach and constant comparison method. Instead of using a pre-drafted codebook, the researcher read and compared the actions mentioned in the materials. Based on the corporate actions, a list of actions was formed. Table 9.1 provides the codebook.

Table 9.1.

Variable	Instruction for Coding
Company	Document the company name
Company sector	• Information technology: internet companies, computers, semiconductors, operating systems. E.g., Microsoft, Intel, IBM • Health care: pharmaceutical companies, health care provider. E.g., CVS, Johnson & Johnson • Financials: banks, investing, insurance, mortgage. E.g., Chase, Fidelity, Geico • Consumer discretionary: products that are not necessary for survival. E.g., Amazon, Bust Buy, Home Depot, Target • Communication services: companies that keep people connected. E.g., Meta, Netflix, Disney, AT&T • Industrials: airlines, military, railroad. E.g., FedEx, Boeing, United Airlines • Consumer staples: companies that provide basic products to life. E.g., Walmart, P&G • Energy: gas, oil, energy transfer. E.g., Chevron, Energy Transfer • Utilities: companies that provide electricity, water, gas to households. E.g., National Grid, Eversource • Real estate: real estate trust fund and realtors. E.g., Boston Properties • Materials: companies that provide raw materials for other companies. E.g., Dow
Publication date	Document the date of the publication
Tone	Corporate tone • The material is written from a company's perspective. • In the format of a news release or statement Personal tone • In the format of a person (CEO, board member, COO, CFO, etc.) • In the format of an open letter to customers or employees.

Two coders coded nine news releases (10.7 percent) separately. The Cohen's kappa for the four categories was 1 (company), 0.89 (company sector), 1 (date of publication), and 1 (tone) respectively. A Cohen's kappa over .8 is considered sound reliability (Lombard, Snyder-Duch, Bracken 2002). Therefore, the codebook was considered reliable.

RESULTS

Among the Fortune 100 corporations, 65 corporations (65 percent) issued news releases, statements, open letters, or corporate blogs on their official website to respond to the murder of George Floyd. Of corporations that touched on the issue, 38 came from a CEO's open letter while 23 corporations used a corporate tone. Another four corporations used multiple tones in different statements.

RQ1 inquired about the specific actions taken by Fortune 100 companies. In these 65 corporations, 42 corporations (42 percent) mentioned specific actions to contribute to the BLM movement. The most common practice was financial contributions from hundreds of thousands to hundreds of millions of dollars, either one-time or over a couple of years. Almost all corporations which took action donated to the BLM movement ($n = 39$, 39 percent), which included donating to nonprofits that are dedicated to racial justice and Black museums. Another form of the donation was to provide funds to Black-owned or minority-owned businesses. Some corporations encouraged employees to donate to the movement by matching employees' donations to a certain amount. An additional four corporations (4 percent) donated volunteer hours to help small businesses.

Some corporations focused more attention on recruiting and retaining diverse employees ($n = 8$, 8 percent). They decided to provide diversity training for HR associates or partner with historically black colleges and universities (HBCUs). Another common practice was to start new initiatives and programs that center on racial equity. Six corporations (6 percent) launched new initiatives to advocate for equality and justice. Four corporations (4 percent) decided to diversify their suppliers so that minority-owned businesses could get more opportunities. The last common practice lies in using media influence. Four corporations (4 percent) mentioned they started advertising and marketing campaigns to advocate for racial equity. Table 9.2 provides the practices.

RQ2 investigated if certain industries were more likely to advocate for racial justice. A chi-square test of independence was performed to understand the relationship between company sectors and willingness to take a stand on

Table 9.2.

Action	Number of Corporations
Donation • To the victim • To nonprofits • To minority-owned business • Match employee donations	39
Reform employee recruitment, training, retention, and promotion	8
New initiatives, programs, and centers that tackle racism	6
Diversify suppliers to offer more opportunities to minority-owned businesses	4
Use media influence to start campaigns focused on racial justice	4

racial justice. The result was significant, χ (9) = 19.03, $p < .05$. A post hoc analysis based on pairwise Z-Tests (Garcia-Perez and Nunez-Anton 2003) indicated that the financial sector was more likely to support the movement than other sectors. In comparison, the energy sector was less likely to speak up for the movement than other sectors.

RQ3 investigated if certain industries were more likely to take action for the movement. A chi-square test of independence was performed to understand the relationship between company sectors and the willingness to take action on racial justice. The result was not significant, χ (9) = 116.14, $p = .06$. Therefore, no specific industry had a stronger willingness to take action during the BLM movement.

DISCUSSION

This study intended to explore the participation of Fortune 100 corporations in the BLM movement after the death of George Floyd in 2020. Specifically, it aimed to reveal common actions taken by these corporations in support of the movement and industry differences. The content analysis revealed interesting findings that could help practitioners to better position their corporations and scholars to understand the gap between academic research and corporate practices.

Inauthentic CSA Practices

At the superficial level, it is satisfying to find that most Fortune 100 corporations (65 percent) showed support for the BLM movement and advocated for racial justice. However, a further look at the statements disclosed that no more than half of the corporations (42 percent) truly joined the movement by providing specific plans. Some corporations only expressed sympathy toward the victim and anger at such an incident. The most common action taken by these corporations was donation (39 percent). There is a long debate on corporate donations in the CSR literature, which frequently discusses the relationship between donation and skepticism. Kim and Lee (2009) found that the amount of donation affected consumers' skepticism and the corporation's credibility. Vlachos et al. (2016) revealed that different frames of donations exerted an influence on consumers' skepticism. To the best of the researcher's knowledge, no study in the CSA literature has discussed the impact of corporate donations on social movements. For a corporation with billions in revenues each year, donating several million dollars seems a convenient and cost-efficient way to join a social movement. It deserves further investigation if making a donation to a social movement could contribute to a social movement and benefit a corporation's reputation.

Some corporations shared more comprehensive plans to advocate for the movement's goals including policy changes, employee recruitment and retention, and new initiatives for racial justice. As Logan (2021) argued, modern corporations emerged and benefited from racialization and racism. From stakeholders' perspectives, more empirical evidence is needed to indicate whether these practices are enough to address racial injustice and racism. This study paves the road for more research on corporate responsibility to race (CRR). CRR requires corporate communication to highlight the impact of racism, improve race relations, and prioritize societal needs over economic gains. Future research could investigate if these practices could satisfy the requirements. If not, what further action could corporations take to address the issue?

Varying Levels of Attention to CSA Across Industries

Ample research has shown the difference in CSR efforts across industries. Young and Marais (2012) reported that companies in high-risk industries put more effort into CSR practices than those in low-risk industries. Similar findings were also revealed by Tagesson et al. (2009), that companies whose manufacturing negatively impacts the environment tend to report more CSR information. When evaluating a corporation's CSR efforts, people also use different standards based on industries. Kim (2011) noted that information technology companies which rely on innovation would be less judged on the basis of their CSR performance. In comparison, consumer staples companies are more likely to be judged on their CSR performance. The findings that companies in different sectors have different levels of CSR involvement apply to the CSA context. The financial sector is more likely to speak up for the BLM movement while the energy sector is less likely to do so. However, regarding the specific actions taken, no industry is more likely to provide a specific plan.

A surprising finding lies in the silence of the energy industry. Out of nine energy corporations on the Fortune 100 list, only one issued a statement on the BLM movement without mentioning any specific action. Due to publics' increasing awareness of climate change, energy corporations heavily engage in CSR and are active in reporting their efforts (Shahbaz et al. 2020; Young and Marais 2012). A lack of involvement of energy corporations in racial injustice might be caused by the perceived fit. Lim and Young (2021) found that the perceived fit between organizational identity and the CSA issue strongly predicted a corporation's reputation. Energy corporations serve all households and are less likely to be associated with racial issues. The management teams of these corporations might not see the link, and thus, kept silent during the 2020 BLM movement. However, CSA differs from CSS because it touches on issues that are not directly related to a corporation's business. Corporations that do not take a stand on these issues will miss the opportunity to engage stakeholders like employees and partners. As people's expectations of corporations continue to change, keeping silent might not be a solution in the future.

LIMITATIONS AND FUTURE RESEARCH

Despite the study providing meaningful results for corporate social advocacy (CSA), it suffers from several major limitations. First, though the researcher documented all communication materials from the corporations' websites, there is no guarantee that all communication efforts have been captured. Some corporations did not publish statements about the movement on their website. Instead, they used social media (e.g., Facebook, Twitter, and LinkedIn) to express their stances. For example, Mark Zuckerberg, the CEO of Meta, expressed his support for the movement on his own Facebook page, but one cannot find such information on Meta's website. Therefore, the sample could not cover all corporations' efforts. Second, though the 2020 BLM movement started in the United States, it generated global discussions and implications outside the United States. Big non-United States corporations equally contributed to the movement and brought even more international influence. Researchers who want to examine the movement from an international perspective should pay more attention to the corporate advocacy outside the United States.

Despite the limitations, this study produced important conclusions for both researchers and practitioners. It also pointed out several new research directions. The researcher invites more investigation into the effect of these practices on both the movement and corporate reputation. The researcher also invites more studies on creative corporate strategies to address racial injustice.

REFERENCES

Agudelo, Mauricio, Lára Johannsdottir, and Brynhildur Davidsdottir. 2020. "Drivers That Motivate Energy Companies to Be Responsible: A Systematic Literature Review of Corporate Social Responsibility in the Energy Sector." *Journal of Cleaner Production*, no. 247 (February 20). https://doi.org/10.1016/j.jclepro.2019.119094.
Austin, Lucinda, Jeanine Guidry, and Michele Meyer. 2020. "#GunViolence on Instagram and Twitter: Examining Social Media Advocacy in the Wake of the Parkland

School Shooting." *The Journal of Public Interest Communications* 4 (1): 4–36. https://doi.org/10.32473/jpic.v4.i1.p4.

Bhattarai, Abha. 2018. "Levi Strauss CEO Takes a Side on Gun Control: 'It's Inevitable That We're Going to Alienate Some Consumers.'" *The Washington Post*, September 10, 2018. https://www.washingtonpost.com/business/2018/09/10/levi-strauss-ceo-takes-side-gun-control-its-inevitable-that-were-going-alienate-some-consumers/.

Black Lives Matter. 2023 "About." Black Lives Matter Website. Accessed March 23, 2023. https://blacklivesmatter.com/about.

Buchanan, Larry, Quoctrung Bui, and Jugal Patel. 2020. "Black Lives Matter May Be the Largest Movement in U.S. History." *The New York Times*, July 3 2020. https://www.nytimes.com/interactive/2020/07/03/us/george-floyd-protests-crowd-size.html.

Carroll, Archie. 1991. "The Pyramid of Corporate Social Responsibility: Toward the Moral Management of Organizational Stakeholders." *Business Horizons* 34 (4): 39–48.

CFT Team. 2023. "The S&P Sectors." Corporate Finance Institute. Accessed March 23, 2023. https://corporatefinanceinstitute.com/resources/knowledge/finance/the-sp-sectors/.

Chen, Andrew, Patricia Dechow, and Samuel Tan. 2021. "Beyond Shareholder Value? Why Firms Voluntarily Disclose Support for Black Lives Matter." Research Collection, School of Accountancy, Singapore Management University. 1–65. Accessed April 24, 2023. https://ink.library.smu.edu.sg/soa_research/1952.

Ciszek, Erica, and Nneka Logan. 2018. "Challenging the Dialogic Promise: How Ben & Jerry's Support for Black Lives Matter Fosters Dissensus on Social Media." *Journal of Public Relations Research* 30 (3): 115–127. https://doi.org/10.1080/1062726X.2018.1498342.

Cohen, Li. 2022. "Disney Heir Blasts Florida's 'Don't Say Gay' Bill After Publicly Coming Out as Transgender." *CBS News*, April 12, 2022. https://www.cbsnews.com/news/charlee-disney-transgender-florida-dont-say-gay-bill/.

Dahlsrud, Alexander. 2008. "How Corporate Social Responsibility Is Defined: An Analysis of 37 Definitions." *Corporate Social Responsibility & Environmental Management* 15 (1): 1–13. doi:10.1002/csr.132.

Dodd, Melissa, and Dustin Supa. 2014. "Conceptualizing and Measuring 'Corporate Social Advocacy' Communication: Examining the Impact on Corporate Financial Performance." *Public Relations Journal* 8 (3): 2–23. http://www.prsa.org/Intelligence/PRJournal/Documents/2014DoddSupa.pdf.

———. 2015. "Testing the Viability of Corporate Social Advocacy as a Predictor of Purchase Intention." *Communication Research Reports* 32 (4): 287–293. doi:10.1080/08824096.2015.1089853.

Edelman. 2022. "Edelman Trust Barometer." Accessed March 23, 2023. https://www.edelman.com/sites/g/files/aatuss191/files/2022-01/2022%20Edelman%20Trust%20Barometer%20FINAL_Jan25.pdf.

Edwards, Lee. 2013. "Institutional Racism in Cultural Production: The Case of Public Relations." *Popular Communication* 11 (3): 242–256. https://doi.org/10.1080/15405702.2013.810084.

Fortune. 2023. "Fortune 500." *Fortune Magazine.* Accessed March 23, 2023. https:// fortune.com/fortune500/.

Gaither, Barbara, Lucinda Austin, and Morgan Collins. 2018. "Examining the Case of DICK'S Sporting Goods: Realignment of Stakeholders through Corporate Social Advocacy." *The Journal of Public Interest Communications* 2 (2): 176–176. https:// doi.org/10.32473/jpic.v2.i2.p176.

Garcia-Perez, Miguel, and Vicente Nunez-Anton. 2003. "Cellwise Residual Analysis in Two-Way Contingency Tables." *Educational and Psychological Measurement* 63 (5): 825–839. https://doi.org/10.1177/0013164403251280.

Howard University School of Law (HUSL). 2023. "Black Lives Matter Movement." HUSL. Accessed March 23, 2023. https://library.law.howard.edu/civilrightshis tory/BLM.

Heffron, Eve, and Melissa Dodd. 2021. "The Impact of Corporate Social Advocacy on Stakeholders' Issue Awareness, Attitudes, and Voting Behaviors." *Public Relations Journal* 12 (4): 1–25. https://prjournal.instituteforpr.org/wp-content/uploads /Heffron_PRJ14.2.pdf.

Johnson, Blair. 2021. "How the Black Lives Matter Movement Enhanced Corporate Governance in 2020." *Emory Corporate Governance and Accountability Review* 8 (1): 99–130. https://scholarlycommons.law.emory.edu/ecgar/vol8/iss1/6.

Jones, Thomas. 1980. "Corporate Social Responsibility Revisited, Redefined." *California Management Review* 22 (3): 59–67. https://doi.org/10.2307/41164877.

Kim, Sora. 2011. "Transferring Effects of CSR Strategy on Consumer Responses: The Synergistic Model of Corporate Communication Strategy." *Journal of Public Relations Research* 23 (2): 218–241. doi:10.1080/1062726X.2011.555647.

Kim, Yeo Jung, and Wei-Na Lee. 2009. "Overcoming Consumer Skepticism in Cause-Related Marketing: The Effects of Corporate Social Responsibility and Donation Size Claim Objectivity." *Journal of Promotion Management* 15 (4): 465–483. http://dx.doi.org/10.1080/10496490903270232.

Lacy, Stephen, Brendan R. Watson, Daniel Riffe, and Jennette Lovejoy. 2015. "Issues and Best Practices in Content Analysis." *Journalism & Mass Communication Quarterly* 92 (4): 791–811. https://doi.org/10.1177/1077699015607338.

Levenson, Eric. 2021. "Former Officer Knelt on George Floyd for 9 Minutes and 29 Seconds—Not the Infamous 8:46." *CNN*, March 30, 2021. https://www.cnn .com/2021/03/29/us/george-floyd-timing-929-846/index.html.

Li, Jo-Yun, Joon Kim, and Khalid Alharbi. 2022. "Exploring the Role of Issue Involvement and Brand Attachment in Shaping Consumer Response toward Corporate Social Advocacy (CSA) Initiatives: The Case of Nike's Colin Kaepernick Campaign." *International Journal of Advertising* 41 (2): 233–257. https://doi.org /10.1080/02650487.2020.1857111.

Lim, Joon Soo, and Cayley Young. 2021. "Effects of Issue Ownership, Perceived Fit, and Authenticity in Corporate Social Advocacy on Corporate Reputation." *Public Relations Review* 47 (4): 102046. https://doi.org/10.1016/j.pubrev.2021.102071.

Livingston, Mercey. 2020. "These Are the Major Brands Donating to the Black Lives Matter Movement." *CNET*, June 16, 2020. https://www.cnet.com/culture /companies-donating-black-lives-matter/.

Logan, Nneka. 2011. "The White Leader Prototype: A Critical Analysis of Race in Public Relations." *Journal of Public Relations Research* 23 (4): 442–457. doi:10 .1080/1062726X.2011.605974.

———. 2021. "A Theory of Corporate Responsibility to Race (CRR): Communication and Racial Justice in Public Relations." *Journal of Public Relations Research* 33 (1): 6–22. doi:10.1080/1062726X.2021.1881898.

Mourão, Rachel, Danielle Brown, and George Sylvie. 2021. "Framing Ferguson: The Interplay of Advocacy and Journalistic Frames in Local and National Newspaper Coverage of Michael Brown." *Journalism* 22 (2): 320–340. https://doi .org/10.1177/1464884918778722.

Munshi, Debashish, and Lee Edwards. 2011. "Understanding 'Race' In/And Public Relations: Where Do We Start and Where Should We Go?." *Journal of Public Relations Research* 23 (4): 349–367. doi:10.1080/1062726X.2011.605976.

Okafor, Anthony, Bosede Adeleye, and Michael Adusei. 2021. "Corporate Social Responsibility and Financial Performance: Evidence from US Tech Firms." *Journal of Cleaner Production*, no. 292 (April 10): 126060. https://doi.org/10.1016 /j.jclepro.2021.126078.

Overton, Holly, Minhee Choi, Jane Weatherred, and Nanlan Zhang. 2020. "Testing the Viability of Emotions and Issue Involvement as Predictors of CSA Response Behaviors." *Journal of Applied Communication Research* 48 (6): 695–713. doi:10 .1080/00909882.2020.1824074.

Parcha, Joshua M., and Catherine Y. Kingsley Westerman. 2020. "How Corporate Social Advocacy Affects Attitude Change Toward Controversial Social Issues." *Management Communication Quarterly* 34 (3): 350–383. https://doi-org.ezp.bent ley.edu/10.1177/0893318920912196.

Park, Keonyoung. 2022. "The Mediating Role of Skepticism: How Corporate Social Advocacy Builds Quality Relationships with Publics." *Journal of Marketing Communications* 28 (8): 821–839. doi:10.1080/13527266.2021.1964580.

Park, Keonyoung, and Hua Jiang. 2023. "Signaling, Verification, and Identification: The Way Corporate Social Advocacy Generates Brand Loyalty on Social Media." *International Journal of Business Communication* 60 (2): 439–463. doi:10.1177/2329488420907121.

Pompper, Donnalyn. 2005. "Difference" in Public Relations Research: A Case for Introducing Critical Race Theory." *Journal of Public Relations Research* 17 (2): 139–169. doi:10.1207/s1532754xjprr1702_5.

Purtell, Rachel, and Katie Kang. 2022. "The Corporate Social Responsibility of Fortune 500 Companies to Black Lives Matter: Strategic Responses on Instagram." *Communication Reports* 35 (2): 120–133. doi:10.1080/08934215.2022.2040559.

Shahbaz, Muhammad, Abdullah Karaman, Merve Kilic, and Ali Uyar. 2020. "Board Attributes, CSR Engagement, and Corporate Performance: What Is the Nexus in the Energy Sector?" *Energy Policy* 143 (August): 111582. https://doi.org/10.1016 /j.enpol.2020.111582.

Sweeney, Lorraine, and Joseph Coughlan. 2008. "Do Different Industries Report Corporate Social Responsibility Differently? An Investigation Through the Lens of Stakeholder Theory." *Journal of Marketing Communications* 14 (2): 113–124. doi:10.1080/13527260701856657.

Tagesson, Torbjörn, Veronica Blank, Pernilla Broberg, and Sven-Olof Collin. 2009. "What Explains the Extent and Content of Social and Environmental Disclosures on Corporate Websites: A Study of Social and Environmental Reporting in Swedish Listed Corporations." *Corporate Social Responsibility and Environmental Management* 16 (6): 352–364. doi:10.1002/csr.194.

Tarin, Carlos, Sarah Upton, and Leandra Hernández. 2021. "We Need to be Better": Race, Outdoor Recreation, and Corporate Social Advocacy." *Frontiers in Communication* 6 (December): 668812. https://doi.org/10.3389/fcomm.2021.726417.

Vlachos, Pavlos, Christos Koritos, Areti Krepapa, Konstantinos Tasoulis, and Ioannis Theodorakis. 2016. "Containing Cause-Related Marketing Skepticism: A Comparison Across Donation Frame Types." *Corporate Reputation Review* 19 (1): 4–21. doi:10.1057/crr.2015.23.

Waymer, Damion. 2010. "Does Public Relations Scholarship Have a Place in Race?" In *The SAGE Handbook of Public Relations*, edited by Robert Heath, 237–246. Thousand Oaks, CA: SAGE Publications.

Waymer, Damion, and Nneka Logan. 2021. "Corporate Social Advocacy as Engagement: Nike's Social Justice Communication." *Public Relations Review* 47 (1): 101031. https://doi.org/10.1016/j.pubrev.2020.102005.

Waymer, Damion, and Joshua Street. 2015. "HBCUs as Relics or Reminders: Race Remains Relevant in a 'Post-Racial' Society? Exploring and Expanding the Role of Memory in Public Relations." *Public Relations Inquiry* 4 (2): 145–162. https://doi-org.ezp.bentley.edu/10.1177/2046147X15588838.

Yim, Myungok. 2021. "Fake, Faulty, and Authentic Stand-Taking: What Determines the Legitimacy of Corporate Social Advocacy?." *International Journal of Strategic Communication* 15 (1): 60–76. doi:10.1080/1553118X.2020.1856853.

Young, Suzanne, and Magalie Marais. 2012. "A Multi-Level Perspective of CSR Reporting: The Implications of National Institutions and Industry Risk Characteristics." *Corporate Governance: An International Review* 20 (5): 432–450. doi:10.1111/j.1467-8683.2012.00926.x.

Chapter Ten

Black Activism from the Ivory Tower

Cultural Betrayal, Sexual Abuse, and Healing for Black Women and Girls

Jennifer M. Gómez

For over 100 years, Black feminist activism has shaped the course of the United States (Leath et al. 2022; Ross et al. 2022), providing the foundation for the 21st century's Black activism (Neville and Cokley 2022; Shaheed et al. 2022). As bell hooks (2014, 110) stated, "To be truly visionary, we have to root our imagination in our concrete reality, while simultaneously imagining possibilities beyond that reality." As such, our activism plays vital roles in defining our experiences as Black women, while demanding substantive change from every system that oppresses us. This dialectic of oppression and resistance (Collins 2022) is also found within education, including at the university (Leath et al. 2022). Simultaneously, Black feminist work produced within academia can be both influenced by and influential for contemporary Black movements (e.g., George Zimmerman's murder of Trayvon Martin, Gómez 2014; Me Too and Black male-perpetrated sexual abuse of Black women and girls, Burke 2021; Gómez 2019f). Amidst the violent and unequal state of the world, a symbiotic relationship of Black feminist activism within and outside of academia can foment a unity in which the oppression that binds us is weakened through our collective resistance. In the current chapter, I briefly detail the context of Black women's experience of sexual abuse in the Black community. I then review my research with cultural betrayal trauma theory (Gómez 2023), which is a framework that centralizes inequality as a primary harm of within-group violence—known as cultural betrayal trauma—in Black and other marginalized communities. Next, I discuss how my CBTT research and public scholarship serve as Black feminist scholar-activism. Then, I detail the need, tenets, and specific strategies of radical healing for Black women who have endured cultural betrayal sexual trauma. Finally, I close with a preview of my upcoming book, detailing specific institutionally courageous

(Freyd 2018) steps that organizations can take to promote both prevention and healing from cultural betrayal sexual trauma for Black women.

THE 'RAPE PROBLEM' IN THE BLACK COMMUNITY

Historically, the "rape problem" in the Black community has been conceptualized as White women falsely accusing Black men of rape, resulting in removal of civil and human rights through incarceration, violence, and murder (Bones and Mathew 2020; Blee 2008; Wells-Barnett 2021). Ignored in this narrative is the very real issue of some Black men raping Black women and girls (Crenshaw 1991). Reasons for this occlusion are multifaceted, including the secondary marginalization (Cohen 2009) that characterizes Black women and girls' lower status and positioning within the Black community. An additional contributor is political intersectionality, whereby sexual violence against Black women and girls is not prioritized in either anti-racist or White feminist movements (Crenshaw 1991). Despite the long history of resistance against rape (McGuire 2010), Black women and girls, along with our experiences of sexual violence, are occluded behind "more important causes" that are defined and circumscribed by Black men and rich White women, respectively.

CULTURAL BETRAYAL TRAUMA THEORY

I created CBTT (Gómez 2012) within the context of Black women and girls' erasure regarding sexual violence in the black community. According to CBTT, within-group violence, such as a Black man sexually abusing a Black girl, includes the implicit harm of cultural betrayal because this violence violates the solidarity needed amongst Black people living in a racist society (Gómez 2023). In addition to contributing to cultural outcomes, such as internalized prejudice, these cultural betrayal traumas may also create vulnerability for Black women and girls' mental, behavioral, and physical health (Gómez and Gobin 2020a). Moreover, cultural group dynamics, such as (intra)cultural pressure, can violently silence Black women and girls who experience cultural betrayal sexual trauma. Examples include some Black people's harassment and discursive violence against Black women who speak about Black men's abuse of them (Burke 2021; Cole and Guy-Sheftall 2003; Gómez 2019f, 2019i; Grundy 2022; Wilson 1994). The empirical findings (Durkee and Gómez 2022; Gómez 2017, 2019a, 2019b, 2019g, 2019h, 2021b, 2021d, 2021e, 2022a, 2022b; Gómez and Freyd 2018; Gómez and Gobin, 2020a; Gómez and Johnson, 2022; Howard Valdivia, Ahrens, and Gómez

2022; McDaniel, Zelenak, and Gómez 2022), including from Black women survivors specifically (Gómez and Gobin, 2022), largely support "to" should be removed the reality of cultural betrayal being a specific harm of within-group violence in the Black community specific harm of cultural betrayal.

BLACK FEMINIST SCHOLAR-ACTIVISM FROM THE IVORY TOWER

Research, such as CBTT, that indicts White Supremacy while centralizing marginalized people and our perspectives can be an act of scholar-activism in and of itself: we demand epistemological legitimacy within an academic environment that more often devalues, degrades, and disregards our knowledge and our ways of knowing (Collins 1991; Gómez 2023). Public scholarship, which is writing, videos, and other works created specifically for our communities and/or the general public, can be another form of scholar-activism. Disseminating my work to people outside of the academy remains an imperative for me. As a student therapist in graduate school, I remember the frustration I felt when I would share with clients the research about the prevalence and impact of sexual abuse: information that academics readily have access to, while people living in the real world typically do not. I find it frightfully unfair, unnecessary, and unethical to confine this information within the self-designated hallowed halls of the academy. Additionally important is the meta-message that is communicated when academics do share our work with the general public; we are imploding the reified 'elite educated class' in service of valuing our work based on its applicability and accessibility to the populations we work with and serve. Through this implosion, "my work" as an academic object becomes "our work" as a tool for societal change and individual, interpersonal, and structural healing.

Over the years, my colleagues and I have produced pieces for our communities and the general public regarding CBTT (Gómez 2016a, 2018b, 2019f), sexual abuse in the Black community (Gómez 2019i; Gómez and Gobin, 2020b), sexual harassment against marginalized women (DePrince and Gómez 2020), racism (Cook and Gómez 2020), racist murder (e.g., Gómez 2014; Gómez and Freyd 2014), the United States' and the field of psychology's role in torture (Gómez 2015c), discrimination in academia (Araral et al. 2021; Brown and Gómez 2022; Gómez 2015d, 2016b, 2018a, 2018c, 2019c, 2019d, 2020), and discriminatory academic policies and practices affecting marginalized college students who experience sexual violence and harassment (Gómez 2015a, 2015b; Howard Valdivia, Ahrens, and Gómez 2022; McDaniel and Gómez, 2021).

My most widely disseminated piece is my article for *The Conversation*, entitled "The Unique Harm of Sexual Abuse in the Black Community" (Gómez 2019f). When I wrote this article, I believed strongly that two things that the U.S. at large does not care about are sexual abuse and Black people. As of March 2023, this article has been read more than 638,800 times. The reach of this work continues through my participation in a filmed panel (Gómez 2021c) with Jamia Wilson, Sheri Sher, Joan Morgan, and Jimmie Briggs to discuss CBTT in reference to the *On The Record* documentary about Russell Simmons' sexual abuse of multiple Black women (Dick and Ziering 2020).

My scholar-activism is vital for my soul-selfhood. As Black women academics, it can feel as though we lose our Blackness and our Black woman personhood in academia because we are living and working within White supremacist norms that create distance and dissonance within ourselves and our community homes. At times, we may even lose credibility with our communities outside of academia when they remove "can" perceive us having been infiltrated by the above. And sometimes and in some ways, they are right. However, there is a Black lining in which we can reclaim and recenter our legacy of Black feminist activism as an integral part of our jobs and lives as academics, thus further dismantling the academic vs. community societally enforced separation.

Through the process and outcomes of my scholar-activism, I am learning that the world is changing. We are not yet living in a world that is peaceful and equitable. Nevertheless, we are existing in a space where such violence and discrimination are becoming harder and harder to ignore, with our activism growing harder and harder to silence. Not only is change coming, so much of the change we need is already here, as is our road to healing.

TRUTH-TELLING AS A PRELUDE TO HEALING

Black Women's Multidimensionality

Before we can discuss radical healing, we must know the importance of truth-telling from the sides of the oppressed (Freire 1970). This provides us with the ability to identify and reject the myths purported by White supremacy (Mills 1997) and misogynoir (Bailey 2016). Perhaps the first step is disrupting homogenous conceptualizations of Black women and girls through instead understanding ourselves and each other as multidimensional beings in all settings. For instance, in academic spaces, I watch some White men performing their self-defined cool-ness, partying, funny, fun, and social selves alongside their defaulted appraisal as Serious Researcher. I have never witnessed Black women academics performing in this same way. However, there are times I notice Black women manicuring themselves in the most positive one-dimensionality of a given space, such as professional at work and sexual at home. Nevertheless, we have models of Black women who bring their full selves to the spaces they occupy, such as President of the American Psychological Association, Dr. Thema Bryant (Tan 2022), who, in her conference presentations, both sings and speaks from her soul to our spirits (Bryant 2021). We can activate the acceptability of our multidimensionality by viewing ourselves as full and complete, while cultivating spaces where our full presence leads to support and not harm (e.g., Gómez 2021f). As such, we can create emotional, psychological, spiritual, and even physical distance between ourselves and those others who dehumanize us.

Black Men's Violence

In tandem with the aforementioned embodiment of truth-telling within our conceptualization of self, truth-telling about Black male-perpetrated sexual abuse against Black women and girls, or cultural betrayal sexual trauma, must happen as well. Given the context of White supremacy and its instantiations, external and internalized violent silencing can be justified through the need to protect Black men and all Black people, while creating an imagined community of unadulterated peace. However, in line with the violent silencing itself, such justification and lies come at the expense of Black women and girls. As integral members of the Black community, that cost to Black women and girls must no longer be acceptable (Gómez 2019i). Therefore, instead of using denial to curate a fallacy of a Black community that is perfect, what if we instead drew from truth? Since we desperately need our community, we can collectively work toward a reality of peace and equality internally that begins with frank acknowledgement of the mistreatment and abuse that Black women and girls are subjected to by members of our very own.

BLACK WOMEN & GIRLS' RADICAL HEALING FROM SEXUAL ABUSE

In the spirit of truth-telling, we can honestly appraise that many therapeutic interventions and even social movements, such as Me Too (Burke 2021), have failed Black women who have experienced cultural betrayal sexual trauma (e.g., Asmelash 2022; Gómez 2023). This failure stems from the White supremacy and intersectional oppression within the work itself (e.g., Crenshaw 1991; Gómez 2023), as well as within dominant society's uptake of the work, as has been the case with rich White women becoming the focus of the Me

Too movement that was created by Black woman advocate and activist Tarana Burke (2021). Given its conceptualization of cultural betrayal sexual trauma as a community-oriented harm due to the role of societal inequalities (Gómez and Gobin 2022), CBTT's downstream implications for healing provide relevant antidotes to the erasure of Black women and girls from the dominant narrative (e.g., Asmelash 2022). Specifically, evidence-informed models of therapy, such as relational cultural therapy (Miller and Stiver, 1997) and the liberation health framework (e.g., Martinez and Fleck-Henderson 2014), can promote holistic mental health and wellness for Black women and girls who have endured intersectional oppression and cultural betrayal sexual trauma. Importantly, posttraumatic growth must never be confined to the four walls of a therapy room, therefore, radical healing in the Black community is paramount. Finally, changing the world as we know it, such as fundamentally altering and sometimes replacing oppressive institutions and systems, are vital to Black women and girls' joyful longevity. Therefore, in this section, I provide implications from CBTT that touch on radical healing in the community and macro-level change to systems and institutions.

Radical Healing in the Black Community

Within the context of mistreatment being normalized (McClelland et al. 2016; Nadal 2018; Papp and McClelland 2021), there is a co-constitutive dialect of oppression and resistance (Collins 2022). Such an independent consciousness is vital and can interrupt the perception or actuality that Black people participate in our own oppression (e.g., Fanon 1963, Friere 1970; Scott 1987). In their psychological framework for radical healing for people of Color and indigenous people, French and colleagues (2020) build upon the trajectory of this dialectical consciousness, with radical healing including ". . . being able to sit in a dialectic and exist in both spaces of resisting oppression and moving toward freedom" (11), while fundamentally understanding that systemic change through social justice is necessary to accomplish both (for a reader on radical healing, see The Psychology of Radical Healing Collective, n.d.).

This psychological framework for radical healing (French et al. 2020) is directly relevant for Black women and girls' healing from cultural betrayal sexual trauma, with resisting oppression being additionally accompanied by resisting the negative impact of violence. In this way, radical healing goes beyond mere coping, such as survival within oppression (Bryant 2022; Watts 2004), to proactive thriving that occurs while resisting the impacts of oppression and abuse (Bryant-Davis 2005; French et al. 2020). Quite deliberately, then, the supposed pathology of oppression and abuse is not found within those victimized (French et al. 2020; Freyd 1996; Gómez, Lewis et al. 2016).

Thus, expanding on the tenets of the psychological framework for radical healing (French et al. 2020), liberation from oppression, trauma, abuse, violence, and pathologizing interpretations of mental health are necessary components of radical healing (French et al. 2020).

Radical Self-Definition

Inside of us lives a need to proactively engage in radical disbelief. To fight for freedom within ourselves that actively externalizes all that is interpersonally, violently, and structurally put upon us. A freedom that is distant, self-determined, and unrelated to the instantiations of inequality all around us. A self-concept and a sovereign microworld within ourselves that we call home. A home that we each return to every day. Therefore, the need for radical healing is deeper than superficial acknowledgement of inequalities. Oppositional ideologies that both challenge White supremacy and make sense of marginalized status, while adapting over time amidst new interpretations of events and social reality (Cohen 2009), are warranted. As such, racial and intersectional domination that is from both outside of and within the Black community (e.g., structural racism, Mills 1997; secondary marginalization, Cohen 2009; cultural betrayal, Durkee and Gómez 2022) are discursively, structurally, institutionally, politically, and psychologically violent. Thus, radical disbelief (hooks 1984) of the oppressive lies stemming from White supremacy (Mills 1997) is necessary for radical healing. The Combahee River Collective engaged in radical disbelief by centering their "shared belief that Black women are inherently valuable, that our liberation is a necessity not as an adjunct to somebody else's but because our need as human persons for autonomy. . . . Our politics evolve from a healthy love for ourselves, our sisters and our community which allows us to continue our struggle and work" (Combahee River Collective Statement, 1977, as cited in Taylor 2017, 18).

In the process of radical healing, we should neither limit ourselves to talking *around* oppression nor relegate ourselves to solely finding solutions within oppression, as if such a context is static and immutable. Secondary marginalization within the Black community (Cohen 2009) perhaps further necessitates specific interrogation of how oppression can operate within proposed or realized solutions. For instance, accountability for sexually abusive Black men within the criminal justice systems need to grapple with how such accountability could reify the discriminatory carceral state (Alexander 2010). Relatedly, we must reject manipulation of such arguments that shield Black male perpetrators from accountability, such as then to-be-confirmed Supreme Court Justice Clarence Thomas' erroneous assertion that he was enduring "high-tech lynching" upon being held to account by Anita Hill for his cultural betrayal sexual harassment of her (e.g., Barbara Ransby, as cited in Taylor 2017; Hill 1997). Within safer spaces, these complex discussions need to be had, as a way to ground (intra)cultural support and community in radical healing. Taken together, truth-telling, oppression complexity, and radical healing require simultaneously learning, re-learning, and internalizing the wisdom and strength that also lives within the Black community's history, present, and future. As such, radical healing occurs with and through the Black community, in which we create peaceful, accountable, and freeing spaces for us all.

Importantly, knowledge, growth, and healing do not come with a mandate of sublime happiness. As such, radical healing should not be pursued as a form of social control in which frustrations, strife, and psychological distress are dulled in the name of toxic happiness (Gómez 2019e). Therefore, distinct from any goals of being happy all the time, radical healing provides the space to heal individually and collectively in ways that both radically accept the depraved aspects of reality, while fostering safety, joy, and freedom for a better individual and collective present and future.

Radical Healing Action

We need not wait for the dominant larger society to grant us with healing mechanisms that are appropriate for ourselves, our experiences, our worldviews, and our individual and collective humanity. As such, we are able to "shift from demanding power from people who do not love us to connecting with the power we already have" (Brown 2018). Therefore, connecting and reconnecting with our history and legacy can provide us with strength, fortitude, and radical hope for our present and future (French et al. 2020; Mosley et al. 2020). For instance, Black women have a long history of identifying, resisting, and thriving through intersectional oppression and sexual abuse (e.g., Crenshaw 1991; McGuire 2010; Mitchell 2018). Through becoming kindred, we reside with and atop giants, drawing from our historical wisdom and perseverance.

In her book *Thriving in the Wake of Trauma: A Multicultural Guide*, Bryant-Davis (2005) discusses how violence, abuse, and trauma affect our safety, self-care, trust, shame and self-blame, anger, sexuality, and more. She additionally provides various strategies for resistance, healing, and thriving, including engaging in activism and the arts (Bryant-Davis 2005). Though engaging in artistic activities can seem daunting when we are not professionals, we must remember that the purpose of the arts ultimately is the process and not the outcome (Gómez 2021a). As such, the arts can produce an outcome that is beautiful in its own right, coming second only to the process in which it was undertaken. This was the case in my choreographing and dancing in *Condemned to Dance: Cultural Betrayal Trauma Theory*—a visual artistic representation of CBTT (Gómez and Johnson-Freyd 2015). Furthermore, psychological empowerment (Ross et al. 2022) is related to activism, with the latter potentially also serving as a kind of self-care (Hickson et al. 2022). Moreover, the Black Love, Activism, and Community (BLAC) Model of Healing and Resilience identifies relationships, spirituality, identity, and active expression as important cultural healing factors.

INSTITUTIONAL COURAGE

Fundamentally, macro-level change, such as eradicating oppressive institutions and systems, is vital for healing. Therefore, it is incumbent on us that ". . . (i)f we don't like the world we're living in, (we can) change it" (Nikki Giovanni, as cited in Tate 1983, 68). My academic book, *The Cultural Betrayal of Black Women and Girls: A Black Feminist Approach to Healing From Sexual Abuse* (Gómez 2023) centers Black women and girls. In the first half of the book, I review basic research in structural racism (e.g., Mills 1997), intersectional oppression (e.g., Crenshaw 1991), and cultural betrayal sexual trauma (e.g., Gómez 2019f); in the second half of the book, I apply this transdisciplinary research to the literatures on culturally competent trauma therapy, radical healing in the Black community, and institutional change for an equal and peaceful society.

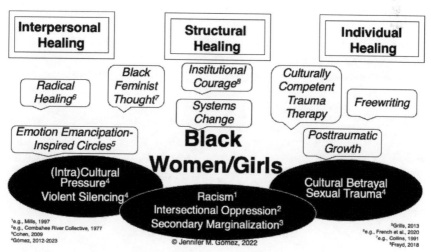

Figure 10.1.   The Cultural Betrayal of Black Women & Girls: A Black Feminist Approach to Healing from Sexual Abuse
© Jennifer M. Gómez, 2022; used with permission

In discussing the need for institutional change, I use Freyd's (2018) concept of institutional courage. Institutional courage protects people who depend on the institution by engaging in moral action (Freyd, 2018). As such, we can apply institutional courage to various settings, such as community-based research, universities, and companies to address and prevent the societal and interpersonal ills negatively impacting Black women (Gómez et al. 2023), such as intersectional oppression (e.g., Combahee River Collective 1983) and cultural betrayal sexual trauma. Expanding from prior work that details concrete steps for institutional courage (e.g., Freyd 2018), the book adapts the Table of Institutional Reparations from Gómez, Smith, and colleagues (2016) in order to organize institutional courage steps (Freyd, 2018), including an example of the step and verifiable outcome(s) of the step. Class 1—Operations describes multiple steps that can provide the foundation for an institutionally courageous institution: operating with transparency; employing checks and balances; complying with laws and with the spirit of the laws; educating individuals, communities, and organizations about sexual harassment, other violence, and racial discrimination; incorporating social justice; and committing budgetary, time, and person power resources to all institutional courage steps. Also engaged with as a matter of course in institutions, Class 2—Assessments deals with organizations' continuous assessments that measure progress, priorities, and potential for future institutional betrayals (Smith and Freyd 2014). Assessments are considered institutionally courageous because of the difficulty in having to know and then address how the organization and its leaders may be harming its members. Finally, Class 3—Reparations are organizations' institutionally courageous responses to institutional betrayal (Smith and Freyd 2014) that serve to both engender healing and alter the institutionally betraying trajectory. Such reparations include bearing witness to those harmed, understanding the problem from the perspective of those harmed, acknowledging wrongdoing, apologizing, cherishing the whistleblower, and correcting/retracting false statements. Taken together, these three classes of institutional courage—operations, assessments, and reparations—provide preemptive, as opposed to solely reactive, institutional norms and practices that serve the organization itself, as well as the members who trust and/or depend on it. Moreover, mobilization with institutional courage (Freyd 2018) can engender systems-level change, including activism and policy, to work toward a world in which equality and peace are common and typical.

CONCLUDING THOUGHTS

It is true that we do not know everything there is to know about Black women and girls' experiences of cultural betrayal sexual trauma. That is where the research and the researchers come into play: to work with members of the community to triangulate empirical data with our individual and collective lived experiences and histories, which can get us closer to a "capital T" Truth. Nevertheless, we must also be aware that the difficulty in finding solutions ". . . is not a knowledge problem. It's a power problem" (personal communication, Darien Alexander Williams, 29 November 2022): the foundational knowledge of Black women's humanity, our worth, and the veracity of some Black males' sexually abusive behavior against us are all self-evident. Why is that information not mainstream? Why does society—and our Black communities—fail to respond to this widespread problem with the urgency that it warrants? Because of power. Or rather, lack of power combined with White supremacist domination. That's where the activism and activists come in: to name the inequality and disrupt the status quo, thus shifting power dynamics at large and small scales within the Black community and outside of it. Such activism has a role, then, in fundamentally changing the world for the better, while simultaneously sustaining and healing ourselves (Hickson et al. 2022; Turner, Harrell, and Bryant-Davis 2022) through reclaiming our power. Finally, for those of us scholar-activists who refuse to adjust ourselves and our work to the oppressive status quo: (Grzanka and Cole 2021), a rallying cry: *may we continually answer the calls to fight for justice using our outsider-within stances (Collins 1991) to transform our worlds from the inside out.*

REFERENCES

Alexander, Michelle. 2010. *The New Jim Crow: Mass Incarceration in the Age of Colorblindness*. New York: The New Press.

Araral, Eduardo, et al. 2021. "Open Letter of Support for Professor Hakeem Jefferson." *Google Blogspot*. https://openletter4profhakeemjefferson.blogspot.com/2021/11/open-letter-of-support-for-prof-hakeem.html.

Asmelash, Leah. 2022. "In Five Years of #MeToo, Here's What's Changed—and What Hasn't." CNN, October 27, 2022. https://www.cnn.com/2022/10/27/us/metoo-five-years-later-cec/index.html.

Bailey, Moya. 2016. "Misogynoir in Medical Media: on Caster Semenya and R. Kelly." *Catalyst: Feminism, Theory, Technoscience* 2 (2): 1–31. https://doi.org/10.28968/cftt.v2i2.28800.

Blee, Kathleen. 2008. *Women of the Klan: Racism and Gender in the 1920s, with a New Preface*. Chicago: University of Chicago Press.

Bones, Paul, and S. Mathew. 2020. "The Power (Threat) of White Women: A Content Analysis of Gender, Race, and Context in Police Calls on Racial Minorities in America." *Journal of Liberal Arts and Humanities* 1 (7): 1–11.

Brown, Adrienne Marie. Personal communication, November 9, 2018.

Brown, Shanique and Jennifer Gómez. 2022. "What BIPOC Professors Need from Students." *Inside Higher Ed, Conditionally Accepted Blog,* March 3, 2022. https://www.insidehighered.com/advice/2022/03/04/advice-how-grad-students-and-others-should-interact-bipoc-women-professors-opinion.

Bryant-Davis, Thema. 2005. *Thriving in the Wake of Trauma: A Multicultural Guide.* No. 49. Westport, CT: Greenwood Publishing Group.

Bryant, Thema. 2021. "Womanist Psychology: Tending Our Gardens: Keynote Address." The Inaugural Psychology of Black Women Conference American Psychological Association (APA) Division 35 Section I (online only). December 3, 2021.

———. 2022. *Homecoming: Overcome Fear and Trauma to Reclaim Your Whole, Authentic Self.* New York: Tarcher Perigee.

Burke, Tarana. 2021. *Unbound: My Story of Liberation and the Birth of the Me Too Movement.* New York: Flatiron Books.

Cohen, Cathy. 2009. *The Boundaries of Blackness: AIDS and the Breakdown of Black Politics.* Chicago: University of Chicago Press.

Cole, Johnnetta, and Beverly Guy-Sheftall. 2003 *Gender Talk: The Struggle for Women's Equality in African American Communities.* New York: One World.

Collins, Patricia Hill. 2022. *Black Feminist Thought: Knowledge, Consciousness, and the Politics of Empowerment.* New York: Routledge.

Combahee River Collective. 1983 (1977). "The Combahee River Collective Statement." In Home Girls: A Black Feminist Anthology, edited by Barbara Smith, 272–282. New York: Kitchen Table: Women of Color Press.

Cook, Joan and Jennifer Gómez. 2020. "Encouraging Bravery and Fortitude in Dismantling the Insidious Stronghold of Racism." *The Hill,* July 3, 2020. https://thehill.com/opinion/civil-rights/505685-encouraging-bravery-and-fortitude-in-dismantling-the-insidious.

Crenshaw, Kimberlé. 1991. "Mapping the Margins: Intersectionality, Identity Politics, and Violence against Women of Color." *Stanford Law Review* 43 (6): 1241–1299. https://doi.org/10.2307/1229039.

DePrince, Anne and Jennifer Gómez. 2020. "Weinstein Trial Begs a Question: Why is the Pain of Women and Minorities Often Ignored?" *The Conversation,* February 19, 2020. https://theconversation.com/weinstein-trial-begs-a-question-why-is-the-pain-of-women-and-minorities-often-ignored-131640.

Dick, Kirby, and Amy Ziering, directors. 2020. *On the Record.* HBO Max Original.

Durkee, Myles, and Jennifer Gómez. 2022. "Mental Health Implications of the Acting White Accusation: The Role of Cultural Betrayal and Ethnic-Racial Identity Among Black and Latina/o Emerging Adults." *American Journal of Orthopsychiatry* 92 (1): 68–78. https://doi.org/10.1037/ort0000589.

Fanon, Frantz. 1963. *The Wretched of the Earth.* New York: Grove Press.

Freire, Paolo. 1970. *Pedagogy of the Oppressed.* New York: Herder & Herder.

French, Bryana, Jioni Lewis, Della Mosley, Hector Adames, Nayeli Chavez-Dueñas, Grace Chen, and Helen Neville. 2020. "Toward a Psychological Framework of Radical Healing in Communities of Color." *The Counseling Psychologist* 48 (1): 14–46. https://doi.org/10.1177/0011000019843506.

Freyd, Jennifer. 1996. *Betrayal Trauma: The Logic of Forgetting Childhood Abuse.* Cambridge, MA: Harvard University Press.

———. 2018. "When Sexual Assault Victims Speak Out, Their Institutions Often Betray Them." *The Conversation,* January 11, 2018. https://theconversation.com/when-sexual-assault-victims-speak-out-their-institutions-often-betray-them-87050.

Gómez, Jennifer. 2012. "Cultural Betrayal Trauma Theory: The Impact of Culture on the Effects of Trauma." *Blind to Betrayal.* https://web.archive.org/web/20221006011353/https://sites.google.com/site/betrayalbook/betrayal-research-news/cultural-betrayal.

———. 2014. "Ebony in the Ivory Tower: Dismantling the Stronghold of Racial Inequality from the Inside Out." *Trayvon Martin, Race, and American Justice: Writing Wrong,* edited by Kenneth Fasching-Varner, Rema Reynolds, Katrice Albert and Lori Latrice Martin, 113–117. Leiden: Brill.

———. 2015a. "Inequality Plays a Role in Campus Sexual Violence." *The Register-Guard* (Eugene, Oregon), October 20, 2015. https://www.registerguard.com/article/20151021/OPINION/310219958.

———. 2015b. "Institutional Failure: An Open Letter to UO Interim President Scott Coltrane." *Daily Emerald,* February 5, 2018. https://www.dailyemerald.com/opinion/guest-viewpoint-dear-president-coltrane/article_fb211bc1-a40b-50d6-bcb4-42ef4cf2503f.html.

———. 2015c. "Psychological Pressure: Did the APA Commit Institutional Betrayal?" *Eugene Weekly* (Eugene, OR), August 6, 2015. https://www.eugeneweekly.com/2015/08/06/psychological-pressure/.

———. 2015d. "The Aesthetics of Social Justice: Appearance Sidetracks our Internal Processes." *Eugene Weekly* (Eugene, OR), October 15, 2015. https://www.eugeneweekly.com/2015/10/15/the-aesthetics-of-social-justice/.

———. 2016a. "Black, Raped, Shamed, and Supported: Our Responses to Rape Can Build or Destroy Our Community." *The Black Commentator,* June 23, 2016. http://www.blackcommentator.com/659/659_campus_rape_gomez_guest.html.

———. 2016b. "UO's Proposed 'Free Speech' Policy Results in Restrictions." *The Register-Guard* (Eugene, OR), November 18, 2016. https://www.registerguard.com/article/20161119/OPINION/311199932.

———. 2017. "Does Ethno-Cultural Betrayal in Trauma Affect Asian American/Pacific Islander College Students' Mental Health Outcomes? An Exploratory Study." *Journal of American College Health* 65 (6): 432–436. https://doi.org/10.1080/07448481.2017.1341896.

———. 2018a. "A Time for Arrogance: A Minority Scholar Describes the Challenges She Experienced on the Academic Job Market." *Inside Higher Ed,* February 15, 2018. https://www.insidehighered.com/advice/2018/02/16/minority-scholar-describes-challenges-she-experienced-academic-job-market-opinion.

———. 2018b. "Black Women and #MeToo: The Violence of Silencing." *The Black Commentator,* December 6, 2018. https://blackcommentator.com/767/767_guest_gomez_black_women_and_metoo.html.

————. 2018c. "Open Essay: Gender Discrimination, Dr. Jennifer Freyd's Lawsuit, and Recommendations for Universities." *Google Blogspot,* December 9, 2018. http://freydlawsuitopenessay.blogspot.com.

————. 2019a. "Group Dynamics as a Predictor of Dissociation for Black Victims of Violence: An Exploratory Study of Cultural Betrayal Trauma Theory." *Transcultural Psychiatry* 56 (5): 878–894. https://doi.org/10.1177/1363461519847300.

————. 2019b. "Isn't It All About Victimization? Cultural Pressure and Cultural Betrayal Trauma in Ethnic Minority College Women." *Violence Against Women* 25 (10): 1211–1225. https://doi.org/10.1177/1077801218811682.

————. 2019c. "Live Up to Your Mission, UO." *The Register-Guard*, November 7, 2019. https://uomatters.com/2019/11/live-up-to-your-mission-uo.html.

————. 2019d. Navigating the Dialectic of Privilege and Pppression. *Inside Higher Ed,* September 12, 2019. https://www.insidehighered.com/advice/2019/09/13/balancing-sense-both-oppression-and-privilege-new-faculty-member-color-opinion.

————. 2019e. "Self-care and Longevity in Research and Clinical Work Regarding Trauma & Inequality." Gómez HOPE Lab Professional Development Series. *Open Science Framework.* osf.io/wpg62.

————. 2019f. "The Unique Harm of Sexual Abuse in the Black Community." *The Conversation,* May 13, 2019f. https://theconversation.com/the-unique-harm-of-sexual-abuse-in-the-black-community-114948.

————. 2019g. "What's In a Betrayal? Trauma, Dissociation, and Hallucinations among High-Functioning Ethnic Minority Emerging Adults." *Journal of Aggression, Maltreatment & Trauma* 28 (10): 1181–1198. https://doi.org/10.1080/10926771.2018.1494653.

————. 2019h. "What's the Harm? Internalized Prejudice and Intra-racial Trauma as Cultural Betrayal among Ethnic Minority College Students." *American Journal of Orthopsychiatry* 89 (2): 237–247. https://doi.org/10.1037/ort0000367.

————. 2019i. "Who's Betraying Who? R. Kelly, Sexual Violence, and the Dismissal of Black Women and Girls." *Google Blogspot,* January 31, 2019. https://culturalbetrayalrkellyblackfemales.blogspot.com.

————. 2020. "Stop Vilifying White Women! Scholars Should Hold Themselves Accountable for Discrimination in Academe." *Inside Higher Ed* February 20, 2020. https://www.insidehighered.com/advice/2020/02/21/scholars-should-hold-themselves-accountable-discrimination-academe-opinion.

————. 2021a. "Arts as Healing from Cultural Betrayal and Sexual Violence." In *In Conversation: Arts & Healing, Part 2*, produced by Andrea Scobie. Michigan Opera Theatre (MOT) At Home Series, Detroit, MI. March 23, 2021. https://www.youtube.com/watch?v=f_aX0-AWMJU.

————. 2021b. "Cultural Betrayal as a Dimension of Traumatic Harm: Violence and PTSS Among Ethnic Minority Emerging Adults." *Journal of Child & Adolescent Trauma* 14 (3): 347–356. https://doi.org/10.1007/s40653-020-00314-0.

————. 2021c. "Cultural Betrayal as a Dimension of Traumatic Harm: Violence and PTSS Among Ethnic Minority Emerging Adults" In *On the Record: A Conversation on Cultural Betrayal Trauma Theory.* Invited panelist at the Bonnie Abaunza

On The Record Social Impact Panel Series. November 21, 2021. https://www
.youtube.com/watch?v=zeYcfff7O_s&t=6s.

———. 2021d. "Does Gender Matter? An Exploratory Study of Cultural Betrayal
Trauma and Hallucinations in Latino Undergraduates at a Predominantly White
University." *Journal of Interpersonal Violence* 36 (3–4): NP1375-1390NP. https://
doi.org/10.1177/0886260517746942.

———. 2021e. "When Solidarity Hurts: (Intra) Cultural Trust, Cultural Betrayal,
Sexual Trauma, and PTSD in Culturally Diverse Minoritized Youth Transi-
tioning to Adulthood." *Transcultural Psychiatry* 59 (3): 292–301. https://doi
.org/10.1177/13634615211062970.

———. 2021f. "Who Is Okay? The Harm of One-Dimensional Appraisals of Women
Scholars During COVID-19 and Beyond." *Advance Journal (Corvallis, Ore.)* 2 (3):
1–9. https://doi.org/10.5399/osu/ADVJRNL.2.3.7.

———. 2022a. "Campus Sexual Harassment, Other Violence, and Racism, Oh My!
Evidence from Black Women Undergraduates for a Culturally Competent University Approach to Title IX." *Feminist Criminology* 17 (3): 368–383. https://doi
.org/10.1177/15570851211062574.

———. 2022b. "Gender, Campus Sexual Violence, Cultural Betrayal, Institutional
Betrayal, and Institutional Support in US Ethnic Minority College Students:
A Descriptive Study." *Violence Against Women* 28 (1): 93–106. https://doi.org
/10.1177/1077801221998757.

———. 2023. *The Cultural Betrayal of Black Women and Girls: A Black Feminist
Approach to Healing from Sexual Abuse.* Washington D. C.: American Psychological Association.

Gómez, Jennifer, and Jennifer Freyd. 2014. "Institutional Betrayal Makes Violence
More Toxic." *The Register-Guard* (Eugene, Oregon), August 22, 2014, A9. https://
www.registerguard.com/article/20140822/OPINION/308229834.

———. 2018. "Psychological Outcomes of Within-Group Sexual Violence: Evidence
of Cultural Betrayal." *Journal of Immigrant and Minority Health* 20 (2018):
1458–1467. https://doi.org/10.1007/s10903-017-0687-0.

Gómez, Jennifer, Jennifer Freyd, Jorge Delva, Brenda Tracy, Lori Mackenzie, Victor
Ray, and Beverly Weathington. 2023. "Institutional Courage in Action: Racism,
Sexual Violence, and Concrete Institutional Change." *Journal of Trauma & Dis-
sociation* 24 (2): 157–170. https://doi.org/10.1080/15299732.2023.2168245.

Gómez, Jennifer, and Robyn Gobin. 2020a. "Black Women And Girls & #Metoo:
Rape, Cultural Betrayal, & Healing." *Sex Roles* 82 (2020): 1–12. https://link
.springer.com/article/10.1007/s11199-019-01040-0.

———. 2020b. "Russell Simmons, Rape, and the Myth of 'Toxic Femininity': What
Black Men Can Do to be Part of The Solution." *Blavity,* June 25, 2020. https://
blavity.com/russell-simmons-rape-and-the-myth-of-toxic-feminity-what-black
-men-can-do-to-be-part-of-the-solution?category1=opinion.

———. 2022 (preprint). "'It Will Always Feel Worse Because It Comes with That
Added 'Betrayal'": Black Young Women Survivors' Reactions to Cultural Betrayal
Trauma Theory." https://doi.org/10.31234/osf.io/hfe6z.

Gómez, Jennifer, and Lars Johnson. 2022 (preprint). "Assessing "Friendly Fire": The Development & Validation of the Cultural Betrayal Multidimensional Inventory for Black American Young Adults (CBMI-BAYA)." https://doi.org/10.31234/osf .io/vea7p.

Gómez, Jennifer, and Sasha Johnson-Freyd, 2015. "Condemned to Dance: Cultural Betrayal Trauma Theory" (Film). *Youtube,* October 26, 2015. https://www.youtube .com/watch?v=X_QwbCkb_m8.

Gómez, Jennifer, Jenn Lewis, Laura Noll, Alec Smidt, and Pamela Birrell. 2016. "Shifting the Focus: Nonpathologizing Approaches to Healing from Betrayal Trauma Through an Emphasis on Relational Care." *Journal of Trauma & Dissociation* 17 (2): 165–185. https://doi.org/10.1080/15299732.2016.1103104.

Gómez, Jennifer, Carly Smith, Robyn Gobin, Shin Tang, and Jennifer Freyd. 2016. "Collusion, Torture, and Inequality: Understanding the Actions of the American Psychological Association as Institutional Betrayal." *Journal of Trauma & Dissociation* 17 (5): 527–544. https://doi.org/10.1080/15299732.2016.1214436.

Grills, Cheryl. 2013. "The Context, Perspective, And Mission of ABPsi: Past and Present." *Journal of Black Psychology* 39 (3): 276–283. https://doi.org/10.1177 /0095798413480685.

Grundy, Saida. 2022. *Respectable: Politics and Paradox in Making the Morehouse Man.* Oakland: University of California Press.

Grzanka, Patrick, and Elizabeth Cole. 2021. "An Argument for Bad Psychology: Disciplinary Disruption, Public Engagement, and Social Transformation." *American Psychologist* 76 (8): 1334–1345. https://doi.org/10.1037/amp0000853.

Hickson, Joniesha, Roddia Paul, Aneesha Perkins, Chiquanna Anderson, and Delishia Pittman. 2022. "Sankofa: A Testimony of the Restorative Power of Black Activism in the Self-Care Practices of Black Activists." *Journal of Black Psychology* 48 (3–4): 448–474. https://doi.org/10.1177/00957984211015572.

Hill, Anita. 1997. *Speaking Truth to Power.* Penguin Random House.

hooks, bell. 1984. *Feminist Theory: From Margin to Center.* Boston: South End Press.

———. 2014. *Feminism is for Everybody: Passionate Politics.* New York: Routledge.

Howard Valdivia, Rebecca, Courtney Ahrens, and Jennifer Gómez. 2022. "Violence Victimization in Latina/O/X Young Adults: The Multiplicative Effects of Cultural and High Betrayal Trauma." *Journal of Family Trauma, Child Custody & Child Development* (2022): 1–23. https://doi.org/10.1080/26904586.2022.2066596 Preprint (accepted manuscript version). https://doi.org/10.31234/osf.io/nt9uf.

Leath, Seanna, Paris Ball, Lauren Mims, Sheretta Butler-Barnes, and Taina Quiles. 2022. "'They Need to Hear Our Voices': A Multidimensional Framework of Black College Women's Sociopolitical Development and Activism." *Journal of Black Psychology* 48 (3–4): 392–427. https://doi.org/10.1177/00957984211016943.

Martinez, Dawn, and Ann Fleck-Henderson, eds. 2014. *Social Justice in Clinical Practice: A Liberation Health Framework for Social Work.* New York: Routledge.

McClelland, Sara, Jennifer Rubin, and Jose Bauermeister. 2016. "Adapting to Injustice: Young Bisexual Women's Interpretations of Microaggressions." *Psychology of Women Quarterly* 40 (4): 532–550. https://doi.org/10.1177/0361684316664514.

McDaniel, Colleen and Jennifer Gómez. 2021. "As Biden Administration Reviews Title IX Regulations, We Are Reminded That Universal Mandated Reporting Creates Increased Risk for Marginalized & LGBT+ Sexual Violence Survivors." *Google Blogspot,* June 26, 2021. https://mcmcd.blogspot.com/2021/06/as-biden -administration-reviews-title.html.

McDaniel, Colleen, Logan Zelenak, and Jennifer Gómez. 2022. "Effect of White Supremacy on White Young People's Blame Attributions in a Male-Perpetrated Acquaintance Rape Vignette (preprint)." https://doi.org/10.31234/osf.io/d6kwa.

McGuire, Danielle. 2010. *At the Dark End of the Street: Black Women, Rape, and Resistance–A New History of the Civil Rights Movement from Rosa Parks to the Rise of Black Power.* New York: Vintage.

Miller, Jean Baker and Irene Pierce Stiver. 1997. *The Healing Connection: How Women Form Relationships in Therapy and in Life.* Beacon Press.

Mills, Charles. 1997. *The Racial Contract.* Ithaca: Cornell University Press.

Mitchell, Koritha. 2018. "Identifying White Mediocrity and Know-Your-Place Aggression: A Form of Self-Care." *African American Review* 51 (4): 253–262. https://doi.org/10.1353/afa.2018.0045.

Mosley, Della, Helen Neville, Nayeli Chavez-Dueñas, Hector Adames, Jioni Lewis, and Bryana French. 2020. "Radical Hope in Revolting Times: Proposing a Culturally Relevant Psychological Framework." *Social and Personality Psychology Compass* 14 (1): e12512-14. https://doi.org/10.1111/spc3.12512.

Nadal, Kevin. 2018. *Microaggressions and Traumatic Stress: Theory, Research, and Clinical Treatment.* Washington D. C.: American Psychological Association.

Neville, Helen, and Kevin Cokley. 2022. "Introduction to Special Issue on the Psychology of Black Activism: The Psychology of Black Activism in the 21st Century." *Journal of Black Psychology* 48 (3–4): 265–272. https://doi.org/10.1177/00957984221096212.

Papp, Leanna, and Sara McClelland. 2021. "Too Common to Count?" Mild Sexual Assault and Aggression Among US College Women." *The Journal of Sex Research* 58 (4): 488–501. https://doi.org/10.1080/00224499.2020.1778620.

Ross, Brianna, William DeShields, Christopher Edwards, and Jonathan Livingston. 1985. "Behind Black Women's Passion: An Examination of Activism Among Black Women in America." *Journal of Black Psychology* 48 (3–4): 428–447. https://doi.org/10.1177/00957984221084779.

Scott, James C. 1987. *Weapons of the Weak: Everyday Forms of Peasant Resistance.* New Haven: Yale University Press.

Shaheed, Janae, Shauna Cooper, Margarett McBride, and Marketa Burnett. 2022. "Intersectional Activism among Black Lesbian, Gay, Bisexual, Transgender, and Queer or Questioning Young Adults: The Roles of Intragroup Marginalization, Identity, and Community."*Journal of Black Psychology*48 (3–4): 360–391. https://doi.org/10.1177/00957984211069058.

Smith, Carly, and Jennifer Freyd. 2014."Institutional Betrayal." *American Psychologist* 69 (6): 575–587. http://dx.doi.org/10.1037/a0037564.

Tan, Rebecca. 2022. "Meet the Psychologist Drawing from the Black Church to Reshape Mental Health Care." *Washington Post,* March 27, 2022. https://www

.washingtonpost.com/dc-md-va/2022/03/27/mental-health-black-baltimore-bryant
/?fbclid=IwAR3a0nOFJNLQyUTovDnwD6RZQxe8Ixp8Ph1sRgrksogyxF-QWKi
WFFbqz7s.

Tate, Claudia. 1983. *Black Women Writers at Work.* London: Continuum Publishing.

Taylor, Keeanga-Yamahtta, ed. 2017. *How We Get Free: Black Feminism and the Combahee River Collective*. Chicago: Haymarket Books.

The Psychology of Radical Healing Collective (n.d.). "Psychology of Radical Healing Syllabus." *The Psychology of Radical Healing Collective*. Accessed April 30, 2023. https://drive.google.com/file/d/1tONPKgCK9Js8vEOzzGvf9FS7jZjTvuRu/view.

Turner, Erlanger, Shelly Harrell, and Thema Bryant-Davis. 2022. "Black Love, Activism, and Community (BLAC): The BLAC Model of Healing and Resilience. *Journal of Black Psychology* 48 (34): 547–568. https://doi.org/10.1177/00957984211018364.

Watts, Roderick. 2004. "Integrating Social Justice and Psychology." *The Counseling Psychologist* 32 (6): 855–865. https://doi.org/1177/0011000004269274.

Wells-Barnett, I. 2021 (1895). *The Red Record: Tabulated Statistics & Alleged Causes of Lynching in the United States*. Redditch, UK: Read Books Ltd.

Wilson, Melba. 1994. *Crossing the Boundary: Black Women Survive Incest*. London: Virago Press.

Chapter Eleven

Racism, Poverty and Health Oh My! The Black Voice

Leading in Unprecedented Times

Melissa Hector

"Racism is a threat to public health and safety, and is a paramount social determinant of health, shaping access to resources that create opportunities for health, including access to food, housing, education, and employment, and is a persistent barrier to health equity" (Walsh 2020). I apply that definition to all Black American people in the United States. Every day, Black people in the United States are living in a crisis continuum consisting of effects from racial injustice. These racial injustices perpetuate and create constant multi-layered pandemics.

The most recent crossroads of pandemics webbed on March 11, 2020 when the World Health Organization declared a pandemic. The novel Coronavirus known as COVID-19 took global precedence. On Friday, March 13th, 2020, the United States Presidential Administration declared a national emergency. Instantly, Black African-Americans became ill at higher rates than any other race in the United States. Through March of 2021 Black Americans died at higher rates than any other race in the United States (COVID Racial Data Tracker, 2023). Life expectancy for the non-Hispanic Black population decreased in 2020 by 4 years, while life expectancy for non-Hispanic White population decreased by 2.4 years (Arias et al. 2021). The United States of America all at once saw the demise of Black health before her eyes. Despaired Black health outcomes are not a new phenomenon. American history showcases periods within the lived experiences of Black Americans where significant events had and continue to have negative and grandiose impacts on the health and wellbeing of Black people living in America.

Throughout the Coronavirus pandemic, it was urgent that community leaders, coalitions and organizations galvanize to insert resources in communities where the pandemic exacerbated quality of life. In the Black community,

Black activists lead the charge to create the possibility of life during the Coronavirus pandemic, much like in the *Dred Scott* case (1857), much like in *Plessy v. Ferguson* (1896), *Brown v. Board of Education of Topeka*, (1954) and throughout the Civil Rights Era of the 1960s. The voice of Black activism was leading in unprecedented times.

What does health activism look like? What does Black health activism mean? The way social constructivism defines activism is to show up to protest-the first thing that most people think activism really stands for. In my opinion, the most difficult form of activism is the long game, institutional activism. It's showing up at a place where society says you do not belong, becoming a change agent within that institution. It is acting as a change agent to bring to the surface the right sets of problems and to create the right sets of solutions. It's ungratifying work because ultimately, people try to push you out, push you down, and don't agree with you. For a lot of people who are successful in that activism, their name never gets out. It requires passion and firm belief to make a very specific kind of difference. In this space of activism, Black health activism, you're in it for the long haul.

Cities like Boston, Massachusetts declared Racism as an Emergency and Public Health Crisis (Walsh 2020), declaring racism in and of itself a broad-reaching and directly negative impact on individual health outcomes. Nationally, local NAACP chapters, historically Black Greek fraternities and sororities and emerging grassroots groups alike came together at the hand of democracy to pump resources into Black communities. This chapter, called "Racism, Poverty and Health Oh My! The Black Voice: Leading in Unprecedented Times," reviews the history of Black health in the United States and the relational transformation of Black health aligned to Black activism. This chapter dives into the evolution of Black activism awareness and involvement in health outcome disparities which Black American people experience. It highlights accountability for disproportionate health outcomes of underrepresented American citizens, specifically Black Americans, and examines a parallel relationship between Black activism and scrutiny of systemic racism as regards health systems and health outcomes for Black people in the United States. This chapter also takes you through a juxtaposition of two periods: the pre-Civil Rights Era through the 1940s–1960s, and the COVID-19 pandemic, highlighting Black leadership as advisors to advance the health and well-being of Black Americans in the United States.

This is the journey of discussing how Black-African American leadership has impacted healthcare, organizations, institutions, and outcomes. As I write through these juxtaposed eras to chronicle this journey, I must acknowledge the people who have historically made institutional and political heroic changes in Black health care possible.

THE HISTORY OF PRESENT ILLNESS

"To talk about why Black people are disparately dying of every disease we have to start with the history."

—Michael Curry, 2022

Healthcare is not mentioned in the United States Constitution. "The United States has not formally codified a right to health, nor does it participate in any human rights treaty that specifies a right to health" (Schweikart 2021).

In 1864, Dr. Rebecca Lee Crumpler, MD graduated from the New England Female Medical College, which later merged with the Boston University School of Medicine (NIH 2015). In doing so she was the first African American woman in the United States to earn a medical degree. At the age of 52 she published *A Book of Medical Discourses* covering the treatment of infants, women and men. A legacy in Black history, it is one of the first medical publications by a Black American in the United States.

In her *Book of Medical Discourses,* Dr. Rebecca Lee Crumpler paves the way for Black leadership in healthcare (NIH 2015). She outlines a set of assessments of what leadership should look like and how institutions should further insert their agency to enhance the health and well-being of Black Americans. Dr. Crumpler worked as a nurse in Charlestown, Massachusetts, near Boston (1852–1860), earned her medical degree and then traveled to the United Kingdom. She then relocated to Richmond, Virginia in 1866 after the Civil War ended (Crumpler 1883). She believed Richmond would be a,

> proper field for real missionary work, and one that would present ample opportunities to become acquainted with the diseases of women and children.
>
> During my stay there nearly every hour was improved in that sphere of labor. The last quarter of the year 1866, I was enabled . . . to have access each day to a very large number of . . . different classes, in a population of over 30,000 colored" (Crumpler 1888, 2).

The National Institutes of Health report that "She joined other Black physicians caring for freed slaves who would otherwise have had no access to medical care, and did so working alongside the Freedmen's Bureau, missionary and community groups, even though Black physicians experienced intense racism working in the postwar South" (NIH 2015) Dr. Rebecca Lee Crumpler's position is one of the earliest documented Black American activist movements to advance the health and wellbeing of Black American people in the United States.

To consider how Black activism has evolved around social awareness and accountability for the disproportionate health outcomes and disparities that

Black American people experience, the first place to start is the relationship between Black Americans and United States health care because that history is still becoming unwrapped in this era. "When we think about why (Black African Americans) won't take a vaccine, we must talk about the history, to talk about why we won't participate in clinical trials, you got to start with history. You talk about why we're desperately dying of almost every disease (to) name, we must start with the history" (Curry, 2022). The relationship with Black-African Americans and healthcare in the United States cannot be explored without the discourse of the history which created the stigma and trauma present in the relationship of Black Americans to the healthcare system in the United States. In *A Book of Medical Discourses*, Dr. Rebecca Lee Crumpler created the start of a legacy for us. She wrote:

> There is no doubt that thousands of little ones annually die at our very doors, from diseases which could have been prevented, or cut short by timely aid. People do not wish to feel that death ensues through neglect on their part. . . .
>
> They seem to forget that there is a cause for every ailment, and that it may be in their power to remove it. My chief desire in presenting this book is to impress upon somebody's mind the possibilities of prevention. (Crumpler 1888, 4)

Dr. Crumpler's documentation paved the way for Black leadership in healthcare. It specifies sets of assessments of what leadership should look like and how institutions should further assert their agency to enhance the health and well-being of Black people in the United States.

Through the course of American slavery, Black people in the United States were subjected to research experiments that happened without any scrutiny by the healthcare system. There are many examples of abuse on Black bodies, and of neglect. Whether it is the Tuskegee syphilis experiment and its 40 years of experimental "research," or the animalistic surgeries on Black female bodies by Dr. James Marion Sims, we must start with the fact that Black Americans come out of experiences of continuous abuse, neglect, undertreatment and mistreatment in the United States healthcare system.

The year 2022 marked 50 years since the nation learned about one of the most shameful atrocities in the history of US medical research. The Centers for Disease Control and Prevention website (2022b) displays the timeline of the "Tuskegee Study of Untreated Syphilis in the Negro Male," showcasing how in 1932, the United States Public Health Service "enrolled 600 Black male sharecroppers from Tuskegee, Alabama and intentionally withheld information and medical treatment from approximately 200 of the 399 Black men who had syphilis while researchers studied how the disease affected their life course" (Haelle 2022). This took place through the late 1960s and early 1970s. When a cure was created, White participants were given the vaccine to treat their syphilis virus while Black participants in this research did not get that treatment. *They were not given a vaccine.* Instead, Black participants were given placebos. "...(G)overnment doctors ... lied over and over again they were being treated for (syphilis)" (Jones and Reverby 2022, 1538). Hundreds of Black Americans died of the syphilis virus—not from a vaccine created to cure this infectious disease.

The Alabama physician Dr. James Marion Sims, often attributed as "the father of modern gynecology" (Domonoske 2018), conducted infamous experimental gynecological surgery exclusively on enslaved Black American women (Washington 2006). Sims operated on one enslaved woman over 30 times; and although it was available, they were given no anesthesia. This of course directly ties into the stereotypical notion that Black people have a higher threshold for pain than any other race (Sabin 2020). It is an ideological fallacy that persists today, confirmed by a recent study conducted at the University of Virginia (Hoffman et al. 2016).

Dr. James Marion Sims practiced on enslaved Black American Women from 1837 through 1853 (Washington 2006). He was a "plantation physician," who had "a partnership in a large practice among rich plantations" (Wylie, 1884). The year 1837 was Sims's first experience treating enslaved Black women. "Medical ethicists and historians say Sims' use of enslaved Black bodies as medical test subjects falls into a long, ethically bereft history that includes the Tuskegee syphilis experiment" (Holland 2017). The only way of hope was going to be pushing through the pain for a better outcome. The only advocacy to be done was by hands in the power of White people. The mistreatment and malpractice of health care on Black bodies lasts decades, causing generational traumatic oppression (Center on the Developing Child 2022).

Almost one hundred years later in 1948, my father, a Black man in America, recalls a childhood memory of White experiment and subjugation in his healthcare:

When I was about 8 years old, I fell out of a tree on Savin Street (Boston, MA). I was getting these pears way up, the branch broke, and I fell. When I woke, my hand was in one direction and my arm was in another direction and there was a rock sticking outside my head. So, I picked up my hand and I walked down the street. This woman picked me up off the ground and carried me and laid me in a hallway. And this is what I remember, there was police officer came and put me on a stretcher and this what they called paddy wagon, a big, long blue police ambulance and the police officer stood on the back of it holding on to these rails and I was laying on the floor . . . took me to the hospital. The other part of that was when they put my wrist back together, I woke up. And I looked around and I was in an amphitheater and all these (White) people were sitting in the audience looking (at me) and taking notes and then they put me back to sleep again. (R. Hector 2022)

The urgent care treatment for my father in 1948 subjected his body to a social study. This is not to be confused with the twenty-first century option to consent to a physician's assistant attending alongside a medical doctor. During this era, hospitals were still segregated by Black and White race. Just two years after my father's childhood injury, in 1950 the famous Charles Drew, the innovator of preserving blood plasma, would succumb to his death. Although researchers suggest "Drew was not denied a blood transfusion at a (White) hospital, that his injuries from his car accident were so severe that the physicians attending him could not save him" (WGBH, 2004), there cannot be any doubt that at the time of his death in 1950, hospitals were in fact segregated, and Black people were only allowed to receive treatment from training students and interns. The question remains that perhaps the physicians attending could not save Charles Drew because they were not certified and qualified, *seasoned* medical professionals.

Much like Dr. Rebecca Lee Crumpler, Dr. Charles Drew used his agency and voice to advocate for the health and well-being of Black-African Americans through his innovation in extending the lifeline of blood plasma. During the times of immediate post slavery and the pre-Civil Rights 1960s era, Black activism in health care did not consist of marching, boycotts, protests or lobbying. Black activism was seen through innovation and documentation. These mechanisms were silent pipelines to elevate and advance the health and well-being of Black Americans. Drew invented improved techniques for storing blood (American Chemical Society 2023). Although others had developed the basic methods for plasma use, Dr. Charles Drew as Medical Director saved many lives, including during WWII. His pioneering research created "the nation's blood banking process and standardized procedures for long-term blood preservation and storage techniques adapted by the American Red Cross" (American Chemical Society 2023). At a time when Black people were not allowed to donate blood, "Drew broke barriers in a racially divided America to become one of the most important scientists of the twentieth century" (American Chemical Society 2023). This milestone inserted opportunity for Black-African Americans to be seen as thought leaders in the health-care industry. Dr. Charles Drew spoke out as an advocate on the struggle as Black-African Americans in America, claiming that,

> while one must grant at once that extraordinary talent, great intellectual strength and unusual opportunity are necessary to break out of this prison of the Negro problem, we believe that the Negro in the field of physical sciences has not only opened a small passageway to the outside world, but is carving a road in many

untrod areas, along which later generations will find it more easy to travel. The breaching of these walls and the laying of this road has not been and is not easy. (American Chemical Society 2023)

This is activism in Black health care: a phenomenal change that he knew, yes, what he was doing was going to serve White people as well. Dr. Drew ultimately helped a lot of Black people who were sick and dying at the time of sickle cell anemia (Sickle Cell Anemia Foundation of Oregon 2022). One in thirteen Black-African American babies are born with sickle cell trait (Centers for Disease Control and Prevention 2022a) along with many other medical conditions that Black Americans were not being treated and cared for.

FACING THE SOCIAL DETERMINANTS OF HEALTH

In 1883 Dr. Rebecca Crumpler wrote in her memoir *A Book of Medical Discourses* that "They seem to forget that there is a cause for every ailment, and that may be in their power to remove it" (4). This truth has been reinforced in the twenty-first century: "Economic, social, and environmental factors influence health more than access to healthcare, although equitable access to such care is of utmost importance" (Health Inequities Task Force 2021, 6). The twenty-first century calls these *social determinants of health*. In 2002, Congress commissioned the Institute of Medicine to conduct a report on the nation's healthcare disparities. It was called *Unequal Treatment: Confronting Racial and Ethnic Disparities in Health Care* (Smedley, Stith, and Nelson 2003). This publication statistically proved that "racial and ethnic minorities receive lower-quality health care than White people—even when insurance status, income, age, and the severity of conditions are comparable" (Bridges 2023). This report memorialized what many had been saying for generations: doctors were not treating Black Americans with fair and equal treatment.

In *Unequal Treatment*, a panel of experts provide evidence and explore how Black African Americans experience the healthcare environment in the United States (Smedley, Stith, and Nelson 2003). The analysis depicts "aspects of the clinical encounter which were shown to contribute to such disparities, including patients" and providers" attitudes, expectations, and behavior."

Here is why that is important. When we consider Black American health disparities or conditions, there must be truth and reconciliation about how we got here, why Black lives are shorter, and why we suffer almost every disease. This is a very particular conundrum. We know life expectancy numbers, we know the racial disparities and outcomes at a national level, we know them even at state levels. Health outcomes for Black-African Americans are direly disparate for Black people in the United States as compared to White and other ethnicities and races. In addition, those with the hands of power in medicine and legislation will tell us, we do not know the underlying reality of what it takes to understand why these disparities are occurring. Black activists will argue otherwise. As Dr. Rebeca Lee Crumpler said in *A Book of Medical Discourses*, those not living the Black-African American experience seem to forget the cause for every ailment, and *it is* in their power to remove it.

Dr. Rebecca Lee Crumpler's publication on health prevention is a very important staple as one of the (if not the only) initial discourse on racism as a direct detriment to health outcomes. Crumpler made public the conversation which aligns Black activism and Black healthcare in the United States. This was well before researchers started talking about social determinants of health. Crumpler in 1864 understood that her people, her Black people, were dying and suffering of almost every disease because of what we now call social determinants of health. Dr. Crumpler understood that if you are housing insecure, and food insecure, if you are living in traumatic situations, violent neighborhoods, if racism at large is impacting your life, your health will be poor.

The Center for Health Information and Analysis (CHIA), an independent agency established by the 192nd legislative session of Massachusetts, "serves as the Commonwealth's primary hub for health care data and a primary source of healthcare analytics that support policy development" (Massachusetts Health and Hospital Association 2022). In November 2022, CHIA published a research brief, "Black and Hispanic Residents Report Higher Likelihood of Potential Reliance on the Emergency Department for Health Care than White Residents in the Commonwealth" (CHIA 2022). This publication determined that Black and Latino residents in Massachusetts rely more on the emergency department (ED) for healthcare treatment than utilization of a clinic for routine care. The CHIA report further established that "the magnitude of the difference in the likelihood of potential reliance on the ED among Black versus White residents is identical to the magnitude of the gap in between residents who reported being in fair or poor health or having an activity limitation, compared with those in good health without any activity limitation" (CHIA 2022, 9). While Massachusetts and other states in the U.S have made significant progress to minimize barriers to accessing and affording care, disparities persist among sub-populations.

When an individual relies on the emergency room for healthcare, that means they are not getting primary care. That means that by the time cancer is found, it is at stage four and not stage one. Reliance on emergency visits means you are not managing your teeth, your mental health, your substance use disorder and overall physical health, because you are getting your healthcare entirely in a three- to-four hour wait in an emergency department. Based on the history, one cannot deny that generations of mistreatment lead to generations of mistrust which lead to habitually limited interactions in the physical healthcare space. Generations of living at or below poverty level lead to generations of normalizing not going to routine doctor visits because work comes first to pay for a place to live, to have lights during the night and food on the table.

Some Black activists argue that although the Civil Rights movement created a wave of advancement in social equality for Black African Americans, the war of equity was so vast it risked leaving out a priority for health care for Black people. The argument could be made that Black activism has not had the intense focus on health equity due to the focus on creating room in other spaces that Black Americans were chronically denied access.

In an interview Michael Curry of the Massachusetts League of Community Health Centers and the National NAACP said,

> So let me bring it back full circle to your point. I think that when you think about all these conditions that have created an inequitable system . . . that's care, that's environment, the fact that we live in worse environments, (like) near landfills and have asthma, so people action, environmental action, which is still people action, generated poor outcomes, poor health outcomes. The problem with (Black) African American activism and I argue this all the time . . . if you go back to the 1960s, we were so focused on integrating lunch counters, and transportation, and desegregating schools. That really the caboose of the movement in healthcare was the caboose of the Civil Rights movement, though part of the movement was healthcare . . . we (should) had talked and prioritized it at the time.. what was most urgent, sitting next to somebody on a bus or getting them access to health care? . . . (Curry, 2022)

As the civil rights movement advanced and Black Americans entered White spaces, more racial barriers taxed the fight for equality. The 1965 passing of Medicare and Medicaid forced hospitals to integrate. "By threatening to withhold federal funding from any hospital that practiced racial discrimination, as required by Title VI of the Civil Rights Act, passed in 1964, Medicare forced the desegregation of every hospital in America virtually overnight" (Sternberg 2015). Hospitals were forced to integrate by money incentives. If you want this money, then you need to comply with the Voting and Civil Rights Acts and you need to now let everybody in your doors and treat everybody. There was not, however, any follow-through to regulate the ingrained biases and prejudice behaviors which continue to affect Black health equality in the United States. There arose a tremendous amount of work needing to take place with internal systems at institutions. Consequently, as health care issues piled up, health disparities among Black people became normal.

Have we become used to poor Black health as a normalization? Fellow Black African Americans, what have you normalized? You can almost guarantee that most of the people in your family will not live past the age of sixty-five, an unfortunate certainty. Cancer gets diagnosed later than White people and Black people are more likely to die. The list continues. We have become numb to police violence, to not being promoted, to not being mayors and governors.

Arline Geronimus, a civil rights lawyer, underscores the evidence of research on social disadvantages that undermine and erode health. She calls this "weathering."

"We as a species are designed to respond to threats to life by having a physiological stress response," Geronimus explains. "When you face a literal life-or-death threat, there is a short window of time during which you must escape or be killed by the predator." Stress hormones cascade through the body, sending blood flowing to the muscles and the heart to help the body run faster and fight harder. Molecules called pro-inflammatory cytokines are produced to help heal any wounds that result. These processes send energy from other bodily systems that aren't enlisted in the fight-or-flight response. . . . That's not important if the threat is short term, because the body's (energy transformation) quickly returns to normal. But for people who face chronic threats and hardships—like struggling to make ends meet on a minimum wage job or witnessing racialized police brutality—the fight-or-flight response may never abate. "It's like facing tigers coming from several directions every day," Geronimus says, and the damage is compounded over time.

As a result, health risks arise at increasingly younger ages for chronic conditions like hypertension and type two diabetes. Depression and sleep deprivation become more common. People are also more likely to engage in dangerous coping behaviors, such as overeating and substance use with drugs and alcohol. (Roeder 2019)

The Harvard University Center for the Developing Child (2023) reported that "A growing body of evidence from both the biological and social sciences connects this concept of chronic wear and tear to racism. This research suggests that constant coping with systemic racism and everyday discrimination provokes the stress response." Racial disparities have a direct impact in chronic illness across the lifespan. Some of that is unequal treatment, some of it is access, some of it is affordability and some of it is that we have become normalized to our health conditions to the point that you can get so used to it, that it doesn't faze you anymore. "The evidence is overwhelming: Black, Indigenous and other people of color in the United States have, on average, more chronic health conditions and shorter lifespans than White people at all income levels" (Harvard University Center for the Developing Child 2023).

A 2017 *Boston Globe* series on race in Boston brought to light a major wealth gap in Massachusetts. In Boston, the median net worth of a Black family is only $8 compared to $247,500 for a White family (Muñoz et al. 2015). The COVID-19 pandemic widened the racial wealth gap even further (Chatterjee 2020). A study by the Boston Foundation released May 2022 shows that 18 percent of Black Massachusetts residents live in poverty, compared to less than 7 percent of White residents (Mattos, Granberry, and Agarwal 2022). Likewise, Black and Brown people are more likely to carry debts that do not show as credit worthy investments such as high rent costs and student loans (Atkins Stohr 2022 a, 2022b, 2022c). The troubling picture painted by the data underscores the need to understand what underserved communities need to succeed and thrive. "It is clear that science cannot address these challenges alone. But science-informed thinking combined with expertise in changing entrenched systems and the lived experiences of families raising young children under a wide variety of conditions can be a powerful catalyst of more effective strategies" (National Scientific Council on the Developing Child 2020, 16–17).

LEVERAGING THE POWER OF COMMUNITIES IN A PUBLIC HEALTH CRISIS: THE COVID CATALYST MOVEMENT

The Boston Equity Now Health Plan in 2021 made the following call: "As we continue our efforts to treat and prevent the spread of infectious disease, we invite you, all of you, to join us in this historic mission of undoing racism and creating a new (nation)" (Health Inequities Task Force 2021, 9).

In that spirit, the Biden Administration implemented the largest adult vaccination program in United States history starting in 2021, with nearly 270 million Americans receiving at least one dose of COVID-19 vaccine (US Department of Health and Human Services 2023). Because of vaccinations and many other efforts, "since the peak of the Omicron surge at the end of January 2022, daily COVID-19 reported cases are down 92 percent, COVID-19 deaths have declined by over 80 percent, and new COVID-19 hospitalizations are down nearly 80 percent" (US Department of Health and Human Services 2023). While we all know that the pandemic only exacerbated the disparities that already existed well before 2020, we also saw that COVID prompted the emergence of new groups and organizations to ensure all community members had the resources they needed to be safe and healthy.

The year 2020 pulled a crossroads of two pandemics, the public health crisis of the Coronavirus and the racism crisis. Boston heard the call to tackle racism and as a response to stop the spread of infection on both ends, initiated policy-based actions to attempt to close gaps in health equity for Black people. On June 12, 2020, former Mayor Martin J. Walsh declared racism a public health crisis (Walsh 2020). This created an Executive Order to address racism as a public health crisis. COVID-19 impacted the health and wellbeing of Black people with wide-ranging and severe disparities. The Boston Health Inequities Task Force (2021) showcased the double pandemic:

> Racial disparities in testing, rates of infection and death rates, access to health care, and vaccinations have been evident throughout the pandemic. The sources of these inequities—rooted in structural racism—were exposed. . . .
> Adding to the fear of the infection, attention focused on acts of police brutality toward Black communities. The murder of George Floyd in the early months of the pandemic galvanized attention and activism on the . . . realities of misconduct that targets communities of color disproportionately. The national reckoning on these matters motivates a more intense scrutiny of the nation's response and accountability to Black American people. . . . Ignoring racism is no longer a viable option. The well-being of residents and the health of our city demand a response (8–9).

Racism as a public health crisis and trauma manifested in many ways during the pandemic. COVID-19 recovery in the United States must continue to protect all Black people from COVID-19 and all other infectious diseases including racism and ensure Black people have the means to recover prosper and through policies, practices, and programs with leadership by federal, national, and state level departments of health and human services.

I have served in the public sector at two government entities over the last decade. Currently, I serve in municipal government at the oldest public health department in the nation, the Boston Public Health Commission (BPHC). I serve as the Director of Equitable and Strategic Initiatives and in this position, I lead and direct all aspects of BPHC's Coronavirus Pandemic community engagement response as well as create and foster internal and external executive level relationships to strengthen BPHC's capacity to best serve residents of Boston. My theory of change is that we must provide all individuals and families the necessary resources they need to live a vital life, to have the most maximized opportunity to lead and live a fulfilled life. I believe all people should have the push and support they need to have access to resources and opportunities that will further enhance the conditions in the environments where they are born, live, learn, work, play, worship, and age (US Department of Health and Human Services 2023)

My leadership serving with the City of Boston first under the Mayor's Office of Health and Human Services (2019) and now at the Boston Public

Health Commission (2022) embodies my theory of change. I created systems to outline intentional access to resources for thousands of residents during the COVID-19 pandemic. Between 2020–2022, I led the City's Youth Development fund which distributed $1.5 million dollars to over fifty youth-serving organizations. This funding initiative enabled non-profit organizations to remain open and provide programs to young people and families when the world was shut down. I co-lead the administration of program selection for the Boston Resiliency Fund, which afforded hard working small businesses and nonprofits the ability to remain open and positively impact communities hit the hardest by the beginning of the Coronavirus pandemic. This $34.6 million distribution led to:

- 960 emergency childcare seats for frontline essential workers
- 1000+ families with infants a month's supply of diapers and formula
- 368,00 bags of groceries and produce to households
- 15,580 gift cards for families to use at local grocery stores etc.
- 8000 Chromebooks for Boston Public School students
- 21 Community Health Centers were supported with Telehealth Services
- 55 unemployed workers were hired to distribute meals
- Free access to COVID-19 testing
- Free access to COVID-19 vaccinations
- 649,000 prepared meals
- 20 local, Black-Immigrant-People of Color-owned restaurants cooking meals
- 55 percent of grantees identify as led by a person of color (City of Boston 2022)

Through acting with urgency and transparency our leadership supported immediate and basic needs of the most impacted communities. My leadership and collaboration at the Boston Public Health Commission created substantial progress over the three years in narrowing the inequities of the COVID-19 era in the City of Boston. The *Beacon Hill Times* (2023) reported on that progress:

> In 2020, Black residents had an age-adjusted mortality rate of 171.2 per 100,000 residents, the highest among any ethnicity . . . COVID-19 mortality rates among Black individuals in Boston are now down to 58.9 per 100,000 residents . . . age-adjusted mortality rates are still significantly higher among Black and Latinx Bostonians than White Bostonians (22 percent and 12 percent higher, respectively) due to COVID-19. (Beacon Hill Times Staff 2023)

As a public servant in City government during this era, I lead a COVID-19 community engagement response, fulfilling the accountability framework of the Boston Health Equity NOW Plan -2021, which calls for "stakeholders to collectively develop, coordinate, and implement strategies to achieve health equity" (Health Inequities Task Force 2021, 13). Under this framework, the Boston Public Health Commission activated a mass-vaccination clinic in the heart of the Blackest neighborhood of the City, Roxbury. This site became activated three months before the State's decision to enlist a large vaccination clinic outside of suburban areas. Through my leadership on this initiative, in collaboration with neighborhood-based community health centers, coalitions and community groups, over one million free COVID-19 vaccinations and free COVID-19 tests were administered to residents in Boston (2021–2022). The clinic lived in the heart of Roxbury, Boston's predominantly Black neighborhood. It was a pillar of access to rebuilding trust, breaking down barriers and providing a sense of hope. The impact of my leadership created strategic partnerships with community-based organizations to open fluid relationships between a government agency, advocates and residents.

Through these community partnerships and coordination with other city departments and elected officials, we advocated for Federal and State funding to bring in an abundance of vaccines for every Black and Brown person in Boston who wanted one. We created open access to vaccination appointments at a time where vaccine appointments were as scarce as toilet paper in March 2020. I stood up the City's first and only Health Equity Vaccine Access (EVA) Line. This was an operation staffed by multi-lingual Black and Brown individuals from the community, providing telephone support for residents who could not find access to a COVID-19 vaccine appointment online. The EVA Line served seniors and people of color. Practices and implementations such as these were pursuant to the exacerbation of COVID-19 on Boston's Black and Brown community in 2020.

We set up mobile COVID-19 testing and vaccination clinics in the backyards of public housing facilities, at churches, and in grocery store parking lots. We partnered with local Community Health Centers to pair the opportunity to serve people with medical professionals who represent their backgrounds and provide access back to routine care. We took a holistic strategy as our approach to ensure a continuum of health care. We set up clinics at outdoor basketball tournaments, music venues and street parades. We handed out free take home test kits at outdoor block parties and after school programs and made PPE available at Boston Public Libraries. Each effort was strategically created to serve in neighborhoods disproportionately impacted by both pandemics—COVID-19 and racism.

In the United States, cities and towns alike must resolve acute health inequities surrounding and preceding COVID-19. To ensure that health inequities are not sustained, a strategic recovery plan must center the most impacted priority populations. The ideology and strategy to recovery must involve economic, social, and health pillars, using a public health approach which ties together opportunities for pivotal stakeholder involvement and collaboration across City and State leadership. We are striving to achieve what the World Health Organization Constitution in 1946 stated, "Health is a state of complete physical, mental, and social well-being and not merely the absence of disease or infirmity" (WHO 2023).

The intersectionality of COVID-19 and the Black Lives Matter movement ushered in a great deal of necessary scrutiny of systematic racism regarding health care outcomes for Black people in the United States. It is unfortunate that it took a pandemic, forcing us to stay home and watch the treatment of Black Americans. We couldn't turn the TV off. We had to watch it repeatedly. One body bag after another. White allies rallied. And Black folks in positions of power got more courage to be empowered. It gave a platform for people to start to move an agenda. It opened the door to some serious activism.

I attended several Black Lives Matter protests throughout Boston, and in 2020 after the murders of George Floyd and Breonna Taylor I witnessed a scene I had never experienced. It was a multitude of young White Americans, chanting, shouting, and filling the streets of Roxbury. A place where I had only seen Black and Brown faces occupying space. I remember walking next to a White person; I saw a marking on their arm, and I asked, "what is FTP?." They responded, with a squint of their eyes ". . . it's FIGHT THE POWER! It's FOR THE PEOPLE! Its F*CK THE POLICE!" . . . "It's whatever you want to combat racism!." For the first time in my generation, I felt that White people wanted to take ownership in the responsibility to respond and perform against the mistreatment of Black people.

Being forced to watch the unfair and unequal treatment of Black people on TV gave us a platform to start to have an honest conversation as a nation about why health inequities exist due to the taint of racism. We have a tendency in this country, driven in large part by White fragility and in some part by internally oppressed Black people, to want to forget the past so we can move on.

> But I tell people all the time, so counterintuitive is that there's almost nothing in society that we build, we try to build on without knowing the past. As a patient, (the doctor) need(s) to know your medical history. If I want to build a building, I need to know the history of the land, I need to know what was here, what's underneath. But for some reason, when it comes to race, we want to forget that it exists. And then pretend that we could just move on without being truthful and honest about all the circumstances. (Curry 2022)

More people are paying attention and more people are organizing who have a lot more power and voice in different organizations to really move the activist agenda. And what we are saying is, now is the time.

> I tell people all the time, if people understood how unfair and unequal our healthcare system is, they would have been in the streets way before George Floyd. And most of us have become weathered to our health conditions. It is not just about no longer eating poor or unhealthy foods or moving out of that neighborhood. Because people have done it and are still sick and are still dying. We got to figure out what environmentally is killing us. We got to figure out who's killing us and what doctors are amputating limbs and not treating us. We need to get rid of them like we need to get rid of bad cops. (Curry 2022)

More and more, there is a consciousness, and it is causing people to start being disruptive about what creates these inequities. In the past organizations and groups like the Medical Committee for Civil Rights (1960) were organizing White liberal activists, Freedom Riders, and Black civil rights activists (Zabel and Stevens 2006). Dr. King is famously known at that convention for saying, ". . . of all the forms of inequity, injustice in health care is the most shocking and inhumane" (Zabel and Stevens 2006, 146). Now is the time that we must be accountable to ourselves to the fact that Black African Americans are dying early at the hand of racism.

Non-transference of wealth, of knowledge, of love—all those things have ripple effects when a 40–50-year-old dies too soon. All those things have an additive effect in a way that cannot be quantified. Black activist groups like the MauMau and the Black Panther Party, mobilized actionable plans to close the gaps in access to basic health and wellbeing that Black people did not have direct access to. These groups created meal programs, clothing drives and book fairs so that Black people could not only have access to basic needs, but so they could see people who looked like them creating real and affective change. If you don't understand me—can you really treat me? We have not cracked a code to say that every person in the United States has access to a physician who looks the way they do. Why? Five percent of doctors in the country are Black (Association of American Medical Colleges 2023). People are more likely to succeed at a task or achieve an accolade when they experience the interaction with that task or accolade with someone who they can connect to their identity. According to the *American Journal of Public Health*, "in the United States, people of color face disparities in access to health care, the quality of care received, and health outcomes" (Hall et al. 2015, e60). Likewise, "Compared with Whites, people of color face more barriers to accessing care, which includes preventive services, acute treatment, and chronic disease management" (e61). Career pipelines in the healthcare industry are significant to save lives of Black Americans. Efforts to support Black American students in this industry cannot stop; their success rests on a vital village to keep them in intended career trajectory.

In Massachusetts during the COVID crisis, leaders of color in significant high-end, decision-making positions chartered the Health Equity Compact (2023) These leaders are curating policy to move health equity in Massachusetts. This is health activism. There are people with power and privilege that can use their privilege to address the inequities in our society and set precedents for other major cities and states to lead more policy reform for health equity. In the context of healthcare and Black activism, we must fight smarter to dismantle racism and agendas affecting the advancement of Black health.

CONCLUSION: RE-IMAGINING
THE BLACK HEALTH MOVEMENT

"Do you know who Charles Drew Is? He revolutionized the way blood plasma gets stored and processed. He essentially invented these processes that saved thousands/ millions of lives. That is what I call Black Activism in the medical context."

—Dr. Carl Donaldson, 2022

At the intersection of Black activism and health care systems there exist several important questions. What remains to be done and can it be achieved? How do we address racist actions in healthcare? What constitutes effective and efficient implementation of anti-racist health-forward policies and decisions? Throughout history there have been leading Black voices that have worked diligently to answer these questions at the individual and institutional level. This has created significant gains to health equality and equity, but there remains a long way to go.

Previous Black leaders in the health space carved pathways toward better health outcomes for Black and all Americans. While individuals like Rebecca Crumpler and Charles Drew contributed to tremendous strides in health care, they also faced severe obstacles. Institutions were slow to accept their findings, integrate holistic change, and see the value of their leadership because of their race. It is important to acknowledge the dual nature of race-based activism within the healthcare space. The opportunity to make large contributions is vast, but there are many racialized personal and professional barriers to achieving equity.

Growing a knowledge of this history while navigating current health system issues allows us to better understand where health systems have continued progress and where they currently falter. As an example, we see that over the long term there have been better life expectancy outcomes. At the same time, the COVID-19 pandemic intensively highlighted existing health inequities shown through disproportionate death and illness outcomes by race.

Through my own efforts as the Director for Equitable and Strategic Initiatives for the Boston Public Health Commission I witnessed this firsthand. The despaired COVID stories are models for what is possible. Let us also honor at some point—it's not where we need to be but the progress we have made has been driven by black activists and community-based organizations. This is a model of what is possible of addressing and readdressing inequalities.

There are victories of building the medical schools where there were none, victories in building hospitals where there were none. Sustaining and yet remaining are critical stories to keep pushing the agenda for Black health equity. We are still not where we need to be, but here are some models of what is possible. Historically, Black people who went to college were educated at Historical Black Colleges and Universities (HBCU's) which created a model of what is possible. Where once the only space where Black Americans could get degrees and medical expertise, White schools are opening to more Black students today.

Black activists have brought attention to a wide range of issues, including police brutality, racial profiling, voting rights, economic inequality, and access to education and healthcare. There are people in positions now in the health equality movement with a conscious awakening to leverage privilege and power, such as myself. Part of my contribution to Black activism in health equity is coming through this pandemic while ensuring a whole constellation of resources are pushed into hands in communities directly and disproportionately impacted by COVD-19. A lot of policy change between 2020–2022 has been propelled by Black activism. Informed by our history, young Black community leaders like myself are equipped and prepared to be in places to push the agenda. We have a very long way to go, but it has not been a wash. We are our ancestors' wildest dreams. We are not coming quietly; we are speaking up and speaking out and not going away. Let us affirm the people who have grounded their health activism in reality. We are in America—the racism depth is there. We will continue to name it and push through it.

There are significant numbers of us who have benefited from the gains of Black activism in health equality. Let us name the successes and chart the path to keep following. We have modeled what is possible to another generation. We are doing advocacy to a much greater community. Black activism advances other categories of marginalized groups of people. If you didn't have some of us here working at it none of us would be here. Black activism influences policy by pushing lawmakers to prioritize issues affecting Black communities and to adopt policies that address these issues. By organizing and mobilizing grassroots support, Black activists have been able to amplify their voices and pressure legislative reform.

Black activism provides a platform for Black voices and perspectives to be heard in policy discussions and decision-making processes, which is critical for ensuring that policies are equitable and address the unique needs and concerns of Black communities. As such, Black activism is an essential driver of social and political change and plays a crucial role in shaping policy outcomes that will dismantle racial inequality.

To serve as an activist and in a position to inform policy as a public health servant, this is the part that has yet to be written and will become fulfilled. I have become the Black activist that is informed by history, personal lived experience and career orientation.

Black activism remains a vital force for progress and change A generation that is conscious. And we are going to keep working at it.

This is the long game.

REFERENCES

American Chemical Society. 2023. "Charles Richard Drew: 'Father of the Blood Bank.'" American Chemical Society. Accessed March 31, 2023. https://www.acs.org/education/whatischemistry/african-americans-in-sciences/charles-richard-drew.html.

Arias, Elizabeth, Betzaida Tejada-Vera, Kenneth Kochanek, and Farida Ahmad. 2022. "Provisional Life Expectancy Estimates for 2021." *Vital Statistics Rapid Release*, no 23, August 2022. Hyattsville, MD: National Center for Health Statistics. doi: https://dx.doi.org/ 10.15620/cdc:118999.

Association of American Medical Colleges. 2023. "Diversity in Medicine: Facts and Figures. 2019." Association of American Medical Colleges. Accessed December 10, 2022. https://www.aamc.org/data-reports/workforce/data/figure-18-percentage-all-active-physicians-race/ethnicity-2018#:~:text=Figure%2018%20shows%20the%20percentage,as%20Black%20or%20African%20American.

Atkins Stohr, Kimberly. 2022a. "Black Grads Aren't Making Bad Decisions about Student Loan Debt." Boston Globe (Online), April 24, 2022. Accessed April 19, 2022. http://ezp.bentley.edu/login?url=https://www.proquest.com/newspapers/black-grads-arent-making-bad-decisions-about/docview/2653812576/se-2.

———. 2022b. "Giving Credit Where It's Due." Boston Globe (Online), April 24, 2022. Accessed April 19, 2022. http://ezp.bentley.edu/login?url=https://www.proquest.com/newspapers/giving-credit-where-due/docview/2653812573/se-2.

———. 2022c. "We Can Solve the Racial Wealth Gap." Boston Globe (Online), April 24, 2022. Accessed April 19, 2022. http://ezp.bentley.edu/login?url=https://www.proquest.com/newspapers/we-can-solve-racial-wealth-gap/docview/2653812574/se-2.

Beacon Hill Times Staff. 2023. "Boston's COVID-19 Metrics Continue to Trend Downward." *Beacon Hill Times*, February 2023. Accessed April 28, 2023. https://beaconhilltimes.com/2023/02/16/bostons-covid-19-metrics-continue-to-trend-downward/amp/.

Bridges, Khiara. 2023. "Implicit Bias and Racial Disparities in Health Care." *American Bar Association Human Rights Magazine* 43 (3). Accessed April 28, 2023. https://www.americanbar.org/groups/crsj/publications/human_rights_magazine_home/the-state-of-healthcare-in-the-united-states/racial-disparities-in-health-care/.

Centers for Disease Control and Prevention. 2022a. "Sickle Cell Disease." Centers for Disease Control and Prevention. Last updated May 2, 2022. https://www.cdc.gov/ncbddd/sicklecell/data.html#:~:text=SCD%20affects%20approximately%20100%2C000%20Americans,sickle%20cell%20trait%20(SCT).

Centers for Disease Control and Prevention. 2022b. "Tuskegee Study–Timeline–CDC–NCHHSTP." Centers for Disease Control and Prevention. Last reviewed December 5, 2022. Accessed December 11, 2022. https://www.cdc.gov/tuskegee/timeline.htm.

Center for Health Information and Analysis (CHIA). 2022. "Black and Hispanic Residents Report Higher Likelihood of Potential Reliance on the Emergency Department for Health Care than White Residents in the Commonwealth." Center for Health Information and Analysis at Mass.gov. Accessed March 29, 2023. https://www.chiamass.gov/assets/docs/r/pubs/2022/Emergency-Department-Reliance-Brief-November-2022.pdf.

Center on the Developing Child at Harvard University. 2022. "How Racism Can Affect Child Development." Center on the Developing Child at Harvard University, April 15, 2022. https://developingchild.harvard.edu/resources/racism-and-ecd/.

Chatterjee, Rhitu. 2020. "How the Pandemic Is Widening the Racial Wealth Gap." NPR, September 18, 2020. https://www.npr.org/sections/health-shots/2020/09/18/912731744/how-the-pandemic-is-widening-the-racial-wealth-gap.

Crumpler, Rebecca. 1888. *A Book of Medical Discourses*. Boston: Cashman, Keating & Co. Printers. Accessed April 27, 2023. https://digirepo.nlm.nih.gov/ext/kirtasbse/67521160R/PDF/67521160R.pdf.

City of Boston. 2022. "Boston Resiliency Fund." City of Boston. Last updated January 18, 2022. https://contactform.boston.gov/departments/treasury/boston-resiliency-fund.

COVID Racial Data Tracker. 2023. "COVID-19 Is Affecting Black, Indigenous, Latinx, and Other People of Color the Most." *The Atlantic Monthly*. Accessed April 17, 2023. https://covidtracking.com/race.

Curry, Michael. 2022. This Era of Black Activism. Interview by author, November 30, 2022.

Domonoske, Camile. 2018. "'Father of Gynecology,' Who Experimented on Slaves, No Longer on Pedestal in NYC." NPR, April 17, 2018. https://www.npr.org/sections/thetwo-way/2018/04/17/603163394/-father-of-gynecology-who-experimented-on-slaves-no-longer-on-pedestal-in-nyc.

Donaldson, Carl. 2022. Black Health Activism. Interview with author, November 17, 2022.

Haelle, Tara. 2022. "The Tuskegee Syphilis Study Revelation 50 Years Later." HealthJournalism.org, August 4, 2022. https://healthjournalism.org/blog/2022/08/the-tuskegee-syphilis-study-revelations-legacy-50-years-later/.

Hall, William J., Mimi Chapman, Kent M. Lee, Yesenia Merino, Tainayah Thomas, Keith Payne, Eugenia Eng, Steven H. Day, and Tamera Coyne-Beasley. 2015. "Implicit Racial/Ethnic Bias Among Health Care Professionals and Its Influence on Health Care Outcomes: A Systematic Review." *American Journal of Public Health* 105 (12): e60–e76. doi: 10.2105/AJPH.2015.302903.

Health Equity Compact. 2023. Our Vision and Mission. Health Equity Compact. Accessed April 17, 2023. https://healthequitycompact.org/about-us/our-vision-and-mission/.

Health Inequities Task Force. 2021. *Health Equity Now Plan.* Health Inequities Task Force. Accessed April 17, 2023. https://www.boston.gov/sites/default/files/file/2021/07/Health%20Equity%20Now%20Plan.pdf.

Hector, R. F. 2022. Being Black in Boston. Interview by author. December 10, 2022.

Hoffman, Kelly, Sophie Trawalter, Jordan Axt and Norman Oliver. 2016. "Racial Bias in Pain Assessment and Treatment Recommendations, and False Beliefs About Biological Differences Between Blacks and Whites." *Proceedings of the National Academies of Science U S A*, 113 (16): 4296–301. doi: 10.1073/pnas.1516047113.

Holland, Brynn. 2017. "The 'Father of Modern Gynecology' Performed Shocking Experiments on Enslaved Women." History Channel, August 29, 2017. Last updated December 4, 2018. https://www.history.com/news/the-father-of-modern-gynecology-performed-shocking-experiments-on-slaves.

Jones, James H. and Susan Reverby. 2022. "50 Years After the Tuskegee Revelations: Why Does the Mistrust Linger?." *American Journal of Public Health* 112 (11): 1538–1540. https://doi.org/10.2105/AJPH.2022.307088.

Massachusetts Health and Hospital Association. 2022. "CHIA." Massachusetts Health and Hospital Association. Accessed April 28, 2023. https://www.mhalink.org/MHA/IssuesAdvocacy/State/RegulatoryAgencies/CHIA/MHA/IssuesAndAdvocacy/StateRegulatoryAgencies/CHIA.aspx?hkey=c7d7bf94-9e1f-4f48-a00b-2c19400d4b67.

Mattos, Trevor, Phillip Granberry and Vishakha Agarwal. 2022. "¡Avancemos Ya! Persistent Economic Challenges and Opportunities Facing Latinos in Massachusetts." University of Massachusetts Boston Gastón Institute Publications. Accessed April 19, 2023. https://bostonindicators.org/-/media/indicators/boston-indicators-reports/report-files/avancemosya_final050222.pdf.

Muñoz, Ana, Marlene Kim, Mariko Chang, Regine O. Jackson, Darrick Hamilton, and William A. Darity Jr. 2015. "The Color of Wealth in Boston." Federal Reserve Bank of Boston. Accessed April 28, 2023. https://www.bostonfed.org/publications/one-time-pubs/color-of-wealth.aspx.

National Institutes of Health (NIH). 2015. "Changing the Face of Medicine: Rebecca Lee Crumpler." U.S. National Library of Medicine, June 3, 2015. https://cfmedicine.nlm.nih.gov/physicians/biography_73.html.

National Scientific Council on the Developing Child. 2020. "Connecting the Brain to the Rest of the Body: Early Childhood Development and Lifelong Health Are

Deeply Intertwined: Working Paper No. 15." Center on the Developing Child at Harvard University, June 2020. https://harvardcenter.wpenginepowered.com/wp -content/uploads/2020/06/wp15_health_FINALv2.pdf.

Roeder, Amy. 2019 "America Is Failing Its Black Mothers." *Harvard Public Health Magazine*, Winter 2019. Accessed November 2, 2022. https://www.hsph.harvard .edu/magazine/magazine_article/america-is-failing-its-black-mothers/.

Sabin, Janice. 2020. "How We Fail Black Patients in Pain." Association of American Medical Colleges, January 6, 2020. https://www.aamc.org/news-insights/how-we -fail-black-patients-pain.

Schweikart, Scott. 2021. "How to Apply the Fourteenth Amendment to the Constitution and the Civil Rights Act to Promote Health Equity in the US." *AMA Journal of Ethics* 23 (3): E235–239. doi: 10.1001/amajethics.2021.235.

Sickle Cell Anemia Foundation of Oregon. 2022. "17th Annual Dr. Charles Drew Blood Drive Highlights Need for Diverse Blood Supply." Sickle Cell Anemia Foundation of Oregon, June 16, 2022. https://sicklecelloregon.org/17th-annual-dr -charles-drew-blood-drive-highlights-need-for-diverse-blood-supply/.

Smedley, Brian Adrienne Stith, and Alan Nelson, eds. 2003. *Unequal Treatment: Confronting Racial and Ethnic Disparities in Health Care*. Institute of Medicine. Washington (DC): National Academies Press. doi: 10.17226/12875.

Sternberg, Steve. 2015. "Desegregation: The Hidden Legacy of Medicare." US-NEWS.com, July 29, 2015. https://www.usnews.com/news/articles/2015/07/30 /desegregation-the-hidden-legacy-of-medicare.

U.S Department of Health and Human Services. 2023. "Fact Sheet: COVID-19 Public Health Emergency Transition Roadmap." U.S Department of Health and Human Services, February 9, 2023. Last modified February 22, 2023. https://www.hhs .gov/about/news/2023/02/09/fact-sheet-covid-19-public-health-emergency-transi tion-roadmap.html.

Walsh, Martin. 2020. "An Executive Order Declaring Racism an Emergency and Public Health Crisis in the City of Boston." Boston.gov. Accessed December 18, 2022. https://www.boston.gov/sites/default/files/file/2021/04/racism-as-public -health-crisis-ocr.pdf.

Washington, Harriet. 2006. *Medical Apartheid: The Dark History of Medical Experimentation on Black Americans from Colonial Times to the Present*. New York: Doubleday.

WGBH. 2004. "Charles Richard Drew." PBS. Accessed September 18, 2022. https:// www.pbs.org/wgbh/theymadeamerica/whomade/drew_hi.html.

World Health Organization. 2023. *Constitution*. World Health Organization. Accessed April 14, 2023. https://www.who.int/about/governance/constitution.

Wylie, W. Gill. 1884. *Memorial Sketch of the Life of J. Marion Sims*. New York: D. Appleton and Company. Accessed April 3, 2023. https://archive.org/de tails/101310238.nlm.nih.gov/page/n13/mode/2up.

Zabel, M. Z and D. P. Stevens. 2006. "What Happens to Health Care Quality When the Patient Pays?" *Quality and Safety in Health Care* 15 (3): 146–7. doi: 10.1136 /qshc.2006.018531.

Chapter Twelve

From Black Dehumanization to Repair

The Long Road Through Death, Poverty, Protests and Policy to Rebuild the Social Contract

Edith Joachimpillai

A recurring theme . . . was the powerlessness of the Negro community. Whether the people were discussing housing, employment, welfare, the poverty program, education or municipal services, they inevitably made the point that no one listens to them, no one consults them, no one considers their needs.

—U.S. Commission on Civil Rights Massachusetts State Advisory Committee, 1967, 5

For 9 minutes and 29 seconds the world watched the murder of George Floyd as Derek Chauvin, a White Minneapolis police officer, knelt on Floyd's neck. Sixty-five years earlier, a set of photographs captured Emmett Till, a fourteen-year-old boy who was brutally beaten, shot, and strung with barbed wire around his neck to a cotton gin fan before being dumped in a river in Mississippi by two adult White men.

There is a continuous nature to the brutality against African Americans in the United States, but both the photos of Emmett Till and the video of George Floyd provided unavoidable evidence of racial injustice on a national scale. Each of their lynchings catalyzed a historic level of awareness and activism in movements toward human and civil rights. The larger movements contained the myriad of issues Black people consistently face in a racist society. Perception of these deaths, however, varied by race and background. While a majority view the deaths as the tragic consequence of a racialized society, others view it as a just outcome due to other factors.

Meanwhile, at a system level, the full range of social, economic, and legal policy failed to produce racial equity, but there has been long-term progress. These systems, which often rely on perception in the aggregate, indicate that there are major barriers to equity including the dehumanizing attitudes that correspond with racism and a deep failure to architect an adequate social contract that would address people's needs in a holistic way.

This chapter evaluates the historical and modern landscape of the social contract to understand the extent of these barriers to racial equity and highlights the policies, often promoted by activists, that can overcome the barriers to growth. It describes the tipping point effect of these two deaths and their ability to garner attention and policy-based activism, discusses the modern consequences of historical dehumanization, and analyzes the landscape of issues that the larger movements aim to address, particularly through the lens of death and poverty. Finally, it assesses how these barriers can be addressed through repairing the social contract and enacting social policy reform.

THE INHUMANITY OF LYNCHING

Emmett Till

On August 28, 1955, Emmett Till, a fourteen-year-old boy, was brutally murdered before being dumped in a river in Mississippi by Roy Bryant and J.W. Milam. David Jackson, a photographer for *Jet* magazine, was permitted by Mamie Till-Mobley, the mother of Emmett Till, to capture a set of photos of Emmett Till's body. Mamie Till-Mobley also insisted on an open casket funeral and declined an offer from a mortician to "touch up" her son's body. "Let the people see what I've seen*"* said Mamie Till-Mobley to the funeral director when she identified her son's body (Gorn 2018, 313). Over four days, around fifty thousand people viewed Emmett Till's body at the Roberts Temple Church of God on the South Side of Chicago.

A few weeks after Emmett Till's funeral, Roy Bryant and J.W. Milam were tried for murder. Justice at the 1955 trial in mid-September hinged on the perceptions of white, male Mississippi. Davis Houck (2005) describes how Emmett Till's death and trial "presented a perceived threat to the South's 'way of life,' a threat understood largely in the context of a looming integration crisis as foreshadowed in the May 1954 *Brown v Board* decision" (228). The racialized portrayal of Emmett Till, Roy Bryant and J.W. Milam ultimately created a climate where Emmett was construed as a menacing male and Bryant and Milam became heroic defenders of the country. Although Bryant and Milam had openly admitted to kidnapping Till, they were acquitted of all charges by an all-white, all-male jury who deliberated for a little over an hour. A few months after the verdict, *Look* magazine published the detailed confessions of the murderers.

As knowledge of what happened to Till spread amongst the African American community, especially through the publication of the photos in *Jet*, it catalyzed a deeper commitment to Black civil rights activism. A few months after Emmett Till's funeral, Rosa Parks refused to move to the back of the bus. Years later she explained to Jesse Jackson that in that moment she "thought of Emmett Till and I couldn't go back" (Library of Congress, n.d.). This act sparked the Montgomery bus boycott, a 13-month mass protest that was coordinated by Dr. Martin Luther King, Jr. His role eventually led him to become a prominent civil rights leader, and the boycotts yielded a ruling from the US Supreme Court that segregation on public buses is unconstitutional. King often preached about one particular motivation for his work: "The crying voices of little Emmett Till, screaming from the rushes of the Mississippi" (King, 1963). In *Stride Towards Freedom*, King's 1958 memoir of the boycott, he mentions that at the time the ". . . Emmet Till case in Mississippi was still fresh in our memories" (King 2010, 171).

Despite the documented brutality, White Americans were largely unexposed to the photos. In *Let the People See*, historian Elliott J. Gorn (2018) explains that the mainstream American press did not reprint the photographs that were in *Jet* and the images were too graphic for television. Gorn's analysis of the period explains that over a few decades, Till's story almost faded into obscurity. "Gorn points out that in the two years following Till's murder, more than 3,000 articles about him were published. Then, 'the whole of the 1960s brought only three hundred articles. In the 1970s, fewer than fifty stories appeared'" (Corrigan, 2018). The mainstream revival of Emmett Till's story only changed because of the rise of African-American studies, which renewed an interest in Black history, and *Eyes on the Prize*, a PBS documentary that opened with the Emmett Till story including the graphic pictures of his body. In fact, Gorn notes that "many White Americans remembered—falsely remembered—the epiphany of Till's ruined face in 1955. (But) few White people saw the photos until thirty years later when the documentary Eyes on the Prize opened with the Emmett Till story. Only then did (his mother's) words, "Let the people see what they did to my boy" begin to be fully realized" (Gorn 2018, 313).

George Floyd

On May 25, 2020, another Black woman would be responsible for sharing the dark reality of racism in America. With the ubiquity of social media use and the social quiet brought on by pandemic lockdowns, Darnella Frazier's video of George Floyd's lynching by Minneapolis police officer Derek Chauvin ricocheted around the globe. Like Mamie Till-Mobley, Frazier found her experience both traumatic and life-changing, but America had changed since 1955 due to the work of extensive activism and persistent Black narratives of injustice. Unlike Till's case, Floyd's case led to the conviction of the individuals involved. In an Instagram post on the first anniversary of Floyd's murder, Frazier explains "If it weren't for my video, the world wouldn't have known the truth. I own that. My video didn't save George Floyd, but it put his murderer away and off the streets" (Hernandez 2021).

Frazier's video did more than lead to the conviction of Derek Chauvin, Tou Thao and J. Alexander Keung. It catalyzed the modern Black Lives Matter movement. It is estimated that on Twitter alone "between May 25 and June 5, 2020, race—and Black Lives Matter—related videos were watched over 1.4 billion times" (Blake 2020). On June 6, 2020, a record 15 million to 26 million people participated in the George Floyd protests in the United States. potentially making it the largest movement in terms of participation in United States history (Buchanan, Bui, and Patel, 2020).

During this period, two types of information spread rapidly due to the modern era of technology. On the one hand, anti-racism information and awareness grew because people were forced to contend with what they had witnessed. This was especially important for White Americans, who continue to constitute the majority of Americans. The viral nature of the video footage of Floyd's lynching, like the photos of Till's lynching, provided unavoidable evidence of the evils of racial injustice. On the other hand, some White Americans had equal access to these modern channels, but the content they witnessed grew and entrenched racist information and attitudes. White supremacy groups, White nationalists, and many prominent conservative figures interpreted the George Floyd lynching very differently and also shared their views on different media and digital platforms. As an example, nearly a year after George Floyd's death, Tucker Carlson's opening monologue on FOX News emphasized George Floyd's criminal record and accused the media of wrongly describing this moment as a racialized one. In Carlson's own words, "George Floyd was murdered because he was Black. That's what they told us. They demanded that we believe that, and if you doubted it in any way, if you had any questions about the facts of the case, then you were effectively as guilty as the racist cop" (Carlson 2021).

With this perception, White supremacists have been empowered to increase violent action. An increasingly important White supremacist idea is accelerationism, which promotes an "increase in civil disorder—accelerate it—in order to foster polarization that will tear apart the current political order. . . . Accelerationists hope to set off a series of chain reactions, with violence fomenting violence, and in the ensuing cycle more and more people join the fray" (Byman 2020). The ultimate goal of accelerationism is for violence to be so pervasive that is commences a race war. *The Washington Post* evaluated data compiled by the Center for Strategic and International Studies to show how domestic terrorism incidents, driven chiefly by far-right extremists, soared in 2021. "More than a quarter of right-wing incidents and just under half of the deaths in those incidents were caused by people who showed support for White supremacy or claimed to belong to groups espousing that ideology, the analysis shows" (O'Harrow Jr., Ba Tran and Hawkins 2021).

The juxtaposition between the observation of a dead Black man in 2020 as a lynching victim by some and as a criminal who was justly punished by others indicates the broad spectrum of perception in America, a spectrum of perception that mirrors the range of opinions about Emmett Till sixty-five years earlier. In fact, Representative Bobby Rush of Illinois described it in the following way: "The metaphorical lynching rope that killed Emmett Till also killed George Floyd and countless others. It extends throughout the history of Black people in America, and it has strangled our nation, preventing America from realizing the promise of its potential" (Hassan 2021). The longstanding perception of Black people as victims by some and criminals by others is directly connected to a history of dehumanization that is woven into contemporary perceptions of race.

DEHUMANIZATION AND
CONTEMPORARY PERCEPTIONS OF RACE

"To dehumanize another person is to conceive of them as a subhuman creature. . . . People can think of others as less than human without ever treating those others badly or describing them in animal-like ways and conversely people can also treat others in cruel and degrading ways . . . without really thinking that they are subhuman beasts. But here, as is the case of physical illness, the symptoms are more or less reliable indicators that the psychological process of dehumanization is at work in the background, so they are important for making the diagnosis."

—David Livingstone Smith, 2020, 19

The United States has an extensive history of dehumanizing Black Americans. One particular form was the "Negro-ape metaphor" created by White explorers in the late seventeenth century (Goff et al. 2008, 292–295). The metaphor arose out of White contact with African peoples who were described as more closely related to apes that to Whites. The link of Blacks to primates also bolstered stereotypes of Blacks as primitive, savage, aggressive and hypersexual. The dehumanization of Black people crystalized between the eighteenth and twentieth centuries with the development of scientific racism is "the recourse to science to justify and rationalize hierarchical comparison between human populations" (Meloni 2017). While both scientific racism and eugenics have been discredited, dehumanizing anti-Black attitudes permeate modern American social consciousness and yield many contemporary consequences

One consequence reified the long-standing difference in American perceptions about the lynchings of Emmett Till and George Floyd. In the case of George Floyd, modern inclusion of Black Americans in polling data allows for an analysis of the differences in racial perception, both in the aggregate and disaggregated by race. The Pew Research Center conducted a survey of US adults the week of June 4–10 in 2020 and asked respondents which factors contributed a great deal to the demonstrations to protest the death of George Floyd (see figure 12.1).

Seventy percent of all respondents felt that anger over the death of George Floyd was a major factor that motivated protesters. However, when the results are disaggregated by race, there are some noteworthy differences in perception. Of Black respondents, 83 percent said that longstanding concerns about the treatment of Black people in the country contributed to the demonstrations. This is almost 20 percentage points higher than every other racial group. Among Whites, 62 percent felt some people were motivated to take advantage of the situation to engage in criminal behavior.

Social psychology, economics, and law have particularly revealed the extent to which dehumanizing, racist, and anti-Black perceptions, stereotypes and policies have contributed to negative outcomes for African Americans in a number of contexts (Hannah et al. 1967, Kerner Commission 1968) including criminal justice (Goff et al., 2008), education quality and access (Goff et al. 2014), health quality and access (Alvidrez et al. 2019; Barr 2019; Stern 2021), income (Shrider et al. 2021), wealth (Derenoncourt et al. 2022; Winship et al. 2021), and housing quality and access (Perry, Rothwell, and Harshbarger 2018; Rothstein 2017).

SOCIAL POLICY GAPS AND GROWTH

Black Americans have life and dignity throughout history. Activists have pushed for change for centuries on a number of issues, mainly centered on opposing anti-Black violence, promoting life sustaining measures, and pushing for anti-poverty policy. In each of those frames, the works of activists have been met with a great deal of resistance. Facing White nationalist organizations and racist policies, Black people in the United States have been met with death and violence in every direction.

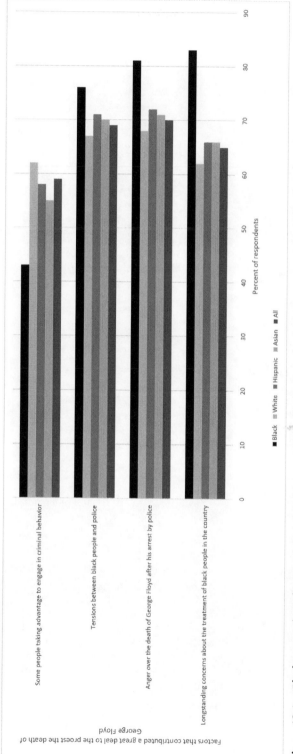

Figure 12.1. **Black perception of motivations behind protests differs from other racial groups (% saying each factor contributed a great deal to the demonstrations to protest the death of George Floyd).**

Violent Death

One of the most overt forms of racialized death and violence is lynching. The Equal Justice Initiative (2017) "has documented 4084 racial terror lynchings in twelve Southern states between 1877 and 1950," in addition to "300 racial terror lynchings in other states during this time period." Modern-day lynchings, like that of Emmett Till, George Floyd and many others, show that Black Americans still have to contend with this dehumanizing type of anti-Black violence. Still, the long arc of history shows that progress is both possible and fragile. Anti-lynching activism predated both killings and wove through and past them without any legislative reaction until March of 2022. On March 29, 2022 the Emmett Till Antilynching Act made lynching a federal hate crime offense (Baldwin III, 2022). There remain many questions about how this legislation will be implemented in practice and some of the unintended consequences of the law. Regardless, it is still a marker of progress to recognize that the extrajudicial killing of Black individuals is a finally a federal offense.

Unmet Basic Needs Hastens Death

Other forms of racism ensure that basic human needs, like economic stability, safe and secure housing, access to quality education, and access to quality health care of Black Americans continue to be unfulfilled. The dehumanization of Black people and codification of anti-Black sentiment in social policy are unequivocally hastening Black death. Throughout history, Black activists, civil rights organizations, and reports about Black life have highlighted the iniquities Black Americans face with regards to their basic needs and described how these iniquities result in hastened death. The National Association for the Advancement of Colored People, a civil rights organization that was formed in 1909 as an interracial endeavor to advance progress for African Americans, has sought justice across a range of issues including criminal justice, health care, education, climate and the economy.

In 1968 the Report of The National Advisory Commission on Civil Disorders, widely known as the Kerner report, emphasized the same issues that the NAACP had advocated as an organization. It explained that that protest directly resulted from White racial attitudes which in turn resulted in pervasive discrimination and segregation, specifically in employment, education and housing, Black migration and White exodus, and Black ghettos. Black Lives Matter, a political and social movement that was founded in 2013, also underscores the racism and inequality experienced by Black people. It started by primarily protesting incidents of police brutality but expanded to affirm all Black lives (across the gender spectrum) and affirm Black humanity.

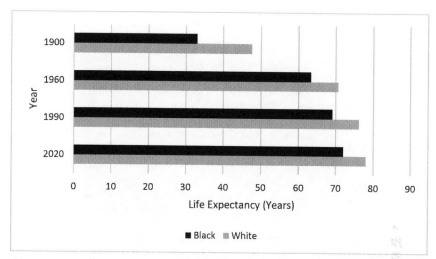

Figure 12.2. Life expectancy at birth (in years) by Hispanic origin and race: United States, 1900, 1960, 1990 and 2020, *Note:* **2020 figures constitute a provisional life expectancy estimate for January through June of 2020.**
Figure created by author, data from: National Center for Health Statistics, National Vital Statistics System, Mortality data (Arias, Tejada-Vera, and Ahmad 2021).

One outcome of inequitable access to basic needs is that there is a life expectancy gap between Black and White Americans. The life expectancy for Black Americans has consistently been lower than that of White Americans in the United States. At the same time, there has been long-term progress on specific measures, like life expectancy by race in the aggregate.

As Figure 12.2 notes, the life expectancy gap at birth between Blacks and Whites was 14.6 years at the turn of the twentieth century, 7.3 years in 1960, 7 years in 1990, and 6 years in 2020. Life expectancy at birth for Blacks has more than doubled since the 1900s, from 33 years to 72 years in 2020 (Arias, Tejada-Vera, and Ahmad 2021; Grove and Hetzel, 2017). There are a number of factors that contributed to declining mortality for all races. Many of the factors were epidemiological drivers, especially during the first half of the twentieth century: "public health measures, improved nutrition, and new medical technologies dramatically reduced the number of deaths from infectious disease . . . (along with) urban sanitation measures, such as . . . water filtration and chlorinationsystems . . . as well as increased resistance to infection from better nutrition" (University of Pennsylvania Wharton 2016).

While life expectancy over the long run illustrates a picture of marked progress, it is important to note the limitations to life expectancy as a measure. First, the provisional life expectancy estimates in the data above do not reflect the entirety of the effects of the COVID-19 pandemic. The second is that life expectancy does not contain any indication of the quality of life. There are cross-country indicators of healthy living years, the number of years that a person is expected to live in a healthy condition, however none are disaggregated by race at the national level.

Race, Poverty and Social Determinants of Health

Social determinants of health can be used to examine racial disparities in outcomes (Barr 2019). According to the Center for Disease Control, social determinants of health are "the conditions in places where people live, learn, work, and play that affect a wide range of health and quality of life risks and outcomes." The US Department of Health and Human Services (HHS) describes five categories as social determinants of health: "economic stability, education access and quality, health care access and quality, neighborhood and built environment, and social and community context" (US HHS n.d.). Poverty falls under the economic stability domain, but also limits access to a number of the categories, like safe neighborhoods, quality health care and education. Poverty rates can highlight the extent to which different races are facing significant barriers to quality of life and positive health outcomes.

Mirroring the overall gains illustrated in life expectancy at birth, poverty rates have been declining in the last three decades across all racial and ethnic

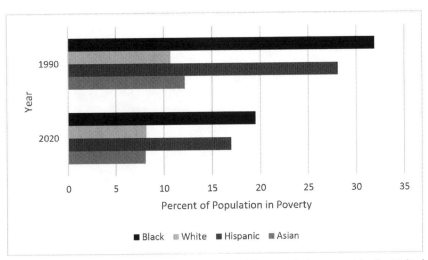

Figure 12.3. Poverty Rate by Race (by percent of the population group) in the United States, 1990 and 2020.
Figure created by author, data from: U.S. Census, U.S. Department of Commerce

identities. The poverty rate decreased by 2.5 percentage points for Whites and 12.4 percentage points for Blacks. Still, there is a notable gap between races. Although the official poverty rate in 2020 was 8.2 percent for Whites in the United States, Blacks continue to have the highest poverty rate in the country at 19.5 percent (Shrider et al. 2021). The Black-White poverty gap, seen through a multi-generational lens, is even more stark. "Three-generation poverty occurs among one in 100 Whites, but it describes the experience of one in five Blacks. Among all Black and White adults who are in their third generation of poverty, 85 percent are Black" (Winship et al. 2021).

The effects that social determinants have on mortality by race and socioeconomic status can create a more accurate and complex picture of the set of issues the most vulnerable Black Americans face toward an equitable quality of life. The National Institute on Minority Health and Health Disparities (National Institutes of Health 2017; Alvidrez et al. 2019) created a research framework the depicts the wide array of health determinants, which includes many social determinants, that are needed to understand and address minority health and healthy disparities and promote health equity as shown in table 12.1.

There are real challenges to data collection and evaluation of each of these social determinants of health. Quantifying the precise individual contribution of social factors such as income, education, and race to health and mortality largely fail because of the interconnected and complex causal pathways involved, despite the clarity that social factors matter in combination. Some suggest that a polysocial risk score, a measure that would remove the need to measure individual influence of social factors and account for the interaction of social factors, could be more useful (Figueroa, Frankt, and Jha 2020). However, a polysocial risk score contains the same type of data collection challenges as well as questions about how to track change over time because of the dynamic nature of these factors (Raphael 2020). Given the breadth and depth of social factors that contribute to outcomes like mortality, what is the path forward? As the polysocial risk score acknowledges, it is the combination of social factors that matters.

The acknowledgment of the interconnected nature of these social factors makes a reevaluation of the social contract in America in a comprehensive way a necessity. A true reevaluation of the social contract requires scrutiny in at least two frames. First, given our history or race-based dehumanization and the related empirical outcomes, adequate comprehensive social contract and social policy reform cannot be race-blind. Secondly, a real repair to the social contract must apply an inclusive and holistic approach. Creating meaningful reforming through these two elements should provide the necessary repair to create a robust and inclusive social contract.

Table 12.1. National Institute on Minority Health and Health Disparities Research Framework

Domains of Influence (Over the Life Course)	Levels of Influence*			
	Individual	Interpersonal	Community	Societal
Biological	Biological Vulnerability and Mechanisms	Caregiver-Child Interaction Family Microbiome	Community Illness Exposure Herd Immunity	Sanitation Immunization Pathogen exposure
Behavioral	Health Behaviors, Coping Strategies	Family Functioning School/Work Functioning	Community Functioning	Policies and Laws
Physical/Built Environment	Personal Environment	Household Environment School/Work Environment	Community Environment Community Resources	Societal Structure
Sociocultural Environment	Socio-demographics Limited English Cultural Identity Response to Discrimination	Social Networks Family/Peer Norms Interpersonal Discrimination	Community Norms Local Structural Discrimination	Societal Norms Societal Structural Discrimination
Health Care Systems	Insurance Coverage Health Literacy Treatment Preferences	Patient-Clinician Relationship Medical Decision-Making	Availability of Health Services Safety Net Services	Quality of Care Health Care Policies
Health Outcomes	Individual Health	Family/Organizational Health	Community Health	Population Health

Notes: *Health Disparity Populations are determined by the following characteristics: Race/Ethnicity, Low Socioeconomic Status, Rural, Sexual and Gender Minority. Other fundamental characteristics include Sex and Gender, Disability, and Geographic Region

Source: National Institutes of Health 2017; Alvidrez et al. 2019.

REPAIR THROUGH AN INCLUSIVE SOCIAL CONTRACT

"We need a new social contract . . . that can repair injustices while transforming the future. This new social contract must be grounded in human rights and based on principles of non-discrimination, social justice, respect for life, human dignity and cultural diversity. It must encompass an ethic of care, reciprocity and solidarity."

—International Commission on the Futures of Education, 2021, 2

The social contract is a theory that was developed Jean-Jacques Rousseau in his treatise *On the Social Contract; or, Principles of Political Right* (1762). Rousseau "reduced" the social contract "to the following terms: 'We, the contracting parties, do jointly and severally submit our persons and abilities to the supreme direction of the general will of all; and in a collective body, receive each member into that body as an indivisible part of the whole" (Rousseau 1893, 25). Rousseau's initial theory also contained a chapter entitled "On Slavery" that expressly determines that the social contract cannot exist alongside slavery. "The terms slavery and justice are contradictory, and reciprocally exclusive of each other" (Rousseau 1893, 20). Although slaves were eventually emancipated, the legacy of slavery persisted and led to a number of modern consequences. The social contract retained a racially sanitized essence of Rousseau's theory as the modern definition of the social contract evolved to "an implicit agreement among members of a society to cooperate for social benefits, by sacrificing some individual freedom for state protection" (Oxford Languages 2023). After World War II, western democracies, including the United States, adopted national social contracts. Over the years, these social contracts required citizens to pay taxes. In exchange, the state provided social safety nets, like unemployment insurance, and redistributive policies, like child tax credits, that narrowed the income gap between owners and workers (Dervis and Conroy 2019). This form of the social contract still did not protect many Americans, and certainly excluded a number of marginalized groups. As Cornel West and Henry Louis Gates, Jr. state in *The Future of the Race* "American society has failed to protect the basic, ostensibly inalienable rights of its people—equal access to education, adequate housing, affordable medical care, and equal economic opportunity—equal access, indeed, to hope . . ." (1997, xii).

As West and Gates mention, the modern social contract should have contained the combination of social safety nets and redistributive policies intended to span the gamut of human needs including education, housing, and employment for all individuals. In the postwar (World War II) period, the benefits of the social contract were almost exclusively extended to White

Americans, ensuring their prosperity and growth. Conversely, the social contract was often explicitly withheld from Black Americans (McGhee 2021). The dual nature of this White-exclusive social contract widened disparities in racial outcomes. The hard-won gains of the Civil Rights Movement and this era of Black activism across a number of civil and human rights issues helped to close outcome gaps, like life expectancy and poverty, but there is further to go and progress has not been immune to retrogression.

The mix of modern political decisions contains consequential effects for Black Americans and Americans at-large. On the one hand, some of these decisions are largely beneficial. The Emmett Till Antilynching Act enacted in March of 2022 finally brought a sense of justice to the lynching of Emmett Till and the nearly 6,500 racial terror and other lynchings that were documented in America. Bryan Stevenson, the director of the Equal Justice Initiative, described the passage of the act as marking "a new day in our country's continuing struggle to provide equal justice to all citizens" (Equal Justice Initiative 2022).

On the other hand, a myriad of historical and recent legislative and judicial decisions has yielded severe negative consequences, particularly for Black Americans. Modern mass incarceration is the cumulative result of the mix of historical and modern decisions in the legal system that have often been centered on a legacy of dehumanizing and criminalizing Black, poor, and other marginalized individuals (Alexander 2012; Kilgore 2015; Hinton 2016; Edelman 2017). In an evaluation of the history of mass incarceration the Brennan Center for Justice explains that the origins of our own legal system worked to guard against the government abuse the country endured through the British legal system by constructing the Constitution to protect the rights of the accused or convicted. In the 19th century French sociologist Alexis de Tocqueville observed that hypocrisy between the United States commitment to administering humane and proportional punishment in its prisons and penitentiaries, yet they maintained a brutal system of slavery. President Richard Nixon's declaration of a "war on drugs" in the 1970s led to the implementation of many punitive policies that disproportionately affected communities of color and caused a staggering escalation in incarceration (Brennan Center for Justice 2018).

The effects of this racialized and income dependent legal legacy remain true in 2023. In 2023, according to the Prison Policy Initiative, "Poverty . . . plays a central role in mass incarceration . . . people of color—who face much greater rates of poverty—are dramatically overrepresented in the nation's prisons and jails. These racial disparities are particularly stark for Black Americans, who make up 38 percent of the incarcerated population despite representing only 12 percent of US residents" (Sawyer and Wagner 2023).

Incarceration had devastating lifelong consequences for current and formerly incarcerated individuals as well as a slew of "hidden victims" including their children, families and communities (Martin 2017; Quandt and Jones 2021). Incarcerated individuals, and particularly those who are non-White, are often subjected to deep human rights abuses and violations as they are subjected to extreme conditions and prevented from having access to reasonable basic goods and services, like food, water, and adequate health care (Southern Prisons Coalition 2022). Additionally, their households and communities are further financially constrained in two important ways. The first is that there is often a loss of potential income due to an incarcerated individual's inability to be employed, especially at a living wage. The second is the sudden cost burden of paying for the incarcerated individual to have access to expensive goods and services (like telephone calls and supplemental food provisions) that are exclusively provided by privatized corporations, who are incentivized by profit, to incarcerated individuals (Sawyer and Wagner 2023). Furthermore, there is a deeply difficult psycho-social effect on the incarcerated individual and their connections (Quant and Jones 2021). These issues do not particularly ease post-incarceration as a formerly incarcerated individual carries a criminal record that can prevent them from access to employment, housing, and much more (Lartey 2023). Activists in this space, many of whom are currently or formerly incarcerated, try to combat these measures through efforts like Ban the Box, a movement to remove the check box that employers often include in job applications. Ban the Box in particular has gain some traction in pockets of the United States but it has yet to be adopted at the national level (Avery and Lu 2021).

There are other more recent legislative and judicial decisions that also disproportionately disserve Black Americans. The John R. Lewis Voting Rights Advancement Act of 2021, which would have curbed voting rights restrictions of minorities, failed to pass the US Senate. The act was designed to reverse *Shelby Country*, a 2013 Supreme Court decision that struck down key portions of the Voting Rights Act of 1965, which had required several states with a history of voting rights discrimination to receive a preclearance from the Department of Justice for any changes to voting laws (Naylor 2022). According to the Brennan Center for Justice at New York University Law, the bill would have modernized and revitalized the Voting Rights Act of 1965 while it strengthened legal protections against discriminatory voting policies and practices (Brennan Center for Justice 2021).

Quite a few major judicial decisions will also yield disproportionately difficult consequences for Black Americans. One decision concerns maternal mortality. The Supreme Court overturned the constitutional right to an abortion on June 24, 2022, which will have a disproportionate impact on Black women and women of color. According to TK Saccoh, a colorism activist who posts on social media as @darkest.hue, "In a country where Black women are already three times more likely to die from pregnancy-related causes, and carrying a pregnancy to term is 33 times riskier than having an abortion, banning abortion could increase maternal mortality by 21 percent and 33 percent in Black women" (Saccoh 2022; Centers for Disease Control and Prevention 2023; Stevenson 2021). Separately, the Supreme Court has also intervened in environmental regulation. It ruled to restrict the Environmental Protection Agency's authority to regulate carbon emissions on June 30, 2022, in *West Virginia v. EPA*. This decision will have a disproportionate impact on Black and Brown communities' mitigation of climate change effects (New York Lawyers for the Public Interest 2022). These are just a few examples of the latest wave of structural policies that have been implemented in response to the latest era of Black activism and will have a disproportionate effect on Black individuals and people of color.

In the face of these and many other often politically motivated policy setbacks, architecting an inclusive social contract would not only renew progress for Black Americans, it would provide a necessary redistribution to uplift other marginalized populations in the United States. To be clear, marginalization happens across a number of frames as outlined in the social determinants of health, but targeting the most vulnerable of our population through effective policymaking often addresses marginalization across different peoples and issues. An effective social contract would acknowledge this reality and create appropriately targeted interventions.

To decide policy priorities for targeting growth, the earlier examination of unmet basic needs that hasten death provides a useful framework. Policies that work across multiple social determinants of health to positively impact life outcomes among marginalized populations should be further tested and expanded. This should be done with an acknowledgement that improvement requires long-term analysis. Domestically, initially focusing reform measures on housing, employment and education policy, to name a few, would uplift Americans who are marginalized due to systemic failings, and therefore target growth for (disproportionately) Black and economically disenfranchised populations. These policy areas must contain a mix of race-conscious and socio-economic conscious best policies. Convergence between Black and other racial groups toward White outcomes would occur if race-conscious policies were employed. At the same time, policies that focus on a socio-economic lens have the effect of "rising tides lift all boats" at lower income levels. Both must occur in tandem to ensure historically marginalized groups that exist in intersectional identities do not fall relatively further behind their peers.

Housing

Healthy, stable and affordable housing in desegregated neighborhoods is an important step toward building racially equitable life outcomes. The World Health Organization defines healthy housing as a "shelter that supports a state of complete physical, mental and social well-being. Healthy housing provides a feeling of *home*, including a sense of belonging, security, and privacy" (World Health Organization 2018, 2). Housing stability can be defined as the extent to which an individual has secure access to housing of reasonable quality (Frederick et al 2014, 964). Affordable housing is defined by the U.S. Department of Housing and Urban Development (2017) as a dwelling where the resident is paying no more than 30 percent of gross income for housing costs. Housing policy reform should include all three of these elements across the mix of housing ownership and occupancy types.

There are a vast set of policy tools that can improve the housing and rental market to provide access to healthy, stable and affordable housing. Jenny Schuetz (2020) highlights a set of three policy tools that would increase the production and access of affordable dwelling units: zoning reform, land value tax, and more housing subsidies. Optimal zoning reforms would occur in high-opportunity communities wherein individuals have stronger access to quality employment and education, allowing for the production of denser and less expensive housing. Zoning reforms at the local level would include removing building height caps and minimum lot sizes as well as overlaying zones that allow for multifamily buildings rather than single-family detached houses. A land value tax would charge a higher tax rate on land and a lower rate on structures. This policy would incentivize owners of expensive land to build more intensively. Each of these policies promote a greater supply of housing units, bring down housing costs over time and allow individuals to move toward lower-poverty neighborhoods.

Even with the expansion of the supply of market-rate housing through these measures, the poorest families would still be priced out of housing. Expanding housing subsidies, like vouchers or the National Housing Trust Fund, would ease the financial stress of the single largest household budget item. In fact, "expanding vouchers is legally and procedurally simple. . . . Low-income families who receive federal housing vouchers rent apartments from private landlords. Families pay thirty percent of their income toward rent, with the remainder picked up by HUD. Vouchers reduce financial stress, crowding and the risk of homelessness among low-income families" (Schuetz 2020, 4).

While the combination of these policies will drive access to housing that is affordable, it alone will not necessarily make housing healthy or stable in a comprehensive way. To accomplish that, housing needs to be located in neighborhoods that provide reasonable access to the basket of goods and services given an individual's needs and resources. In a discussion about housing and neighborhoods Brendan O'Flaherty explains, "When you buy a house or rent an apartment, you acquire a bundle of goods—shelter, neighbors, voting and trash disposal rights, land, parking spots, landline telephone connections, cable TV or a satellite dish, Internet connections, electrical wires, closets, bathrooms, furnace, sewer and water connections or facilities, propinquity to various medical facilities, protection from various dangers" (2020, 256). The proximity of housing to an affordable comprehensive basket of goods and services must be considered in addition to making housing itself affordable. O'Flaherty goes on to note:

> In particular the housing you buy has a big influence on your child's friends and where they go to school . . . how long your commute to work is and where you look for a job . . . your opportunities as a child for studying and playing; your exposure to contagious diseases, mold, and various allergens . . . which doctors you see and what hospitals you visit, especially in emergencies; what stores you shop at and what kinds of food are available in them . . . and what people think of you when they see your address. (2020, 256–257)

Research on mobility and economic outcomes confirms the effects on children of exposure to these better-served neighborhoods over their incomes and the net positive returns for taxpayers (Chetty et al. 2016).

Employment

Employment provides earnings that can allow an individual to purchase a specific basket of goods and services. Without stable earnings at a reasonable rate and level, it is difficult for an individual to acquire the minimum basket of goods and services to live and maintain a dignified life. The US Bureau of Labor Statistics (BLS) assesses unemployment rates by race and provides it as an annual average in percent. In 2023 it produced a report of 2021 rates which reflected a labor market that was continuing to recover from the impact of the COVID-19 pandemic (US BLS 2023). While the overall unemployment rate averages 5.3 percent and the national rate for Whites was 4.7 percent, the national rate for Black Americans was 8.6 percent. The US BLS indicated that racial disparities, which are the vastest between Black and White Americans, include factors like "education attainment; occupations and industries in which the groups work; the geographic areas of the country in which the groups are concentrated, including whether they tend to reside in urban and rural settings; and the degree of discrimination encountered in the workplace" (US BLS

2023). Like housing, it is clear that employment outcomes are deeply interwoven with many elements of life and there is no single source of solutions that will make the gap in outcomes between races converge.

There are a number of questions that arise when trying to close the employment and earnings gap between Blacks and Whites. If such a vast set of factors can explain the gap, what are the best set of policies that can start to produce convergence in employment and earnings outcomes? As explained in the housing section, in the shorter run relocating individuals to high opportunity communities creates more and better access to employment and greater earnings. This proximity also has the potential to minimize cost burdens like commuting costs.

At the same time, it is clear that relocation alone is not sufficient to generate enough earnings for the full basket of goods and services required to live in a dignified way in the modern age. First and foremost, there are many racialized and non-racialized barriers that prevent equitable outcomes. One barrier is the racial gap that exists in hiring, pay, and promotion (Bornstein 2022). Another barrier is the lack of access many marginalized groups have to specific types of reskilling of labor can efficiently and effectively stabilize employment and earnings for individuals. Creating structures for reskilling would again necessitate a rearchitecting of the social contract. Like the New Deal, the government can provide the service of stabilizing society through providing opportunities to work. The United States could also further invest in a nationally structured unemployment office system that aids individuals reskill and coordinates employment placement for those who are seeking opportunities in the labor market.

Beyond these barriers it is also important to note that the measured positive economic consequences of mobility that have been captured by the economic literature to date are not the only important factors to consider. There are a mix of effects on other social, economic and health related factors. As an example, mobility also causes changes in access to cultural community and kinship which can have damaging mental health effects on families and children. Additionally, an overemphasis on metropolitan development while avoiding rural revitalization can limit our ability to smooth production in times of volatility (like a lack of local agricultural production during COVID yielding price instability in food-related commodities), causing issues in our complex economic and social ecosystem.

Education

Stabilizing access to basic human goods and services through housing and income stability provides the best opportunity for education to be effective for a given person in a number of ways (Reardon 2011; Brennan et al. 2014). Strengthening integration into existing high opportunity communities and better utilizing resources in a race-conscious way to build high opportunity areas and communities would lift health and life outcomes, remove some naturally-occurring cross-racial barriers to cross-cultural understanding, and likely improve mental health outcomes enough to allow for better learning. In a globalized world with a great deal of technological expansion, the United States must invest in preparing individuals for the future of work. That future will require our educational frameworks to profoundly shift toward human-forward, cross-cultural, and individualized instruction. Leveraging the racial diversity of the United States, which will continue to increase over the next three decades, with the right investment in this new form of education can put current and future Americans on the frontier of the future of work.

Other Policy Areas Related to the Social Contract

As aforementioned, social determinants of health indicate that a number of factors like health, immigration, crime, and other social policy areas are deeply intertwined with other factors like housing, employment and education. The three social policies that were selected for deeper analysis set an important initial framework through which other elements of social policy were considered. The reason for this is because, from a human frame, many of the outcomes due to these interrelated social issues can begin to improve through addressing core human dignity needs. That said, large sets of reforms are required in each of these other social policy areas and more to create equity in outcomes. The intricate interrelated nature of these policies also means that adequate reforms in these areas have the potential to create positive spillover effects. As an example, automatic expungement of individuals with certain marijuana convictions, especially as states legalize the use of marijuana could decrease incarceration and recidivism while potentially augmenting access to the stable housing and job opportunities by removing the extensive burdens of a criminal record (Vinopal 2021).

There is one last potential policy that is necessary to address when discussing social welfare improvements for Black Americans: reparations for slavery. Reparations is a form of justice-based redress for egregious injustices. As a form of justice in itself, any form of reparations is a tangible acknowledgement of historical injustice and an attempt to provide repair and reconciliation. So far, there have only been small and local forms of reparations for the descendants of enslaved Black Americans in the United States (Davis 2023). As a form of economically addressing the ills faced by the Black community in a nationally comprehensive manner, particularly those who are descendants of chattel slaves, it is highly dependent on both the architecture of the reparations and public perception. Rashawn Ray and Andre Perry argue that atonement for slavery requires reparations for Black Americans (Ray and Perry 2020). *From Here to Equality* by William A. Darity Jr. and A. Kristen Mullen (2020) explains that the United States has not taken the steps to justify forgiveness for the historical injustice of slavery. This lack of atonement prevents African Americans from collectively forgiving the past. Restitution, in the form of financial reparations is the "appropriate form of redress" (3). Darity and Mullen provide a framework for reparations at the national level. Using this proposal, Darity and Mullen state,

> We have clear metrics for determining when restitution has been achieved that we do not have for establishing the same for atonement. Specifically, restitution for African Americans would eliminate racial disparities in wealth, income, education, health, sentencing and incarceration, political participation, and subsequent opportunities to engage in American political and social life. It will require not only an endeavor to compensate for past repression and exploitation but also an endeavor to offset stubborn existing obstacles to full back participation in American political and social life. (3)

INTERNATIONAL LENS

The same arc of history that was described for the United States can also loosely be applied from an international frame. Black, indigenous, and people of color have been subject to dehumanizing forces throughout history. A heritage of slavery and colonialism combined with racist and destructive eurocentric policies has demonstrably led to a divergence in outcomes between developed nations, which are primarily White, and developing nations, which are primarily Black and Brown. Some of the policy consequences of historical western expansion include ecological destruction for western resource accumulation, a growing imbalance of income and wealth among nations which was exacerbated by protectionist western policy, and a spread of violence and disease from European military dominance. Through a history of White supremacy, death, and poverty, developing nations have also had a strong history of protest and revolution that has resulted in a specific kind of progress, a redistribution of power and resources. Artifacts of racist structural policy are yielding the same issues of centuries past in our modern epoch. Ecological and biodiversity destruction is generating climate change. A global capitalist system premised on extractive processes is producing economic disruption. An inadequate ability to handle epidemic disease is producing a pandemic on a global scale. All of these issues are transnational threats. Disproportionately

Black and Brown communities around the world face the most immediate and intense effects of these threats.

The transnational challenges of the modern era require global coopera-tion in addition to national and local action. In addition to national social contracts, an inclusive and adequate international social contract must be established globally to address the range and scope of modern challenges. Just as the failure of the United States to reflect an inclusive social contract prevented the country from enacting strong social safety nets and produced bad outcomes for the American population at large, inadequately addressing vulnerable populations globally will be a precursor to the spread of conse-quences in a way that is geographically unpredictable, especially given the confluence of issues. It is only through solidarity and a more equitable and redistributive investment in each other toward humanization and human dig-nity that we can all contend with these existential threats.

CONCLUSION

Love, hate, both true,
I describe you.
Correctly is the hardest part,
writing it, a silent art.

—Jackson McCloy, 2013, 33

Understanding and combating one of the great American and global chal-lenges of the twenty-first century requires undoing historical race-based dehumanization to promote life and dignity. This process, however, is fraught with varied racial perceptions, difficult and intensive emotions, and intricate philosophical, economic, legal, and policy work. Examining the periods surrounding the deaths of Emmett Till and George Floyd dramatically high-lighted the extent to which this is true. An outpouring of grief produced mass protest movements and struck two distinct generations. At the same time, a myriad of subsequent policies created, inhibited, and blocked progress for Black and all Americans. The ones that often create progress are the result of activists who center their efforts on humanizing Black people and assuring they have access to their basic needs toward a dignified life. The ones that inhibit and block progress reify historical dehumanizing stereotypes and often center their messages around threats to the White race. These messages incul-cate fear and lead many White Americans to violent actions and ends in order to preserve a constructed racial hierarchy. Removing the barriers that dehu-manizing attitudes creates would allow us to recognize our shared humanity and construct an inclusive social contract that equitably and adequately serves everyone, regardless of initial life circumstance.

REFERENCES

"1960 to 2021 Annual Social and Economic Supplements, Table 13: Number of Families Below the Poverty Level and Poverty Rate." n.d. Historical Poverty Tables: People and Families—1959 to 2020. U.S. Census. https://www.census.gov/data/tables/time-series/demo/income-poverty/historical-poverty-people.html.

Alexander, Michelle. 2012. *The New Jim Crow*. New York: The New Press.

Alvidrez, Jennifer, Dorothy Castille, Maryline Laude-Sharp, Adelaida Rosario, and Derrick Tabor. 2019. "The National Institute on Minority Health and Health Disparities Research Framework." *American Journal on Public Health* 109 (51): 16–20. https://doi.org/10.2105/AJPH.2018.304883.

Arias, Elizabeth, Betzaida Tejada-Vera, and Farida Ahmad. 2021. "Provisional Life Expectancy Estimates for January through June, 2020." 010. Vital Statistics Rapid Release. U.S. Department of Health and Human Services, Center for Disease Control and Prevention, National Center for Health Statistics, National Vital Statistics System. https://www.cdc.gov/nchs/data/vsrr/VSRR10-508.pdf.

Avery, Beth, and Han Lu. 2021. "Ban the Box: U.S. Cities, Counties, and States Adopt Fair-Chance Policies to Advance Employment Opportunities for People with Past Convictions." National Employment Law Project. https://s27147.pcdn.co/wp-content/uploads/Ban-the-Box-Fair-Chance-State-and-Local-Guide-Oct-2021.pdf.

Baldwin III, Robert. 2022. "Experts Warn the New Anti-Lynching Law May Not Actually Help Prevent Hate Crimes." *NPR*, April 2, 2022. https://www.npr.org/2022/04/02/1090474718/anti-lynching-law-hate-crimes.

Barr, Donald A. 2019. *Health Disparities in the United States: Social Class, Race, Ethnicity, and the Social Determinants of Health*. Third edition. Baltimore: John Hopkins University Press.

Blake, Sam. 2020. "George Floyd Protest Videos Were Watched Over 1.4 Billion Times In The First 12 Days of Unrest." *Dot.LA*, June 12, 2020. https://dot.la/george-floyd-video-2646171522.html.

Bornstein, Stephanie. 2022. "Confronting the Racial Pay Gap." *Vanderbilt Law Review* 75 (5) (10): 1401–1460. http://ezp.bentley.edu/login?url=https://www.proquest.com/scholarlyjournals/confronting-racial-pay-gap/docview/2738244564/se-2.

Brennan, Maya, Patrick Reed, and Lisa A. Sturtevant. 2014. "The Impacts of Affordable Housing on Education: A Research Summary." Center for Housing Policy. https://nhc.org/wp-content/uploads/2017/03/The-Impacts-of-Affordable-Housing-on-Education-1.pdf.

Brennan Center for Justice. 2021. "The John Lewis Voting Rights Advancement Act Fact Sheet," December 22, 2021. https://www.brennancenter.org/our-work/research-reports/john-lewis-voting-rights-advancement-act.

———. 2018. "The History of Mass Incarceration," July 20, 2018. https://www.bren nancenter.org/our-work/analysis-opinion/history-mass-incarceration.

Buchanan, Larry, Quoctrung Bui, and Jugal Patel. 2020. "Black Lives Matter May Be the Largest Movement in US History." *The New York Times*, July 3, 2020. https://www.nytimes.com/interactive/2020/07/03/us/george-floyd-protests-crowd -size.html.

Byman, Daniel. 2020. "Riots, White Supremacy, and Accelerationism." *Order from Chaos* (blog). June 2, 2020. https://www.brookings.edu/blog/order-from-chaos /2020/06/02/riots-white-supremacy-and-accelerationism/.

Carlson, Tucker, dir. 2021. "Everything the Media Didn't Tell You about the Death of George Floyd: The Trial of Derek Chauvin Is Not an Open-and-Shut-Case." *Tucker Carlson Tonight*, March 11, 2021. Fox News. https://www.foxnews.com/opinion /tucker-carlson-george-floyd-death-what-media-didnt-tell-you.

Centers for Disease Control and Prevention. 2023. "Working Together to Reduce Black Maternal Mortality," April 3, 2023. https://www.cdc.gov/healthequity/fea tures/maternal-mortality/index.html.

Chetty, Raj, Nathaniel Hendren, and Lawrence F. Katz. 2016. "The Effects of Ex- posure to Better Neighborhoods on Children: New Evidence from the Moving to Opportunity Experiment." *American Economic Review* 106 (4): 855–902. 10.1257 /aer.20150572.

Corrigan, Maureen. 2018. "'Let the People See': It Took Courage To Keep Emmett Till's Memory Alive.'" National Public Radio, October 30, 2018. https://www.npr .org/2018/10/30/660980178/-let-the-people-see-shows-how-emmett-till-s-murder -was-nearly-forgotten.

Davis, Allen J. 2023. "Reparations in the United States." University of Massachusetts Amherst Library. Last updated March 21, 2023. https://guides.library.umass.edu /reparations.

Darity, William A., and A. Kristen Mullen. 2020. *From Here to Equality: Reparations for Black Americans in the Twenty-First Century*. Chapel Hill: The University of North Carolina Press.

Derenoncourt, Ellora, Chi Hyun Kim, Moritz Kuhn, Moritz Schularick. June 2022. "Wealth of Two Nations: The U.S. Racial Wealth Gap, 1860–2020." NBER Work- ing Paper 30101, National Bureau of Economic Research, Cambridge, MA. http:// www.nber.org/papers/w30101.

Dervis, Kemal, and Caroline Conroy. 2019. "How to Renew the Social Contract." Brookings Institution, June 25, 2019. https://www.brookings.edu/opinions/how-to -renew-the-social-contract/.

Edelman, Peter. 2017. Not a Crime to Be Poor: The Criminalization of Poverty in America. New York: The New Press.

Equal Justice Initiative. 2017. "Lynching in America: Confronting the Legacy of Racial Terror." Equal Justice Initiative. Third edition. https://lynchinginamerica .eji.org/report/.

———. 2022. "Antilynching Act Signed into Law," March 29, 2022. The Equal Jus- tice Initiative. https://eji.org/news/antilynching-act-signed-into-law/.

Figueroa, Jose, Austin Frankt, and Ashish Jha. 2020. "Addressing Social Determinants of Health: Time for a Polysocial Risk Score." *Journal of the American Medical Association* 323 (16): 1553–54. https://doi.org/10.1001/jama.2020.2436.

Frederick, Tyler J., Michal Chwalek, Jean Hughes, Jeff Karabanow, and Sean Kidd. 2014. "How Stable Is Stable? Defining and Measuring Housing Stability." *Journal of Community Psychology* 42 (8): 964–979. https://doi.org/10.1002/jcop.21665.

Goff, Phillip, Jennifer Eberhardt, Melissa Williams, and Matthew Jackson. 2008. "Not Yet Human: Implicit Knowledge, Historical Dehumanization, and Contemporary Consequences." *Journal of Personality and Social Psychology* 94 (2): 292–306. DOI: 10.1037/0022-3514.94.2.292.

Goff, Phillip, Matthew Jackson, Brooke Di Leone, Carmen Culotta, and Natalie DiTomasso. 2014. "The Essence of Innocence: Consequences of Dehumanizing Black Children." *Journal of Personality and Social Psychology* 106 (4): 526–45. DOI: 10.1037/a0035663.

Gorn, Elliott. 2018. *Let the People See: The Story of Emmett Till*. Oxford University Press.

Grove, RD, and AM Hetzel. 2017. "Life Expectancy at Birth, at Age 65, and at Age 75, by Sex, Race, and Hispanic Origin: United States, Selected Years 1900–2016." National Center for Health Statistics, National Vital Statistics System. https://www.cdc.gov/nchs/data/hus/2017/015.pdf.

Hannah, John, Eugene Patterson, Frankie Freeman, Erwin Griswold, Theodore Herburgh, Robert Rankin, and William Taylor. 1967. "A Time to Listen. . . . A Time to Act: Voice from the Ghettos of the Nation's Cities." U.S. Commission on Civil Rights. https://play.google.com/books/reader?id=yHIZAAAAIAAJ&pg=GBS.PP4&hl=en.

Hassan, Adeel. 2021. "Emmett Till's Enduring Legacy." *The New York Times*, December 6, 2021. https://www.nytimes.com/article/who-was-emmett-till.html.

Hernandez, Joe. 2021. "Read This Powerful Statement From Darnella Frazier, Who Filmed George Floyd's Murder." *NPR*, May 26, 2021. https://www.npr.org/2021/05/26/1000475344/read-this-powerful-statement-from-darnella-frazier-who-filmed-george-floyds-murd.

Hinton, Elizabeth. 2016. From the War on Poverty to the War on Crime: The Making of Mass Incarceration in America. Cambridge, MA: Harvard University Press.

Houck, Davis. 2005. "Killing Emmett." *Rhetoric and Public Affairs* 8 (2): 225–62. doi:10.1353/rap.2005.0078.

International Commission on the Futures of Education. 2021. *Reimagining Our Futures Together: A New Social Contract for Education*. New York: UNESCO. https://unesdoc.unesco.org/ark:/48223/pf0000379707.locale=en.

Kerner Commission. 1968. Report of the National Advisory Commission on Civil Disorders. Washington: US Government Printing Office.

Kilgore, James. 2015. Understanding Mass Incarceration: A People's Guide to the Key Civil Rights Struggle of Our Time. New York: The New Press.

King, Jr., Martin Luther. 1963. "What a Mother Should Tell Her Child, Sermon Delivered at Ebenezer Baptist Church." The King Center. https://kinginstitute.stanford.edu/encyclopedia/till-emmett-louis.

290 *Edith Joachimpillai*

———. 2010. *Stride Toward Freedom: The Montgomery Story*. Beacon Press.

Lartey, Jamiles. 2023. "How Criminal Records Hold Back Millions of People," April 1, 2023. https://www.themarshallproject.org/2023/04/01/criminal-record-job-housing-barriers-discrimination.

Library of Congress. n.d. "Rosa Parks, The Bus Boycott." Accessed June 28, 2022. https://www.loc.gov/exhibitions/rosa-parks-in-her-own-words/about-this-exhibition/the-bus-boycott/emmett-till-with-his-mother/.

Livingstone Smith, David. 2020. *On Inhumanity*. Oxford: Oxford University Press.

Louis Gates Jr., Henry, and Cornel West. 1997. *The Future of the Race*. New York: First Vintage Books.

Martin, Eric. 2017. *Hidden Consequences: The Impact of Incarceration on Dependent Children*. Washington D.C.: National Institute of Justice, U.S. Department of Justice. https://www.ojp.gov/pdffiles1/nij/250349.pdf.

McCoy, Jackson Original Book. 2013. *Thoughts from My Notebook*. Private Collection, Concord, 33.

McGhee, Heather. 2021. *The Sum of Us*. London: Oneworld.

Meloni, Maurizio. 2017. "Scientific Racism." *The Wiley Blackwell Encyclopedia of Social Theory*, December 4, 2017. https://doi.org/10.1002/9781118430873.est0324.

National Institutes of Health. 2017. "The National Institute on Minority Health and Health Disparities Research Framework." National Institutes of Health, National Institute on Minority Health and Health Disparities. https://www.nimhd.nih.gov/about/overview/research-framework/nimhd-framework.html.

Naylor, Brian. 2022. "The Senate Is Set to Debate Voting Rights. Here's What the Bills Would Do." *NPR*, January 18, 2022. https://www.npr.org/2022/01/18/1073021462/senate-voting-rights-freedom-to-vote-john-lewis-voting-rights-advancement-act.

New York Lawyers for the Public Interest. 2022. "Supreme Court Decision Signals Need for Strong Implementation and Adequate Funding for New York's Landmark Climate Law." https://www.nylpi.org/wp-content/uploads/2022/07/WV-v-EPA-Decision-Statement.pdf

O'Flaherty, Brendan. 2015. *The Economics of Race in the United States*. Cambridge: Harvard University Press.

O'Harrow Jr., Robert, Andrew Ba Tran, and Derek Hawkins. 2021. "The Rise of Domestic Extremism in America: Data Shows a Surge in Homegrown Incidents Not Seen in a Quarter-Century." *The Washington Post*, April 12, 2021. https://www.washingtonpost.com/investigations/interactive/2021/domestic-terrorism-data/.

Oxford Languages. 2023. "Social Contract." Oxford University Press. Accessed April 26, 2023. https://www.google.com/search?rlz=1C1CHBF_enUS858US858&sxsrf=APwXEdf6cbw5SmBpZxkwLZAYT7JpjN-ckA:1682421354500&q=social+contract&si=AMnBZoE_SgVdNzFvWI74rwHkJYEEHjGHEzPK36c8qbZsfkOwULO-ANivTtTrxcG8zCXxQiHpdlIGEKIQry4Cehhh3wcmy4wIZUzDV5yrW__0Leffil TPEs%3D&expnd=1&sa=X&ved=2ahUKEwjy8sn588T-AhW4kYkEHazuArgQ2v4IegQIFRAP&biw=1368&bih=761&dpr=2#bsht=Cgdic2h3Y2hwEgQIBDAB.

Parker, Kim, Juliana Menasce Horowitz, and Monica Anderson. 2020. *2020 Pew Research Center's American Trends Panel Wave 68 June 2020 Final Topline:* Pew

Research Center. https://www.pewresearch.org/social-trends/wp-content/uploads/sites/3/2020/06/PSDT_06.12.20_protest.report-TOPLINE.pdf.

Perry, Andre M., Jonathan Rothwell, and David Harshbarger. 2018. "The Devaluation of Assets in Black Neighborhoods: The Case of Residential Property." Brookings Institution and Gallup. https://www.brookings.edu/wp-content/up loads/2018/11/2018.11_Brookings-Metro_Devaluation-Assets-Black-Neighbor hoods_final.pdf.

Quadt, Katie Rose and Alexi Jones. 2021. "Research Roundup: Incarceration can cause lasting damage to mental health." May 13, 2021. Prison Policy Initiative. https://www.prisonpolicy.org/blog/2021/05/13/mentalhealthimpacts/.

Raphael, Kate. 2020. "Addressing Social Determinants of Health: Time for a Polysocial Risk Score." *Harvard Global Health Institute*, April 22, 2020. Accessed April 26, 2023. https://globalhealth.harvard.edu/addressing-social-determinants -of-health-time-for-a-polysocial-risk-score/.

Ray, Rashawn, and Andre M. Perry. 2020. "Why we need reparations for Black Americans" Brookings Institution. https://www.brookings.edu/policy2020/big ideas/why-we-need-reparations-for-black-americans/?amp.

Reardon, Sean F. 2011. "The Widening Academic Achievement Gap Between the Rich and the Poor: New Evidence and Possible Explanations" In *Whither Opportunity? Rising Inequality, Schools, and Children's Life Chances*, edited by Greg J. Duncan and Richard J. Murnane, 91–116. New York: Russell Sage Foundation.

Rothstein, Richard. 2017. *The Color of Law: A Forgotten History of How Our Government Segregated America*. Liveright Publishing Corporation.

Rousseau, Jean-Jacques. 1762. *Du Contrat Social; Ou, Principes Du Droit Politiques*. Paris, France.

———. 1893. *The Social Contract: Or Principles of Political Law*. Translated by Peter Eckler. New York: Peter Eckler.

Saccoh, TK (@darkest.hue). 2022. "A Supreme Court draft opinion with the decision to overturn Roe v. Wade was recently leaked." Instagram, May 9, 2022. https://www.instagram.com/p/CdWFTWHr98P/?igshid=MDJmNzVkMjY=.

Sawyer, Wendy and Peter Wagner. 2023. "Mass Incarceration: The Whole Pie 2023." March 14, 2023. Prison Policy Initiative. https://www.prisonpolicy.org/reports /pie2023.html#community.

Schuetz, Jenny. 2020. "To Improve Housing Affordability, We Need Better Alignment of Zoning, Taxes, and Subsidies." *Policy 2020*, January 2020. Brookings Institution. https://www.brookings.edu/wp-content/uploads/2019/12/Schuetz_Pol icy2020_BigIdea_Improving-Housing-Afforability.pdf.

Shrider, Emily, Melissa Kollar, Frances Chen, and Jessica Semega. 2021. "Income and Poverty in the United States: 2020, Current Population Reports. P60–273. U.S. Census." U.S. Department of Commerce. https://www.census.gov/content/dam /Census/library/publications/2021/demo/p60-273.pdf.

Southern Prisons Coalition. 2022. "The United States of America's Compliance with the Convention on the Elimination of All Forms of Racial Discrimination: 107th Session of the Committee on the Elimination of Racial Discrimination." July 14th,

2022. https://www.naacpldf.org/wp-content/uploads/Report-on-Southern-Prisons -Final-Copy-7.14.22-5pm.pdf.

Stern, Alexandra. 2021. "Cautions About Medicalized Dehumanization." *American Medical Association Journal of Ethics* 23 (1): 64–69. 10.1001/amajethics.2021.64.

Stevenson, Amanda Jean. 2021. "The Pregnancy-Related Mortality Impact of a Total Abortion Ban in the United States: A Research Note on Increased Deaths Due to Remaining Pregnant." *Demography* 58 (6): 2019–2028. 10.1215/00703370-9585908.

U.S. Department of Housing and Urban Development. 2017. "Defining Housing Affordability." U.S. Department of Housing and Urban Development. https://www .huduser.gov/portal/pdredge/pdr-edge-featd-article-081417.html.

U.S. Bureau of Labor Statistics. 2023. "Labor Force Characteristics by Race and Ethnicity, 2021." U.S. Bureau of Labor Statistics, January 2023. https://www.bls .gov/opub/reports/race-and-ethnicity/2021/home.htm.

United States Commission on Civil Rights Massachusetts Advisory Committee. 1967. "The Voice of the Ghetto; Report on Two Boston Neighborhood Meetings." United States Commission on Civil Rights Massachusetts Advisory Committee. https:// babel.hathitrust.org/cgi/pt?id=hvd.32044031984487&view=1up&seq=5.

U.S Department of Health and Human Services. n. d. "Social Determinants of Health." U.S Department of Health and Human Services, Office of Disease Prevention and Health Promotion. Accessed June 29, 2022. https://health.gov/healthy people/priority-areas/social-determinants-health.

University of Pennsylvania Wharton. 2016. "Mortality in the United States: Past, Present and Future." University of Pennsylvania Wharton School of Business. Accessed April 26, 2023. https://budgetmodel.wharton.upenn.edu/issues/2016/1/25 /mortality-in-the-united-states-past-present-and-future.

Vinopal, Courtney. 2021. "As More States Legalize Marijuana, People with Drug Convictions Want Their Records Cleared." PBS Newshour, May 5, 2021. https:// www.pbs.org/newshour/nation/as-more-states-legalize-marijuana-people-with -drug-convictions-want-their-records-cleared.

Winship, Scott, Christopher Pulliam, Ariel Shiro, Richard Reeves, and Santiago Deambrosi. 2021. "Long Shadows: The Black-White Gap in Multigenerational Poverty." AEI, Brookings. https://www.brookings.edu/wp-content/uploads/2021/06 /Long-brendShadows_Final.pdf.

World Health Organization. 2018. "WHO Housing and Health Guidelines." World Health Organization. Accessed April 26, 2023.

Appendix

ANTI-BLACK ENVIRONMENTAL RACISM
AND ENVIRONMENTAL JUSTICE ACTIVISM

Alkon, Alison Hope and Julian Agyeman. 2011. *Cultivating Food Justice: Race, Class, and Sustainability*. Cambridge, MA: MIT Press, 2011.

Allen, Barbara L. 2001. "Saving St. Gabriel: The Emergence of a New African-American Town." *Contemporary Justice Review* 4 (2): 145–159. https://search -ebscohost-com.ezp.bentley.edu/login.aspx?direct=true&db=a9h&AN=5458134& site=ehost-live.

Black, Sara Thomas, Richard Anthony Milligan, and Nik Heynen. 2016. "Solidarity in Climate/Immigrant Justice Direct Action: Lessons from Movements in the US South." *International Journal of Urban and Regional Research* 40 (2): 284–98. DOI:10.1111/1468-2427.12341.

Blanton, Ryan. 2011. "Chronotopic Landscapes of Environmental Racism." *Journal of Linguistic Anthropology,* 21(21): E76–E93. doi: https://doi.org/10.1111/j.1548 -1395.2011.01098.x.

Bullard, Robert, ed. *The Quest for Environmental Justice: Human Rights and the Politics of Pollution*. Berkeley: Counterpoint, 2005.

Bullard Robert, Paul Mohai, Robin Saha, and Beverly Wright. 2007. *Toxic Wastes and Race at Twenty 1987–2007: Grassroots Struggles to Dismantle Environmental Racism in the United States*. Cleveland, OH: United Church Christ Justice Witness Ministry.

Bullard, Robert and Beverly Wright. 2009. *Race, Place, and Environmental Justice after Hurricane Katrina: Struggles to Reclaim, Rebuild, and Revitalize New Orleans and the Gulf Coast.* New York: Routledge.

Burgess, Laura Dillon, Glenn S. Johnson, and Steven C. Washington. 2014. "An African American Community and the PCB Contamination in Anniston, Alabama: An Environmental Justice Case Study." *Race, Gender & Class* 21 (1): 334–361. http://

ezp.bentley.edu/login?url=https://www.proquest.com/scholarly-journals/african
-american-community-pcb-contamination/docview/1690371878/se-2.

Byrnes, W. 2014. "Climate Justice, Hurricane Katrina, and African American Environmentalism." *Journal of African American Studies* 18 (3): 305–14. doi:10.1007
/s12111-013-9270-5.

Chambers, Stefanie. 2007. "Minority Empowerment and Environmental Justice." *Urban Affairs Review* 43 (1): 28–54. doi:10.1177/1078087407301790.

Checker, Melissa A. 2002. "'It's in the Air': Redefining the Environment as a New Metaphor for Old Social Justice Struggles." *Human Organization* Human Organization 61 (1): 94–106. doi: https://doi.org/10.17730/humo.61.1.10dwpu3mqj1c8guw.

———. 2005. *Polluted Promises: Environmental Racism and the Search for Justice in a Southern Town*. New York: NYU Press.

———. 2020. *The Sustainability Myth: Environmental Gentrification and the Politics of Justice*. New York: NYU Press.

Coleman Flowers, Catherine. 2020. *Waste: One Woman's Fight Against America's Dirty Secret*. New York: The New Press.

Colsa Perez, Alejandro, Bernadette Grafton, Paul Mohai, Rebecca Hardin, Katy Hintzen and Sara Orvis. 2015. "Evolution of the Environmental Justice Movement: Activism, Formalization and Differentiation." *Environmental Research Letters*, 10 (10): 1–12. DOI 10.1088/1748-9326/10/10/105002.

Dillingham, Heather. 2008. "Determining the Current Status of the Environmental Justice Movement: Analysis of Revolutionary Actions." *Harvard Journal of African American Public Policy* 14: 37–50. https://search-ebscohost-com.ezp.bentley
.edu/login.aspx?direct=true&db=a9h&AN=32966840&site=ehost-live.

Ezeilo, Angelou and Nick Chiles. 2019. *Engage, Connect, Protect: Empowering Diverse Youth as Environmental Leaders*. Gabriola Island: New Society Publishers.

Farrugia, Rebekah. 2020. *Women Rapping Revolution: Hip Hop and Community Building in Detroit*. Oakland: University of California Press.

Fields, Kimberly. 2018. "Beyond Protest: The Effects of Grassroots Activism on Maryland and Pennsylvania's Responses to Environmental Justice." *Environmental Justice* 11(1): 15–28. https://doi.org/10.1089/env.2017.0022.

Finney, Carolyn. 2014. *Black Faces, White Spaces: Reimagining the Relationship of African Americans to the Great Outdoors*. Chapel Hill: UNC Press.

Frankland, Peggy. 2013. *Women Pioneers of the Louisiana Environmental Movement*. Jackson: University of Mississippi Press.

Fuller, Trevor K. 2015. *Environmental Justice and Activism in Indianapolis*. Lanham, MD: Lexington Books.

Gioielli, Robert. 2014. *Environmental Activism and the Urban Crisis: Baltimore, St. Louis, Chicago*. Philadelphia: Temple University Press.

Gomez, Antoinette M., Fatemeh Shafiei, and Glenn S. Johnson. 2011. "Black Women's Involvement in the Environmental Justice Movement: An Analysis of Three Communities in Atlanta, Georgia." *Race, Gender & Class* 18 (1): 189–214. http://
ezp.bentley.edu/login?url=https://www.proquest.com/scholarly-journals/black-wo
mens-involvement-environmental-justice/docview/913374728/se-2.

Griffith Spears, Ellen. 2014. *Baptized in PCBs: Race, Pollution, and Justice in an All-American Town*. Chapel Hill: University of North Carolina Press.

Guild, Joshua B. and Jeff Whetstone. 2021. "Malik Rahim's Black Radical Environmentalism." *Southern Cultures* 27 (1): N.PAG. doi:10.1353/scu.2021.0007.

Hines, Revathi. 2007. "Race, Environmental Justice, and Interest Group Mobilizations: Hazardous Waste and the Case of Sumter County, Alabama." *Western Journal of Black Studies* 31 (1): 50–57. https://search-ebscohost-com.ezp.bentley.edu/login.aspx?direct=true&db=a9h&AN=36291672&site=ehost-live.

———. 2015. "The Price of Pollution: The Struggle for Environmental Justice in Mossville, Louisiana." *Western Journal of Black Studies* 39 (3): 198–208. https://search-ebscohost-com.ezp.bentley.edu/login.aspx?direct=true&db=a9h&AN=113913887&site=ehost-live.

Johnson, Glenn. 2005. "Grassroots Activism in Louisiana." *Humanity & Society* 29 (3–4): 285–304. https://doi.org/10.1177/016059760502900308.

Johnson, Rebecca. 2019. "A Lot Like War: Petrocapitalism, 'Slow Violence,' and the Struggle for Environmental Justice." *Social Justice* 46 (1): 105–118. https://www.jstor.org/stable/26873840.

Kohl, Ellen. 2022. "Making the Invisible Visible: Telling Stories to Animate Environmental Injustices." *ACME: An International E-Journal for Critical Geographies* 21 (1): 33–48. https://search-ebscohost-com.ezp.bentley.edu/login.aspx?direct=true&db=a9h&AN=155666403&site=ehost-live.

Lee, Tsuey-Ping. 2020. "Pursuing Justice in a Community Experiencing Environmental Injustice: The Practice of Community Revitalization." *Contemporary Justice Review* 23 (4): 337–53. doi:10.1080/10282580.2019.1700365.

Lerner, Steve. *Diamond: A Struggle for Environmental Justice in Louisiana's Chemical Corridor*. Cambridge, MA: MIT Press, 2005.

Lucas-Darby, Emma. 2012. "Community Benefits Agreements: A Case Study in Addressing Environmental and Economic Injustices." *Journal of African American History* 97 (1/2): 92–109. doi:10.5323/jafriamerhist.97.1–2.0092.

Mandell, Rebecca, Barbara Israel, and Amy Schulz. 2019. "Breaking Free from Siloes: Intersectionality as a Collective Action Frame to Address Toxic Exposures and Reproductive Health." *Social Movement Studies* 18 (3): 346–63. doi:10.1080/14742837.2018.1556091.

Miller Hesed, Christine, and David Ostergren. 2017. "Promoting Climate Justice in High-Income Countries: Lessons from African American Communities on the Chesapeake Bay." *Climatic Change* 143(1–2): 185–200. doi:https://doi.org/10.1007/s10584-017-1982-4.

Pauli, Benjamin. 2019. *Flint Fights Back: Environmental Justice and Democracy in the Flint Water Crisis*. Cambridge, MA: MIT Press.

Pavel, Paloma. 2009. *Breakthrough Communities: Sustainability and Justice in the Next American Metropolis*. Cambridge: MIT Press.

Pellow, David and Robert Brulle, eds. 2005. *Power, Justice, and the Environment: A Critical Appraisal of the Environmental Justice Movement*. Cambridge, MA: MIT Press.

Penniman, Leah. 2023. Black *Earth Wisdom: Soulful Conversations with Black Envi-*
ronmentalists. New York: Amistad Publishing.

Pope, Blaine, Ernie Smith, Samuel Shacks, and Joyce Keith Hargrove. 2011. "Booker
T. and the New Green Collar Workforce: An Earth-Based Reassessment of the
Philosophy of Booker T. Washington." *Journal of Black Studies*, 42(4), 507–529.
2011.https://doi.org/10.1177/0021934710380204.

Poblete, JoAnna. 2021. "Women Community Warriors of St. Croix." *Women, Gender,*
and Families of Color 9 (1): 83–101,124. http://ezp.bentley.edu/login?url=https://
www.proquest.com/scholarly-journals/women-community-warriors-st-croix
/docview/2630322560/se-2.

Rainey, Shirley, and Glenn Johnson. 2009. "Grassroots Activism: An Exploration of
Women of Color's Role in the Environmental Justice Movement." *Race, Gender*
& Class 16 (3/4): 144–73. https://search-ebscohost-com.ezp.bentley.edu/login.aspx
?direct=true&db=8gh&AN=48383554&site=ehost-live.

Rector, Joseph. 2022. *Toxic Debt: An Environmental Justice History of Detroit.* Chapel Hill: University of North Carolina Press.

Schelhas, John, and Sarah Hitchner. 2020. "Integrating Research and Outreach for
Environmental Justice: African American Land Ownership and Forestry." *Annals*
of Anthropological Practice 44 (1): 47–64. doi:10.1111/napa.12133.

Schneller, Andrew, Saima Hannan, Haja Isatu Bah, Sophia Livecchi, and Stacy Pet-
tigrew. 2022. "Environmental Justice Is Exhausting: Five Decades of Air Pollution
and Community Advocacy at Ezra Prentice Homes in Albany, New York." *Local*
Environment 27 (12): 1514–35. doi:10.1080/13549839.2022.2113869.

Sobey, Allyssa. 2014. "Long Exposure: Environmental Racism and Activism in
Institute, West Virginia." Masters Thesis. West Virginia University. https://doi
.org/10.33915/etd.6686.

Stein, Rachel, ed. 2004. *New Perspectives on Environmental Justice: Gender, Sexual-*
ity, and Activism. New Brunswick, NJ: Rutgers University Press.

Sze, Julie. 2006. *Noxious New York: The Racial Politics of Urban Health and Envi-*
ronmental Justice. Cambridge, MA: MIT Press.

Tajik, Mansoureh and Meredith Minkler. 2007. "Environmental Justice Research and
Action: A Case Study in Political Economy and Community-Academic Collaboration." *International Quarterly of Community Health Education* 26 (3): 213–31.
https://search-ebscohost-com.ezp.bentley.edu/login.aspx?direct=true&db=8gh
&AN=26589049&site=ehost-live.

Waldron-Moore, Pamela, Anthony McKinney, Ariel Howard, and Amanda Brown.
2007. "A Question of Social Justice: The Case of Louisiana Communities and
their Struggle for Environmental Sustainability." *Gender & Class* 14 (3): 154–
174. http://ezp.bentley.edu/login?url=https://www.proquest.com/scholarly-journals
/question-social-justice-case-louisiana/docview/218859110/se-2.

Ward, Brandon. 2021. *Living Detroit: Environmental Activism in an Age of Urban*
Crisis. New York: Routledge.

Williams, Teona. 2021. "For 'Peace, Quiet, and Respect': Race, Policing, and Land
Grabbing on Chicago's South Side: The 2018 Clyde Woods Black Geographies
Specialty Group Graduate Student Paper Award." *Antipode* 53 (2): 497–523.
doi:10.1111/anti.12692.

BLACK ATHLETE ACTIVISM

Anderson, Shaun. 2023. *The Black Athlete Revolt: The Sport Justice Movement in the Age of #BlackLivesMatter*. Lanham, MD: Rowman & Littlefield Publishers.

Black, Wayne, Ezinne Ofoegbu, and Sayvon Foster. 2022. "#TheyareUnited and #TheyWantToPlay: A Critical Discourse Analysis of College Football Player Social Media Activism. *Sociology of Sport Journal* 39 (4): 352–361. https://doi.org/10.1123/ssj.2021-0045.

Boykoff, Jules, and Ben Carrington. 2020. "Sporting Dissent: Colin Kaepernick, NFL Activism, and Media Framing Contests." *International Review for the Sociology of Sport* 55 (7): 829–49. doi:10.1177/1012690219861594.

Brown, Drew, ed. 2020. *Sports in African American Life: Essays on History and Culture*. Jefferson, NC: McFarland & Company.

Bryant, Howard. 2018. *The Heritage: Black Athletes, A Divided America, and the Politics of Patriotism*. Boston: Beacon Press.

Burin, Eric. 2018. *Protesting on Bended Knee: Race, Dissent, and Patriotism in 21st Century America*. Grand Forks: Digital Press at The University of North Dakota.

Carr, Brett. 2018. "Kaepernick's Kneel: Performance, Protest, and the National Football League." *Callaloo* 41 (3): 4–17. doi:10.1353/cal.2018.0049.

Colombo-Dougovito, Andrew, Tracey Everbach, and Karen Weiller-Abels. 2022. *Not Playing Around: Intersectional Identities, Media Representation, and the Power of Sport*. Lanham, MD: Rowman & Littlefield Publishers.

Coombs, Danielle Sarver, and David Cassilo. 2017. "Athletes and/or Activists: LeBron James and Black Lives Matter." *Journal of Sport & Social Issues* 41 (5): 425–44. doi:10.1177/0193723517719665.

Cooper, Joseph. 2021. *A Legacy of African American Resistance and Activism Through Sport*. Bern: Peter Lang.

Cooper, Joseph, Charles Macaulay, and Saturnino Rodriguez. 2019. "Race and Resistance: A Typology of African American Sport Activism." *International Review for the Sociology of Sport* 54 (2): 151–81. doi:10.1177/1012690217718170.

Cramer, Linsay. 2019. "Cam Newton and Russell Westbrook's Symbolic Resistance to Whiteness in the NFL and NBA." *Howard Journal of Communications* 30 (1): 57–75. doi:10.1080/10646175.2018.1439421.

Crooks, Delando, Alvin Logan, Daniel Thomas III, Langston Clark, and Emmitt Gill. 2022. "Legal and Political Activism: The Next Wave of Student-Athlete Protest." *Sport, Education & Society*, January, 1–14. doi:10.1080/13573322.2021.2023490.

Cunningham, George B. and Michael R Regan, Jr. 2011. "Political Activism, Racial Identity and the Commercial Endorsement of Athletes. *International Review for the Sociology of Sport* 47 (6): 657–669. DOI: 10.1177/1012690211416358.

Druckman, James, Adam Howat, and Jacob Rothschild. 2019. "Political Protesting, Race, and College Athletics: Why Diversity Among Coaches Matters." *Social Science Quarterly* (Wiley-Blackwell) 100 (4): 1009–22. doi:10.1111/ssqu.12615.

Edwards, Ashley and M. Elizabeth Thorpe. 2019. "The Dilemma of Being Colin Kaepernick: A Rhetorical Analysis of the #takeaknee Protest Using Heider's Balance Theory." *Iowa Journal of Communication* 51 (1): 71–110. https://search

-ebscohost-com.ezp.bentley.edu/login.aspx?direct=true&db=ufh&AN=139348455 &site=ehost-live.

Edwards, Harry. 2018. *The Revolt of the Black Athlete: 50th Anniversary Edition.* Urbana: University of Illinois Press.

Gill, Emmett. 2016. "'Hands up, Don't Shoot' or Shut Up and Play Ball? Fan-Generated Media Views of the Ferguson Five." *Journal of Human Behavior in the Social Environment* 26 (3/4): 400–412. doi:10.1080/10911359.2016.1139990.

Gill, Emmitt, Langston Clark, and Alvin Logan. 2020. "Freedom for First Downs: Interest Convergence and The Missouri Black Student Boycott." *Journal of Negro Education* 89 (3): 342–59. https://search-ebscohost-com.ezp.bentley.edu/login .aspx?direct=true&db=a9h&AN=147634892&site=ehost-live.

Graber, Shane M., Ever Figueroa, and Krishnan Vasudevan. 2020. "Oh, Say, Can You Kneel: A Critical Discourse Analysis of Newspaper Coverage of Colin Kaepernick's Racial Protest." *Howard Journal of Communications* 31 (5): 464–80. doi:10 .1080/10646175.2019.1670295.

Hartmann, Douglas. 2019. "The Olympic 'Revolt' of 1968 and its Lessons for Contemporary African American Athletic Activism." *European Journal of American Studies* 14(1): 1–25. https://doi.org/10.4000/ejas.14335.

Hawkins, Daniel, Andrew Lindner, Douglas Hartmann, and Brianna Cochran. 2022. "Does Protest 'Distract' Athletes From Performing? Evidence From the National Anthem Demonstrations in the National Football League." *Journal of Sport & Social Issues* 46 (2): 127–55. doi:10.1177/01937235211043647.

Howell, Charlotte E. 2021. "The 2020 National Women's Soccer League Challenge Cup Anthem Protests: The Limits of Symbolic White Allyship." *Velvet Light Trap: A Critical Journal of Film & Television* 87 (Spring): 76–79. https://search -ebscohost-com.ezp.bentley.edu/login.aspx?direct=true&db=a9h&AN=149476016 &site=ehost-live.

Intravia, Jonathan, Alex Piquero, and Nicole Leeper Piquero. 2018. "The Racial Divide Surrounding United States of America National Anthem Protests in the National Football League." *Deviant Behavior* 39 (8): 1058–68. doi:10.1080/0163 9625.2017.1399745.

Intravia, Jonathan, Alex R. Piquero, Nicole Leeper Piquero, and Bryan Byers. 2020. "Just Do It? An Examination of Race on Attitudes Associated with Nike's Advertisement Featuring Colin Kaepernick.'" *Deviant Behavior* 41 (10): 1221–31. doi: 10.1080/01639625.2019.1604299.

Jacob, Frank, ed. 2020. *Sports and Politics: Commodification, Capitalist Exploitation, and Political Agency.* Berlin: Walter de Gruyter GmbH.

Jones, Brittany, and Joel Berends. 2023. "Enacting Antiracist Pedagogy: An Analysis of LeBron James and Doc Rivers' Antiracist Discourse." *Equity & Excellence in Education*, January, 1–16. doi:10.1080/10665684.2022.2158392.

Kido Lopez, Jason. 2020. "Branding Athlete Activism." In *Race and Media: Critical Approaches*, edited by Lori Kido Lopez, 67–78. New York: NYU Press.

Knoester, Chris, David Ridpath, and Rachel Allison. 2022. "Should Athletes Be Allowed to Protest During the National Anthem? An Analysis of Public Opinions

Among U.S. Adults." *Sociology of Sport Journal* 39 (1): 23–34. doi:10.1123 /ssj.2020-0153.

Lewis, Apryl. 2018. "Pariahs of the Sports World: Reclaiming Autonomy Against White Supremacy Through Protest." *Callaloo* 41 (3): 114–23. doi:10.1353/cal .2018.0060.

Long Anderson, Mia, ed. 2023. *Social Justice and the Modern Athlete: Exploring the Role of Athlete Activism in Social Change*. Lanham, MD: Lexington Books.

Martin, Lori Latrice. 2018. "The Politics of Sports and Protest: Colin Kaepernick and the Practice of Leadership." *American Studies Journal* 64 (January): 1–12. doi:10.18422/64-06.

McClearen, Jennifer, and Mia Fischer. 2021. "Maya Moore, Black Lives Matter, and the Visibility of Athlete Activism." *Velvet Light Trap: A Critical Journal of Film & Television,* no. 87 (Spring): 64–68. https://search-ebscohost-com.ezp.bentley.edu /login.aspx?direct=true&db=a9h&AN=149476012&site=ehost-live.

McCoy, Dorian. 2023. "Black Student-Athletes, Contemporary Student-Athlete Activism, and Critical Race Theory." *New Directions for Student Services* 2022 (180): 39–49. https://doi.org/10.1002/ss.20446.

McGrath, Rory, ed. 2021. *Athlete Activism: Contemporary Perspectives*. New York: Routledge.

Montez de Oca, Jeffrey. 2021. "Marketing Politics and Resistance: Mobilizing Black Pain in National Football League Publicity." *Sociology of Sport Journal* 38 (2): 101–10. doi:10.1123/ssj.2021-0005.

Niven, David. 2021. "Who Says Shut Up and Dribble? Race and the Response to Athletes' Political Activism." *Journal of African American Studies* 25 (2): 298–311. https://link-gale-com.ezp.bentley.edu/apps/doc/A667960860/EAIM?u=mlin_m _bent&sid=bookmark-EAIM&xid=c898be88.

Piper, Timothy. 2022 "#NoJusticeNoLeBron and the Persistence of Messianic Masculinity in Black Athlete Activism." *International Journal of Communication* [Online] 16 (2022): 1197–1219. Gale Academic OneFile, link.gale.com/apps/doc /A699363131/AONE?u=mlin_m_bent&sid=bookmark-AONE&xid=1e68d9ef.

Piquero, Alex R. 2018. "Linking Race-Based Perceptions of Gangs to Criminals and Athletes." *Society* 55 (3): 237–42. doi:10.1007/s12115-018-0244-z.

Pradhan, Sean and Marianne Marar Yacobian. 2022. "Interception!: Sports Fans' Responses to Social Justice Activism by Minoritized Players in the National Football League (NFL)." *The International Journal of Sport and Society* 14 (1): 25–44. doi:https://doi.org/10.18848/2152-7857/CGP/v14i01/25-44.

Ratchford, Jamal. 2012. "'Black Fists and Fool's Gold: The 1960s Black Athletic Revolt Reconsidered' The LeBron James Decision and Self-Determination in Post-Racial America." *Black Scholar* 42 (1): 49–59. doi:10.5816/blackscholar.42.1.0049.

Rounds, Christopher D. 2020. "The Policing of Patriotism: African American Athletes and the Expression of Dissent." *Journal of Sport History* 47 (2): 111–127. doi:10.1353/sph.2020.0025.

Ruck, Rob. 2021. "Reflections on African Americans in Baseball: No Longer the Vanguard of Change." *Race and Social Problems* 13: 172–181. https://doi.org/10.1007/ s12552-021-09333-4.

Ruffin II, Herbert. 2014. "'Doing the Right Thing for the Sake of Doing the Right Thing': The Revolt of the Black Athlete and the Modern Student-Athletic Movement, 1956–2014." *Western Journal of Black Studies* 38 (4): 260–78. https://search-ebscohost-com.ezp.bentley.edu/login.aspx?direct=true&db=a9h&AN=100700659&site=ehost-live.

Ryle, Robin. 2020. *Throw Like a Girl, Cheer Like a Boy: The Evolution of Gender, Identity, and Race in Sports.* Lanham, MD: Rowman & Littlefield.

Sanderson, Jimmy, Evan Frederick, and Mike Stocz. 2016. "When Athlete Activism Clashes With Group Values: Social Identity Threat Management via Social Media." *Mass Communication & Society* 19 (3): 301–22. doi:10.1080/15205436.2015.1128549.

Serazio, Michael and Emily Thorson. 2020. "Weaponized Patriotism and Racial Subtext in Kaepernick's Aftermath: The Anti-Politics of American Sports Fandom." *Television & New Media* 21 (2): 151–68. doi:10.1177/1527476419879917.

Steele, David. 2022. *It Was Always a Choice: Picking Up the Baton of Athlete Activism.* Philadelphia: Temple University Press.

Tenjido, Daniela. 2020. "Shut Up and Dribble: The Racial Subordination of the Black Professional Athlete." *St. Thomas Law Review* 33 (1): 27–54. https://search-ebscohost-com.ezp.bentley.edu/login.aspx?direct=true&db=a9h&AN=152785770&site=ehost-live.

Thomas, Etan. 2018. *We Matter: Athletes and Activism.* Brooklyn: Akaschic Books.

Thomas, Michael and Jamie Daniel. 2022. "Playing Offense: How Athletes are Impacting a Changing Administrative State." *Administration & Society* 54 (10): 2101–2120. https://doi.org/10.1177/00953997221102612.

Thomas, Michael and James Wright II. 2022. "We Can't Just Shut up and Play: How the NBA and WNBA Are Helping Dismantle Systemic Racism." *Administrative Theory & Praxis* (Taylor & Francis Ltd) 44 (2): 143–57. doi:10.1080/10841806.2021.1918988.

Towler, Christopher, Nyron Crawford and Robert Bennett. 2020. "Shut Up and Play: Black Athletes, Protest Politics, and Black Political Action." *Perspectives on Politics* 18 (1): 111–127. doi:10.1017/S1537592719002597.

Williams, A. Lamont. 2022. "The Heritage Strikes Back: Athlete Activism, Black Lives Matter, and the Iconic Fifth Wave of Activism in the (W)NBA Bubble." *Cultural Studies/Critical Methodologies* 22 (3): 266–75. doi:10.1177/15327086211049718.

Zirin, Dave. 2021. *The Kaepernick Effect: Taking a Knee, Changing the World.* New York: The New Press.

BLACK CHURCH ACTIVISM

Anderson, Kami J. 2020. "A Place for Authentic Spirit: Building and Sustaining A 'Beloved Community' For Spiritual Transformation Outside the Church." *Journal of Communication & Religion* 43 (3): 29–36. https://search-ebscohost-com.ezp.bentley.edu/login.aspx?direct=true&db=ufh&AN=147726334&site=ehost-live.

Ayers, Danielle and Reginald Williams, Jr. 2013. *To Serve This Present Age: Social Justice Ministry in the Black Church.* King of Prussia: Judson Press.

Barber, Kendra H. 2015. "Whither Shall We Go? The Past and Present of Black Churches and the Public Sphere." *Religions* 6 (1): 245–65. doi:10.3390/rel6010245.

Barnes, Sandra L. 2005. "Black Church Culture and Community Action." *Social Forces* 84 (2): 968–94. doi:10.1353/sof.2006.0003.

———. 2006. "Whosoever Will Let Her Come: Social Activism and Gender Inclusivity in the Black Church." *Journal for the Scientific Study of Religion* 45 (3): 371–87. doi:10.1111/j.1468-5906.2006.00312.x.

Barron, Charrise. 2020. "Bridging Liturgies in the Black Lives Matter Era." *Liturgy* 35 (4): 51–57. doi:10.1080/0458063X.2020.1832851.

Baumann, Roger. 2016. "Political Engagement Meets the Prosperity Gospel: African American Christian Zionism and Black Church Politics." *Sociology of Religion* 77(4): 359–85. http://www.jstor.org/stable/44282050.

Booker, Vaughn. 2021. "Mothers of the Movement: Evangelicalism and Religious Experience in Black Women's Activism." *Religions* 12: 141. https://doi.org/10.3390/rel12020141.

Cameron, Christopher, and Phillip Sinitiere, eds. 2021. *Race, Religion, and Black Lives Matter: Essays on a Moment and a Movement.* Nashville: Vanderbilt University Press.

Deal, Heather E. 2022. "Christian Congregations and Social and Political Action: A Review of the Literature." *Social Work & Christianity* 49 (3): 289–301. doi:10.34043/swc.v49i3.303.

Delehanty, John D. 2016. "Prophets of Resistance: Social Justice Activists Contesting Comfortable Church Culture." *Sociology of Religion* 77(1): 37–58. http://www.jstor.org/stable/44282005.

Edwards, Elise M. 2017. "'Let's Imagine Something Different': Spiritual Principles in Contemporary African American Justice Movements and their Implications for the Built Environment." *Religions* 8(12): 256. https://doi.org/10.3390/rel8120256.

Franklin, Robert M. 2015. "Rehabilitating Democracy: Restoring Civil Rights and Leading the Next Human Rights Revolution." *The Journal of Law and Religion* 30(3): 414–427. https://doi.org/10.1017/jlr.2015.22.

Gunning Francis, Leah. 2015. *Ferguson and Faith: Sparking Leadership and Awakening a Community.* St. Louis: Chalice Press.

———. 2021. *Faith After Ferguson: Resilient Leadership in Pursuit of Racial Justice.* St. Louis: Chalice Press.

Harris, Angelique and Omar Mushtaq. 2022. *Womanist AIDS Activism in the United States: "It's Who We Are."* Lanham, MD: Lexington Books.

Harris-Lacewell, Melissa V. 2007. "Righteous Politics: The Role of the Black Church in Contemporary Politics." *CrossCurrents* 57 (2): 180–96. https://search-ebscohost-com.ezp.bentley.edu/login.aspx?direct=true&db=a9h&AN=26338022&site=ehost-live.

Hendrickson, Hildi. 2021. *Building Beloved Communities: The Life and Work of Rev. Dr. Paul Smith.* Athens, GA: University of Georgia Press.

House, Christopher A. 2018. "Crying for Justice: The #BLACKLIVESMATTER Religious Rhetoric of Bishop T.D. Jakes." *Southern Communication Journal* 83 (1): 13–27. doi:10.1080/1041794X.2017.1387600.

Hudson, Willie. 2018. "Black Theology and Hip-Hop Theology: Theologies of Activism and Resistance." In *Taking It to the Streets: Public Theologies of Activism and Resistance,* edited by Jennifer Baldwin, 87–100. Lanham, MD: Lexington Books.

Johnson, Sandra. 2022. *Standing on Holy Ground: A Triumph Over Hate Crime in the Deep South.* New York: St. Martin's Press.

Johnson, Terence. *We Testify With Our Lives: How Religion Transformed Black Radical Thought From Black Power to Black Lives Matter.* New York: Columbia University Press, 2021.

Little Edwards, Korie and Michelle Oyakawa. 2022. *Smart Suits, Tattered Boots: Black Ministers Mobilizing the Black Church in the Twenty-First Century.* New York: NYU Press.

Massingale, Bryan. 2017. "White Supremacy, the Election of Donald Trump and the Challenge to Theology." *Concilium* (00105236), 3 (June): 65–73. https://search-ebscohost-com.ezp.bentley.edu/login.aspx?direct=true&db=a9h&AN=126437372&site=ehost-live.

McCormack, Michael. 2021. "'Breonna Taylor Could Have Been Me': Bearing Witness to Faith in Black (Feminist) Futurity at the Speed Art Museum's Promise, Witness, Remembrance Exhibit." *Religions* 12 (11): 980. doi:10.3390/rel12110980.

McMickle, Marvin. 2014. *Pulpit and Politics: Separation of Church and State in the Black Church.* Valley Forge, PA: Judson Press.

Mingo, AnneMarie. 2021. "Black and Blue: Black Women, 'Law and Order,' and the Church's Silence on Police Violence." *Religions* 12 (10): 886. doi:10.3390/rel12100886.

Monroe, Irene. 2009. "Taking Theology to the Community." *Journal of Feminist Studies in Religion* 25(1): 184–90. https://doi.org/10.2979/fsr.2009.25.1.184.

Moultrie, Monique. 2023. *Hidden Histories: Faith and Black Lesbian Leadership.* Durham: Duke University Press.

Royles, Dan. 2020. *To Make the Wounded Whole: The African American Struggle against HIV/AIDS.* Chapel Hill: UNC Press.

Sharpton, Al. 2020. *Rise Up: Confronting a Country at the Crossroads.* New York: Hannover Square Press.

Slessarev-Jamir, Helene. 2011. *Prophetic Activism: Progressive Religious Justice Movements in Contemporary America.* New York: NYU Press.

Smith, R. Drew. 2013. *From Every Mountainside: Black Churches and the Broad Terrain of Civil Rights.* Albany: SUNY Press.

———. 2021. "The Diminished Public, and Black Christian Promotion of American Civic Ideals." *Religions* 12(7): 505. doi:10.3390/rel12070505.

———. 2022. "Black Religion and Reparations: Pragmatic Trajectories and Widening Support." *Religions* 13 (12): 1169. doi:https://doi.org/10.3390/rel13121169. http://ezp.bentley.edu/login?url=https://www.proquest.com/scholarly-journals/black-religion-reparations-pragmatic-trajectories/docview/2756781240/se-2.

Smith, R. Drew, William Ackah, Anthony G. Reddie, and Rothney S. Tshaka, eds. 2015. *Contesting Post-Racialism: Conflicted Churches in the United States and South Africa*. Jackson: University Press of Mississippi.

Sutton, Madeline and Carolyn Parks. 2013. "HIV/AIDS Prevention, Faith, and Spirituality among Black/African American and Latino Communities in the United States: Strengthening Scientific Faith-Based Efforts to Shift the Course of the Epidemic and Reduce HIV-Related Health Disparities." *Journal of Religion and Health*, 52(2), 514–30. doi: https://doi.org/10.1007/s10943-011-9499-z.

Theoharris, Liz, ed. 2021. *We Cry Justice: Reading the Bible with the Poor People's Campaign*. Minneapolis: Broadleaf Books.

Index

305

Morris, Aldon, 97, 160, 167
Morrison, Toni, 193
Movement for Black Lives (M4BL), 2,
    6, 23–24, 47
Mullen, A. Kristen, 285
Munshi, Debashish, 213
Murray, Pauli, 20
Murthy, Dhiraj, 28

NAACP. *See* National Association for
    the Advancement of Colored People
Nash, Diane, 18
National Action Network, 46, 56
National Advisory Commission on Civil
    Disorders, 92, 272
National Association for the
    Advancement of Colored People
    (NAACP), 20, 46, 49–50, 55, 56, 60,
    105, 272
National Coalition of Black Lesbians
    and Gays, 147
National Football League (NFL),
    129–30
National Housing Trust Fund, 281
National Incident Management
    Standards (NIMS), 86, 92, 96
National Institute on Minority Health
    and Health Disparities, 275, *276*
National Institutes of Health, 245
National Urban League, 56
NBC, 75, 79, 86
New England Female Medical College,
    245
New Florida Majority, 60
The New Jim Crow (Alexander), 2, 46
New York Age (periodical), 110
New York City Anti-Violence Project,
    151
New York City Police Department
    (NYPD), 140–41, 151, 153
New York City Pride, 148–49, 151
New York Times (periodical), 60, 61,
    151
Nexis Uni database, 50, 54, 58
Ng, Mark, 148

Nike, 211, 212
Nixon, Jay, 74, 79
Nixon, Richard, 279
Nollywood, 115
Nova, Zazu, 140, 142, 143, 145, 154
Nummi, Jozie, 98

Obama, Barack, 75
Obergefell vs. Hodges, 147
O'Brien, Cecelia, 55
Ocala Banner (periodical), 53
O'Flaherty, Brendan, 282
O'Neal, John, 170
On the Freedom Side (Hogan), 47
"On the Purpose of Education" (King),
    159–60
On The Record (documentary), 228
On the Social Contract (Rousseau), 277
Operation PUSH, 46
oppositional gaze, 106–7
Orlando Sentinal (periodical), 53
#OscarsSoWhite campaign, 3
Outkast Reader (Bradley), 194

Palestine, Dream Defenders solidarity
    with, 59–60
Palm Beach Post (periodical), 55
Parcha, Joshua M., 212
Parks, Gordon, 111–12
Parks, Rosa, 18, 267
Parsons, Talcott, 163, 171, 176
"passing," 175–76
"Pedagogical Cinema" (Goldfarb), 115
Pendas, Gabriel, 53, 54, 55
Perry, Andre, 285
Pew Research Center, 23, 33, 34, 270
PFLAG, 150
Philadelphia AIDS Task Force, 147
Philadelphia Gay News (periodical),
    147
photography. *See* camera, uses of
"Pictures and Progress" (Douglass), 104
Pillow, Travis, 55
Pinderhughes, Dianne, 200
Pittsburg Courier (periodical), 110

About the Editors and Contributors

ABOUT THE EDITORS

Edith Joachimpillai, BS is a Principal Managing Partner at Copper and Cobalt, a global consulting firm based in the Boston area. Edith formerly worked for the Brookings Institution in the Global Economy and Development Program on issues including the Eurozone crisis, scaling up a United Nations-funded girls education program in Uttar Pradesh, India, the Paris Agreement for Climate Change, and "Technology, Productivity, and the Future of Growth." In 2020, she co-led the #BlackAtBentley initiative to call out experiences of racism from students at her alma mater. She is a member of the NAACP in Cambridge and Merrimack Valley, Massachusetts and serves on the board of Sustainable Westford, a sustainability driven non-profit in eastern Massachusetts. She earned a Bachelor of Science degree in Economics-Finance with minors in mathematics and Mandarin at Bentley University.

Mary Marcel, PhD is Associate Professor of Information Design and Corporate Communication at Bentley University. She and Kiana Pierre-Louis of Northeastern University School of Law led an NEH-funded research seminar entitled "From Scapegoats to Citizens: This Era of Black Activism" at Bentley in 2021–2022 which was the genesis of this edited volume. She helped to establish the Multicultural Bisexual Lesbian and Gay Studies program at UC Berkeley, now under the Department of Gender and Women's Studies. Formerly she worked at New England Research Institutes on disparities in health outcomes for African American women with HIV/AIDS and breast cancer. She has published on news framing and biases in coverage of the priest-sex crisis in *Women's Studies in Communication*, and on news coverage of the

319

murders of transgender women of color in *Local Violence, Global Media: Feminist Analyses of Gendered Representations.*

ABOUT THE CONTRIBUTORS

Greg Austin, PhD is senior Lecturer in African American Studies in the Department of Gender and Race Studies at the University of Alabama. Dr. Austin has for more than ten years taught a wide range of courses at the undergraduate and graduate level that address issues of race, gender, and sexuality. His research focuses on health policy, the courts, race and sexuality. He is interested in the place of the Black academic in contemporary conversations about AIDS/HIV, reproductive rights, the COVID pandemic, Black masculinity, and the law.

Joe Feagin, PhD is the Ella C. McFadden Professor in Sociology at Texas A&M. Focusing on issues of racism and sexism, his research includes *Racial and Ethnic Relations* (Ninth edition; Prentice-Hall, 2011 with Clairece Booher Feagin); *Latinos Facing Racism: Discrimination, Resistance, And Endurance* (Paradigm Publishers, 2014 with J. Cobas); *The White Racial Frame* (Third edition; Routledge, 2020); *Yes We Can: White Racial Framing and the Obama Presidency* (Second edition, Routledge, 2013 with A. Harvey-Wingfield); *White Party, White Government: Race, Class, and U.S. Politics* (Routledge, 2012); *Racist America* (Second edition; Routledge, 2010); and *Two-Faced Racism: Whites in the Backstage and Frontstage* (Routledge, 2007; with L. H. Picca). He is a past president of the American Sociological Association.

Jennifer M. Gómez, PhD is an Assistant Professor at Boston University School of Social Work and Center for Innovation in Social Work & Health, Board Member and Chair of the Research Advisory Committee at the Center for Institutional Courage, and lead co-editor of the 2021 special issue of *Journal of Trauma & Dissociation—Discrimination, Violence, & Healing in Marginalized Communities.* As a 2021–22 Fellow at the Stanford University Center for Advanced Study in the Behavioral Sciences (CASBS), Dr. Gómez wrote her first book, *The Cultural Betrayal of Black Women & Girls: A Black Feminist Approach to Healing from Sexual Abuse* (APA 2023). Dr. Gómez' goal for her research is to identify avenues of hope and healing for individuals, families, communities, institutions, and society. https://jmgomez.org; Twitter: @JenniferMGmez1.

Moussa Hassoun, JD is an attorney in New York City who has organized with BIPOC Queer people for years on a wide range of issues. Over several years, Moussa created an online collaborative network of Queer activists located throughout the Middle East, the US, and Canada dedicated toward sharing resources and campaign tactics. Over the past five years, he has volunteered to represent Queer BIPOC asylees in their pursuit of asylum due to persecution in their countries of origin. Moussa has also organized low income BIPOC tenants to avoid evictions, co-founded a street safety campaign to advocate for greater public transportation services and improve street safety, and helped organize support for local businesses during the COVID-19 pandemic. He lives in Brooklyn.

Melissa Hector, MS, MBA is the Director of Equitable and Strategic Initiatives at the Boston Public Health Commission. Ms. Hector led community initiatives under three Mayors in the Office of Human Services for the City of Boston. Since her appointment in 2019, she has worked with internal and external partners to develop a COVID-19 health equity community engagement framework. She is a certified DEI trainer, who received her BA in Media and Culture from Bentley University, MS Global Studies and International Affairs from Northeastern University, and Social Impact MBA from Boston University. Ms. Hector grew up in Boston's neighborhood of Roxbury. In her spare time, she promotes health awareness and self-confidence through her volunteer run/walk meetup group *Curvy Girls Run*.

Carly Jennings, MS is a doctoral candidate in Sociology at Texas A&M University and also holds an MS in Educational Human Resource Development. Her research agenda centers African American homeschooling, and includes Black parenting, American schooling's institutional racism, the Black Lives Matter movement, and teacher education. Carly has taught in public and private schools, as well as private homes, in English and Spanish, in the USA and in Panama to students of all ages and varying levels of literacy. Other research interests include racial aesthetics and epistemic erasure. During the Social Justice Summer of 2020, Carly Jennings's research and analysis of the Black Lives Matter movement and hegemonic attempts at degrading the BLM message was featured in a special issue of ASA Footnotes newsletter, found at https://www.asanet.org/news-events/footnotes/jul-aug-2020 /features/love-note-launched-movement

Utz McKnight, PhD has spent the last ten years as Chair of the Department of Race and Gender Studies at the University of Alabama. Before this he was a multi-year visiting professor in African American Studies at UC Berkeley. As an academic activist, he has been central to the renaming the buildings at the University of Alabama, the apology by the faculty senate for owning slaves that worked on the campus, supporting the Hallowed Grounds Tour of the campus, and many of the initiatives that improved Black student retention and graduation rates over two decades. He is currently Associate Dean for DEI in the College of Arts and Sciences, and author of four books on the subject of race.

Jozie Nummi, PhD teaches at Bemidji State University as an Assistant Professor of Sociology and Gender Studies. She earned her PhD in Sociology at Texas A&M University. She researches gender inequalities, social movements, and social media. She teaches sociology and gender studies courses to provide students with the skills necessary to participate in a global world. Her research analyzes protests, policing, and social media platforms through an intersectional lens to affect social change. She has published on the #BlackLivesMatter movement in *Sociological Forum* and on gendered strategies following natural disasters.

Anne Warfield Rawls, PhD is Professor and Chair of Sociology, Bentley University, Research Professor, Siegen University (Center for Media of Cooperation) and Director of the Garfinkel Archive. Publications include *Tacit Racism* (2020, co-authored with Waverly Duck), and *Black Lives Matter: Ethnomethodological and Conversation Analytic Studies of Race and Systemic Racism in Everyday Interaction* (co-edited with Kevin Whitehead and Waverly Duck). Some recent publications on Race include "'Fractured Reflections' of High Status Black Male Presentations of Self: Non-Recognition of Identity as a Tacit form of Institutional Racism" (2017, co-authored with Waverly Duck); "Playing the Interrogation Game: Rapport, Coercion, and Confessions in Police Interrogations"(2017, with Gary David and James Treinum); and "Problems Establishing Identity/Residency in a City Neighborhood during a Black/White Police/Citizen Encounter: Revisiting Du Bois' Conception of 'The Submissive Man'" (with Waverly Duck and Jason Turowetz, 2018).

Joyce Hope Scott, PhD is Clinical Professor of African American Studies at Boston University where she teaches courses in African American literature, and history and black popular culture. Prof. Hope Scott is a former Scholar of the Oxford Round Table, and former Fulbright Scholar/Professor to Burkina Faso and the Republic of Bénin, West Africa. She is Co-Founder/Co-Director of the International Network of Scholars and Activists for Afrikan Reparations

(INOSAAR), current President of the Boston Pan African Forum (BPAF), and the "Fellow on Africa" at the Center for African, Caribbean and Community Development at UMass/Boston. Dr. Hope Scott developed and organized the event "Restorative Justice and Societal Repair: A Symposium on Global Racism and Reparations" at Boston University in 2020. She is an Invited Consultant to the United Nations Office of the High Commissioner for Human Rights' Regarding Human Rights Resolution on Accountability, Remedy and Redress for transatlantic slavery, colonialism and systemic racism.

David Stamps, PhD is an Assistant Professor in Information Design and Corporate Communication at Bentley University. He earned his PhD from the University of California at Santa Barbara and M.A. from the California State University at Northridge. His research examines the role of media's presentation of racialized and gendered stereotypes and how these depictions affect various groups in terms of their affective, behavioral, and cognitive responses. His work bridges critical race, feminist, and social scientific intellectual traditions and utilizes thematic and data analyses to uncover nuanced communication experiences among audiences. Dr. Stamps has published in *Communication Studies*, the *Journal of Social and Personal Relationships, Advances in Journalism and Communication*, the *Journal of International and Intercultural Communication, Journalism and Mass Communication Quarterly*, and the *Howard Journal of Communications.*

Amorette T. Young, PhD teaches in the Departments of Ethnic, Gender and Transborder Studies and Sociology at Pima Community College. She earned her PhD in Sociology at Texas A&M University. Her research interests focus on immigrant detention practices and maltreatment, mass incarceration, connections between bureaucratic oversight and state violence, and the long-term health and other effects of incarceration. Dr. Young has published in *VOLUNTAS: International Journal of Voluntary and Nonprofit Organizations, The Social Science Journal*, and the *International Journal of Sociology and Social Policy.*

Ziyuan Zhou, PhD is an assistant professor for the Department of Information Design and Corporate Communication at Bentley University. He earned his PhD in Communication and Information Science at the University of Alabama. His research focuses on the protection of stakeholders during organizational crises and the application of emerging technologies in public relations. Dr. Zhou's work appears in leading corporate communication journals including *Public Relations Review, Journal of Communication Management*, and *Corporate Communication: An International Journal.*